Praise for *Everyday Surveillance*

"This insightful and wonderfully accessible book shows how surveillance has radically transformed just about every aspect of s~~~~~~~~~~~~~~~~~~~~~~~~~~~~~~~~
online worlds, surveillance defines and m~~~~~~~~~~~~~~~~~~~~~~
edition of *Everyday Surveillance* is the p~~~~~~~~~~~~~~~~~
and their consequences." —**Torin Monahan**, ~~~~~~~~~~~~~~~~~~~

"George Orwell was wrong. The modern p~~~~~~~~ of sur~~~~~~~~ ~~~'~ ~~~ ~~~~~~~~~~~~ thousands upon thousands of 'Tiny B~~~~~~~~~~~~~~~~~~~~~~~~~~~~~~~~~~~~~~~ William G. Staples offers a compelling account of the rise of private surveillance— complementing but also complicating the watchful eye of the State—and the equanimity with which this has been greeted by the public." —**Simon Chesterman**, dean, National University of Singapore Faculty of Law

"Staples blends sophisticated social theorizing with a keen eye for the minute ways that surveillance touches our day-to-day lives. In the process he brings to light the often otherwise invisible powers of contemporary monitoring practices." —**Kevin D. Haggerty**, University of Alberta

"Through incisive analysis, *Everyday Surveillance* charts the various ways that surveillance shapes the postmodern moment: from the routinized gathering of data by 'smart' technologies when we shop, work, travel, or protest, to new categories of punishment that blur the line between incarceration and freedom—where those under house arrest are subject to 'participatory monitoring' with the expectation that they come to supervise themselves. Through interviews and observations, Staples offers a 'sociology of the postmodern' that is a wide-ranging, historically grounded, and theoretically informed engagement with the techniques of surveillance and social control." —**Simone Browne**, University of Texas at Austin

"The beauty of this book? It's true to its title. Surveillance is demystified. It's not an occasional or remote occurrence but an intrinsic aspect of all our everyday lives. We are challenged to understand and come to terms with a culture of surveillance in which 'Big Brother is us.' Staples guides us between the multifaceted vigilance of digital systems and the enhanced visibility of our mundane life-paths, noting subtle shifts from modern to postmodern practices. This book deftly draws attention to the key questions that we discount to our detriment." —**David Lyon**, Queen's University, Canada

"This book is very well written. . . . It offers a fascinating chronicle of the rage to invent new forms of surveillance, as well as pithy conceptualizations that organize the empirical materials nicely. As such, it clearly meets Staples's stated goal of providing an accessible undergraduate textbook." —*Social Forces* (praise for a previous edition)

"The suggestion made by *Everyday Surveillance* that a 'quiet revolution' is occurring in which we are all targets is a thought-provoking one. It reminds us that we all are responsible for encouraging surveillance by being seduced by its promises, fearing the consequences without it, and heralding it as society's salvation. The book flags some new directions in which the study of visual, informational, and communication technologies might profitably head." —*British Journal of Criminology* (praise for a previous edition)

Everyday Surveillance

Everyday Surveillance

Vigilance and Visibility in Postmodern Life

Second Edition

William G. Staples

ROWMAN & LITTLEFIELD
Lanham • Boulder • New York • Toronto • Plymouth, UK

Published by Rowman & Littlefield
4501 Forbes Boulevard, Suite 200, Lanham, Maryland 20706
www.rowman.com

10 Thornbury Road, Plymouth PL6 7PP, United Kingdom

British Library Cataloguing in Publication Information Available

Library of Congress Cataloging-in-Publication Data

Staples, William G.
Everyday surveillance : vigilance and visibility in postmodern life / William G. Staples. — Second edition.
pages cm.
Includes bibliographical references and index.
ISBN 978-0-7425-4109-2 (cloth : alk. paper) — ISBN 978-0-7425-4110-8 (pbk. : alk. paper) — ISBN 978-1-4422-2629-6 (electronic)
1. Social control—United States. 2. Electronic surveillance—Social aspects—United States. 3. United States—Social conditions—1980– 4. Privacy—United States. I. Title.
HN59.2.S698 2014
323.44'820973—dc23
2013022176

Printed in the United States of America

For Lizette, still and always, my brave companion of the road

Contents

Preface

An extraordinary decade has passed since I first published *Everyday Surveillance*. During that time, four hijacked planes crashed into the World Trade Center, the Pentagon, and a field in Pennsylvania killing more than 3,000 people; the United States engaged in wars in Iraq and Afghanistan; and we faced a near global financial collapse. Most recently we endured an astonishing week that began with the bombings at the Boston Marathon and left that major metropolitan area and much of the country on edge. These events have rattled our social and political institutions, undermined our sense of security, and brought about increased fear and uncertainty.

In the aftermath of the September 11, 2001, attacks, the Bush administration ushered in the "War on Terror" and with it an unprecedented level of state surveillance and monitoring of the population. As part of the government's sweeping Homeland Security agenda, including the USAPATRIOT legislation, federal, state, and local agencies were empowered to scrutinize the lives of ordinary citizens in extraordinary ways. Pressured by the Bush administration to bypass civil liberties and skirt formal legal channels, a secret and illegal wiretapping program authorized the National Security Agency (NSA) to collect phone records and even listen in on calls to or from the United States. In 2007, the essential elements of the Bush program were made legal by Congress with the proviso of greater oversight by the Foreign Intelligence Surveillance Act (FISA) Court. To this day, continuing under the Obama administration, the NSA is engaged in the systematic collection of what most would consider "personal" data of the American public. This situation has prompted many to declare that George Orwell's government-run, "big brother" surveillance state has finally arrived and has contributed to the idea that after 9/11, "everything changed."

Yet for a number of us who have been studying surveillance practices historically, developments after 9/11 reflect much deeper social and cultural changes that have been going on for some time now. As David Lyon states, "The attacks brought to the surface a number of surveillance trends that had been developing quietly, and largely unnoticed, for the previous decade and more." So while legislation and other actions in the post-9/11 period dramatically enhanced the state's ability to keep a close eye on the public and contributed to the notion that "everything has changed," a better characterization might be "more of the same," albeit with a shift in the scope and quality of social monitoring. In my view, one of the more fascinating and yet troubling developments in this period is how, in the time of crisis, the state was able to turn to private corporations for their support in facilitating the collection of information about the populace: I call this "big brother" meets his "tiny brothers."

What I have been doing for the past two decades is documenting the appearance of what I call postmodern surveillance practices. These relatively mundane, microtechniques of social monitoring and control—the "tiny brothers"—include the activities of large commercial enterprises that specialize in collecting, processing, aggregating, and storing comprehensive and detailed information about us. So, rather than building their own politically dubious surveillance network, evidence suggests that, in the post-9/11 period, state security agencies were able to turn to these corporate accomplices—for example, as many as fifty telecommunications, Internet, and data brokerage companies—and buy access to the enormous amount of data that they had already collected about the citizenry. For instance, Acxiom, Inc., which maintains its own database on about 190 million individuals and 126 million households in the United States, worked with the government to provide information on eleven of the nineteen 9/11 hijackers. Similarly, cell phone companies have reported that in 2013 they responded to more than 1.3 million demands from various law enforcement agencies for subscriber information including the content of text messages and caller locations.

The extent of this corporate teamwork was made glaringly public when Edward Snowden, a 29-year-old former technical assistant for the CIA and employee of the defense contractor Booz Allen Hamilton, and former employee of other private contractors including computer giant Dell, spoke out about the scope and workings of the NSA surveillance activity. One such program, codenamed MAINWAY, contains "metadata" (descriptive characteristics, not content) for hundreds of billions of telephone calls placed with the largest corporate telephone carriers in the United States. Yet, while technically classified, Snowden's revelations about these programs were not really as startling as they were portrayed in the media: the existence of MAINWAY and other programs has been publicly known since 2005 and, again, under authorization of the FISA Court, their core activities have been carried out within the parameters of current law.

Although the events of 9/11 and its aftermath force us to pay attention to the institutional level of the security state and what figures to be a reconstitution of state power within its complex web of affiliations with civil society, I maintain that the state still does not have a monopoly over the practice of watching people. I continue to focus on the more commonplace strategies used by governmental, but even more likely, private organizations and individuals that target and treat the body as an object to be watched, assessed, and manipulated. These are local knowledge-gathering activities often enhanced by the use of new information; visual, communication, and medical technologies that are increasingly present in the workplace, the school, the home, and the community. In this book I argue that, although our inherited, modern ideas about the nature of human beings, deviance, and social control continue to shape the ways in which we keep a close watch on people, a new set of meanings, attitudes, and practices is taking hold that is constituted by and indicative of conditions of postmodernity.

Sociologist Wendy Griswold points out that we study culture when we observe a community's pattern of meanings; its enduring expressive aspects; its symbols that represent and guide the thinking, feelings, and behavior of its members as they go about their daily lives. The word surveillance, in the most general sense, refers to the act of keeping a close watch on people. The purpose of this book is to examine the meanings, attitudes, and behaviors surrounding the ways in which people in the United States are being watched, monitored, and controlled in their everyday lives. This book was written to be accessible to a wide audience of students, scholars, and the interested public. While deeply informed by the work of social theorists and other scholars, the text is relatively free of academic jargon. My intent is to challenge the reader to deliberate on a salient and important topic and consider it from what is likely to be an alternative vantage point. My hope is that you will find the book enjoyable, informative, and worthy of considerable discussion and debate.

This edition of this book was supported, in part, by a research leave provided by Dean Danny Anderson of the College of Liberal Arts and Science and the sabbatical leave program of the University of Kansas. I appreciate very much the work of my research assistants Melissa Irwin and Alex Myers and help from Sheridan Stewart and Corinne Legleiter. I would also like to recognize the people who were willing to share with me their work, lives, and experiences that have become part of this book. While many of their identities remain hidden, their effect has been profound. I could not possibly name all the colleagues, students, friends, and audience members who have offered valuable feedback on this and my other projects. Your support and encouragement has been a source of inspiration and perseverance. I am especially grateful to my partner Lizette Peter for taking the time away from her own work to read, edit, and comment on the entire manuscript; I promise to return the favor. Finally, thanks to the staff of Rowman & Littlefield for all their assistance, especially my editor, Sarah Stanton, for her support and, most of all, patience.

W. G. Staples
Lawrence, Kansas

Chapter One

Everyday Surveillance

Throughout the United States, thousands of offenders are placed under "house arrest," their movements monitored electronically by a transmitter attached to their ankle or a computer placed in their home. In a number of cities, police deploy mobile fingerprint scanners to check the immigration status and criminal records of day laborers. In several states, prison inmates are issued radio frequency ID–enabled (RFID) wristbands to track their movements in the facility. In New York City, a digitized courtroom collects myriad information about a single defendant that is kept in an electronic file. Most "clients" in community corrections programs are subjected to random drug testing.

At the same time:

More than 70 percent of major U.S. employers engage in some form of electronic monitoring of workers. At Walt Disney World in Florida, a biometric "measurement" is taken from the finger of "guests" to make sure that a multi-day ticket is used by only one person. School districts around the country have issued RFID student badges that monitor a pupil's movements on campus. A company in Arkansas has constructed the world's largest consumer database containing detailed information on about five hundred million consumers worldwide. And about 90 percent of U.S. manufacturers test workers for drugs.

These examples illustrate a blurring distinction between the surveillance and social control practices of the official justice system and those existing in the everyday lives of ordinary people. How are we to understand these developments? Are they simply "advances" in our struggle against possible illegal, deviant, or problematic behavior or do they signal the rise of what might be called a "culture of surveillance"? What kind of society has produced these practices, and why do we appear so willing to adopt or permit them? The purpose of this book is to explore these and other questions about the emergence of new forms of pervasive monitoring in contemporary society.

A while ago I sat in the café section of a large, suburban bookstore talking with a friend. She asked me what I was working on these days and I told her that I was writing a book about social control in contemporary life. At this she said, "You mean about crime and prisons?" "No," I said, "not really. More like the issue of surveillance." "Oh," she replied, "so you are looking into how the government spies on people?" To many of us, including my friend, issues of discipline, social control, and surveillance tend either to revolve around the criminal justice system or to invite the image of George Orwell's notorious Big Brother. Yet as important as our vast prison system and the activities of domestic "spying" organizations are, I am most interested here in the relatively small, often mundane procedures and practices, the "tiny brothers," if you will, that are increasingly present in our daily lives. These techniques exist in the shadow of large institutions; they are not ushered in with dramatic displays of state power; nor do they appear as significant challenges to constitutional democracy. The methods I want to consider are the evermore commonplace strategies used by both public and private organizations to influence our choices, change our habits, "keep us in line," monitor our performance, gather knowledge or evidence about us, assess deviations, and in some cases, exact penalties. I argue that it is these routine kinds of surveillance and monitoring activities that involve many more of us than does life in a state prison or a National Security Agency (NSA) "warrantless wiretapping" of our phone conversations.

The practices I have in mind range along a continuum. They begin on one end of the spectrum with the "soft," seemingly benign and relatively inconspicuous forms of monitoring and assessment such as those used in the very bookstore where I sat with my friend. In that business, as in thousands across the United States, a "security" system chronicled our interaction with video cameras while the store's spatial arrangement was designed for optimal surveillance of customers and employees alike. Computerized checkout stations kept track of inventory, calculated store performance figures, assessed the credit worthiness of patrons through remote databases, collected personal information about customers so they could be targeted for marketing campaigns, monitored the log-on and log-off times of employees, and calculated the average number of customers those employees processed per hour. All of this was accomplished "behind the scenes" as it were, without disruption to the manufactured ambiance of soft leather chairs, the "narrowcast" background music, and the sound and smell of cappuccino brewing.

At the "hard" end of the spectrum are the most obtrusive and confrontational practices—often taking on the qualities of what I call "surveillance ceremonies"—that may begin with the assumption of guilt, are often designed to uncover the truth about someone's behavior, to test an individual's character, and, more generally, to make them consciously aware that they are indeed being watched and monitored. This element was also present at the corporate bookstore I visited with my friend since the employees there were subjected to pre-employment drug testing and we were also aware that the merchandise was "tagged" so that we could be electronically "frisked" as we walked through the observable sensor gates at the exit. Other "surveillance ceremonies" include the use of lie detectors, pre-employment integrity tests, mobile fingerprint scanning, drug and alcohol testing, electronically monitored "house arrest," and the use of metal detectors and various body scanners.

Between these soft and hard types of surveillance lies a vast array of techniques and technologies that are designed to watch our bodies, to monitor our activities, habits, and movements, and, ultimately, to shape or change our behavior.[1] These procedures are often undertaken in the name of law and order, public safety, fraud prevention, the protection of private property, or "good business practice"; other measures are initiated for an individual's "own good" or benefit. But no matter what the stated motivation, the intent is to mold, shape, and modify actions and behaviors.[2] Surveillance and social control of this type, *sans* "big brother," is not orchestrated by a few individuals; it is not part of a master plan that is simply imposed on us. Rather, in my view, *we are all involved and enmeshed within a matrix of power relations that are highly intentional and purposeful; arrangements that can be more or less unequal but are never simply one-directional.*

The subjects of this book, then, are the cultural practices that I call "meticulous rituals of power." Most generally, I include those microtechniques of surveillance and social monitoring that are often enhanced by the use of new information, communications, and medical technologies. These are knowledge-gathering strategies that involve surveillance, information and evidence collection, and analysis. I call them meticulous because they are "small" procedures and techniques that are precisely and thoroughly exercised. I see them as ritualistic because they are often embedded in organizational procedures, faithfully repeated, and quickly accepted and routinely practiced with little question or resistance. And they are about power because they are intended to entice, cajole, prod, discipline, or outright force people into behaving in ways that have been deemed appropriate, normal, beneficial, productive, or lawful.

So while these techniques may be "small," monotonous, and even seemingly trivial, they are not without effect. In this way, meticulous rituals are the specific, concrete mechanisms that help maintain unbalanced and unequal relationships between clusters of individuals (e.g., between managers and workers, teachers and students, store employees and customers, parents and children, police officers and suspects, probation officials and offenders) and, in a larger sense, between individuals and the public and private organizations where these rituals take place. Meticulous rituals often operate in such a way as to create a form of "information asymmetry" where one person, group, or organization gains important information about a person and uses it as leverage to modify their behavior. On the "softest" end of my spectrum, this information may be offered up "voluntarily," as in the case of someone who uses a geolocation social network application on their cell phone to announce to their friends their whereabouts and are then prodded by advertisers to patronize businesses in that area. At the "hardest" end of the spectrum, information may be taken on demand of formal authority such as a community corrections officer ordering a client to submit to a drug test.

"OK," you may say, "so what is really new here? Hasn't society always had ways of keeping people in line? Aren't these 'meticulous rituals' just newer, perhaps more effective ways of doing what we have always done to ensure social order?" In some ways, yes, they are logical extensions of "modern" approaches to the problems of crime, deviance, and social control, and they may indeed be more efficient at accomplishing these societal goals. Yet, at the same time, they have qualities that make them fundamentally new, and, I want to argue, more *post*modern in design and implementation. That is, I see these strategies as a product of our contemporary period of history that contains profoundly new and distinctive patterns of social, cultural, and economic life. Therefore, I argue that there are at least four defining characteristics of *post*modern meticulous rituals of power and surveillance that set them apart from *modern* methods of social control. First, consider the following.

In the past, the watchful eyes of a small shopkeeper may have deterred a would-be shoplifter; her surveillance was personal, not terribly systematic, and her memory, of course, was fallible. She was more likely to know her customers (and they her), to keep a "closer eye" on strangers, and to "look the other way" when she saw fit (and to make a call to say, an offending juvenile's parents later). This kind of "personal" social control was once typical of small communities or close-knit societies where people certainly watched one another very diligently and where a shared, customary culture, as well as fear of ridicule or exclusion, was a powerful inducement to conformity.[3]

By contrast, the part-time employees of the large corporate bookstore where I sat with my friend have less interest in watching for thieves; their huge number of customers is an anonymous horde. Here, store management relies on subcontracted security personnel as well as the faceless and ever-ready video security cameras positioned in the ubiquitous black domes in the ceiling. Video—one of the defining features of postmodern society—projects a hyper-vigilant "gaze," randomly scanning the entire store day and night, recording every event, and watching *all* the customers, not just the "suspicious ones." Moreover, the cameras are also positioned to watch the employees, who must now be monitored both for their productivity as workers and as potential thieves themselves. In this way, the surveillance practiced at this store has become oddly democratic; everyone is watched, and no one is trusted.

So, the first characteristic of postmodern surveillance is that it tends to be systematic, methodical, and automatic in operation. It is also likely to be impersonal in that the "observer" is rarely seen and is anonymous and often not an individual at all but rather what I call some form of "data sponge": a computerized system, video camera, scanner, barcode reader, drug-testing kit, RFID chip, or automated tracking system of some kind. Once collected, the data may become part of a permanent record in the form of a digital file of some kind. In fact, the role played by highly efficient digital databases is crucial. The storage capacity of these machines is now boundless, spatially efficient, and incredibly inexpensive. Corporate personnel files, hospital, mental health, and substance abuse agency records, as well as insurance company databanks, join all those demographic, financial, credit, and consumer habits information to create what is now called "big data"; massive conjoined datasets that can be used to create "virtual" data-based identities of us as well as new analytic tools used to "mine" these data in search of patterns and to sort people into different categories. Once created, our "virtual doppelgängers" are, as Mark Poster suggests, "capable of being acted upon by computers at many social locations without the least awareness by the individual concerned yet just as surely as if the individual were present somehow inside the computer."[4] For example, credit ratings may be destroyed or medical benefits denied without personal input or influence of the individual involved.

Second, meticulous rituals of power often involve our bodies in new and important ways, and I want to distinguish two primary tactics of bodily monitoring. I agree with Donald Lowe when he writes, "As living beings, we are more than body and mind, more than the representations and images of our body. We lead a bodily life in the world."[5] My thesis is that these bodily lives are shaped, manipulated, and controlled by a set of ongoing practices that compose our daily lives as workers, consumers, and community members.

The first tactic I want to distinguish has to do with types of surveillance and monitoring that enhances our visibility to others. We seem to be entering a state of permanent visibility where our bodies and our behaviors are being monitored, tracked, or watched continuously, anonymously, and systematically. This kind of surveillance happens when people engage in such diverse activities as driving a company truck, accessing a "free" wireless "hotspot" in a coffee shop, using a credit card, or simply walking down a public street. These instances signify different forms of visibility: the company vehicle is equipped with digital sensors that track the driver's activities and movements; the wireless access point collects historical data on how frequently a customer visits that cafe; the credit card purchase leaves a digital trail of the user's activities and whereabouts; and public and private surveillance cameras positioned along the street signify to anyone who gains access to the image, that a particular individual was on the street on a particular day at a certain time. Add to these transit swipe cards, electronic tolling devices, cell phone location beacons, card-key access points, and even smart parking meters, and our visibility—or at least our whereabouts—to others is being systematically recorded and stored. The methodical, technology-driven, impersonal gaze has become a primary mechanism of surveillance in our society, and it is fixed on our bodies and their movements.

A second tactic of bodily surveillance and social control relates to new developments in science, technology, and medicine. These intersecting fields are making the human body infinitely more accessible to official scrutiny and assessment. This means that the ability of organizations to monitor, judge, or even regulate our actions and behaviors *through* our bodies is significantly enhanced. It also means that it becomes less important to trust anyone to speak the truth or to "tell us what we need to know." In this way, the body is treated as an "object" that holds proof of identity or evidence of possible deviance. On the soft side of my spectrum of social control, we see that corporations are using medical data collected on employees in their "wellness" and exercise clinics to confront the "unhealthy lifestyles" of those not conforming to prevailing standards (about, for example, tobacco use or appropriate weight). Meanwhile, at the hard end of the spectrum, DNA samples are being systematically collected on most people who come in contact with the justice system and permanently stored in a vast database. The body, I contend, is a central target of many postmodern surveillance techniques and rituals.

The third defining characteristic of postmodern meticulous rituals relates to a shift in the location of surveillance and social control. Since the early nineteenth century, our primary method of dealing with lawbreakers, those thought to be insane, deviant, criminal, and even the poor, has been to isolate them *from* the everyday life of the community—as in the case of the mental asylum, reformatory, modern prison, and the poorhouse. Yet the kinds of practices I am most concerned with here attempt to impose a framework of accountability on an individual *in* everyday life. Although, obviously, removing the most "troublesome" people from society is still a significant means of formal social control (after all, in the United States, we "mass incarcerate" more people, at a rate per one hundred thousand of the population, than any country on the planet),[6] today we also attempt to regulate and "treat" a variety of behaviors, conditions, and "lifestyles" associated with substance and alcohol (ab)use, sexual offenses, "dysfunctional" families, and a host of psychological or psychiatric disorders and medical conditions.

Under this thinking, the segregative or quarantine model of social control developed in the nineteenth century, while, again, still very much with us, is increasingly considered by many to be too costly, ineffective, and outmoded. The incentive in recent years has been to develop new ways to control and "keep an eye on" the variety of problematic individuals and deviants through an evolving network of "community corrections" programs; regulatory welfare, health, and social service agencies; as well as in schools and other community institutions. And new developments in the forensic, medical, and computer and information sciences—generated by corporate research and development, universities, and the military/security industrial complex—are creating more remote, more flexible, and more efficient ways of making this happen. For example, consider the "accountability" regimes enforced through intensive supervision programs in the criminal justice system that monitor the behavior of "substance abusers" living in the community with random drug and alcohol tests. Or, we find that school truants, who were once sent to a juvenile detention center, are now ordered to carry a handheld GPS tracking device and required to key-in a numeric code five times throughout the day.

Finally, as new forms of social control are localized in everyday life, they are capable of bringing wide-ranging populations, not just the official "deviant," under their watchful gaze. As I indicated earlier, trust is becoming a rare commodity in our culture. The notion of "innocent until proven guilty" seems like a cliché when people are apt to be subjected to disciplinary rituals and surveillance ceremonies because aggregate statistical data suggests that they have a higher probability for being offenders (e.g., "flying while Muslim" or "driving while black"). Data generated through surveillance techniques can produce whole classes of individuals who are deemed "at risk" for behavior, whether any one particular individual has engaged in such behavior or not. These data, of course, are then used to justify even closer surveillance and scrutiny of this group, thereby increasing the likelihood of uncovering more offenses; and so it goes.[7] In the context of these changes, social control becomes more about predicting deviance—always assuming that it will, indeed, happen—rather than responding to a violation after it has occurred. Therefore, when put in place, ritualistic monitoring and surveillance ceremonies often blur the distinction between the official "deviant" and the "likely" or even "possible" offender. Indeed, what distinguishes the convicted felon from the college athlete from the discount store cashier if each is subjected to random drug screening? One consequence of this blurring is that we may be witnessing a historical shift from the specific punishment of the individual deviant, *post*offense, to the generalized surveillance of us all.

So, it would seem that while these meticulous rituals are "more of the same," they are, in other respects, strikingly new; and this, I propose, is how we should come to understand them. In other words, we need to see how the world we are creating today is a product of both our modern historical past and our *post*modern cultural present.[8] This historically grounded perspective has two advantages. First, if we connect these "new" disciplinary techniques to significant long-term processes and trends, we can see the continuity of social life and can understand that contemporary developments reflect an ongoing struggle to deal with problems and issues set in motion by the birth of the modern age. Second, by looking at how differently we have responded to the problems of social order in the past, we can also see that matters of deviance and social control are not fixed categories but are changing, socially constructed ideas. Therefore we begin to realize that what is defined as "deviant" behavior or as a "social problem" today—as well as what seems like appropriate responses to them—may not have been considered worthy of attention one hundred or even twenty years ago.

These long-term changes I refer to are some of the major themes that have come to characterize the period of modernity (from around the late eighteenth century until the middle of the twentieth century) and have had considerable influence on our strategies of social control. These themes include the increasing rationalization of social life; the rise of large centralized states and private organizations; and strongly held beliefs in reason, rationality, and the certainty of "progress." This modern faith in our power to shape the world was grounded in our apparent ability to control and to "know" nature through the physical sciences. This rational model of science was increasingly applied to the manipulation of "man" through the knowledge of the "human sciences" such as medicine, public health, criminology, psychology, sociology, and demography. In other words, with the birth of the modern era, human beings—our bodies, minds, and behaviors—became the *subject* or topic of scientific inquiry as well as the *object* or target of its knowledge. Thus, we see in the modern era the gradual disappearance of public torture, stigmatization, and banishment as primary means of punishment and social control, and their replacement by rationally organized reformatory institutions such as the prison, the poorhouse, and the asylum. Rather than seek retribution and public punishment, these institutions would isolate the offending individual and introduce behavioral modification—the transformation of the individual criminal, deviant, or the poor—through the administration of techniques of knowledge and power; techniques frequently developed by those in the human sciences. It is this relationship—between knowledge and power—that is central to the operation of meticulous rituals. Many of these influences are still with us today and continue to shape social life.[9]

Yet, much like the fairly gradual movement from so-called *pre*modern to modern times, the character of social change in the last half of the twentieth century is such that, while elements of this older modern social order are still with us—lodged in various social institutions and practices—it has been giving way to new patterns and practices in social, cultural, and economic life. This *postmodernization* of societies, especially in the United States, originating in developments since World War II and more intensely since the early 1970s, is characterized by fragmentation and uncertainty as many of the once-taken-for-granted meanings, symbols, and institutions of modern life seemingly dissolve before our eyes. Time as well as social and geographical spaces are highly compressed by rapidly changing computer/media and advanced technologies, information storage and retrieval, and scientific and medical knowledge. Ours is a culture deeply penetrated by commodities and consumer "lifestyles." In our day, consumption rather than production has become the wellspring of society, while highly bureaucratic (although increasingly "decentralized") state agencies attempt to order and regulate social life. What is "real" in this culture is presented to us through the mass media in video imagery that has become the primary source of our cultural knowledge. In much of this media, we are offered a nonstop barrage of "crisis-level" social problems, leaving us to wonder "what the world is coming to." In turn, we are left cynically mistrusting each other and furthering the disintegration of public life and discourse. This cultural hysteria creates a fertile ground for those selling "science" and "advanced" technological fixes that they claim will ease our fears. Under these conditions, rather than trust the actions and judgments of others, we turn to more depersonalized, pervasive, and what appear to be more predictable means of surveillance and social control. In essence, we are seduced into believing that, given the apparent tide of problems we face, subjecting ourselves to more and more meticulous rituals is an unfortunate but necessary condition. The forgoing conditions form what I will refer to simply as "the everyday life of the postmodern," and it is in this cultural context, I believe, that we continue to struggle with problems and issues that arose during the early nineteenth century.

As an example of how our current disciplinary practices are a product of both our historical past and our cultural present, let us consider an incident that took place a few years back in my hometown. In this case, a school bus driver was accused of physically restraining an unruly child on his vehicle. In short order, the driver was fired, and much debate took place in the local newspaper about the child's supposed "bad" behavior on the bus, the reported good reputation of the driver, and about the way school district administrators handled the case. It was clear that no one trusted anyone's account of what actually transpired on the bus that day. A few months later, right before the beginning of the new school year, there was an announcement that each of the district's fleet of buses would be equipped with a video camera "black box." The bus company claimed that, on any given day, just three video cameras would be rotated among all the district's buses and that, given the design of the boxes; neither the students nor the drivers would know when their bus was equipped with a camera. The bus company's manager stated that the use of the cameras would "help to improve student discipline" as well as ensure that the drivers follow "proper procedures."

Now, the principle behind the rotating camera is not new; it originates with a design by Jeremy Bentham dating from 1791 called the panopticon (from the Greek, for "all-seeing"); a design for a central guard tower inside a prison or reformatory. The tower was planned in such a way that prisoners were never quite sure whether a guard was present or not and would have to assume that they were being watched. The inmates, in effect, would watch themselves, internalizing, if you will, the watchful gaze of their keeper. It was a simple, even elegant, solution to the problem of disciplining people in an enclosed space—a dilemma brought about with the birth of the asylum, the modern "solution" to criminal behavior, madness, poverty, and the like. The evolution of this idea more than two hundred years later—deployed in a postmodern context—produces a technological design, routinely applied in the everyday life of schoolchildren and their adult supervisors, none of whom apparently are trusted to act responsibly. Inexpensive video technology—and our willingness to define schoolchildren's behavior on a bus as being so problematic that it warrants "objective" surveillance rather than personal monitoring—makes the use of this new form of social control possible. Curious about what people thought of the cameras, I casually spoke with friends and others in the community about the new policy. Most seemed shocked at the idea at first, but then, in resignation, many conceded that it was probably a "good idea" for the "safety" of everyone involved. I see the new disciplinary techniques, then, both as a product of important, long-term processes set in motion more than two centuries ago and as shaped by a newly emerging cultural context. My goal, echoed nicely by Best and Kellner in writing about their own work, is to "grasp the continuities and discontinuities with the earlier modern era, while mapping the changing threats, and promises now before us."[10]

One challenge I make to the modernist "grand narrative" of the inevitability of historical progress is to assert that the last two hundred or so years of "reforming" justice practice has unequivocally produced a system that is more "just" or more "humane" than the brutal, public punishment that came before it. In other words, I want to challenge the idea that, simply put, we keep building a better mousetrap. Rather, I want to argue that the modern attempt to transform, mold, shape, and "rehabilitate" the criminal, the deviant, and the poor in the name of more effective and even "progressive" social policy may, in fact, be seen as a more general model for the rational ordering of the entire society—intended or not. That is, I am concerned here with a process, set in motion in the early nineteenth century, whereby the enforcement of ever-finer distinctions between what is "acceptable" and "unacceptable" behavior has become part of all our daily lives, and not just the lives of those who break the law. Ultimately, I will show how we are building a culture of surveillance when we infuse daily life with practices that constantly assess our behavior, judge our performance, account for our whereabouts, and challenge our personal integrity.

As I have argued in this chapter, postmodern surveillance practices, these meticulous rituals of power, have four defining characteristics:

1. They are increasingly technology-based, methodical, automatic, and sometimes anonymously applied, and they usually generate a permanent record as evidence.
2. Many new techniques target and treat the body as an object that can be watched, assessed, and regulated.
3. The new techniques are often local, operating in our everyday lives.
4. Local or not, they manage to bring wide-ranging populations, not just the official "deviant" or suspect, under scrutiny.

These characteristics form an "ideal type" postmodern meticulous ritual of power. An ideal type is not "ideal" as in desirable, but rather it is the "pure form" of a social phenomenon; it is an analytical construct that serves as a benchmark to compare the similarities and differences of concrete cases. In what follows, I use this ideal type to identify practices that resemble this pure form of meticulous ritual and I locate the settings where these practices take place. The location is crucial since I argue that in recent times we are seeing the spread of disciplinary practices throughout social life where surveillance and social control strategies that were once aimed at people who had broken the law are now as well targeted at those simply *capable* of transgressing social norms and laws. So, in my analysis, I demonstrate this blurring distinction as I begin each chapter by highlighting examples from, and sometimes move back and forth between, the world of criminal justice and our everyday postmodern lives.

The plan for the book is as follows: I begin chapter 2 by focusing on the work of the late French philosopher Michel Foucault (1926–1984). It is from Foucault, a pioneering social theorist, that I take the idea to concentrate on the small, seemingly benign rituals at the intersection of power, knowledge, and the body. In his strikingly original book, *Discipline and Punish: The Birth of the Prison*, Foucault presented a political history of two basic forms of discipline: the physical torture associated with the "Age of the Sovereign" and, later, the emergence of the asylum, a product of modernity.[11] Building on Foucault's analysis, I chart the evolution of disciplinary practices and surveillance techniques from the invention of the asylum on and, by taking up where Foucault left off, I hope to extend his study of modern social control into the *post*modern era. In chapter 3, I focus on new forms of surveillance that systematically watch and monitor our bodies and behaviors; I show how our communities, homes, schools, and workplaces are increasingly infused with meticulous rituals and surveillance ceremonies. In chapter 4, I turn my attention to practices that treat the body itself as the site and source of evidence and knowledge or, alternatively, that attempt to take control of the body through the use of various technologies. In chapter 5, I consider the postmodern qualities of the Internet and examine a number of surveillance and social control practices developed for and facilitated by the Web. Finally, in chapter 6, I return to considering the important issues and questions I have raised throughout the book about these contemporary developments, assess their consequences, and modestly suggest at least one strategy should we decide to confront the culture of surveillance we are creating.

BEFORE WE MOVE ON

My goal for this book is to offer a theoretically informed description and examination of a variety of surveillance and disciplinary techniques that have become part of our contemporary lives. My agenda is not explicitly "for" or "against" these practices but rather to engage the reader in a process of critical thinking: I want to raise important questions and problems, express them clearly, gather relevant information, use abstract ideas to interpret that information effectively, and to come to well-reasoned conclusions about how surveillance and disciplinary practices actually operate. In my experience, the topic of this book generates passionate feelings that can lead quickly to what are called "normative judgments" or the commonplace view that some things are decidedly "better" than others. So, in this case, it might be a hasty assessment about whether, say, surveillance cameras in public places are a "good" or "bad" thing. These value-laden determinations often turn on a crude cost-benefit analysis of perceived usefulness of the cameras versus a sense of potential harm from their installation. Although, ultimately of course, values are critically important in, for example, drafting public policy regarding the installation of video surveillance, premature normative judgments tend to close off further consideration, impede deeper analysis, and limit our ability to see the "big picture." For the sake of understanding, I encourage the reader to "suspend" their normative judgments and approach the text with a "beginner's mind," that is, with an attitude of openness and lack of predeterminations.

Let me try also to make a few other points clear from the outset. I am neither a technological determinist nor a neo-Luddite. That is, I do not believe that technology "drives" social life or that it is inherently "bad." I do assume, however, that technologies are social products, created and implemented within a complex milieu of cultural, political, and economic influences. [12] In this book I attempt to uncover those influences as they relate to the actual workings of disciplinary power, its daily practices, rituals, and minute procedures, and how those workings are often bound up with the use of new technologies. Moreover, I am *not* suggesting that there is no need for social control in society or that shoplifting, drug abuse, or violent crime are not real problems with real victims. Of course they are. I lived in Los Angeles for a decade and witnessed firsthand the crime, violence, and chronic social problems that seem to define the hard edge of urban life in the United States. But the issues I am raising are of broader sociological concern and have to do with that "big picture" of where we are going as a culture and with the balance of power, if you will, within that larger society. In other words, I want to look at the evolution of surveillance as an entry point to observing and understanding our changing attitude and practice toward discipline and social control in general.

By implying that surveillance is becoming more universal and thus oddly more democratic, I am *not* suggesting that we are all necessarily subject to the same quantity or quality of social control or that it does not have differential effects. Historically and cross-culturally, the amount and character of monitoring, discipline, and punishment that individuals are afforded have varied considerably by such defining characteristics as age, racial and ethnic categories, class, and sex. We see, therefore, teenagers more likely to be subjected to police scrutiny, the poorly dressed to reap more inspection by store security, and women to experience more informal and formal social control of their bodies.[13] Without question, this continues today. My point is that there are more impersonal, more methodical, and more technology-driven forms of surveillance and social control in our society than ever before, and today's forms and their sheer volume are enveloping even those who might have been previously immune.[14] For example, the surveillance camera positioned in the bookstore I discussed earlier where I sat with my friend does not differentiate or discriminate whose image it captures; breathalyzers are administered to all the students attending the prom, and no employee is exempt from a health "screening" program.

For those who have traditionally been the target of more monitoring and control than others, these developments serve only to intensify and increase the amount of ritualized regulation and monitoring already in their daily lives. Moreover, as David Lyon points out, surveillance often supports a process of "social sorting."[15] That is, some surveillance practices should be considered not only as potential threats to individual privacy and liberties but, from a sociological perspective, they may operate as a powerful means of creating and reinforcing social differences and enhancing the life chances of some while diminishing those of others. For instance, "data mining" techniques can tell a bank that certain "high-value" customers should be offered low-interest loans and personal services and advice while other "low-value" ones are charged higher interest rates and fees or are even discouraged from becoming a customer at all.

Reflecting on the simultaneous modern and postmodern world we live in today, I should also point out that my analysis is centered on a "sociology of the postmodern" period rather than "postmodern sociology." The former approach applies a blend of both classical and contemporary social theory and methods for example, the ideas of Max Weber (1864–1920) on the functioning of bureaucracy along with the insights of Jean Bauldriard (1929–2007) regarding our inability in a mediated culture to distinguish reality from fantasy, or David Harvey (1935–) who views postmodernity as a new stage of global capitalism. By contrast, the latter tactic—postmodern sociology—tends to be associated with more avant-garde ways of writing and thinking about the social world that are more artistic than traditionally analytical in style.

This book was written as an essay-argument rather than as a typical academic monograph. Fitting this style, it is filled with anecdotal evidence, journalistic accounts, and my own and others' research of contemporary surveillance practices. I use this pastiche of material as my primary data for several reasons. First, like many sociologists, I see culture as inconsistent, contradictory, and complex; it simply defies the more linear, "cause and effect" models associated with "scientific" inquiry. Does this mean that I do not need empirical evidence to support my claims? Hardly. It simply means that my objective is, as Diana Crane states, "to interpret a wide range of materials in order to identify what might be described as an underlying 'gestalt.'"[16] Therefore, I take recorded culture to be both a window into society as well as a legitimate source for the interpretation of social meaning.

Second, my goal is to offer an account of how ordinary people experience, live with, and actually contribute to the new surveillance practices. Sociology is sometimes referred to as "slow journalism" since it often takes quite some time to conduct formal studies, collect data, and publish findings. By bringing in and referencing the work of professional journalists, I hope to weave together accounts of the current, lived experiences of average citizens and the power of sociological theory and analysis.[17] And third, while I recount the stories of particular individuals in my narrative, I also try to support my arguments by referencing, where available, broader trends as indicated by government reports and data, pertinent legal cases, changes to federal and state laws, the results of national opinion polls, industry-wide trends and assessments, and relevant scholarship and debate.

Finally, readers will notice my frequent use of quotation marks on words and phrases without necessarily citing sources (when I am indeed quoting someone in particular, I do indicate the source). The use of these marks in this way is both stylistic and substantive. Some of this punctuation simply references everyday colloquialisms. Yet others are intended to alert the reader to the socially constructed nature of language and to suggest that meanings are inherently unstable and potentially contested. Expressions such as "substance abuse," "dysfunctional family," "at risk," and "learning disability" are labels created by those who claim professional expertise or are used by those in positions of authority. Readers should decide if they agree with the meanings evoked by this language or if they wish to contest their legitimacy.

Chapter Two

The Scaffold, the Penitentiary, and Beyond

In the colony of Virginia during the 1760s, the theft of a hog would bring twenty-five lashes well laid on at the publick whipping post; for the second offense he was set two houres in the pillory and had both ears nailed ther to, at the end of the two hours to have the ears slit loose; for the third offence, death. [1]

Yet by the 1830s,

Within an atmosphere of repression, humiliation, and gloomy silence, the Auburn Penitentiary convict performed an incessantly monotonous round of activity. He arose at 5:15 and as soon as his cell was unlocked, he marched out holding three pieces of equipment: a night tub used for calls of nature; a can for drinking water; and a wooden food container. Holding this paraphernalia in his left hand, he laid his right hand on the shoulder of the felon who occupied the next cell and marched in lock-step across the court yard to his workshop. [2]

Here we have two very different forms of punishment. What happened to bring about this radical change? For years, many legal scholars and progressive historians advanced the idea that the "invention" of the modern penitentiary was a product of a deep, humanitarian impulse on the part of reformers, state officials, and citizenry. From this perspective, the ritualized torture on the public scaffold used in Europe and the whipping post favored in the United States were, quite suddenly, deemed barbaric and unenlightened and, if one reads the rhetoric of the reformers of the nineteenth century, this theme is certainly evident. Yet, in the late twentieth century, a number of scholars came to question this interpretation of history. One significant figure in that debate was Michel Foucault.

Foucault argued that while indeed the penal reformers of the eighteenth century may have set out to reduce the ferocity of punishment—along with its public spectacle—they did not necessarily aim to punish *less* but, rather, to punish *better*. In other words, their intent was to make punishment and the system of justice more efficient and effective. Punishment, under their plan, would be rationally organized and proportional to the crime; deterrence, rather than retribution, would be its central purpose. These ideas helped set in motion a series of "reforms" by which the "soul" as well as the body of the offender became the target of punishment. The perpetrator would now be sent away for years to a modern asylum, such as the celebrated Auburn penitentiary in New York State, to be subjected to an institutional regime that would strip him of his individuality, isolate his mind, and discipline his body. (The term "penitentiary" has roots in Latin, meaning "regret for one's actions.") Under this new idealized plan, the staff would watch the miscreant's every move and accumulate knowledge of the circumstances of his crime, his family background, and life history. This institutional regime would break him of his bad habits and transform him into a model citizen. Punishment would succeed when the inmate had been "rehabilitated."

But Foucault, in a book entitled *Surveiller et punir: Naissance de la prison* and translated from the French as *Discipline and Punish: The Birth of the Prison*, questions the very notion that all this "rehabilitation" necessarily meant "progress" and the more "humane" treatment of the offender.[3] Indeed, we might want to ask ourselves: Is more or less physical pain the only yardstick of benevolence? Of suffering? Of human dignity? On what basis and with what values do we assess whether a criminal is treated more "humanely"? On what scale, for example, do we place "twenty-five lashes well laid on" versus being locked in a cell twenty-three hours a day for life in a "super max prison"? I am not advocating a return to physical punishment but rather questioning the philosophical and ethical basis on which claims of "justice" and "humanity" have been asserted. Such assertions can often appear quite contradictory. Take the case of the young American in Singapore a few years back who was sentenced by authorities there to six lashes from a rattan cane for vandalism. Following the sentence there were cries of brutality and "inhumane" treatment from U.S. officials. Curiously, at nearly that same time, a criminologist and longtime death penalty proponent in New York was calling for the substitution of lethal injection for the electric chair to carry out that state's then return to executions. He claimed that the injections were a "painless and nonrepulsive way of doing justice."[4] This suggests that, for some, even a death sentence can be considered "humane" as long as it is "painless."

With the purported "march of progress," then, while it may be said that social control has, in some ways, become more "gentle," it may also be true that it has become more widespread and more invasive. What do I mean? Simply this: that changes began in the early nineteenth century to make justice more "efficient" set in motion a process whereby the authority to judge an individual's behavior has been extended well beyond any legal offense committed. Since that time, a complex machinery of organizations, institutions, and practices (e.g., myriad kinds of jails, prisons, courts, halfway houses, boot camps, community corrections programs; as well as "correctional" techniques such as probation and parole, fines, restitution, house arrest, community service, work release, and day-reporting centers) has been developed and is now part of the justice system. The result has been a proliferation of the number of crimes it is possible to commit as well as the number of "judges" to assess them. These judges are the armies of personnel who appear as "expert" authorities—probation and parole officers, wardens, psychiatrists, social workers, criminologists, penologists—along with their diagnoses, assessments, evaluations, and classifications. In fact, rather than simply responding to a specific behavior or infraction, this kind of judgment goes beyond simply what someone has done and extends to the very core of who he is. In other words, this "power to punish," as Foucault called it, assesses something other than crimes alone. It judges what kind of persons offenders are and whether they measure up to the kind of person society expects them to be. It is about, in essence, the enforcement of "normalcy" and the attempt to isolate, restrict, and control; or better yet, eliminate all social, physical, and psychological "irregularities."

Seen in this way, a fellow who stole a hog in the colony of Virginia was simply punished for his crime. No one expected him, as part of his penalty, to reflect on his inner self or to become a productive worker. No one really cared if he came from a "dysfunctional" family, if he had a "personality disorder," or if he was a good candidate for "rehabilitation." While there is little doubt that torturing the hog thief was a brutish act, there were limits to how much pain and punishment could be exacted on him without killing him (which, of course, effectively ended the process of punishment). His body was all he had to offer; it was all that the authorities could take from him. Yet, at some point, it was decided that the thief had more to give; it was not enough that he simply stop stealing hogs. Reformers, philosophers, jurists, religious leaders, and state officials—liberal utopians and conservative pragmatists alike—began to argue that, with the right program, the criminal, the deviant, the delinquent, and even the poor could be "morally reformed" from the inside out. Why did all of this come about? Where did these influential people ever get the idea that, in the name of "doing good," "saving" someone, or "getting tough," they could change an individual's behavior by remaking the self, indeed, by "improving" the offender's "character" with the appropriate reform program or with "moral guidance"? What happened, I want to argue, is that forms of punishment and justice such as the public whipping post, like other "premodern" social practices, were swept away with the birth of the modern era. To understand the kind of disciplinary techniques we practice today, we need to understand them in a historical context, and this demands that we interrogate the very meaning of modernity.

BIRTH OF THE MODERN

The roots of modernity lie in the post-Renaissance period from the mid-sixteenth century until about the early 1800s, a period often referred to as the Enlightenment. From this age came a fundamental break from medieval tradition and religious dogmas. Unfettered by such constraints, the idea emerged that autonomous, universal, human "reason," not simply God's laws, would bring certainty, hope, and progress to the world. Indeed, the Enlightenment is credited with giving birth to a near-utopian vision of a future in which human emancipation and "enlightened" thinking would prevail. As these ideas and practices took hold, more traditional forms of social, economic, and cultural life began to crumble under the weight of changes in economic organization, scientific experimentation, and the rise of democratic states and rational law. This movement intensified and culminated in the birth of the modern era—for our purposes, from around the turn of the nineteenth century and continuing through the first half of the twentieth century. We can summarize the main themes and characteristics of modernity as follows:

- An increased rationalizing or calculating attitude toward social life based on notions of efficiency, predictability, control, and discipline, epitomized by the emergence of the factory and machine-based capitalism.
- The progressive differentiation of social life in the division of labor, specialization of occupation, and separation of the "public" and "private," "home" and "work" life.
- The rise of large-scale state and private organizations and bureaucracies as well as large, urban centers.
- The acceleration or "compression" of time-space relations, a fast-paced world that was made "smaller" by emerging modes of transportation and communication.
- The rise of a relatively large middle and professional class with its own self-interest, sensibilities, and culture.
- The development of the "human sciences" such as psychology, psychiatry, sociology, criminology, demography, statistics, and public health.

- The institutionalization of the belief in progress, driven by the idea that scientific knowledge, objective reasoning, and technology could harness nature and change social life and human existence for the better.

Modernity's achievements were considerable. It gave birth to democratic movements in the West that increased personal freedoms and liberties for most, eventually including those not owning property, minorities, and women. Governments regulated social and economic relations and put in place rational systems of law, justice, monetary exchange, compulsory schooling, and social welfare systems. Driven by the dynamic and technology-based system of capitalism, transportation, communication, and utility systems proliferated, while literacy expanded, consumer goods became readily available, and the standard of living increased. Scientific experimentation, medical discoveries, and public health and sanitation movements helped wipe out common diseases and reduce various forms of human suffering. These developments were certainly progress but they were not the whole picture; modernity has always had its detractors.

Karl Marx (1818–1883) wrote about the devastating poverty, exploitation, and alienation that he saw in nineteenth-century capitalism, pointing out that not everyone benefitted equally from the new arrangements. The French sociologist Emile Durkheim (1858–1917) considered how increasing geographic and class mobility and the loss of tradition in culture were likely to produce a feeling of anomie, or normlessness, on the part of many. The German social scientist Max Weber (1864–1920) offered the view that modernity's distinctive "formal rationality"—as epitomized in large, bureaucratic organizations represented an "iron cage" that would ultimately entrap us. An even darker view is found in the writings of anti-Enlightenment philosopher Friedrich Nietzsche (1844–1900).

Nietzsche offered a direct challenge to the optimistic worldview of the Enlightenment and the so-called advances of modernity. For Nietzsche, this period's "progress," the claims of the discovery of absolute "truths," and its scientific and technical "innovation" were more about what he called the "will to power"; the human drive to dominate nature and the environment. While Nietzsche praised the critical spirit of the Enlightenment, he disputed those who claimed to have discovered universal moral codes and systems of reason, since he believed that, given the diversity of human nature, such codes could not apply to everyone. This meant that individuals asserting lawlike standards must necessarily place themselves—morally, socially, and culturally—above others, thereby dominating them. From a Nietzschean perspective, the history of recent human experience is not a simple procession of higher universal morals and higher standards of reason. Rather, driven by the desire for some ultimate "truth" and knowledge, humans have produced one system of domination after the other. As it was once put, we "progressed" in the twentieth century, for example, from "the slingshot to the megaton bomb." Even Albert Einstein wrote in a letter to a friend, "Our entire much-praised technological progress, and civilization generally, could be compared to an axe in the hand of a pathological criminal."[5] In this view, knowledge cannot be separated from power. The ideological system of Enlightenment, based on notions of reason, rationality, and progress, is seen as just that: another ideology, another interpretation of reality, advanced by one group over others, rather than some ultimate, final "truth."

For Nietzsche, then, as well as for Weber and later for Foucault, the post-Enlightenment period is one of increasing domination *masked in a guise of emancipation and humanitarianism*. As philosopher Steven Best writes, "Awakening in the classical world like a sleeping giant, reason finds chaos and disorder everywhere and embarks on a rational ordering of the social, attempting to classify and regulate all forms of experience."[6] Foucault suggested that rather than a utopian dream of freedom, late eighteenth-century politicians, philosophers, and jurists offered instead a blueprint for a military model of society in which discipline and self-control would become central organizing themes. Uniform precision, bodily discipline, rigid hierarchies, and "the drill" designed to mold and shape the body would become techniques of social control that could easily be adapted beyond the military camps, barracks, monasteries, and the *Hôtel-Dieu de Paris* where the poor were once confined, places where these techniques were discovered and perfected. The modern individual was born, according to Foucault, into a sea of regulations, petty rules and subrules, and fussy inspections, a world where the supervision of the smallest fragments of life and of the body are carried out.[7]

With Enlightenment zeal, late eighteenth-century ideologues turned their attention from the control of nature to the manipulation of "man" by way of the emerging knowledge of the human sciences. This movement is reflected in the early writings in penology and criminology, psychology, neurology, and demography and, in many ways, continues today as a fundamental assumption of these fields of study. In other words, in new and important ways, human beings—our bodies, minds, and behaviors—became the *subject* of scientific inquiry and the *object* of its passions. The human sciences, then, helped to create a regime of power that examines and describes human behavior in terms of "norms"; by setting out what is "normal" they also create the idea of "abnormal" and deviant. The rise of the human sciences as a topic of inquiry is closely linked with the emergence of new "disciplinary technologies" designed to treat the human body as an object to be assessed, analyzed, broken down, and improved.[8] The experiences that Foucault saw as the most vulnerable to the process of normalization, scientific inquiry, and official scrutiny were madness, criminality, poverty, and "deviant" sexual practices.

This is a crucial turn of events. Rather than focusing on dominating the world around them, late Enlightenment scholars turned the will to power on human beings. Rational and scientific knowledge and discourses (i.e., systems of language overlapping with cultural practices), embedded within bureaucratized organizations, provided the means to sort and classify, regulate, exclude, and even eliminate any human behavior deemed outside an increasingly narrow definition of "normal." Some would argue that, say, Nazi Germany or Stalinist Russia were, rather than some aberration in the course of human progress, a natural outcome of the rational, calculating mind of modernity. As Foucault once said, both regimes "used and extended mechanisms already present in most other societies. More than that: in spite of their own internal madness, they used to a large extent the ideas and the devices of our political rationality."[9]

It would seem that this is the historical context of how we in the West got the idea that we could, regardless of an individual's particular "defect," reconstruct a more idealized person if only he could be subjected to the right disciplinary regime.

CASTLES OF OUR CONSCIENCE

This mentality and the emergence of the modern disciplinary institution are patently evident in the United States.[10] In addition to their sudden revulsion to violence, what became clear to reformers in the late eighteenth and early nineteenth centuries was that the use of the village whipping post or stocks was a messy business and, increasingly, a political liability in postrevolutionary America. These inherited English criminal statutes were a constant reminder of monarchical political oppression while those involving "cruel" sanctions were not applied consistently, making criminal justice arbitrary and ineffectual. In these early years, "a jury, squeezed between two distasteful choices, death or acquittal, often acquitted the guilty," according to historian Lawrence Friedman.[11] This kind of "jury lawlessness" sometimes provoked vigilante justice, endangering the establishment of rational-legal authority and, therefore, the political power of the new government. A more predictable, orderly, and democratic set of punishments was needed to support the new political regime. We see, then, the emergence of a new discourse of crime and new forms of punishment.

Inspired by the writings of, among others, the influential Italian criminologist Cesare Beccaria and his new "science of man," *Homo criminalis*, people such as Dr. Benjamin Rush (1745–1813), who was a signer of the Declaration of Independence, set out to reinvent criminal justice practices. The new discourse on crime and punishment that he promoted was celebrated in a now well-known set of principles:

- Punishment must be consistent and not arbitrary.
- Punishment should be a deterrent to future criminality.
- There should be temporal modulation, since punishment can function only if it comes to an end.
- Each crime and each penalty would be clearly laid out in a classification scheme.
- The guilty should be only one of the targets of punishment, for punishment is directed above all at the potentially guilty.

The bodies of condemned offenders were now the property of society rather than of the king. Such ideas were infused with the notion of the social contract: that crime was an attack on society itself and that punishment should right the wrong done to the community and restore offenders to their proper places in it. Criminal justice would be rational, not emotional, according to the reformers. It would approach the mind and soul of the criminal and not just the body.

For a while, it was deemed that performing public works was the best treatment for the offender. In Philadelphia, for example, the application of the city's "wheelbarrow" law of 1786 put ragged, shaven-headed, chain-gang prisoners to work cleaning the streets under the watchful eye of armed guards. But the sight of these men became increasingly distasteful to the good citizens of the city as the convicts went about "begging and insulting the inhabitants, [and] collecting crowds of idle boys," and they became the sport of others who tormented the prisoners incessantly. The law of March 27, 1789, soon sequestered prisoners to conditions of more private punishment at the Walnut Street jail.[12] Here the prisoners were subjected to a "moral" regime of solitary confinement, hard labor, diet control, and bodily hygiene. Yet not long after it was built, conditions at the jail deteriorated; inspectors began pardoning prisoners to alleviate overcrowding, abuses and neglect were exposed, and serious riots took place. The result was unanimous condemnation of the Walnut Street jail. But rather than scrap the experiment with incarceration, authorities pressed on and called for the building of new, larger state penitentiaries. Undertaking the most ambitious public works program in Pennsylvania's history to date, the western and eastern facilities were erected by the laws of 1817 and 1821, marking the beginnings of Pennsylvania's prison "system." The situation was similar elsewhere, as other states increased their commitment to institutional punishment.

This turn to rationally organized reformatory institutions and the new "science of man" influenced society's response to other behaviors as well. Before about 1825, the majority of poor and dependent people had been customarily cared for in noninstitutional ways. Those close to the center of town life might stay in their own homes with the help of the community or were placed with relatives, friends, or fellow church members. Those on the social margins were "boarded" with townsfolk, with a widow perhaps, at a negotiated price. Later, communities made direct payments to people in their homes while some able-bodied poor might be "auctioned off" to farmers and others and were put to work for their keep. Yet, after the 1820s, these apparently flexible and informal arrangements began to break down under the weight of expanded commercial development, the erosion of social cohesion in small towns, the attraction of wealth, and the increasing stratification of towns and villages. Townsfolk, particularly those of the middle and upper classes, became less willing to take in and board the increasing number of strangers and outsiders appearing in their area.

In New York, for example, an influential report by the secretary of state in 1824 estimated the total number of the state's poor to be 22,111 and the cost of providing for them to be close to $500,000. The report advocated the establishment of a system of county poorhouses, or almshouses, modeled after the "House of Industry," which had been erected in Rensselaer County in 1820. The idea was that each inmate would work to his own ability as a means of stimulating industry and sharing the expense of his maintenance. These houses of employment would ideally be connected to a workhouse or penitentiary "for the reception and discipline of sturdy beggars and vagrants." Street beggary would be entirely prohibited. By 1835, almshouses appeared in fifty-one out of fifty-four state counties.

The principal advantages of the poorhouse seem clear. It isolated the dependent from the growing middle-class community that increasingly considered the pauper an idler and troublemaker. Rather than have the indigent scattered around town in private dwellings or, worse yet, begging on street corners, the almshouse centralized relief administration and provided for more effective surveillance of their activities by one overseer. However, before long, the "new" system of county indoor relief was itself in crisis. For what was hailed as the final solution to dependency revealed itself as yet another administrative, jurisdictional, and financial mess. In New York, annual reports from throughout the state to the legislature uncovered shocking abuse of inmates. Idleness was pervasive, especially in the larger houses. Economic depressions between 1837 and 1843, and later between 1857 and 1858, combined with the dramatic increase in immigration, placed an incredible burden on relief agencies. State governments, grappling to gain some rational control over the system and its expenditures, began to create central administrative agencies to coordinate the activities of public charities. Massachusetts was the first to create a state board of charities in 1863. Later that year, New York established its board. By 1873, boards had been set up in Illinois, Pennsylvania, North Carolina, Rhode Island, Michigan, Wisconsin, Kansas, and Connecticut.

One important development that followed the establishment of these state boards was the process of classifying and segregating the population of the almshouses and moving inmates into facilities designated for their particular "defect." Reformers, once again deploying rational thought and armed with new studies from the human sciences and the experiences of doctors and wardens of the new institutions, contended that the care and control function of the poorhouse could be enhanced if each class of dependent had its own particular needs addressed, since the mixing of such classes had created conditions that were detrimental to all. This "classification" movement attempted to extend administrative rationality and planning by isolating each particular class of deviants and dependents, not only to physically separate them from each other but also to gain more effective surveillance, observation, and control. Gender, age, and mental and physical capacities were the basis of boundaries among the new facilities, which prevented, through the restriction of both social and sexual contact, the procreation of what were commonly called the "defective classes." Once so isolated, each facility could engage in a more exacting process of distinguishing the degree of each class's "rehabilitative" potential. Whereas custodial care was all that could be expected for the very old, the very young, the infirm, or the completely helpless, others, including recalcitrant children, healthy deviants, and the slightly feeble, could be educated and trained to labor both inside and, eventually, outside the institution.

The first group of dependents affected by the movement for separation was the insane. By 1881, there were six state hospitals for the acutely and chronically insane in New York, for example. Between 1850 and 1869, thirty-five new hospitals were opened in other states and, by 1890, fifty-nine others came into existence, with the post-1870 hospitals increasingly larger in size. Children were similarly drawn away from the mixed almshouses where they were, for the most part, "badly fed, badly clothed, badly taken care of, and exposed to the degrading influence of those in immediate charge of them," according to reformer Louisa Lee Schuyler.[13] Specialized juvenile correction facilities—houses of refuge, reformatories, and training schools—expanded both the classification scheme and the system of care and control of dependent and troublesome children. Not only were children increasingly institutionalized in segregated facilities, but the legal mechanisms by which they got there changed as well. The juvenile court represented one more manifestation of the increasingly bureaucratic system of social control and the trend toward administrative reform and rationality. Within twenty-five years of the adoption of the first juvenile court legislation in Illinois in 1899, juvenile courts were established in every state but two. Although perhaps more ceremonial than substantive at first, the juvenile court evolved to possess broad-sweeping jurisdiction over the lives of children under the age of sixteen. The court's ideological foundation rested on the notion of *parens patriae*, or parental care, and thus the legal institution was charged with protecting and providing for the needs of delinquent, dependent, and neglected youth.

The darker side of the reform story, however, was the regulation of family life by the state along with few alternatives to an institutional response to youthful misconduct. By 1940, juvenile courts in the United States handled 200,000 delinquency cases alone, not including the dependent and neglected—a rate of 10.5 per 1,000 of those between the ages of ten and seventeen. By 1955, the corresponding figures were 431,000 cases with a rate of 21.4 per 1,000. In comparing figures from the U.S. Bureau of the Census for juvenile correctional facilities between 1923 and 1950, we see that these populations rose from 27,238 in 1923 to 30,496 in 1933 and to 40,880 by 1950. The corresponding rates per 100,000 of those in the population under age eighteen were 65.7, 72.3, and 88.8, respectively.

Specialized facilities were also developed for the "feebleminded" and the epileptic. "Mental defectives" were further classified as "teachable" or "unteachable." Concerned with the "hereditary factor" in the proliferation of crime, pauperism, and mental deficiency, reformers and state welfare administrators sought to isolate its source, which, according to one reformer, was "the unrestrained liberty allowed to vagrant and degraded women." They urged the creation of an institution for such women, which, if not for reformation, could at least cut off the line of pauper descendants. In New York, the campaign resulted in 1887 in the House of Refuge for Women at Hudson, where "all females between the ages of fifteen and thirty years who had been convicted of petty larceny, habitual drunkenness, of being common prostitutes, frequenters of disorderly houses or houses of prostitution" were to be placed. Suitable employment was to be provided, which would encourage "habits of self supporting industry" and "mental and moral improvement." This facility was soon filled to capacity and three other women's reformatories were erected in the state by the late 1890s.

According to the view I want to take here, the inventions of the penitentiary, the poorhouse, and the mental asylum were not *simply* chapters in a long humanitarian crusade. Driven by ideas having their origins in Enlightenment reason and progressive convictions, a constellation of influential philosophers, jurists, reformers, religious devotees, and state authorities aided in the creation and expansion of a system of social control for modern society not possible in the premodern, classical age. Ironically then, it might be argued, that in the name of "humanity" and "emancipation," progressives created *more* formal social control, not less. Reformers, interested in punishing more effectively and more certainly, went beyond the surface of the skin into the very heart and soul of the deviant. In doing so, they approached the criminal, the deviant, and the poor as objects to be manipulated whereas just a short time before, the community had confronted the "impenitent sinner" as deserving of corporal punishment or, in the case of the poor, simply as a poor person who had been "reduced to want."

Under the authority of the state and "in the name of the people," these reformers— increasingly from middle and professional classes—asserted a new system of universal "moral" principles and a new discourse on crime and punishment, placing themselves as "experts" at the center of justice practice. Reflecting the central themes of modernity, disorderly and ill-defined forms of public torture and stigmatization ceremonies were replaced by rationally organized legal codes as well as reformatory institutions such as prisons, poorhouses, and asylums that this new social class would run and supervise. As part of their new program, rather than seek retribution, they removed punishment from public view and placed it behind the walls of the institution. The "dangerous rogue," sent away to places like the Auburn penitentiary, was to be subjected to a mostly secular, military-like apparatus that would transform him (or a woman sent to a "House of Refuge") into a newly refined democratic subject: "A diligent, literate laborer; a moderate, self-interested citizen."[14] And, as I have shown, it was soon asserted that the poor could be made "industrious," the deviant turned from their unusual ways, and the insane brought back to reason. Listen to these notions in the words of some of these early reformers:

> You take a child; you must not expect to make her, without care, and instruction and patience, a useful domestic. Encourage what you may find good in her, and in punishing her faults, consider how you should endeavor to correct those of your own children.—Boston Children's Aid Society, *Reminiscences of the Boston Female Orphan Asylum* (1844)

> To make a vagrant efficient is more praiseworthy than to make two blades of grass grow where one grew before.—E. Stagg Whitin, *Penal Servitude* (1912)

> Outside the walls a man must choose between work and idleness—between honesty and crime. Why not teach him these lessons before he comes out?— Thomas Mott Osborne, *Society and Prisons* (1916)

DISCIPLINE AS A TECHNIQUE

The modern era gave birth to a range of discourses, techniques, and practices that were designed to mold and shape the body as well as the mind. These practices involve a distinctly modern form of social and political constraint that Michel Foucault called "disciplinary power"; a kind of power that is *exercised* as a technique rather than *held* as a commodity. It is a *strategy*, a set of tactics that circulate within a network of relations. This is a radical alternative to traditional sociological conceptions of power. Most theories assert that power is possessed by the "powerful" who control material and social resources; for example, the owners of capital or political elites. "Power" is assumed to emanate from these resources and these theories often take for granted that knowledge is either politically neutral or necessarily liberating. Such "resource" theories of power are very important, no question about it. They are especially helpful in aiding our understanding of, say, the perpetuation of social classes or other forms of material inequality. Unfortunately, however, they are often "reductionistic" in that they reduce all forms of social power to class domination or to the more "macrostructures" of the economy, political authority, or the state. In doing so, they may tell us very little about the "micro level," the concrete ways in which individuals, their bodies and behaviors, are controlled and shaped in everyday life. The exercise of discipline is one of the ways that we can actually see power put into effect. This is a subtle argument. Foucault is *not* suggesting that disciplinary power is without political effect or that it does not create or contribute to asymmetrical advantage for one individual or group in relation to another. Disciplinary power may augment, and may even be intimately bound with, other forms of political, social, and economic resources but it cannot be simply reduced to or subsumed by them.

Disciplinary power then can appear "bidirectional," not simply operating from the "top down" but circulating throughout the social body. That is, it does not simply flow directly from the highest levels of the government or ruling elites and imposed on the masses, but may be developed and practiced by a wide range of people in a host of institutional or organizational sites as well as everyday settings. Rather than being concentrated in the hands of just a few, disciplinary power appears nearly everywhere, dispersed and fragmented. In this view, *we are all involved and enmeshed within a matrix of power relations that are highly intentional and purposeful; arrangements that can be more or less unequal but are never simply one-directional.*

Let's stop to consider two contemporary examples. First, drug-testing programs in the workplace and the cases of Samuel Allen and Daryl Kenyon. Allen is a highly paid president of the international division of a large corporate sporting goods store with more than ten thousand employees. Kenyon, on the other hand, works on the production line at a large office furniture manufacturer. Despite their obvious differences in pay, status, and authority, both men were required to offer hair samples to be tested for drugs when they were hired and both consented to and endorsed the testing programs at their respective companies.[15] Second, think of your local police force. Although officers can exercise considerable authority over the citizenry, they must, to function legitimately in the eyes of the public, discipline themselves with bureaucratic rules and regulations, a rigid hierarchy of command, and the close monitoring and evaluation of each other's actions.

The exercise of disciplinary power is often continuous, automatic, and anonymous (think of the surveillance video camera). It is extensive and thorough, and it is capillary as well, meaning that it extends out to the remotest corners of society. It seeks to discipline individuals efficiently and effectively, with the least amount of physical force, labor power, and expense. Knowledge, in Foucault's scheme, is intrinsic to the spread and proliferation of disciplinary power. Knowledge is not equal to power, nor is power the same as knowledge; each presupposes the other. Again, consider drug testing. Such tests are a disciplinary ritual that uses scientific knowledge *of* the body to derive knowledge *from* the body. This information is then used as the basis to judge or to take action against an individual. Without knowledge, power is exercised capriciously; yet without the capacity to punish, knowledge is meaningless.

Finally, disciplinary power is often productive and not simply repressive. This is a crucial point. If disciplinary power operated only in a top-down, repressive fashion, it would meet with far more resistance and have limited effects. Instead, proponents of disciplinary techniques stress the obvious advantages of their deployment, thus appeasing opposition (e.g., "Police surveillance cameras will enhance public safety"; "Drug testing will make workplaces more productive"). Like water seeking its own level, when resistance appears, disciplinary power finds a way around it, incorporates or coopts it. The techniques of disciplinary power are also "corrective" and agents may employ rewards or privileges to accomplish the goal of modifying behavior. For example, supervision on a factory floor may have been set up to avoid theft but the knowledge gathered from the monitoring may also be used to enhance employee's skills and productivity (this is echoed in the now ubiquitous recording you hear when you call a company, "This call may be monitored for your protection and for training purposes."). In such cases, workers may be encouraged to use the workplace surveillance system to their own advantage by becoming "better" workers. Suspected substance users are told to use the company's random drug tests to help keep themselves "clean," while "motivated" students are persuaded to utilize a teacher's tracking system to meet goals and complete their work.

It is during the modern era that, according to Foucault, a variety of these relatively modest disciplinary procedures were devised in the new institutions by the doctors, wardens, and schoolmasters who were out in the provinces far removed from the center of state power. It was these individuals who were the first to confront problems of managing large numbers of people in confined spaces. By mimicking military discipline and with the help of the knowledge of the emerging human sciences, these institutional administrators established detailed, micromethods for the efficient supervision and surveillance of inmates, patients, and students to produce obedience and conformity. These methods include strict posture and machinelike movements such as in the "lockstep-and-silence" system; monotonous uniforms; the separation and classification of people by their crimes, diseases, and abilities; podiums and orderly lines of desks so it took only one master to observe an entire classroom; and even the smallest architectural details, such as large dividers between bathroom stalls to prevent sexual misconduct. Enclosure was not just about confinement but also permitted the partitioning of internal space into an orderly grid that, in turn, used architecture to disperse bodies and refine classifications (wings, wards, cells, classrooms, desks, etc.) where, as Foucault states, "each individual has his own place; and each place its individual."[16]

The control of time and space was crucial in these institutions; every minute of every day and every activity of the inmates were monitored and scheduled. It was in these closed disciplinary organizations where, for the first time, people were treated as "cases" about which authorities attempted to build extensive dossiers including life histories, family backgrounds, and rehabilitative progress. There were also series of micropenalties established to scan conduct and ensure social control. Offenses such as lateness, absences, inattention, impoliteness, disobedience, poor attitude, and lack of cleanliness were subjected to light physical punishments, minor deprivations, and petty humiliations. By specifying the minutest details of every day, disciplinary power made almost any behavior punishable and thus the object of attention, surveillance, and control.

Disciplinary power is further enhanced by the use of more ritualized knowledge-gathering activities such as "the examination." Here, case files are built out of the often-mundane details of people's lives and activities. Two key procedures are used to build these files. One is "hierarchical observation," which involves surveillance, information collection, and analysis as a central organizing principle of the institution. Disciplining individuals through observation requires the delegation of supervision. Here, individuals carry out the act of watching others while they themselves are being watched. The other key procedure is "normalizing judgment," which entails the assessment of an individual's behavior set against some standard or ideal (i.e., "normal") where all conduct lies between two poles, "good" and "bad," and can be judged—with small, graduated distinctions—along a continuum. Foucault argued that the goal of these procedures was to forge what he called "docile" bodies: mute, obedient individuals who have been subjected, transformed, and improved.

This notion of docility is very important to the ideas presented in this book, for it is the ultimate aim of most forms of social control. The opposite of docility is rebellious, wild, and disagreeable behavior. Robert Emerson and Sheldon Messinger refer to the "politics of trouble" when they point out that most behavior that comes to be labeled deviant, problematic, or disagreeable originates with people causing "trouble" for others or by feeling troubled themselves.[17] No matter what its stated purpose—to "help," "cure," "punish," or "rehabilitate"—social control that is aimed at the juvenile delinquent, the unemployed, the mentally ill, the nursing home resident, or the recalcitrant worker is intended to render that individual docile; that is, manageable, submissive, teachable, tractable, and pliable. The "politics of trouble" are echoed in the commands, "Keep in line," "Don't talk back," "Eat your dinner," "Don't make noise," "Don't cause problems," "Work harder."

BENTHAM'S PANOPTICON

Amid the array of disciplinary practices that emerged in the modern era, Foucault chose to highlight what he considered to be an exemplar in the operation of disciplinary technology: the panopticon. In 1791, British utilitarian philosopher, economist, and jurist Jeremy Bentham (1748–1832) printed a collection of letters he had exchanged with his brother, an architect living in Russia, under the long-winded yet telling title *Panopticon; or, The Inspection-House: Containing the Idea of a New Principle of Construction Applicable to Any Sort of Establishment, in Which Persons of Any Description Are to Be Kept under Inspection; and Particular to Penitentiary-Houses, Prisons, Poor-Houses, Lazarettos, Houses of Industry, Manufactories, Hospitals, Work-Houses, Mad-Houses, and Schools with a Plan of Management Adapted to the Principle.* The detailed architectural design for the panopticon called for the construction of a building with a central tower that contained the "inspector's lodge." Around the lodge, in a circular form, was a set of peripheral cells with windows in the rear and front of each cell so that, in effect, the cell space was backlit. The prisoner—or lunatic, pauper, schoolboy, or other inmate—could then be subjected to the constant observation of the person occupying the lodge.[18] Bentham himself anticipated the "politics of trouble" when he emphasized that the goal of docility could be easily achieved with the panopticon design "[n]o matter how different or opposite the purpose: whether it be that of punishing the incorrigible, guarding the insane, reforming the vicious, confining the suspected, employing the idle, maintaining the helpless, curing the sick, [or] instructing the willing."[19]

The panopticon reversed the principles of the dungeon; it was about light and visibility rather than darkness and isolation. Yet, the person under inspection would be kept in the dark, in another sense, as the lodge would be constructed with an elaborate Venetian-blind effect that Bentham called the "inspector's lantern": a sort of one-way mirror that masked the presence or absence of an observer. Bentham devised this part of the lodge because, according to his very efficient plans, the inspector would also function as the institution's bookkeeper. Yet if he performed this task, his lamp would give away his presence to the inmates. Therefore, Bentham designed the lantern so that the only thing the inmates could see was a dark spot at the center of the aperture. With this scheme, the inmates may or may not be under constant surveillance; they just think or imagine that they are. As Bentham states, they are "awed to silence by an invisible eye."[20] The inmates have therefore internalized what Foucault called *le regard*, or the "gaze" of the authorities and, in effect, they watch and render themselves docile. In this way, power operates without coercion, force, or violence, automatically and continuously, whether or not the tower is occupied at all. As Foucault characterizes the invention, "The Panopticon is a machine for dissociating the see/being seen dyad: in the peripheric ring, one is totally seen, without ever seeing; in the central tower, one sees everything without ever being seen."[21] Bentham's technology created the illusion of an all-seeing, all-knowing "God" that was, in reality, nothing more than a dark spot in the lantern. In Bentham's words, "in a Panopticon the inspector's back is never turned." And he asserted the productive benefits of his design for the "inspection-house" in the opening lines of his treatise: "Morals reformed—health preserved—industry invigorated—instruction diffused—public burdens lightened . . . all by a simple idea in architecture!"[22]

Although Bentham spent years trying to convince British authorities to adopt his panopticon, they never did build it, at least not in an unadulterated form. Yet, one could argue that this did not diminish its importance; a number of its principles were embraced and the plans stimulated considerable discussion about new techniques for surveillance and social control. For Foucault, the panopticon was not only "a cruel, ingenious cage" where inhabitants collaborated in their own subjection, it was emblematic of the times in which it was produced; its significance lay *in the very idea* that such a design was thought to be necessary or desirable at that historical moment. Indeed, he called it the "birth certificate" of the new "disciplinary society"[23] and "a generalizable model of functioning; a way of defining power relations in terms of the everyday life of men (*sic*)."[24] The panopticon remains both an important symbol of modern disciplinary technology and a basic principle on which many forms of contemporary surveillance operate (e.g., the video cameras rotating among school buses mentioned in chapter 1).[25]

PANOPTICISM AND THE "SWARMING OF DISCIPLINARY MECHANISMS"

Let me summarize Foucault's contribution to our understanding of modern social control. Influenced by a radical critique of Enlightenment reason, Foucault chose to study the relationships among experiences such as madness and criminality, the knowledge produced by the new "sciences of man," and the manner in which power was exercised on bodies and "souls" through meticulous rituals developed and deployed in institutions like asylums and penitentiaries. It was in those institutions that he saw the fullest realization of the military model of society emerging in the modern era. In other words, life in the penitentiary, reformatory, and poorhouses was conceived as an idealized version of a utopian, bourgeois society; a machinelike, disciplined culture, set on obedience, order, and uniformity and bent on "normalizing" what was deemed to be aberrant behavior. The shaping, molding, and construction of "docile bodies" would be accomplished through the use of various "disciplinary technologies." These techniques ranged from the "lockstep" to ritualistic examinations with their "hierarchical observations" designed to instill the gaze of authorities and produce self-control and "normalizing judgments" that set the behavioral standards to be upheld.

In *Discipline and Punish*, Foucault set out the early modern origins of disciplinary power within the confines of closed, disciplinary institutions. This early political project was directed primarily at the criminals, deviants, and delinquents of the lower rungs of society. Yet, this is only the beginning of what was to come. Soon after a subtle shift began: from panopticon to *panopticism*; from punishment directed at people who had broken the law to a form of social control imposed on all those *capable* of violating the law. Foucault calls the process the "swarming of disciplinary mechanisms." Here, he means that disciplinary microtechniques that were developed in the modern institutions began to reach out from those organizations, linking up with other institutions and practices, creating a larger, macroweb of social control. "While on the one hand," Foucault states, "the disciplinary establishments increase, their mechanisms have a certain tendency to become 'de-institutionalized,' to emerge from the closed fortresses in which they once functioned and to circulate in the 'free' state; the massive, compact disciplines are broken down into flexible methods of control, which may be transferred and adapted."[26]

In Foucault's portrait of the nineteenth century, schools begin to supervise the conduct of parents as well as of children, the hospital monitors not only inmates and patients but other inhabitants of the district, too, and relief officials "oversee" not just the poor but their entire extended families, as well. Remember, disciplinary power is capillary; it expands out, colonizes, and moves to the tiniest reaches of social life. Once this happens, we have a society where much of everyday life is filled with meticulous rituals of power involving surveillance, examinations, and knowledge-gathering activities. This creates, according to Foucault, "[a] subtle, graduated, carceral net, with compact institutions, but also separate and diffused methods," which he sees as far more effective than the "arbitrary, widespread, badly integrated" practices of the classical age.[27] We see, then, "an increasing ordering in all realms under the guise of improving the welfare of the individual and the population . . . this order reveals itself as a strategy, with no one directing it and everyone increasingly enmeshed in it, whose only end is the increase of power and order itself."[28]

In Foucault's account, the foundation of this kind of disciplinary society was in place in Europe as early as the seventeenth century. I argue in this book that we have witnessed, in the last half of the twentieth century, at least in the United States, the proliferation and intensification of social monitoring and surveillance techniques and technologies that mark a shift from exceptional punishment—that is, the disciplining of a particular individual for committing a particular offense—to more generalized forms of social control and monitoring of wide swaths of the population. I want to argue here that the conditions that constituted modern social control practices have been transformed and that alternative disciplinary technologies and discourses have taken hold. In short, I argue that we have witnessed the emergence of a new regime of social control—a regime that retains many of the modern institutions and practices of the past while, at the same time, is both a product and a reflection of contemporary postmodern culture. Therefore I see an increasing tension between two practices of social control. As Foucault states:

> At one extreme, the disciplinary-blockade, the enclosed institution, established on the edges of society, turned inwards towards negative functions: arresting evil, breaking communications, suspending time. At the other extreme, with panopticism, is the disciplinary-mechanism: a functional mechanism *must improve the exercise of power by making it lighter, more rapid, more effective, a design of subtle coercion for a society yet to come.*[29]

POSTMODERNIZATION

It seems clear that we have witnessed, beginning after World War II (and more intensely since the early 1970s), significant changes in the organization of Western society and culture. Some social theorists think that these changes reflect an "exhaustion" of modernity and signal the beginning of a new "postmodern" period of history. Most scholars, however, would acknowledge that this transition is happening while many "modern" institutions and practices remain in place.[30] Accordingly, I tend to agree with Fredric Jameson and others who argue that the postmodern era reflects the "cultural face" of a more developed stage of capitalism.[31]

Just what are the conditions that make up postmodernity? We best see its characteristics by comparing them with the dimensions of modernity I offered earlier; see table 2.1.

I indicated in chapter 1 that ours is a culture deeply penetrated by commodities and consumer "lifestyles." As Donald Lowe writes, most of us "no longer consume commodities to satisfy relatively stable and specific needs, but to reconstruct ourselves in terms of the lifestyles associated with the consumption of certain commodities."[32] Generated by corporate marketing

Table 2.1. Comparison of the Characteristics of Modernity and Postmodernity

Modernity	Postmodernity
Rationalization of social life epitomized by the rigid predictability and control of the factory and machine-based capitalism (Fordism).	"Flexible" movements in use of labor, manufacturing organizations, markets, products, organizational innovation, and "service" economy (Post-Fordism).
Division of labor, specialization, and clear separation of the "public" and "private," gender roles, home and work life, and the like. Relatively stable nation-state boundaries, hierarchy and colonialism.	Blurring of boundaries. Implosion of once taken-for-granted meanings, symbols, and institutions of modern life: work, marriage, family, health, sexuality, intimacy, gender, privacy, etc., often combined with nostalgia for the past. Shifting global boundaries and power centers and de-colonialization.
Rise of large-scale, centralized state and private organizations and bureaucracies as well as urban space.	Increasing de-centralization, e.g., public housing, "community" corrections and policing, public schools, corporate divisions, and suburbanization.
"Compression" of time-space relations. Fast-paced world made "smaller" by new modes of transportation and communication.	Intensified time-space compression creating intense disorientation and disruption in cultural and social life. A dominant video culture; the commodification of sexuality and desire and a celebration of consumer lifestyles.
Large middle and professional class with its own self-interest, sensibilities, and culture. It becomes the dominant cultural definition culminating in the 1950s.	Increasing challenges to middle-class "nuclear family" from women, gays, ethnic and religious groups, as well as cultural diversity with acknowledged "different voices."
Rise of the "human sciences" modeled after the physical sciences aimed at "knowable man" through individuality, consciousness, and behavior.	Collapse of "grand narratives" and a turn away from the scientific approach to understanding society; rise of feminist, cultural studies agendas that take gender, class, race and ethnicity to be central to any analysis of society.
Utopian belief in progress driven by the idea that scientific knowledge, objective reason, and technology could harness nature and change social life and human existence for the better.	Increasing skepticism of progress and of those who assert its possibility; criticism of scientific knowledge and rationality.

strategies such as the latest "concept" in "upscale, casual dining restaurants," companies sell us images of how we want to see ourselves as much as they market actual products (e.g., Banana Republic: "Giving each person a chance to discover and create his or her own city style"; Anthropologie: "A one-of-a-kind and compelling shopping experience that makes women feel beautiful, hopeful and connected"; and Mercedes Benz: "MB is a lifestyle: an experience that transcends the road and raises expectations"). The economic viability of the United States and, as was made clear in the "Great Recession of 2008," the entire global economy, is now dependent on our willingness to purchase these prized lifestyle insignias. For many of us, time spent at work has become little more than a means to fulfill what is now defined as our patriotic duty to consume; a notion President George W. Bush asserted during the economic collapse following September 11, 2001. And when we do go to work, it may be to a "virtual" company that "flexibly" hires consultants and "temp" workers for its labor force, "outsources" its manufacturing needs, and changes its organizational structure and ownership like a chameleon.

Increasingly, time as well as social and geographical space is highly compressed by rapid transportation, mobile, high-speed communication, computer technologies, and information storage and retrieval. But while the world seems "smaller," resembling in many ways the "global village" that Marshall McLuhan suggested was coming, it may also be experienced as incoherent and contradictory. We may have, with the click of a mouse, for example, access to a staggering amount of information; yet, many of us are unable to judge the veracity of the content. We can deploy the Internet to read about an election halfway around the world but not know who sits on our own city council. And we may have vast entertainment networks that can deliver seemingly endless content but we may find that, as the title of an old Bruce Springsteen song suggests, there are "fifty-seven channels (and no-thin' on)." Each day brings us startling scientific and medical knowledge that, unfortunately for most, does little to help us cope with our everyday lives. As Vaclav Havel, the playwright, political dissident, and former president of the Czech Republic, once stated:

> [W]e find ourselves in a paradoxical situation. We enjoy all the achievements of modern civilization that have made our physical existence on this earth easier in so many important ways. Yet we do not know exactly what to do with ourselves, where to turn. The world of our experiences seems chaotic, disconnected, confusing. There appear to be no integrating forces, no unified meaning, and no true inner understanding of phenomena in our experience of the world. Experts can explain anything in the objective world to us, yet we understand our own lives less and less. In short, we live in the postmodern world, where everything is possible, and almost nothing is certain.[33]

The uncertainty Havel describes is exacerbated by the blurring of boundaries between the once taken-for-granted meanings, symbols, and institutions of modern life such as work, marriage, family, health, sexuality, intimacy, gender, and privacy.[34] Moreover, an underlying anxiety may be created from our increasing inability to distinguish "fact" from fiction and the "real" from the "simulation of the real." Some argue that the "language of the visual," or "videocy," is rapidly replacing modern forms of literacy based on oral and written traditions. Postmodern society, according to one theorist, only knows itself through its own reflection in the camera's eye and through experience that may be replaced by its visual representation. In postmodern culture, we learn to identify with the simulated world of television more readily than we do with the "real" world around us.

Another analyst suggests that television or video has a unique ability to break down the distinction between "here and there, live and mediated, personal and public" and has thus severed the links between social and physical space. This may lead to a sense of "placelessness."[35] I find myself not terribly surprised when my students frequently cite examples from and find meaning through the media they consume, often speaking confidently and as if from experience, about one social issue or another based on their viewing "knowledge." "Jen," for example, a precocious junior from Chicago, declared in one of my classes that she understands what it must be like to live under surveillance because she is an avid viewer of the reality TV show, *Big Brother.* Another, "Nick," an upper-middle-class senior from suburban Kansas City, told us that he likes the gritty HBO series *The Wire* because of what he claims is its "brutal realism." Yet Nick has never walked the hard streets of west Baltimore and, in fact, has no frame of reference to compare these "real" streets to their fictional portrayal, no matter how realistically they are depicted.

Within the flood of images presented in the media, how do we separate "investigative journalism" from "docudramas," *Real Cops* from the "breaking news" story, or "live" CNN coverage of an international skirmish from a *Modern Marvels* episode about advanced weaponry?[36] In this context, authenticity begins to lose its anchoring points. Making matters worse, the field of professional journalism seems to be melting before our eyes as traditional, "old" media sources such as newspapers, magazines, journals, and network television are losing their market share, or shifting formats away from expensive news bureau-based coverage and investigative reporting, or simply going out of business.[37] Replacing print media, the once venerable "fourth estate," a crucial "pillar of democracy," is a plethora of "new media" outlets and online news sites, webzines, and "blogs" of every political persuasion, as well as "collaborative" and "contributory" media sites, open-access cable channels, Twitter feeds, and the like that are controlled and staffed by a range of dubiously qualified characters, from high profile media "personalities" to "citizen journalists." Some argue that this glut of alternative sources represents a "thousand flowers blooming," an empowering movement that breaks the stranglehold of old media as the filter of information. Yet, this postmodern "decentering" of news and information has other possible consequences as this multisourced "information overload" can contribute to the kind of postmodern bewilderment Havel describes. Moreover, without professional training, ethics, and journalistic standards in play, questions of authenticity and dependability are constantly present; or, alternatively, the media production may be unabashedly political and partisan. Desperate for some unifying theme, many people simply pick the outlets that reflect back and thus reinforce their existing worldview—politically right or left wing, Christian fundamentalist, or what have you—segmenting themselves into comfortable media enclaves that insulate them from alternative viewpoints.[38]

The "new media(ated)" postmodern culture has a tremendous effect on our ability to make informed political and policy decisions. Video journalists, sensational talk show hosts, and those behind slick marketing campaigns have become, according to Norman Denzin, the new "intellectuals" and "historians" who hold a near monopoly on the presentation and interpretation of politics, social issues, and problems. "They have turned news into entertainment and their commentary into instant analysis," says Denzin.[39] Twenty-four hours a day, hours and hours of cable news formats, TV "news magazines," and other sensationalized formats turn everyday life into a theatrical drama where the most compelling stories are those that recount lives filled with uncertainty and unpredictability. They point to the next burgeoning "crisis" that threatens to make you or me its latest victim: your daughter may be a drug user, your ex-husband a child molester, or your study partner a rapist. Meanwhile, as industry representatives readily admit, local TV news stations typically follow the adage, "if it bleeds, it leads," where seemingly every segment begins with the most gruesome murder and mayhem stories. Broadcasts are often littered with the word "you," attempting to personalize the events and tragedies. "Imagine if it were *you* dropping your baby off at the sitter, only to have him killed." "If *you* were accidentally exposed to the HIV virus, would *you* want to be able to take a potent medicine to prevent getting AIDS?"[40]

My point is not to suggest that life's tragedies are simply media illusions. Rather, my argument is that what may actually be a relatively rare occurrence is easily sensationalized into an apparent widespread "social problem," creating a level of fear, anxiety, and mistrust that distorts our ability to make informed policy and political decisions. For example, despite the fact that the nation's crime rate, both for property and violent offenses, fell between 2004 and 2007, the percentage of Americans telling opinion pollsters that they thought that there was more crime in the United States than the year before rose from 53 percent in 2004 to 71 percent in 2007.[41] When asked, "Generally speaking, would you say that most people can be trusted or that you can't be too careful in dealing with people?" the proportion of Americans saying that "most people can be trusted" has fallen precipitously, from 46 percent in 1972 to only 33 percent in 2008.[42]

It is very easy to be swept up in the fear; everyone is vulnerable. When my son was young, I found myself hesitating to leave him at a city park as I would have nightmares of his picture ending up on a milk carton. Yet, despite the reported hundreds of thousands of missing children each year publicized by activist groups such as the National Center for Missing and Exploited Children, the number of kids taken by strangers is actually relatively small, three to four hundred a year. Although even one kidnapping is obviously awful, most missing children either are teenage runaways or are taken by one parent in a messy divorce. Look closely at the fear campaigns of organizations such as the infamous Partnership for a Drug-Free America public service announcements (e.g., cracking the egg in the frying pan: "This is your brain. This is your brain on drugs.") that ask you to pick out the "drug dealer" from a full-page newspaper ad of laughing, squeaky-clean, white, middle-class, preadolescents. As the "director of creative development" for the group once stated about their controversial ad campaigns in the past: "They are not pretty. They are not nice. They are not polite. They are designed to disturb and upset people."[43] Or think of the sensational case of accusations of child molestation at a preschool that results in teachers throughout the country not even daring—or even being allowed—to give a child a hug. Do we challenge the politicians who for a time were claiming that homicidal teenage "super predators" were stalking the streets when, at the same time, 80 percent of the counties in the country did not register a single homicide committed by a juvenile?[44]

A COMMUNITY *OF* CORRECTIONS?

As I have suggested previously, the arrival of many aspects of cultural postmodernism are concomitant with fundamental changes in the nature of contemporary capitalism. It is no coincidence that we observe these cultural shifts taking place after the 1970s; a decade characterized by economic stagnation and declining corporate profits. Replacing the half century old so-called Fordist-Keynsian social compact that underwrote a modicum of social benefits and income security for the poor and working people, a new neoliberal "regime of accumulation" emerged which sought economic deregulation, a retrenchment of the welfare state, a move to more "market-driven" social policy, and a new emphasis on "individual responsibility."[45]

Picking up on these changes, the new "intellectuals" constructed an individualized discourse on social problems that centered on the epidemic of crime and drug use, the disintegration of the nuclear family, or the laziness of homeless men and "cheating" welfare mothers that helped create nostalgia for the "good ol' days" of perceived cultural stability. This lamenting for an idealized past—in part, a backlash against the racial and social gains of the

1960s—became an important ideological plank in the platform of the New Right as it captured political power in the 1980s. Here, we saw a coalition of right-wing politicians and religious fundamentalists (re)construct their version of the ideal citizen, who personified the sacred values of religion, hard work, health, and self-reliance. But this agenda was aided as well by both "New Democrats" such as Bill Clinton, who claimed to be tough on crime, drugs, and welfare "dependency," as well as "liberals" who were willing to use the power of the state to enforce programmatic solutions to these social issues.[46]

We therefore began a far-reaching campaign to regulate not only the traditional crimes of person and property but also to control and "treat" a variety of behaviors, conditions, and "lifestyles" associated with substance (ab)use, alcohol consumption, "eating disorders," tobacco use, sexual promiscuity and "deviance," teenage pregnancy, out-of-marriage births, domestic violence, child abuse and neglect, "dysfunctional" families, various psychological or psychiatric disorders, and other medical conditions such as ADHD and diseases such as HIV/AIDS. And yet, we see at the same time a rejection of the practicality and effectiveness of the modern asylum where "nothing works" and where "rehabilitation" is a waste of time and money. In our day, the prison has lost the capacity to summon images of moral redemption and discipline. Not only does the ideology of reformation no longer conceal the reality of daily life on the inside, but the gaze of television and the cinema has taken us inside the asylum, offering us a drama of hopelessness and chaos, as well. As Loïc Wacquant writes, "the contemporary prison is geared toward brute neutralization, rote retribution, and simple warehousing—by default if not by design."[47]

The essentials of America's late twentieth-century moral panic are best illustrated by the almost obsessional focus of the "war on drugs" of the 1980s. As pointed out, the "Reagan-Bush administrations . . . needed a way to redefine American social control policies in order to further their broader political aims. . . . Substance abuse was the problem they decided upon."[48] Here we saw a public discourse that held the defective character of the individual drug user responsible for nearly all the ills of contemporary society (and not, of course, poverty, poorly funded schools, or the ill-effects of deindustrialization) and helped justify a new politics of repression. This political agenda was underwritten by strategically cutting federally sponsored community mental health programs while allocating massive funds for a growing "substance abuse" sector.[49] Restrictive plea bargaining and longer, determinate sentences for drug-related offenses soon overwhelmed the country's courts, jails, prisons, and probation and parole departments and sent authorities searching for new ways to control drug-arrest populations.[50] Within the swirl of the "crisis," our video culture brought us publicity stunts, or what David Altheide called "gonzo justice," such as the Los Angeles

Police Department's use of a "battering ram," mounted on a military tank, to crash into suspected (and sometimes mistaken) crack-cocaine houses.[51]

While such media spectacles held public attention, authorities were quietly introducing new disciplinary techniques, administered through an evolving network of local public and private substance abuse and "community corrections" bureaucracies, and through what I will describe in chapter 3 as "intensive supervision programs." Supported by state subsidies to local agencies, these programs are intended to divert prison-bound, nonviolent felons from state institutions (a tactic known as "deinstitutionalization"). These "intermediate sanctions"—including house arrest, boot camps, intensive supervision, community service, work release, restitution, day-reporting centers, and day fines—emphasized a new rationality centered on the sorting and classifying of offenders into finer categories of risk and dangerousness.

Proponents argue that these individuals are "better off" in the community, since they are "free" to participate as "productive" members of society. I contend that this movement has, in effect, inserted the power to judge and punish more deeply into the daily life of the community, "deinstitutionalizing," along with the offender, the disciplinary procedures and mechanisms of the prison. Once individuals become enmeshed in these organizational webs, their bodies, behaviors, movements, and actions can be monitored and controlled through a structure of bureaucratic accountability and disciplinary technologies and rituals such as drug testing, electronic monitoring, curfews, "surprise" work visits.

Given the control intensity of these kinds of programs, haven't we then moved the disciplinary mechanism of the prison—the "gaze" of authorities, the surveillance, the judgments, the case files—into the community?[52] And having done so, haven't we blurred the boundary between the modern penal institution and the everyday life of the postmodern? Politicians, the public, and even the "clients" may think that such programs are "better" than doing time in prison (which, of course, was supposed to be "better" than public torture), but, again, what standard is being used to make these claims? Foucault argued that the enclosure of institutions permitted the control of time and space that was essential for the effective and efficient application of disciplinary power. It created an orderly "grid" that placed each inmate in a visible square of light. I argue, and illustrate in the following chapters, that such a grid is being built in the community, where the exercise of power is local and decentralized, methodical, and nearly automatic, as it is set within a framework of bureaucratic rules and regulations. Computers and telecommunication devices evoke the gaze of the state, while the body is monitored for evidence of deviant activity. As I argue, to contend that the emergence of new disciplinary practices is rooted in the postmodern is not to suggest that "modern" institutions or practices we have inherited will disappear anytime soon. After all, we are still incarcerating people at an unprecedented rate.

Rather than replacements, these new applications should be seen as extensions of disciplinary power that invest, colonize, and link up preexisting forms. I describe this process in more detail in the following chapters.

But what do programs for convicted felons have to do with the rest of us? I want to argue that there are certain consequences for our society and culture as a whole that stem from recent policies. Foucault tells us to look to judicial practice to observe changing attitudes about discipline, social control, and surveillance in other spheres of society. In studying modern social control, he saw, for example, important similarities between the rational organization and monotonous routine of prison life and the shop floor of the new factories. Today, I argue, programs like "community corrections" tend to normalize the presence of formal social control in everyday life. Such a presence—even though initially targeting people in the justice system—raises our tolerance for social control and provides models for other institutions and organizations to emulate. When combined with the rampant fear and mistrust generated by a sensationalizing media, the consequence is that we are more willing to condone, even insist, that we adopt more and more surveillance ceremonies and disciplinary practices that soon become routine and commonplace. For example, drug screening was well established in the community corrections system before the Supreme Court ruled that, even without probable cause, any student participating in public school athletics could be randomly tested. Likewise, while we have community-based "electronic monitoring" of convicted felons, we also see that employers tether employees with a variety of electronic gadgets or monitor their activities through their computers, with video cameras, handheld data-entry devices, or other forms of electronic leashes. While prisons have armed guards, metal detectors, and video surveillance cameras, so does the Sunrise Multiplex movie theater in Valley Stream, New York, and so does Mount View High School in West Virginia. These parallels are too significant to ignore.

Even prisons themselves "blend in" to everyday life as they are made indistinguishable from other community institutions. In Lockhart, Texas, a small factory no different from the others on Industrial Boulevard makes computer circuit boards and air conditioners. Its "employees" are actually inmates doing time in the medium-security prison run by Wackenhut Corrections Corporation. Other facilities are designed to simulate suburban, high-tech industrial parks and often are referred to as "campuses." In Los Angeles, neighborhood-based, privately run "microprisons" holding illegal immigrants look no different from the surrounding apartment complexes—both have locked gates and bars on the windows. Meanwhile, in downtown Los Angeles, the Metropolitan Detention Center appears to be just another interesting architectural building or luxury hotel to those who drive by it every day. In this facility, guards sport preppy blue blazers as they ride elevators from floor to floor. As one inmate told author Mike Davis years back, "Can you imagine the mind fuck of being locked up in a Holiday Inn?"[53]

In the chapters that follow, I draw on examples from and move back and forth between the official justice system and the everyday life of the post-modern. In doing so, am I suggesting that "everything is a prison"? No, of course not. I do, however, want to argue and illustrate how the lines between these two spheres of social life are increasingly blurred by the use of new surveillance and disciplinary practices and that the kind of scrutiny once reserved for those involved in the justice system is becoming commonplace in many of our everyday lives. We see, in a number of cases, that various surveillance techniques and technologies are first deployed on those who are under direct authority and with few rights—prisoners, military personnel, the institutionalized, and other socially marginalized people—and then these applications soon gravitate to everyday use. Sometimes this is a highly strategic move while at other times it is a form of "mission creep" where these meticulous rituals of power are put in place for one goal and then are adapted for other purposes. And we also see how contemporary corporate capitalism and university research and development generates new information and communication technologies that are "smaller, lighter, cheaper, and faster" and form the basis of many surveillance gadgets and data sponges. My goal is to show how these new meticulous rituals of power are constituted by and indicative of conditions of postmodernity, and I employ the ideas and concepts developed by Michel Foucault and other theorists to help us understand these developments. Next, in chapter 3, I focus on new forms of surveillance that systematically watch and monitor our bodies and behaviors and I show how our communities, homes, schools, and workplaces are increasingly infused with meticulous rituals and surveillance ceremonies.

Chapter Three

The Gaze and Its Compulsions

Disneyland is presented as imaginary in order to make us believe that the rest is real.—Jean Baudrillard[1]

Court TV: Watching the Real Life Drama of Justice . . . Just the reality of real reality television.—Advertisement, *New York Times*

Clarissa: thirty-two-year-old European-American waitress, two kids, drug habit. She tells me that she slept through a 7:56 a.m. call from the DOC computer. She was exhausted since she was woken up by four calls since midnight. Missing the last call meant that she had to drive the fifteen miles from home to the House Arrest Center to be body searched, have an alcohol breath test, provide urine for a drug test, and offer an explanation of why she had not answered her phone.—Staples, field notes

"Clarissa" was one of a couple of dozen people, "clients" as they are called, that I interviewed a few years ago who were living under "house arrest" in the Kansas City metro area.[2] Under the system being deployed in this community corrections program, Clarissa needed to respond to random phone calls from a Department of Corrections computer to prove she was home when she was scheduled to be. Officials had installed a small computerized unit in the house attached to her phone line. The calls demanded that she complete a drill of answering the phone within the first three rings, saying her name and the time, and blowing into an alcohol tester that is built into the machine. While she did this, the device took her picture and compared it to a reference photograph stored on a central computer.

Much like the mixed-up world of Disneyland referenced by Jean Baudrillard at the beginning of this chapter, Clarissa's experience of "doing time at home" is a patchwork of preceding eras and futuristic possibilities. It is a pastiche of the institutional confinement of the past and the more fantastical possibility of being closely monitored in everyday life. Hers is a virtual world where the values of order, authority, justice, discipline, freedom, consumption, work, and self-help are all celebrated, simulated, and presented. For example, when I asked another arrestee, "Jill," a working-class woman in her early thirties with five children who was convicted of drunk driving, what it is like to live under house arrest, she told me:

> Ahm [long pause] . . . of course nobody likes to be monitored, like, twenty-four hours a day, you know, but it's better than sitting in jail. And at least under house arrest you can provide for your family and if you're, you're not out there doing what you're, you're not supposed to be. . . . As long as you're following your schedule and you're honest with the house arrest officer on where you are going to be and what you are going to be doing, then you shouldn't have any problems. . . . House arrest can actually be a beneficial thing to a person. You know, for one, you're proving to the community that you can survive, be a part of the community.

The practice of house arrest strikes me as a bit of what Baudrillard once called the "hyperreal." How so? Hyperreality occurs in a postmodern culture when there are seemingly no longer any "real," stable reference points. For example, while "electronic monitoring" is judged by proponents to simulate the confinement experience of being in jail, in practice, this disciplinary technique bears little relation to *any* reality. We are told that offenders are "free" to participate in everyday life, yet their movements are highly regulated, the random gaze creating anxiety and, yes, obedience and docility.[3] Is this real freedom or a simulation? Clarissa is permitted to live at home, but is it "home," or is it "prison"? Is she a "convict" or simply a "client"? Is her home a "private" space or a simulation of the private that can come under the scrutiny of authorities? These dichotomies no longer make much sense and have been blurred to the point of nondistinction. If house arrest *is*, and at the same time *is not*, "home," "prison," "private," or "freedom," then what is it?

Most of the people I spoke with had their own versions of what house arrest is all about. "Johnny," an articulate college student who was involved in an "alcohol-related" car wreck, told me, "I'd say the whole thing doesn't even really make sense because you would automatically assume that if you were at home, why do you call it house *arrest*?" "Frank" told me flat-out that, "Well, it's just home and jail more or less. You know it's just strict accountability," says the forty-eight-year-old mechanic. He adds, "I don't know any other way to put it." "You might as well say you're locked-down at home," declared "Jolene," a convicted check forger and recently single mother of one, "You're locked-down, you can't even go nowhere." "Peter" told me, "It is a lot like jail because, it's all, I *have* to be home." And Jill, quoted earlier, confessed that her ten-year-old son was upset when she told him she would be on house arrest because the boy thought his mother would have to wear a ball and chain around her ankle like he had seen on TV cartoons.

This jumble of ideas is evident when justice officials discuss just what "house arrest" means. One advocate calls the concept a "winner" because it enables a person to maintain "the semblances of a normal life—even hold a job" (in other words, a simulated "normal" life). Another is critical, since agencies often fail to provide clients with "the kind of counseling they need to re-enter society." But aren't they already in society? Apparently not, according to the Superior Court of Arizona. The court ruled that a person under house arrest may be prosecuted for "escape" for unauthorized leaves, just as a prisoner may be prosecuted for breaking out of prison.[4] So then, "house arrest," this odd-sounding contradiction in terms, has become part of the discourse and practice of justice officials who have normalized this simulation as accepted public policy. A client's home is characterized in this new discourse as simply another "correctional setting." It becomes, then, a "virtual" prison.

Within the hyperreality of house arrest, clients are rendered docile not through isolation and transformation of their "souls" during their *segregation* from society but rather through the surveillance of their bodies during *integration* into everyday, postmodern life. During the industrial age of the nineteenth century, the "prison" (i.e., social segregation) and punishment were premised on the denial of "freedom" (i.e., social integration) and on the production of "useful" bodies trained to labor. Yet the social, cultural, and economic conditions of late capitalism shatter this theorem. Today, "useful" bodies are primarily consuming ones, and everyday life is marked by our dependency on the commodities that signal our desired lifestyles.

As "Peter," a salesman in his early thirties with a pregnant fiancé and two kids, told me about house arrest, "I guess the biggest thing to why I need it or like it, is because it's either making money for my family or not. If I go to jail, there's whole lotta stuff, I mean . . . I have to be able to go to work to pay the mortgage payments, car payments, and all this stuff." Therefore, if formal, coercive social control is increasingly weaved into social integration rather than to segregation, then "freedom" becomes simply that which can create a simulation of freedom.

SPIDER-MAN MEETS THE MATRIX

The brainchild of a New Mexico judge (who, it is said, was inspired by the use of a similar device in a Spider-Man comic book), "electronically monitored home confinement" programs now tether an estimated seventy thousand individuals throughout the country to central monitoring systems installed by community corrections officials.[5] "It's just a given that business is going to grow," said one stock analyst about a decade ago speaking of the corporations that produce the devices. "These are the companies working to solve a social problem. They are going to help develop the industry and the state-of-the-art equipment that is going to be necessary."[6] Indeed. In the thirty or so years that electronic monitoring has been around, the technology has changed dramatically. While many jurisdictions still deploy the original ankle bracelet—the type that made headlines when it was worn by celebrities such as Martha Stewart, Paris Hilton, and Roman Polanski—that limits an individual's movement to no more than 150 feet or so from a monitoring box, new versions can monitor drug and alcohol use through perspiration and provide active global positioning system (GPS) tracking.

For example, the Tattle Tale™ Generation III Alcohol and Marijuana Sensing House Arrest Ankle Bracelet,

> works with Bluetooth® enabled handsets which transmit the GPS location of the offender, and the data from the ankle bracelet sensors. The GPS and sensor data is transmitted through the Sprint or Verizon wireless network communication system to an internet user interface. Using the Internet user interface, private service providers, as well as probation departments, parole officers and court officials can monitor active GPS data for each offender, track the historical GPS, time and location information, and monitor the current and historical status of each sensor on the ankle bracelet.[7]

Another system based on voice biometrics called ShadowTrack® is actually marketed to offenders themselves as well as correctional officials.

> "ShadowTrack has been helping individuals with their House Arrest needs for over 10 years," claims their webpage. "If you have been sentenced to home detention or you are looking for an alternative to incarceration, then Shadow-Track® electronic monitoring system is your ideal solution. The Shadow-Track® voice biometrics program is an inexpensive means to fulfill your obligation to the court and allows you to stay close to your family."[8]

Whether offering one's voice up to the machine, "carrying the state around on your ankle," as one inmate at a Midwestern state penitentiary characterized it to me, or paying for your own house arrest as many are required to do, this kind of decentralized control encourages "participatory monitoring" whereby those being watched may become active "partners" in their own surveillance.[9]

Electronic monitoring is a disciplinary technology that has much in common with the past. Like Bentham's panopticon, the anklet device permits near-constant surveillance of movement. Twenty-four/seven monitoring brings the one-dimensional gaze of authorities onto an offender's body; the contemporary equivalent of the prisoner exposed before the inspector's lodge. Yet while Bentham's panopticon was an archetype of modern discipline—and the anklet device a logical extension of it—this new technique is, at the same time, quintessentially postmodern in design and implementation. The contemporary cybernetic life-world creates a new partitioning—a new "grid" of power—that extends into the everyday, in and through the gaze of community corrections. This grid comes about because the anklet device no longer requires the division of space through architecture. Indeed, this exercise of power can operate more freely, down to the trivial extremities and the remotest corners of everyday life, rather than be confined, like the offenders themselves, within the walls of the modern asylum. Instead of subjecting the body to a regimented system of institutional discipline and control, this disciplinary technology is located on the body itself. Disciplinary power then has been deinstitutionalized and decentralized. And unlike the somewhat primitive panoptic tower that could practically view only a limited number of cells, this cybernetic machine is capable of creating an infinite number of confinements. As Foucault states, "like so many cages, so many small theaters, in which each actor is alone, perfectly individualized and constantly visible."[10]

The modern asylum once stood as a grand monument of state power for all to see. But house arrest technology follows new principles of postmodern disciplinary power; it is nearly invisible, yet it works quietly, constantly, and efficiently. It replaces the heaviness of the fortress with the simple, economic geometry of the semiconductor. As Foucault claims, "The panoptic schema makes an apparatus of power more intense: it assures its economy (in material, in personnel, in time); it assures efficacy by its preventive character, its continuous functioning and its automatic mechanisms."[11] The technologically driven marvel of house arrest alters the cost equation of prison construction and administration. Compared with the price tag of building and operating prisons—currently more than $50,000 per inmate per year—electronic monitoring systems require a small initial investment, few personnel to administer, and the cost to operate is typically charged to the "clients" themselves. With electronic monitoring, we now have in our grasp an inexhaustible supply of relatively inexpensive, disciplinary "spaces." (This notion played out recently when law enforcement officials and politicians in California and a few other states pushed for initiatives that would require convicted sex offenders to be tracked by GPS satellite systems *for life*, even after they finish their parole. Also, Governor Arnold Schwarzenegger proposed a $48 million program to expand a pilot program in San Bernardino that uses anklet devices for violent parolees to Los Angeles, Sacramento, and Fresno. "The worst of the worst will get [global positioning] bracelets so we know exactly where they are and what they are doing," said Schwarzenegger.)[12]

With the extended reach of such community-based programs, the authority to judge an individual goes far beyond the walls of the prison that may have formally held him or her. Now the gaze and surveillance of authorities can go straight into an individual's home, school, or workplace and can evaluate, assess, and enforce, if necessary, the person's "progress" on the road to becoming a model citizen. This kind of power is, indeed, capillary, circulating freely, far below the central administration of the state and out to the most distant regions of society, and exercised by low-level criminal justice bureaucrats and technicians armed with a new discourse of accountability and what are referred to by practitioners as "case-management devices"; devices that foster and maintain unbalanced and unequal authority relationships.

Anyone who thinks that "doing time at home" is "easy time" knows little about these new programs. One official told me that being sentenced to a community corrections program was, in many ways, much "harder time" than sitting in a jail cell. For example, consider the intensive supervision programs (ISPs) now operating in many communities throughout the country. These are designed for adult, nonviolent felons so that they may, according to one report, "remain in the community while becoming responsible, accountable, and self-supporting." One ISP requires a minimum of four contacts per week between a client and an intensive supervision officer (ISO) during the first year in the program. During this time, the ISO is charged with directing daily job searches, verifying employment through the provision of pay stubs, initiating at least one monthly meeting with employers or training/education providers (not including unannounced visits), coordinating community service work (forty hours per week for those unemployed; five hours for those employed), collecting court-ordered restitution, initiating client curfews (enforced by means of electronic monitoring if deemed necessary), running weekly computerized record checks, and performing random drug and alcohol tests on all participants. After successfully completing the first eight months in the program with no "major violations," an offender may progress to less-intensive surveillance "at the discretion of the ISO."[13]

I spent some time talking with directors and intensive supervision staff of several community corrections programs and I took a monitoring tour with one agency's "surveillance officer" (his official title). "Pete," a twenty-year veteran of law enforcement and military policing, is responsible for checking up on program clients (both juveniles and adults) on weekends and evenings. He does so by driving around the largely rural county, stopping in on clients at random times, making sure they are at home as scheduled, generally checking up on them, and performing drug and alcohol tests. (I discuss these techniques in more detail in chapter 4.) Pete records his findings on a clipboard, jotting down the results of the tests as well as noting that the client was "watching TV" or had a "friend visiting," and the like. Sometimes he would "double back" on a client fifteen or twenty minutes after his first visit to, as he put it, "keep 'em honest."

From the eyes of an outsider like me, Pete's ritualized visits to a client's home—sometimes as late as 11:30 p.m.—had an absurd and unnerving quality. I kept trying to imagine what it would be like to have someone knock on my door this late at night for what amounts to a very personal inspection. Indeed, it seemed clear to me that, while not exactly a prison, an offender's home was transformed into a "correctional setting" in terms of the loss of privacy and the institution-like rituals that occurred with Pete's arrival. Despite this, every client I observed greeted Pete in a friendly manner as he walked—without hesitation or invitation—into their homes. It was obvious that these people knew "the drill" of Pete's visits, just as they knew the surveillance ceremonies of alcohol and drug testing. His showing up seemed as normal to them as the arrival of the mail carrier. I was also struck by how much Pete knew about their lives—not only the typical things that were likely to be in their files but also the numerous details about their friends, their habits, their likes and dislikes, their medical and family histories, who among them were likely to be the "success stories" and who were likely to "screw up." And "screw up" they do. One measure of the difficulty of the program is, according to its director, the fact that 50 percent of adult clients fail to complete their contract with the court (this appears to be typical of other programs throughout the country). Given what he called the "intrusive" nature of the surveillance program—as he states, "We're out there every night, weekends and holidays"—it seems it would be difficult not to "screw up."

Moreover, as one program director told me, once such programs are put in place, judges begin to assign what he considered to be "inappropriate" offenders to the program, such as "low-risk" misdemeanants, juveniles waiting for hearings, and adults convicted of nonaggravated sex offenses. Previously, these people would have been released or would have done short jail time had the program not been available. But once people are under the constant gaze of authorities, other infractions may be uncovered; files get thicker and the minor offender becomes the "known drug user" or the kid with "serious problems." These people, of course, are deserving of even more surveillance, and so it goes. The process has the effect of "widening the net" of the justice system and drawing in people who might not otherwise have been there. Interestingly, after being told that an increasing number of "sex offenders" was being assigned to one program, I asked officials why someone convicted of a sex crime should be tested regularly for alcohol (a legal substance) and drug use. No one could give me a defensible answer, saying only that it was "part of the program."

Once established, then, programs like intensive supervision become general disciplinary tools that are used to let certain individuals "know we're watching even when they don't know we're watching," whether that form of surveillance is "appropriate" for them or not. Finally, Pete told me, with little hesitation, that the ISP was "obviously better than putting them away." He repeatedly stressed the "productive" and "self-training and discipline" capacities of the community corrections scheme throughout our conversations. When I asked him, for example, what he thought his clients felt about wearing an electronic anklet device, he said, "They appreciate that it's an option for them rather than prison." He went on to relate stories about clients who themselves had requested to be in the program to "clean up" from drugs or to "stop running with the wrong crowd."

"INTERVENTION OPPORTUNITIES"

As suggested in chapter 2, I see these new community-based forms of surveillance to be an extension of the disciplinary power first deployed in closed institutions. Once lodged in the community, however, they begin to reach out, to invest, colonize, and link with other organizations and practices. This is clear when we see the blurring distinctions among the legal, justice, and social welfare functions of these programs. For example, during one of my rounds with Pete, the surveillance officer, he received a cell phone call from a police dispatcher (Pete is not a law enforcement officer) who asked him questions about, and later had him call, one of his clients concerning a domestic dispute at her house. For advocates and administrators, this is the "productive" aspect of "inter-agency cooperation," "information sharing," and "efficient service delivery." Yet it is also these very activities that produce a more finely woven, integrated network of social control.

Another community corrections program I looked at has, in addition to the ISP, nearly a dozen other programs that it administers (and will even contract out to neighboring counties) including domestic violence intervention, rape crisis, victim-witness assistance, homes for children "at risk," educational services for clients, and the Family Training Program (FTP). The stated goal of the FTP component is to prevent the incarceration of the adult offender by tracking not only the offender but family members, as well. The program involves an "in-home" style of intervention. Yet, despite the best intentions of its practitioners, it is a model that, I argue, significantly facilitates and enhances the exercise of disciplinary power. With this view in mind, consider how proponents characterize their activities. A report from the community corrections agency describes the FTP this way:

> By improving the stability of the offender and his/her family, there is a much higher likelihood that the offender will be productive and avoid additional criminal behavior that would result in incarceration. This goal is obtained by physically working in the home and teaching new parenting skills and child management skills to parents who have exhibited weaknesses in these areas. . . . This is accomplished by a therapist of the Family Training Program

going into the home and providing intense therapy within the home setting. In addition to scheduled appointments, the therapist will make intermittent unannounced visits in order to gain a more realistic view of the family's interaction and the use of the new skills. [14]

In fact, the "home-based" and "family preservation" models have become quite popular throughout what one could call the penal/health/welfare complex. For example, some see the supposedly therapeutic agendas of community mental health programs this way:

Practitioners constantly seek innovative ways to improve service delivery to high-risk children and families who are isolated and unlikely to seek help at an agency. Home-based practice is rapidly becoming an alternative to practice in office settings [providing for] . . . enhanced assessment and intervention opportunities. [15]

Home visits [that] allow therapists . . . direct observation of a family in the natural environment of their home can bring into focus more quickly the significant dynamics in the family and can help guide treatment. Therapy moved into the home setting occurs in a heightened reality context that includes the possible participant-observer role of the therapist, more active involvement of family members, and the opportunity for immediate analysis of family members' actual behavior. [16]

These kinds of home-based models, then, provide the means by which caseworkers, therapists, and others extend the gaze of disciplinary power into the daily lives of clients. As "experts," they are charged with making normalizing judgments not only about their clients but also about their entire families. (Are they "functional" or "dysfunctional"? Are they "multiproblem"? Do they have "borderline" personalities? Are they "at-risk"? Do they have the correct "parenting skills"? Do they use drugs? Do the kids go to school?) And even if, as individuals, these well-intentioned, dedicated professionals do not want to become the "eyes of the law," they are compelled, by law, to report any illegal behavior they observe to the appropriate authorities. Or take the situation where social welfare officials are trying to decide whether a child should be "reintegrated" back into a home after the parents have been deemed "unfit." "This is when the team has to decide to let go," according to one social worker I spoke with. (The "team" in this particular program is made up of the core members of what is called a "wraparound" treatment model that brings in welfare caseworkers, individual and family therapists, agency lawyers, and a host of other professionals.) In this case, the previously "unfit" family must meet the standard of the supposedly more "functional" foster family the child may be living with. The possibility of "letting go" creates considerable anxiety on the part of the social worker because "[i]t's hard to extract the kid out of this great home and put him back in with borderlines." While most of us might be able to identify cases of, say, physical abuse, one has to wonder what criteria are used to determine who is "borderline" and who is not. Just where is the line between a "functional" versus an "unfit" family? Who gets to decide what "parenting skills" are appropriate, while other skills are not? The fact remains this is not a science but a series of socially constructed judgments of "normality." I wonder how many American families could survive the assessment and be labeled as living in a "great home" if our behaviors were constantly observed, scrutinized, and clinically diagnosed.

THE JUSTICE FISHBOWL

With community policing and corrections, neighborhood detention centers, offenders under arrest in their own homes, and the proliferation of in-home social welfare models, we see disciplinary power leaching into everyday life. To reiterate Foucault, this is the process whereby the "massive, compact disciplines—the jail, the prison, the poorhouse, and the mental hospital—are broken down into flexible methods of control, which may be transferred and adapted."[17]

The next logical step in "decentralizing" the penal/heath/welfare complex is to bring courts to the local level as well. One model—simply riddled with postmodern themes—was opened in New York City's Times Square district in 1993. Instead of dispensing justice from a stately nineteenth-century court building—a fixed and firm symbol of the American legal system—this specialized "boutique" court called the Midtown Community Court is run out of a nondescript office building and deals only with street hustlers, graffiti artists, prostitutes, and shoplifters who traditionally had been dismissed by uptown courts too busy with felony cases. The court, partially financed by private developers who have spent billions rehabilitating the once seedy district into a tourist mecca, processes more than fifteen thousand of these so-called "quality-of-life offenders" a year. It was characterized in one media story as a "computer-driven laboratory," a "fishbowl," rather than simply a court, a "restoration center" that puts a "judge under the same roof as city health workers, drug counselors, schoolteachers and nontraditional community service outlets." The court's designer, John Feinblatt, went on to help found the Center for Court Innovation and is currently Criminal Justice Coordinator for the Mayor of New York. The center now boasts nearly two dozen "demonstration projects" around New York City including specialized Attendance Court, Brooklyn Domestic Violence Court, Manhattan Family Treatment Court, Parole Reentry Court, and others.

At the Midtown Community Court, a computer is at the center of the information management system. It acts, according to one writer who observed the court,

> as the receptor for an elaborate system of remote feeds which, when combined, create the equivalent of a three-inch court file that can be accessed from a single screen. The process usually begins with a beat cop issuing a complaint to an offender, complete with a date for him or her to appear in court. Copies of the complaints are sent to the Manhattan DA's office, which in turn faxes them to the court. . . . When the defendant arrives in the new courthouse, his presence is noted on large screens that hang in the entrance way like airport flight monitors, displaying the names of all those scheduled to appear that day. . . . In addition, a dozen monitors jam the interior well of the courtroom. . . . If all has worked, the faxed complaint from the DA's office has been scanned into the computer and can be pulled up from any of those monitors. Ditto the defendant's rap sheet, which gets fed into the database by an online hookup with the state's Division of Criminal Justice. . . . Before long, an interviewer approaches the defendant with a laundry list of queries: Does he or she have a drug habit, a home, a job? Each answer is typed into a laptop computer. . . . By now thousands of bits of information about a single defendant are swimming around the electronic file folder.[18]

As Feinblatt said in 1993, "We know very little about the 100,000 people who come through this system. In three years, we're going to know a whole lot more."[19]

TRANSPARENCY

trans·par·ent adj \tran(t)s-'per-ənt\
1a (1): having the property of transmitting light without appreciable scattering so that bodies lying beyond are seen clearly: pellucid (2): allowing the passage of a specified form of radiation (as X-rays or ultraviolet light) b: fine or sheer enough to be seen through: diaphanous
2a: free from pretense or deceit: frank b: easily detected or seen through: obvious c: readily understood d: characterized by visibility or accessibility of information

—Merriam-Webster

If postmodern culture is characterized by an implosion of previously accepted *boundaries*, we see as well the disintegration of the *barriers* that once offered us some form of sanctuary from the intrusions of others. "Such a society," according to Ronald Corbett and Gary Marx, "is transparent and porous. Information leakage is rampant. Barriers and boundaries—distance, darkness, time, walls, windows, and even skin, which have been fundamental to our conceptions of privacy, liberty and individuality—give way."[20] This condition has been brought about, in part, by the emergence of what Marx dubbed more than twenty years ago as the "new surveillance": an optical revolution engendered by a dizzying array of digitized, computer/video/ tele-communication devices that have made watching and monitoring deftly pen-etrating yet often seamless and hidden. Extensive research and development of night-vision technology, auditory devices, and telecommunications moni-toring capabilities now means that the state, as well as private organizations and even individuals, have an arsenal of surveillance gadgets at their dispo-sal. In the next few sections I introduce some of these devices and show how the new technologies, often first deployed by military and policing agencies, end up leaching into our everyday lives.

The video camera, for example, has fundamentally altered the nature of policing as well as the entire U.S. justice system. For example, ever since the evening of March 3, 1991, when four Los Angeles police officers were secretly videotaped beating unarmed motorist Rodney King, law enforce-ment officials began to experiment with installing video cameras in police cars. It was argued that the same device used to expose this atrocity would now "protect" both the officers and their suspects. "I think they have the ability to bring credibility back to law enforcement," stated one law enforce-ment chief about the use of such cameras a short time after the King beating. "When you're on TV, you don't do bad things. The officer acts his best and the actions are documented." In the twenty or so years since the King inci-dent, videocams, mounted on the dashboards of patrol cars, have become a central feature in the daily lives of the police and those they encounter. Activated automatically whenever an officer turns on the car's flashing lights, the devices are a "real asset to everyone involved," according to one law enforcement official. "Tapes can be played in court," states a news article, "to give jurors an unadulterated account of the crime. Instead of hearing disputed testimony about a drunk driver's impaired driving, for in-stance, jurors could see the car weaving. The footage also serves for unim-peachable evidence of evaluating deputies. Video of an officer's conduct—correct or incorrect—could be used in training."[21]

Footage has become a routine feature in courtrooms, mostly used as evi-dence in drunken driving cases and in the seemingly endless loops on shows like *World's Wildest Police Videos* which center on the "unbelievable" be-havior of "crazy drivers" and other "bad guys" rather than the police them-selves. Yet the camera does not discriminate; its gaze is both controlling and productive as it attempts to discipline the conduct of both suspects as well as the police. The visual technology not only empowers the calculated gaze and watches and renders the suspect docile but, as Foucault put it, it also "con-stantly supervises the very individuals who are entrusted with the task of supervising."[22] It provides an elegant solution to the question: "Who is guarding the guards?" demonstrating the role of "hierarchical observation" as each individual carries out the act of watching others while one is also being watched.

But the latest versions have police cruisers bristling with technology. Motorola Solutions designs police cars with seven video cameras to cover every angle of interaction between a cop and the public. Outward facing cameras use infrared technology to automatically scan license plates and compare them instantly against a database of stolen cars, known felons, scofflaws, etc. The system can scan as many as ten thousand plates a shift and the data are constantly uploaded to a central server and stored, keeping track of what cars were where and when. Another camera aimed at the backseat records an arrestee's words and actions. Like other technologies, videocams have become so inexpensive and small they can be used almost anywhere. Wireless, miniature cameras are being worn by police across the country to document their interaction with the public. The cameras are small enough to clip to a collar, a cap, or an officer's sunglasses and all the digital images can be uploaded to a central server at the end of a shift. Yet, when William A. Farrar, the police chief in Rialto, California, released plans to have his officers wear the new video cameras, "it wasn't the easiest sell," he told a reporter, because some older officers were "questioning why 'big brother' should see everything they do." (Interestingly, the American Civil Liberties Union [ACLU] has come out in support of *these* cameras.)[23] "Motorola Solutions envisions officers wearing not only video cameras, but also heart-rate monitors so police operators know when the officer is in a high-stress situation, and sensors that record whenever they release the strap on their pistol holster." All these data would get fed back and stored on servers, too.[24]

Video technology is also being used in documenting interrogations and confessions, undercover investigations, lineups, crime scenes and their reenactments, the testimony of victims and witnesses and the physical condition of suspects during booking, lockups, and on and on. One interesting use of the videocam has been to link judges and defendants during preliminary hearings and other procedural steps in the justice system. Rather than take the time and incur the cost of transporting numerous offenders to the courthouse from correctional facilities, the participants merely view each other on a monitor—constituting a sort of efficient "virtual" *habeas corpus*, if you will. Just imagine yourself as a defendant, watching your own preliminary hearing on a video screen while the television in the game room blares reruns of a gritty "reality" justice show or has live coverage of today's "trial of the century." The process of "justice" becomes yet another videoscape in the day-to-day world of the postmodern. Another justice-based "reality show" has appeared in several locations around the country. Here, "deadbeat parents" are called out in public as their pictures are posted on the screen and an announcer narrates the person's height, weight, race, last known occupation, and number of minor children. One pitch tied to the syndicated show asserts that:

> Over \$22 billion of court-ordered child and general support payments is currently owed to various custodial parents throughout the United States. Divorce, legal separation or abandonment by male or female parents has reached epidemic proportion during recent years resulting in the remaining custodial parent often being placed in the position of totally inadequate funding to care for a child or children. Using a national television program, Most Wanted Deadbeat Parents will feature specific "deadbeat" parents who have abandoned their responsibility and children physically and financially and who have failed to comply with court ordered support payments. Very similar to the successful "America's Most Wanted®" program, "Most Wanted Deadbeat Parents" will seek the help of the viewing public to locate the "deadbeats."[25]

After years of resisting the intrusion of the camera into the sacrosanct courtroom and police precinct, it seems that some authorities have embraced them as a public relations tool. For example, following the Rodney King beating, the Los Angeles Police Department turned to network TV to help put their officers in a better light. Broadcast in 120 markets nationwide, *LAPD: Life on the Beat* was on the air for four years. Producers of the thirty-minute show, featuring video footage of officers supposedly going through their shift, claim that it is "the most accurate representation of law enforcement on television." Yet critics contended it was simply propaganda for the department.[26] Likewise, after several years of resistance, in the mid-1990s New York City permitted the cable channel *Court TV* (now called *truTV* and claiming to be "television's destination for real-life stories told from an exciting and dramatic first-person perspective and features high-stakes, action-packed originals that give viewers access to places and situations they can't normally experience") to film a series called *The System* in and around the 101st Precinct in Far Rockaway. Videocam operators ride along with police, film arrests and bookings, and follow defendants through trial "like a nonfiction version of the NBC long-running franchise drama *Law and Order*," according to one news article. But wait: Wasn't *Law and Order* supposed to be a "reality" drama based on the "true" stories of the justice system? Then was the filming of *The System* a case of life imitating art that, itself, was supposed to be imitating life? An official from the police commissioner's office stated at the time that the filming will "help to tell a less-sensational story about the lives of officers and the true nature of police work." It also provided a way of keeping his own eye on his officers in a department with a long history of allegations of police brutality, corruption, and other illegal behavior.[27]

POWER SEEING

With the end of the Cold War and its emphasis on large nuclear arsenals and the heavy steel of traditional military hardware, we now have "peace-keeping" missions, insurgency-based conflicts in Iraq and Afghanistan, and the "War on Terror" and protection of the "homeland." The focus now is on intense "intelligence-gathering" and surveillance capabilities and the use of "smaller" and "lighter" technologies designed to monitor and root-out the parties or potential terrorists involved. In what others have dubbed "postmodern conflicts," traditional nation-state enemies have been replaced by fragmented "militant" groups and militias that often lack a central authority to engage.[28] The result is that a good segment of the "military industrial complex" is morphing into a "security industrial complex" where established defense contractors and new corporate players have found a lucrative market in the multibillion dollar surveillance and "security" business.

One exemplary model was set up during the international armed conflict that took place in Bosnia and Herzegovina in the mid-1990s. The U.S. military command post there, saturated with the latest technologies developed by corporate contractors, was called "Battlestar." Here is how one journalist described the installation:

> There is a system called "power-seeing," and what it allows is them to take satellite photographs that already exist and put them over maps and create, basically, 3-D layouts so that, in fact, before anybody actually went into Bosnia, people down to the company command level had actually practiced with power-seeing flying through the route they were going to take, and see things down to the scale of buildings and intersections and railroads. And, it's like a video game. You have a joystick and you can kind of weave your way through. We went out on a night patrol, and a lot of people have global positioning satellite readers. So, they know exactly where they are. And, everybody, virtually, has one kind of night-vision goggle. And, it's a camera [as well] and you have two eye pieces. In the eye pieces you see kind of a green and white representation of the landscape.[29]

Today, devices developed for and the lessons learned in conflicts like Iraq and Afghanistan are slowly making their way into law enforcement departments at a variety of levels and therefore it is increasingly likely that U.S. citizens may find themselves subjected to their gaze. In fact, we have been witnessing the "militarization" of the nation's police forces, something that has serious constitutional implications. Paramilitary SWAT teams deploying army-style weapons, tactics, training, uniforms, and the like, originally set up for life-threatening and emergency situations such as hostage takings, bank robberies, and threats of terrorism, are increasingly used for issuing routine warrants and in other nonviolent cases and crimes. Since 1990, a number of federal programs have been in place to facilitate the transfer of "surplus" military hardware to the law enforcement agencies, supposedly justified to "fight drugs." The war on drugs clause has since been dropped and replaced with "terror." To date, $2.6 billion worth of equipment—everything from bayonets, helicopters, armored vehicles, and night-vision gear—has been provided to all fifty states, four U.S. territories, the District of Columbia, and hundreds of federal and tribal law enforcement agencies.[30] "As long as it's not a cannon, they'll probably get it," according to the person who was determining if the requested equipment is appropriate for the department.[31]

"Power seeing" seems like an operative term when one considers all the devices being deployed to make just about any kind of barrier, wall, or container transparent and open for inspection. For example, thermal imaging technology like that used in "night-vision" goggles is moving from military applications to law enforcement and even more everyday uses. The National Guard began using thermal imaging technology in the Pacific Northwest to ferret out marijuana growers by sensing the heat seeping from "grow lamps" in homes, attics, and barns. (A hiccup in the tactic occurred in 2001 when the Supreme Court ruled, in *United States v. Kyllo* [533 U.S. 27 2001], that the technology explored the details of a private home that would have been unknowable but for physical intrusion and, as such, the technique constitutes a "search" as defined in the Fourth Amendment.)

Now, thermal imaging devices, following the adage of "smaller, lighter, cheaper, and faster," are handheld and often issued to police and fire departments and used in everything from structural analysis of machinery, paranormal investigations, and the monitoring of poultry houses. At Logan International Airport in Boston, a security system pairs *VistaScape* Security Data Management software with infrared cameras from *Flir Systems* to stream video images from atop the airport control tower. "Abnormal movements or objects show up on a PC screen as potential threats," asserts one article on the system, and continues, "While guarding against the remote threat posed by terrorists, the cameras will help [the airport authority] stay on top of more mundane intruders such as graffiti artists and, possibly, rats in some of the tunnels beneath the airport."[32] On another front, the U.S. army has been aggressively funding the development of "Sense through the Wall" technologies that use radar to detect motion on the opposite side of a barrier. They recently awarded Raytheon and L3 multimillion dollar contracts to build "STTW" handheld units, a big step toward making walls "functionally transparent," a long-standing goal of the Pentagon's Defense Advanced Research Projects Agency. The U.S. Department of Justice has its own funding stream to develop the technology.[33]

We can list other examples of police embracing new technologies:

- The LAPD's upgraded 911 system allows callers to use text messages to ask for help. Other police departments use Twitter, monitor chat rooms, and surveil other social media to find out about raves, underground parties, or gang meets.
- Mobile phone handsets send out a signal called a "ping" to the closest cell tower every few minutes and the towers forward the location of the phone back to the network. Phone companies will assist police who have a subpoena for phone records that they can obtain simply with a phone call. The process of keying in a mobile phone number and having the last known location pop up on a screen can take less than a minute.
- NYPD detectives occupy the "Real Time Crime Center" that has a fifteen-foot-high video screen that can show maps, diagrams, satellite pictures, and surveillance camera images. Information available includes criminal complaints, criminal background, previous home addresses, as well as names of individuals who have visited someone in prison, aliases, and the nicknames of known criminals.
- The Montgomery County Police Department north of Houston has purchased a $300,000 Vanguard Shadowhawk unmanned aerial vehicle (UAV) or "drone" with a grant provided by the Department of Homeland Security. Unlike some of the other police drones currently in operation, this machine has the capability to shoot tear gas and rubber bullets, as well as "taser projectiles."
- Concerned that the commercial trucks that go in and out of the city each day could be used as terrorist weapons, NYPD has established checkpoints where the trucks are screened and subjected to several tests including mobile radiation detectors.
- State troopers, port authority personnel, National Guard units, and prison correctional staff have been issued "ion scanners" designed to detect minute trace amounts of drugs or explosives from a variety of surfaces. These portable devices are passed over the logbooks of long haul truck drivers, used to scan bulk cargo, waved over the kitchen tables of suspected dealers, and used to scrutinize visitors to prisons.
- A Denver area school district is implementing a SWAT (Security with Advanced Technology) system that would enable law enforcement to observe video footage from inside a school that could be transmitted to command centers and patrol cars. Cameras would be installed and images would be transmitted through an antenna from the school's roof; there are about 750 cameras already installed in the district.
- A $138 million, fifty-seven-mile system of sensors that will incorporate radar, video motion detectors, thermal imagers, and closed-circuit television is being erected around the perimeters of John F. Kennedy International, LaGuardia, Newark Liberty International, and Teterboro airports.

- Chicago police acquired a new, $2.1 million helicopter through Homeland Security funds that features night-vision instrumentation, a gamma radiation detector designed to help find "dirty bombs," a LoJack detection system for pinpointing stolen automobiles, as well as a special map system with video cameras that can downlink images to the city's 911 emergency center.
- The Worcester County, Massachusetts, sheriff's office has launched Iris Recognition Biometric Technology, which allows individuals to be identified by a unique eye scan. Sheriff Guy W. Glodis says the technology will be especially helpful in identifying missing children and seniors with Alzheimer's disease or other forms of dementia.[34]

The issue of transparency became a significant news story in 2010 when the Transportation Security Administration (TSA) began widespread installation of millimeter wave scanners and backscatter X-ray devices, generally referred to as "full-body scanners" at U.S. airports. These devices create a ghostly, seminude image of a person's body to reveal any objects without physically removing clothes. The TSA argued that the scans are effective at detecting explosive devices that evade traditional metal detectors and are faster and less invasive than a physical body search. Yet, there was considerable backlash against the scanners from the public and a number of privacy rights groups, who asserted a wide range of objections, including that they were an invasion of privacy and emit dangerous levels of radiation. Some people even argued that the machines produced child pornography when deployed on children.

Passengers who refuse to submit to the scanners, like John Tyner, a thirty-one-year old Californian, are instead offered the traditional metal detector and a "basic pat-down." Tyner decided to video his interaction over his refusal with TSA officials on his cell phone at a security checkpoint in San Diego. For unexplained reasons, Tyner was also asked to consent to an additional "groin check" by a TSA security guard and can be heard telling the official, "You touch my junk and I'm going to have you arrested." Tyner's story contributed to an attempt to organize a nationwide "Opt Out Day" protest on the Wednesday before Thanksgiving, considered the busiest travel day of the year, when travelers were urged to refuse the scans and demand the pat-down instead. The idea was to slow down the security screening process and produce long delays; the protest never materialized.[35] But the installation and proliferation of these kinds of technologies has been happening for some time, post 9/11. Schiphol Airport in the Netherlands was the first airport in the world to implement this device on May 15, 2007. At least one New Jersey PATH train station used full-body scanners during a two-week trial in 2006. Full-body scanners have been installed in at least one Florida courthouse and are starting to appear in courthouses around the United States. I suspect that soon, the use of these or other similar scanning technologies will become as routine and mundane in their use as the traditional metal detectors.

While law enforcement personnel rave about the next generation of weapons in their war on crime, others contend that the technology is subject to abuse and is prone to error, making many of the new devices a threat to our constitutional rights. For example, in one case, nightclub owner Antoine Jones was being investigated by the FBI and D.C. Metropolitan Police Department for narcotics crimes. During the investigation, a GPS device was installed on Jones's car without a valid warrant and the device tracked his movements 24 hours a day for four weeks. Jones was later convicted but appealed his case based on the idea the GPS device violated the Fourth Amendment's unreasonable search and seizure clause. The case ended up in the Supreme Court and the justices unanimously ruled that the government's installation of the device constituted a "search" under the Fourth Amendment and because it was "warrantless" it was inadmissible evidence. The court did not address whether such a search would be unreasonable and therefore a violation of the Fourth Amendment.

EVERYTHING IS GETTING "SMARTER"

Meanwhile, as we look beyond the justice system, we can see other practices and technologies being put in place in everyday life that mimic these kinds of monitoring and surveillance capabilities. It seems that a good number of technologies and "data sponges" earn the prefix "smart" to alert us to the fact that they are often automated, remotely operated, collect and store information, and are integrated into larger, networked systems. "Smart" homes, power grids, phones, appliances, and the like earn this moniker for these reasons. So, we now have, for example, intelligent transportation systems (ITS), or "smart highways," that apply advanced technologies in electronics, communications, computers, control, sensing, and detecting in an attempt to rationally regulate traffic flows, or alert drivers to accident scenes and other tie-ups through real-time information. Nearly every major metropolitan area in the United States has ITS operational centers that resemble the "Battlestar" installation during the Balkan War cited earlier (in fact, engineers at one center refer to the space as the "war room").[36] Here, "video walls" offer dozens of screens of closed circuit television (CCTV) images of roadways and intersections, data from road sensors, weather conditions and the like, and a variety of software programs are deployed to model, predict, and control traffic flows.

In Los Angeles, the city's Automated Traffic Surveillance and Control (ATSAC) computer-based traffic signal control system monitors traffic conditions and system performance, selects appropriate signal timing (control) strategies in 3,100 signalized intersections. Sensors in the street detect the passage of vehicles, vehicle speed, and the level of congestion. CCTV cameras with pan, tilt, zoom, and half-mile range have been installed in 270 locations.[37] In his study of these types of systems, Torin Monahan notes how "mission creep" sets in when such capabilities are built into the infrastructure: the systems are interlinked and accessible to personnel beyond a particular center, engineers routinely listen in on police radios and provide information to police about suspects and their cars, and the centers are typically designated as "emergency operations centers" related to "national security interests." As Monahan points out, "Transportation flows are increasingly monitored and controlled with systems of diverse technologies, yet it is difficult to envision the data generated by traveling; how others might be interpreting, sharing, and responding to those data; and how mobilities or experiences might be altered based upon individual or automated responses to those data."[38]

Another program, the California Air Resources Board, the state's air-quality management and regulatory agency, has installed remote-sensing devices that project beams of both infrared and ultraviolet light across a roadway. As a vehicle passes by, its tailpipe emissions absorb some of the light. A sensor receives the light and a computer calculates the vehicle's emissions level while a video camera captures the vehicle's license plate and a computer logs and digitizes the emissions and license plate information. Identification of the owner from the vehicle plate number means that an inspection notice—or ticket—might soon arrive in the mail.[39] In the last few years, hundreds of E-ZPass-type systems that automatically deduct tolls from vehicles that have a transponder mounted on the windshield have been installed around the country. In Kansas, when a similar system was installed, highway authorities mailed out twelve thousand transponders in the first week. Users marveled at the new system. "I just can't believe how convenient it is," one man stated. "The arm swings up and away we go, and wave to everyone else waiting in line."[40] U.S. Department of Transportation is working on a plan to have a national standard for the devices so that they would work on roads across the country.

Getting ahead of the line, however, comes with a trade-off. These systems, based on RFID technology (discussed next), are, of course, generating historical time, date, and location data of each toll collected offering the opportunity to monitor the movements of individual drivers, information a variety of public and private organizations might find useful. For example, cash-strapped state departments of transportation might be cajoled into selling the information to auto insurance companies so they could assess their relative risk of insuring someone based on the person's driving habits. Other uses for such "geolocation" data have emerged, as well. Lynne Gold-Bikin, a

Pennsylvania divorce lawyer, used E-ZPass records to prove a client's husband was being unfaithful: "He claimed he was in a business meeting in Pennsylvania. And I had records to show he went to New Jersey that night." Of the twelve states that are part of the E-ZPass system, seven state agencies are willing to provide electronic toll information in response to court orders in criminal and civil cases, including divorces. The Illinois Tollway received dozens of subpoenas in 2012. Electronic toll records were also used as evidence in the murder case against Melanie McGuire, a New Jersey nurse convicted of killing her husband and disposing of his remains in Chesapeake Bay. Prosecutors used toll records to document her travels to the area.[41]

Other roadway devices have proliferated, as well. For more than twenty years, "red light" cameras have been deployed in twenty-six states and the District of Columbia. Mounted on poles at intersections and some deployed in mobile units, the cameras are connected to the traffic signal and to sensors that monitor traffic flow just before the stop line. A series of photographs or a video clip shows the red light violator prior to entering the intersection on a red signal, as well as the vehicle's progression through the intersection. Cameras record the date, time of day, time elapsed since the beginning of the red signal, vehicle speed, and license plate. Tickets typically are mailed to owners of violating vehicles based on a review of photographic evidence.[42]

Cars themselves have been getting "smarter," too. Numerous automobile manufacturers now offer an onboard communications system, such as General Motors' OnStar, which has over six million subscribers. The equipment, referred to in the industry as "active tracking," can call a live operator who can give directions and other assistance; it can also automatically alert police if an air bag is deployed, remotely unlock the vehicle, and track the vehicle's whereabouts. Similar systems are available by Ford, Lexus, BMW, and others. While OnStar claims that it is not possible for them or anyone else to listen to conversations in a car without the knowledge of the occupant, they did announce in 2011 that they had started retaining all the information collected by the system so that it could be sold to third parties, possibly insurance companies.[43]

In 2012, the National Highway Traffic Safety Administration proposed regulations requiring car manufacturers to include event data recorders (EDRs)—similar to airplane "black boxes"—in all new cars and light trucks. Yet, in reality, automakers have been installing these devices for years. EDRs can monitor speed, driving habits, locations visited and distances traveled, seat belt utilization, number and weight of passengers carried, and as many as fifteen other different data measurements. The idea behind this is to gather information that can help investigators determine the cause of accidents and lead to safer vehicles. But data collected by EDRs are being introduced in lawsuits, criminal cases, and high-profile accidents. For example, when former New Jersey governor Jon Corzine was seriously injured in a crash while being driven by a state trooper, the SUV's recorder showed the vehicle was traveling ninety-one miles per hour on a parkway where the speed limit was sixty-five miles per hour and Corzine was not wearing his seat belt. "Right now we're in an environment where there are no rules, there are no limits, there are no consequences and there is no transparency," said Lillie Coney, associate director of the Electronic Privacy Information Center, a privacy advocacy group. "Most people who are operating a motor vehicle have no idea this technology is integrated into their vehicle."[44]

Progressive Auto Insurance has devised an incentive program based on "behavioral economics" to encourage people to hand over their driving habits data to the company for the possibility of reduced rates. Called "Snapshot®" and "Pay As You Drive®," the company says that it is a "unique insurance program that gives you a personalized rate based on your driving. The better you drive, the more you can save, up to an extra 30 percent off our rate." Progressive offers free use of a device like a computer USB drive that plugs into a vehicle onboard computer port. While attached, the device records the (1) time of day you drive, (2) number of miles you drive, and (3) how hard you brake. Snapshot is about making "normalizing judgments" about "good" and "bad" driving risk, not "good" and "bad" driving skill.[45] On the commercial side, Teletrac specializes in management of vehicle fleets in "food and beverage, construction, cable and telecommunications, chemical, energy and mining, food, government, HVAC, mobile workforce, passenger transport, tree/lawn/garden, towing, trucking, utilities and waste management." Teletrac's Fleet Director® includes:

> electronic driver logs (hours of service), on-board navigation, lane guidance and two-way messaging, it is the premier software for fleet tracking intelligence. Tracking more than 200,000 vehicles in 75 countries, Teletrac saves fleet owners time and money while reducing their carbon footprint. Teletrac customers report up to 30% lower fuel usage, an average of 15% less driver overtime, 12% higher productivity and less unauthorized vehicle use. . . . Teletrac software currently processes over 25 billion data transactions daily through its cloud-based platform and real-time tracking capabilities.[46]

Another interesting little data sponge that has made its way into our daily lives is the "smart card," a credit card–sized plastic card with a computer chip embedded in it. The chip can be either a microprocessor with internal memory or a memory chip with nonprogrammable logic. The smart card can be read by being "swiped" through a reader or by remote radio frequency. Smart cards have the ability to store large amounts of data including biometrics, carry out on-card functions such as encryption and digital signatures, and interact "intelligently" with a smart card reader, thus keeping track of where and when the card has been deployed. The Smart Card Alliance, an industry trade group, works "to stimulate the understanding, adoption, use and widespread application of smart card technology. The Alliance invests heavily in education on the appropriate uses of technology for identification, payment, and other applications and strongly advocates the use of smart card technology in a way that protects privacy and enhances data security and integrity." In 2012, more than 6.9 billion cards were shipped worldwide. Some examples of their use in the United States:

- The U.S. government personal identity verification (PIV) card being issued by all federal agencies for employees and contractors
- The ePassport being issued by the Department of State.
- Payment cards and devices being issued by American Express, Discover Network, MasterCard, and Visa.
- Transit fare payment systems currently operating or being installed in such cities as Washington, D.C., Chicago, Boston, Atlanta, San Francisco, and Los Angeles.
- The subscriber identity module (SIM) used in mobile phones.
- Pay (satellite) TV security cards in set-top boxes for cable and satellite television subscribers. [47]

A few years ago, my university, in a deal struck with a local bank, issued "smart" student and staff identification cards with problematic success. Not given any choice about our participation in the use of the cards, students and faculty lined up as if we were being booked at the local police station and had our digital pictures taken by bank employees dressed in embossed bankwear. Others harangued us with sales pitches about their bank's services, filling our hands with leaflets. When I raised questions about who would have access to the pictures, I was told simply they were "property of the bank." Not long after, I began receiving solicitations in the mail from the bank as well as ones from several other businesses that were specially targeted at the university community and could be traced back to the bank and its database. Ironically, after the cards failed to work properly on campus buses, they were quickly renamed "dumb cards" and were vilified in the university newspaper.

As mentioned previously, another "smart" data sponge being deployed in a variety of contexts is RFID technology. RFID is yet another technology initially developed for military use and later adapted for commercial and other purposes. One might characterize RFID as a barcode on steroids. A tag, some as small as a grain of rice, is attached to an object and radio-frequency electromagnetic fields permit the wireless transfer of stored information on the chip as it passes by an RFID reader (also called "interrogators" or "scanners"). Anything that has been "chipped" in such a way can be counted, tracked, and processed. Unlike a barcode, the tag does not need to be within line of sight of the reader and can be embedded in the tracked object. Here are some examples of the current uses of this technology:

Manufacturing A major tire manufacturer is going to insert RFID tags into its tires. The tags will store a unique number for each tire, which will be associated with the car's vehicle identification number.

Pharmaceuticals Pharmaceutical companies have embedded RFID chips in drug containers to track and avert the theft of highly controlled drugs, such as OxyContin.

Airlines Continental Airlines uses RFID tags to track passenger bags, while Delta Airlines is tagging customer bags with RFID technology to reduce the number of lost bags and make it easier to route bags if customers change their flight plans.

Restaurants A premier coffee chain is considering using RFID chips and readers to enable its suppliers to make after-hour deliveries to stores, which avoids the disruption of staff members during work hours.

Toll Roads Many tolls roads in the United States use RFID technology to collect fees without the need for toll booth personnel.

Retail ExxonMobil uses RFID technology for its "SpeedPass," which instantly collects payment at gas stations from a tag on a driver's keychain, while Wal-Mart is requesting that all their suppliers apply RFID tags to all cartons of goods delivered.

Seaports Three seaport operators in the United States, which account for 70 percent of the world's port operations, agreed to deploy RFID tags to track daily arriving containers.

Government The U.S. Department of Defense is planning to use RFID technology to trace military supply shipments.

Corporate and Municipal Australia placed RFID tags in employee uniforms to aid in deterring theft. The same idea would work well in a corporate environment to help control desktop computers, networking equipment, and personal digital assistants or handheld computers.

Credit Card Visa is combining smart cards and RFID chips so people can conduct transactions without having to use cash or coins.

Banks The European Central Bank is considering embedding RFID chips in Euro notes to combat counterfeiters and money launderers. This also would enable banks to count large amounts of cash in seconds.

People Tracking The United Nations uses RFID technology to track the movements of its personnel.[48]

Inventory, consumer products, passports, pets, cattle, library books, patients in hospitals, and nursing home residents have all been tagged with RFID chips. Correctional facilities in California, Virginia, Michigan, Illinois, Ohio, and Minnesota have deployed RFID tracking systems to help manage inmates. As we see in other cases, the benefits of this technology seem manifest and are overwhelmingly "positive" and productive. Delivery companies improve their "logistics," retailers keep better track on inventory, the right patient has his gallbladder removed, and Fluffy the missing dog is identified and returned home to his worried family. Yet, the RFID empowered gaze is too tempting not to exploit, too compelling not to find other uses to monitor actions or assess and change behavior.

Reading a recent book titled *Spychips: How Major Corporations and Government Plan to Track Your Every Purchase and Watch Your Every Move*, even *I* thought the authors, Katherine Albrecht and Liz McIntyre, were engaging in a bit of hyperbole when they wrote:

> In a future world laced with RFID spychips, cards in your wallet could "squeal" on you as you enter malls, retail outlets, and grocery stores, announcing your presence and value to businesses. Reader devices hidden in the doors, walls, displays, and floors could frisk the RFID chips in your clothes and other items on your person to determine your age, sex, and preferences. Since spychip information travels through clothing, they could even get a peek at the color and size of your underwear. [49]

Yet, the more I researched RFID, the more examples I found to suggest that this future may not be far off. For instance, J.C. Penney has placed RFID tags on 100 percent of its merchandise and multiple interrogators and Wi-Fi will have customers checking out their own merchandise. 7-Eleven convenience stores are testing a system installed at its checkout counters that has consumers automatically "checking in" when they enter the store through their cell phone. The store can collect the name and spending habits linked to each phone's number, coupons sent to the phone can be personalized based on a particular customer's past purchases, and employees can be alerted that a specific individual had arrived and therefore offer a personalized greeting. The Department of Veterans Affairs has installed RFID systems at 152 medical centers and 1,400 ancillary facilities to provide real-time location of patient and staff movements, asset management, sterile processing, temperature and humidity tracking, as well as the "tracking of staff hand-hygiene procedures," all stored in a centralized database. [50]

Meanwhile, a business professor at Baylor University employed RFID to study NASCAR fans' "engagement" with various sponsors. Lured by the opportunity to have their names entered in a drawing for VIP status at future races, attendees were offered an RFID-enabled card that was activated by providing their name, contact information, and login information for Facebook. Tapping the credential against a Fish Technologies reader attached to an Apple iPad resulted in a visitor's picture being posted to their Facebook wall. Fans were then told that they had to visit each of twelve widely dispersed RFID-enabled "Tap Towers," where they had to scan their "RFID credential" against a reader. Each tower was branded with the name of a famous NASCAR driver and was located strategically close to a sponsor's promotional display. The RFID cards created a record of visits to the kiosks and enabled participants to post more pictures of themselves to Facebook. The use of the sweepstakes drew visitors to locations where they had visual contact with the sponsors, while RFID tracked and confirmed their location. Following the event, researchers e-mailed questionnaires to each participant, asking them about the promotional information or activity they observed including games and music provided by the race's sponsors, which included Ford Motor Company and the U.S. Army.

Northern Arizona University (NAU) employs RFID tags embedded in student identification cards to automate attendance tracking for classes exceeding fifty students. Administrators at NAU argue that instructors are already generating attendance records manually and this step simply automates the process and saves time. They also claim that research shows that students who attend classes on a regular basis tend to perform better academically than those who do not (duh!). Federal stimulus funds paid for the interrogators and the attendance system software, which collects ID numbers as students hold their cards up to the readers upon entering a classroom and then forwards this information to the instructor for her class attendance records.

In another interesting application, West Virginia University has installed refillable water bottle kiosks that clean and refill reusable water bottles for "free." Each user pays a one-time fee to purchase a water bottle fitted with an RFID tag that is coded with their "activation" information including their gender, age, interests, and the like. During the minute or so it takes to clean and refill the bottle, the kiosk's video screen displays advertising matched to that user's demographic information it scans off the RFID tag on the person's registered bottle. A student whose interests include the outdoors might be shown advertisements for a sporting goods store. An advertiser pays a fee according to the total number of times that its advertisements are viewed.[51]

VIDEO ANALYTICS

Few of us stop to think about just how often, on any given day, we are being monitored, filmed, or having our digital image captured by cameras. But it's not simply a kind of one-way, big brother surveillance that is going on. As a society, we have become obsessed with the gaze of the videocam, not only because we perceive that it brings us "security," but also because we seem fascinated by the visual representation of ourselves and others. This "serious" and "playful" fascination with the camera's eye results, I argue, in the normalization of the gaze in everyday life. As videocams are used around the house to capture our foibles and to make us stars on *You Tube* or *America's Funniest Home Videos*, they make us more and more comfortable with, and even drawn to the idea of, having our image captured. Mark Andrejevic speaks to this seduction when he analyzes the "reality" television shows, *The Real World* and *Road Rules*. Andrejevic writes, "Big Brother may have been portrayed as hostile and forbidding during the Cold War era but he is currently receiving a glossy Hollywood makeover as a poster boy for the benefits of high-tech surveillance. . . . [He] has to win public acceptance as a nonthreatening—even entertaining and benevolent—pop-culture icon."[52]

Taken to the next audacious level, a few years after these shows ran, another "reality" contest series appeared simply titled *Big Brother*. Here, a group of strangers live together in a house "outfitted with dozens of cameras and microphones recording their every move 24 hours a day, seven days a week. One by one, the HouseGuests will vote each other out of the house until at the end of three months the last remaining HouseGuest will win the grand prize." Weekly tasks and competitions are set out at big brother's direction and a "diary/confession room" is where housemates supposedly reveal their thoughts, feelings, and votes for eviction. And to show just how much a fan of the old Orwellian character you are, you can even buy "big brother" T-shirts and coffee mugs.

The proliferation of video means that we can all be "on film," just like our cherished cultural icons of television and the cinema, so much so that a men's clothing store advertisement reads: "You are on a video camera an average of 10 times a day. Are you dressed for it?" A state of permanent visibility looms as cameras and their recorded images blanket everyday life. Today, the ubiquitous video "security" camera stares blankly at us in apartment buildings, department and convenience stores, gas stations, libraries, parking garages, automated banking outlets, buses, and elevators. No matter where you live you are likely to encounter cameras; some places simply bristle with them. By one estimate, there are thirty million police surveillance cameras now deployed in the United States—many of them installed with funds from the Department of Homeland Security   shooting four billion hours of footage a week.[53]

Following up on the work of some geographers who set about mapping the video surveillance presence on the streets of midtown Manhattan, the New York chapter of the American Civil Liberties Union (NYCLU) has conducted several surveys of cameras monitoring public space. In 2005, the NYCLU counted 4,176 cameras in lower Manhattan alone; an increase of 443 percent from their 1998 survey. These are part of a widespread plan called the Lower Manhattan Security Initiative or sometimes, "Project Sentinel," that resembles London's "Ring of Steel," an extensive web of cameras, license plate readers, radiation detectors, and roadblocks to deter would-be terrorists. There are also 4,313 cameras in the New York subway system and according to one estimate, two-thirds of large apartment and commercial buildings utilize camera surveillance. Since the last survey, New York City has required all nightclubs to install cameras at their entrances and exits. Citibank's video system monitors every branch in Manhattan and its suburbs and a quarter of a million New Yorkers pass these bank cameras every day. On a recent visit to the city, I noticed on a side street not far from the 9/11 memorial site a mobile panopticon-like guard tower, a couple of stories high with tinted glass to mask its occupant's presence and surveillance cameras mounted on the roof; it was a stunning sight.[54]

For New York City, a previous and potential future target of terrorism, this level of surveillance seems "justifiable." Yet, we find that Chicago now has ten thousand cameras; Baltimore, five hundred; another five hundred in Charlotte, North Carolina; and they have appeared as well in places like Carlsbad, California; Elmore, Ohio; and Williamsport, Pennsylvania. Sugar Creek, Missouri, a tiny town of about four thousand, has a cluster of automated cameras to cite speeders while Minneapolis has a database of millions of license plate numbers collected from plate-reading cameras. Each plate number recorded, along with the corresponding GPS location data, date, and time, is held for up to a year. In Chicago, 911 calls have been integrated into the city's surveillance system. Within seconds of a call to police, a video image of the caller's location appears on the dispatcher's computer screen. When an officer arrives on the scene, s/he is directed to the particular suspect or activity via radio by the dispatcher watching the video. Ray Orozco, the executive director of the Chicago Office of Emergency Management and Communications, states, "We can now immediately take a look at the crime scene if the 911 caller is in a location within 150 feet of one of our surveillance cameras, even before the first responders arrive." In addition to the city's camera network, Orozco said, the new system can also connect to cameras at private sites like tourist attractions, office buildings, and university campuses. But nothing so high-tech for the impoverished city of Flint, Michigan. There, officials are pining for surveillance cameras but can't afford the half-million or so price tag to install about a dozen units around town. In response, they have developed a tax deductible, "adopt-a-camera" program: for $30,000 the city will put your company's name or logo on the bulletproof box the camera sits in.[55]

The arguments about why we need all this watching are heard over and over again, most of them centered on notions of "security" and "safety." Despite the fact that 99 percent or more of the activity recorded is of law-abiding behavior, the police and the public seem convinced that if one thief or assailant is caught because of video surveillance then it is well worth the expense, the intrusion into public space, and even possible abuses of the systems. High-profile instances where video cameras actually turn out to be useful, such as in the April 2013 bombing event in Boston, only serve to reinforce these opinions.[56]

But this faith that surveillance technology will provide us consistent and effective public safety is misplaced. First, research suggests that whatever deterrent effect may be produced by such cameras, the result is that crime is often displaced to other areas. Second, some will say that the cameras make them feel "safe" but I would suggest that this is a false sense of security that actually works to undermine their alertness to their surroundings. An assault, for instance, can take place in a matter of seconds and the perpetrator long gone before the police are alerted and someone arrives. Third, video cameras are notoriously bad at providing useable evidence; poor image quality, limited camera angles, and a ball cap or hoodie can thwart a positive identification. Finally, many cities hire operators who are not police nor are they well trained. Even with a relatively small system, operators will have to view millions of "pictures" per day in control rooms miles away from the site, and this means that the "situated knowledge" of the scene is lost. In fact, operators cannot hear sound and they have no real understanding of what is happening on the street. With such limited knowledge, operators often develop a set of what Clive Norris and Gary Armstrong call "working rules" and tend to find "suspicious" behavior in all the "usual suspects": groups of men, teenagers, and people of color.[57]

Interestingly, it was Great Britain that seemed to get the ball rolling with systematic public video monitoring. In 1986, owners of an industrial park in the moderately sized market town of King's Lynn set up just three cameras to counteract a rash of burglaries. According to the owners, after two years the problem "virtually disappeared." Local officials were so enamored with the cameras that they went about installing Great Britain's first centralized urban video surveillance system, or CCTV. Initially, forty-five cameras monitored a community center, seventeen car parks, and the streets in both an industrial park and a housing complex. King's Lynn got a lot of attention and the media flocked to see big brother in action. Much like the nineteenth-century advocates of a more rational system of justice, the police in King's Lynn asserted that the cameras provide more efficient and more effective social control. They cited, for example, the case of children playing on their bikes in a car park when one decided to write graffiti on a wall. Alerted by the cameras, the police arrived, confronted the juvenile, and made him clean up the wall. This way, the police claim, "the whole incident—crime, detection, and restoration—was over in less than five minutes, and dealt with informally, without the child having to be taken to the police station." Moreover, like the all-seeing, all-knowing "god" of the panopticon, the mere presence of the camera's gaze appears to have the power to expedite "justice." Police say that the tapes from the system are rarely needed in court because "most people who are caught on tape confess as soon as they are told of the tape's existence, without even seeing it."[58]

Following developments in King's Lynn, a representative of one manufacturer of CCTV equipment predicted that, within five years, "Every town in Britain will have a similar system." He was right and one tragedy a few years later motivated public officials further and galvanized the support of the citizenry: the abduction, torture, and murder of two-year-old James Bulger by two ten-year-old boys. CCTV in a shopping center in Liverpool had captured a low-resolution image of Bulger being led away by the two boys, one of them identified in the eerie image that was played over and over again in the media. Today, Great Britain leads the world in the use of public surveillance cameras, especially when one takes into consideration the size of the population: there are nearly two million police cameras operating in public spaces in the United Kingdom, which averages to about one camera for every thirty-two people and a typical citizen being seen by as many as seventy CCTV cameras a day.[59]

Although all this watching by the authorities appears quite "big brother-ish," and we should indeed debate the implications of extensive state-run surveillance systems, other "tiny brothers" operate to enhance the seemingly apolitical goal of "risk management" and no debate is ever considered. For instance, one journalist doing research for a story described such a system operating in a local supermarket:

> Earlier this year, on a hot summer afternoon, I left my Brooklyn apartment to do some shoplifting. I cruised the aisles of the neighborhood grocery store, a Pathmark, tossing items into my cart like a normal shopper would—Frosted Mini-Wheats, Pledge Wipes, a bag of carrots. Then I put them on the belt at checkout. My secret was on the lower level of the cart: a 12-pack of beer, concealed and undetectable. Or so I thought. Midway through checkout the cashier addressed me, no malice in her voice, but no doubt either. "Do you want to ring up that beer?" . . .
>
> The beer was identified by an object-recognition scanner at ankle level—a LaneHawk, manufactured by Evolution Robotics—which prompted the cashier's question. Overhead, a camera recorded the incident and an alert was triggered [on the desktop of a "store loss prevention" agent] miles away on Staten Island. He immediately pulled up digital video and later relayed what he saw to the man. "You concealed a 12-pack of Coronas on the bottom of the cart by strategically placing newspaper circulars so as to obstruct the view of the cashier." Busted.[60]

This supermarket chain deploys a system developed by StoreVision called *Store-Ctrl* that "allows management to more efficiently supervise POS [point of sale] activity and to identify and reduce shrinkage due to theft, poor training, cashier errors, etc." In some of their stores, as many as 120 cameras are operating, monitoring both customers and employees; members of management "can log on via the Web and see what any one of them is recording in real time. An executive on vacation in Brussels could spy on the frozen-food aisle in Brooklyn."[61]

You might decide to throw a birthday party for your child at a local Chuck E. Cheese pizza/entertainment outlet "Where a Kid Can Be a Kid®." But behind the cute little mouse who assures you that "wholesome family fun" will be had by all, employees and customers are videotaped in all its 510 locations. Jeff Strege, the director of risk management for CEC Entertainment, which operates Chuck E. Cheese's restaurants, claims that the cameras have been valuable in reducing the number of fraudulent worker compensation claims among the company's seventeen thousand employees as well as liability cases involving customers. "We've made a number of claims literally vanish once we produce the video footage to show that what the claimant says, whether it's an employee or a guest . . . didn't really happen," he said. Even though some states limit the "security" camera coverage to a smaller-than-desired area, "it can still go a long way toward reducing the number of dubious work comp claims." "If you have pretty much 75% coverage, and they happen to fall and claim an injury in the other 25%, it becomes very suspicious that (the injury) wasn't recorded," said one security expert.[62]

Should you find yourself or a loved one in need of in-patient psychiatric care, the Millwood and Hickory Trail Hospitals in Texas are dedicated to "the overall vision of UHS [Fortune 500 health care management corporation, Universal Health Services, Inc.] which includes creating a safe and effective environment for patients, employees, visitors, and the general public." The company D-Link ("Building Networks for People") goes on to describe how it enhanced this "vision" and "managed risk" at the facilities through a new surveillance system. It's worth quoting at length:

> Ongoing and new staff training as well as round-the-clock patient monitoring is crucial to improving patient care while reducing risk. Having an ineffectual surveillance system severely limited the ability of the hospitals to deliver the top-level training needed to fulfill their mission. In addition, dispute resolution and litigation over patient handling in the facilities often hinged on inadequate picture quality and eyewitness accounts that resulted in higher legal fees and were limited in preventing future incidents through visual training. Also, both locations had experienced theft of hospital supplies and even an employee assault in the parking lot. Clearly, a dramatic change was required.
>
> Results of the new surveillance system were immediate and profound—from locating an unsupervised delusional patient to catching a parking lot purse snatcher, the legal fees saved through accurate audio and video footage have been significant. Improvements in risk reduction as well as improved training and event resolution . . . Millwood and Hickory Trails hospitals are realizing the benefits of creating an environment that is safe, effective and profitable for all.[63]

On the other side, the *presence* of cameras may be *verboten* when they have the potential to challenge the legitimacy of those in authority or have an economic interest that would be undermined. Emily Good of Rochester, New York, was arrested after videotaping the arrest of a man at a traffic stop from her front yard. On her film the officer is heard saying, "I don't feel safe with you standing behind me, so I'm going to ask you to go into your house." When she did not leave, the officer said, "You seem very anti-police," and arrested her. In Maryland, Anthony Graber was ticketed for speeding on his motorcycle and taped the interaction of the traffic stop with his motorcycle helmet-cam. He posted the video on YouTube showing an enraged off-duty, out-of-uniform officer pulling him over and aiming his gun at Graber. Prosecutors later got a grand jury indictment against Graber on felony wiretap charges.[64] A student at Malibu High School in California secretly videotaped a teacher who "lost control" of his class and raised his voice while students laughed at him. The student posted the video on YouTube. This and several other incidents had administrators discussing what technologies they would permit students to carry and about restricting access to YouTube at school. Animal rights advocates have used video recording on farms and in meat processing plants to expose illegal or inhumane treatment of animals. But a number of states have or are considering laws to stop the practice. One business advocacy group has offered a "model" bill, "The Animal and Ecological Terrorism Act," which prohibits filming or taking pictures on livestock farms to "defame the facility or its owner." Violators would be placed on a "terrorist registry."[65]

Finally, expecting parents planning to capture the birth of their child with a video camera may be in for a surprise. Many hospitals have banned video recording in delivery rooms out of concerns about medical malpractice suits and "protecting the privacy of the medical staff, many of whom have no desire to become instant celebrities on Facebook or YouTube." In one case, a baby born at the University of Illinois Hospital ended up with shoulder complications and permanent injury. The jury had been shown video taken by the father of a nurse-midwife using what appeared to be excessive force leading to a settlement with the family of $2.3 million. Massachusetts General Hospital in Boston also bans cameras during births, said Dr. Erin E. Tracy, an obstetrician there who also teaches at Harvard Medical School. "When we had people videotaping, it got to be a bit of a media circus."[66]

A CULTURE OF VOYEURS

The term *voyeur* comes from French meaning, "one who looks." Norman Denzin suggests that, "The postmodern person is a restless voyeur, a person who sits and gazes (often mesmerized and bored) at . . . [a] screen. This is a looking culture, organized in terms of a variety of gazes." So, we find out that, ironically, while surveillance footage may turn out to be, as they claimed in King's Lynn, United Kingdom, "rarely needed" for the justice to be served, the images are being gobbled up as voyeuristic entertainment. Seeing a potential market a few years back, one enterprising young man decided to purchase footage from insurance companies, security firms, and local governmental authorities such as those from police cruisers. "Caught on Tape" and the sequel "Really Caught on Tape" contain snippets of things like a man being beaten during a store robbery, supposed drug dealers bashing each other with pipes, office workers having sex in a storeroom. The producer of the tapes claimed, oddly, that they were created as a form of protest against the surveillance cameras, but he admitted they were also making him some money. "We sold 60,000 in the first morning," he said, and they ordered another 125,000 copies of the sequel. "When it comes down to video journalism—and that is what we claim to be—we're total hypocrites."[67]

Of course, this kind of thing was only the beginning. With the proliferation of cameras—not only those installed specifically for surveillance purposes but also the small, portable, and inexpensive ones—and the ability to post video on hundreds of websites, the likelihood of anyone appearing on video somewhere has increased exponentially. "Caught on Tape" segments have become standard fare on local and national news outlets, a variety of tabloid and cable shows, and in hundreds of sites across the Internet. "Dramatic" police chases, "terrifying" car crashes, and "frightening" armed robberies are played over and over. Paparazzi stalk "celebrities" of every stripe, offering up the most intimate and unflattering images they can get to the seemingly insatiable market for the latest "dish" on their so-called private lives. Alternatively, we find that a number of celeb's "private sex tapes" mysteriously end up in the hands of the media, thereby keeping publicity-seeking "personalities" on the front page or boosting sagging careers. Two thousand twelve Republican presidential candidate Mitt Romney was secretly recorded telling attendees at a $50,000-a-plate fund-raising dinner that 47 percent of Americans are "victims" who are "dependent upon government" and "pay no income tax." Some campaigns have set out young staffers known as "trackers" with video cameras to watch a rival candidate's every move and hopefully catch them making a political gaffe.

While we are likely watched and monitored ourselves, we are also called to join in on the watching. Programs such as *America's Most Wanted* appeal to the public to "join the force," as it were, and to provide information about criminals on the loose. Mimicking this style, a TV station in Kansas City, Missouri (like numerous others across the country), regularly runs "real" surveillance footage in its popular "Crime Stoppers" segment, calling on the public to provide information about incidents. (When no images are available, they simply offer a "reenactment" of the crime with actors and props, dramatizing its threat.) Some locales offer citizens the ability to jack into public CCTV systems so that anyone can join the watching, looking for criminal activity or identifying the wanted. Lili Berko argues that this kind of access and the proliferation of devices increases the "pool of watchers" and fundamentally changes our role in the surveillance gaze. "In this way," she states, "the postmodern panopticon moves beyond Bentham's model . . . in which individuals enjoy the possibility of becoming the owners and operators of the personal and professional seeing machines."[68]

Indeed, if watching someone else's generated images lacks the "real," voyeuristic experiences you may crave, you can always pick up a gadget or two and start spying on your own. Dozens of vendors sell those "personal and professional seeing machines." For example, the Spy Store—"Our plug and play spy gear, spy equipment, and surveillance equipment is designed for quick set-up and easy-use by individuals, business, and law enforcement"— sells an amazing array of relatively inexpensive devices: alarm clocks, power receptacles, and table lamps with embedded miniature cameras, infrared night-vision cameras, and audio/video under-door viewers. Heck, you can even swing by Wal-Mart and buy a Swann PenCam 4GB Mini Video Camera and Recorder for $61 or a Q-See Outdoor 30-foot Night Vision camera for $72. But we hardly need to go out of our way to buy "spy" gadgets when video cameras are built into our everyday devices such as personal computers, laptops, smartphones, and tablets, and inexpensive pocket-sized digital camcorders that can record 120 minutes of high-definition video have us filming anytime, anywhere. Such consumerism highlights a postmodern paradox: that the gaze is increasingly secured through the very products and services that we are seduced into buying. Is this what David Lyon once called "pleasurable" surveillance?[69]

In addition, a lot of that footage can be uploaded and distributed worldwide through websites such as YouTube. In 2011, YouTube had more than one trillion views or around 140 views for every person on earth. Forty-eight hours of video are uploaded to the site every minute, resulting in nearly eight years' worth of content deposited there every day.[70] Google has set about video recording the streets of the world with cars driving around with cameras mounted on them in support its "Street View" in the Google Maps platform. If you have ever used this productive application, it can be quite helpful navigating a city or finding an address. Yet, these indiscriminate recordings have also captured men leaving strip clubs, protesters at an abortion clinic, sunbathers on private property, and identifiable people passed out on sidewalks. While no one can expect to have "a reasonable expectation of privacy" in a public space, I argue we tend to assume a reasonable expectation of *anonymity* in these spaces and not be systematically recorded and possibly identified without control over these images. Kevin Bankston, for example, thought that was the case. Bankston, who just happens to be an attorney at the Electronic Frontier Foundation and advocate for digital privacy, was amazed when a snippet of him smoking outside his San Francisco office was found on Amazon's now-defunct A9.com map service. His family was not aware that Bankston was an occasional smoker. Astonishingly, a couple of years later Bankston was again filmed outside his office, this time by Google's Street View. Today, a web search for "Kevin Bankston smokes" reveals more than twenty thousand links. "I felt somewhat embarrassed and a bit spied upon," said Bankston. "I am now thoroughly outed as a cigarette smoker."[71]

"Pleasurable surveillance" seems to be evident when we see how the operators who have been entrusted to deploy the seeing machines for "legitimate" surveillance purposes end up using them for their own gratification and/or the objectifying of female bodies by men.[72] Here, the broad notion of cultural voyeurism is intensified into a psychosexual condition where gender plays a defining role. Among the many, many examples, we find in Tuscaloosa, Alabama, a traffic camera commandeered by Alabama State Troopers, which plays a continuous loop on a local cable channel, used to zoom in on several college-aged women's breasts and buttocks as they walked down the street. A professor of constitutional law at the University of Alabama stated, "If it is for traffic purposes, then it should be used as such and not for the self-gratification of a trooper."[73] In Arizona, two members of Fort McDowell Casino's regulatory office were fired when one man used the "point, tilt, zoom" (PTZ) capabilities of the casino's surveillance cameras "to photograph the breast area of patrons and employees" and to generate photographs on printers hooked to the cameras.[74] In New York City, a tape surfaced from a police helicopter hovering over the East Village during a protest march. As one news report described the tape: "The police dutifully survey the area, but then they focus on a couple in a passionate embrace kissing and fondling each other on a roof top terrace. On the recording, the police infra-red scope stays on the scene for a while and then pulls away, but then comes back a second time and even third time to watch the couple. It then follows the woman and the warm footprints her bare feet left behind." Jeffrey Rosner, fifty-one, one of the two people filmed on the roof stated afterwards, "When you watch the tape, it makes you feel kind of ill," he said. "I had no idea they were filming me—who would ever have an idea like that."[75] And finally, two FBI workers are accused of using surveillance equipment to spy on teenage girls as they undressed and tried on prom gowns at a charity event at a West Virginia mall. The two men were working in an FBI satellite control room at the mall when they positioned a camera on temporary changing rooms and zoomed in for at least ninety minutes on girls dressing for the Cinderella Project fashion show. An organizer said, "I can't even begin to put words around what I consider an unspeakable act, the misuse of surveillance by a branch of our government in a place we felt so secure," she said. "Never in a million years would we have thought something like this would happen. We're in shock."[76]

Our obsession with the gaze of the videocam leads to some amazing behavior and ironic contradictions. For a while now, there have been reports of teenagers and young people who went about filming their own deviant and criminal activities. Here, personal exhibitionism plays out as the other side of the coin of cultural voyeurism (see chapter 5). While seemingly illogical, this behavior reflects the video-centeredness of this generation and how the camera, and typically the Internet, facilitate what Charles Derber calls "the pursuit of attention" and "the democratization of celebrity, where ordinary people can garner huge attention for their mistakes, crimes, traumas, and tragedies."[77] This phenomenon was presented in cable shows like *Jack Ass*, which featured young people performing various dangerous, crude, self-injuring stunts and explicit public displays and pranks considered "sick," "epic," and "dope" by the mostly male audience. Web searching the topic of people filming their own such behavior produces dozens and dozens of examples. In one instance, several teens ranging in ages from sixteen to nineteen in St. Paul, Minnesota, filmed themselves committing a variety of hooligan acts including pushing people off bikes, knocking down joggers, taking hats off people's heads. Not only did they film it, they used their real names, and then uploaded the six-minute video to YouTube. They were promptly arrested.[78] In Florida, a number of young men videotaped themselves breaking into stores and destroying the interiors and merchandise. The purported ringleader posted the video on his Facebook page.[79] In New Jersey, a twenty-year-old man and a seventeen-year-old boy filmed an assault on a homeless man. As the older one attacks the fellow, the boy filming eggs him on and at one point the man is punched in the face and knocked to the ground and the two laugh. Like the others, the film was posted to YouTube. Alerted to the existence of the video, local police were able to identify the assailant and both were arrested.[80] In a more high-profile case, the Abu Ghraib prisoner abuse scandal of 2004 went "viral" when cell phone videos and photos emerged of the young guards at the facility in Iraq torturing and humiliating prisoners. Not only did they generate the evidence that would ultimately convict them, the tapes and photos brought worldwide condemnation of the United States and our role in the invasion of Iraq.[81]

Finally, malfunctions, poor video quality, ineffectiveness, and incompetence plague the practical application of the looking machines and undermine their promised security and "solutions" to what ails us. For instance, portable surveillance cameras purchased by the police in Charlotte, North Carolina, were intended to record criminal activity in several tough neighborhoods. "We shot alleged prostitutes going up to cars . . . vehicles . . . Johns," one police officer said. "And we came back and it's not downloadable." Hours of evidence were lost because the cameras or the computers that drive them didn't work. "Has it helped you?" asked a reporter to the cop, "No, not at all. It's been virtually useless to us at this point."[82] Seventy-four cameras were installed in San Francisco's high-crime neighborhoods as city officials faced a rising tide of murders. The results: they found that homicides within 250 feet of the cameras were virtually eliminated. However, homicides in areas from 250 feet to 500 feet actually increased. "It shows that if people are going to commit a crime they can just go around the corner from a camera to do it," police Commissioner Joseph Alioto-Veronese said. "This system will only work if we plan on having a camera every 100 feet, which is just not realistic."[83]

But even if they had that many cameras, one wonders if it would really help. In our nation's capital, the D.C. Council authorized the placement of cameras to aid police in their investigations of violent crimes. "Generally, the State's Attorney's Office has not found them to be a useful tool to prosecutors," said spokeswoman Margaret Burns. She added, "They're good for circumstantial evidence, but it definitely isn't evidence we find useful to convict somebody of a crime." Burns related the experience in Baltimore where prosecutors kept detailed statistics from the first nine months of the camera program. It seems that most of the five hundred cases forwarded to prosecutors were minor "quality-of-life" crimes rather than violent offenses and 40 percent of those cases were dropped or dismissed. "We have not used any footage to resolve a violent-crime case," said Burns, also noting that the police sometimes misidentify suspects because the cameras produce "grainy" and "blurry" images.[84] Finally, some time ago, authorities in my hometown installed cameras at the county treasurer's office; they were apparently concerned about the possibility of confrontations with irate taxpayers. One employee, who had been there twenty-seven years, could not remember a single situation that had ever gotten out of hand but still claimed, "It's an added feeling of safety." The county treasurer herself said, "I feel more comfortable with them on." In bitter irony, not long after they began filming themselves and the daily line of bored but hardly hostile taxpayers, burglars broke into the building one night through a basement door and stole, among other things, several thousand dollars of the treasurer's own money that she inexplicably kept in a file drawer. The video cameras, however, were useless; they were routinely shut off at night.[85]

WE HEAR YOU

As with the proliferation of video, audio recording has become more common as well. Audio surveillance technologies have been added to the "security" arsenals of a variety of organizations while smartphones as well as inexpensive and miniature digital recorders may be deployed in everyday exchanges. And with ubiquitous voicemail systems, our conversations and messages are frequently recorded and stored in digital formats, generating a history of conversations and files that can easily be passed on to others and even edited and changed. While it is illegal in most states to engage in "eavesdropping" in public, workplaces, or stores, these laws are skirted by peculiar "consenting laws," using signage to alert people that they are indeed being recorded or by giving notice to employees that audio surveillance is being used. In the cultural context of messy divorces, child custody disputes, political smear campaigns, and sexual harassment lawsuits, the notion of "watching what you say" has taken on a whole new meaning.

In the early 1990s, Dunkin' Donuts franchises had installed fairly sophisticated listening technology in its stores, for example, and more than three hundred in the state of Massachusetts had audio monitoring on the premises. A Dunkin' Donuts corporate spokesperson asserted at the time that the systems are there to increase security and to keep employees "on their toes," not to listen in on customers.[86] Yet, they changed their tune when a New Hampshire woman filed a class action suit claiming that the local store had violated the privacy rights of both employees and customers. The suit claimed that the manager of the store "pointed the audio surveillance device in her direction" to listen to her conversation because the manager's girlfriend was apparently romantically involved with the woman's soon-to-be ex-husband. The bad publicity forced the corporation to request that all franchisees shut off the devices.[87] Nonprofit Goodwill Industries of Texas added audio recording to its video surveillance system in its retail stores. The company that sold them the systems, Barix ("The Voice of Simplicity"), claims that, "Since the implementation, the security team can address the thief while he is on the site and let him know he is recorded. A 99% reduction of theft and vandalism is the result, with savings in the range of $10,000 per week for Goodwill."[88]

Meanwhile, public buses in San Francisco; Athens, Georgia; Baltimore; Eugene, Oregon; Traverse City, Michigan; Hartford, Connecticut; and Columbus, Ohio, have been equipped with sophisticated audio surveillance systems to listen in on the conversations of passengers. In San Francisco, a federal Homeland Security grant has covered the $5.9 million contract to install the surveillance system on 357 buses and trolley cars over four years, with an option for 613 more vehicles.[89] In another development, manufacturer Illuminating Concepts has invested in what they call their "Intellistreets" system. Here, wireless, networked, and remote-controlled streetlights have a number of "homeland security features" that include the capability of recording conversations and a "built-in speaker [that] can broadcast emergency information," states a press release. It goes on, "SmartSite luminaires can be equipped with a variety of cameras and sensors to ensure real-time 24/7-security coverage. The sensors detect a variety of threats that enable rapid response from emergency personnel or help prevent crime and gain control of the streets." A company public relations video has the system announcing security messages: "pay attention please . . . please stand by for a public safety announcement," and "this is a security alert." The streetlights have been installed in Detroit, Chicago, and Pittsburgh but the Intellistreets "surveillance hubs" could find their way into "retail malls, sports venues, [and] on college campuses."[90]

Today, recording of personal conversations is becoming commonplace. I had my own encounter with this a couple of years ago with a student. As department chair, I had to file academic misconduct charges against a young man who frequently interrupted and essentially harassed one of my graduate teaching assistants. I had several meetings with him concerning his behavior and, later, in a judicial board hearing, he announced he had recordings of me discussing the charges. I guess he fancied himself engaged in the kind of gonzo tactics associated with political "activist" James O'Keefe. While my colleagues in the room got a chuckle out of the idea that the student had secretly taped "the surveillance guy," I told him to go ahead and circulate the transcripts of the recording he had. The hearing committee had no interest in reading them, however, and found him guilty of academic misconduct.

Lawyers frequently record conversations with clients, witnesses, or the opposing counsel. Attorneys who use this tactic claim that they need the data as insurance against witnesses who might recant a story or fellow bar members who might back out on a deal. Thirty-nine states permit making recordings of exchanges as long as *one party* to the conversation—such as the person doing the taping—"consented" to it. Some argue that the technology has become so easy to use and the practice is so widespread that people should simply assume it is being done; thus it is not deception at all. "Perhaps in the past," one lawyers' association ethics committee member stated, "secret recordings were considered malevolent because extraordinary steps and elaborate devices were required. . . . Today, recording a telephone conversation may be accomplished by the touch of a button, and we do not believe that such an act, in and of itself, is unethical."[91]

"Assume it is being done," is the advice of lawyers representing employers in discrimination complaints. In fact, one-third of employees who go to the U.S. Equal Employment Opportunity Commission's (EEOC) Houston office to file discrimination grievances bring secretly made recordings of conversations with their bosses or with human resources personnel.[92] In another case, dozens of waiters and dishwashers at the Boathouse Restaurant in Central Park recorded hundreds of workplace conversations, including ones with the owner threatening to close the restaurant if the workers unionized. The employees claimed that "supervisors routinely threatened and retaliated against them for trying to organize a union"; after they took the recordings to the newspaper, sixteen of the staff supporting the union campaign were abruptly fired.[93] Other examples: In 1997, Lucianne Goldberg, a staunchly Republican literary agent, encouraged Linda Tripp to record her conversations with her friend and ex-White House intern Monica Lewinsky resulting in the impeachment of the president. According to ESPN, New Orleans Saints general manager Mickey Loomis had the ability to eavesdrop on the game day communications of opposing coaches. The Saints denied the allegations, threatening legal action against the network. [94] Actor Alec Baldwin left a two-minute long, ranting message berating his eleven-year-old daughter for not answering her phone for a court-ordered conversation. The message was submitted as sealed evidence for a custody hearing between Baldwin and his ex-wife but somehow the recording was leaked to the press. [95] Ginni Thomas, wife of Supreme Court justice Clarence Thomas, left an odd message for Anita Hill about the accusations of sexual harassment Hill made against her husband nearly twenty years ago.

HOME SWEET HOME

Increasingly, U.S. households are awash with intruder alarms, security systems, motion detectors, video cameras, and fenced perimeters. Taking these security techniques to the next level, the fastest-growing residential communities in the nation are private, usually gated, fiefdoms where, at some, visitors are video recorded as they arrive. About twenty-eight million Americans live in an area governed by a private community association. Here, the enforcement of "normalcy" is taken to new heights. These serene fortresses have a plethora of rules and regulations that govern everything from the color you can paint your house to the type of toys that can be left in your driveway. Developers and residents appear obsessed with creating a perfect world, where all things are controlled and predictable. Here is how one journalist described a private suburban development near Seattle:

> There are no pesky doorbellers, be they politicians, or girl scouts, allowed inside this community. . . . A random encounter is the last thing people here want. There is a new park, every blade of grass in shape—but for members only. Four private guards man the entrance gates twenty-four hours a day, keeping the nearly 500 residents of Bear Creek in a nearly crime free bubble. And should a dog try to stray outside its yard, the pet would be instantly zapped by an electronic monitor. [96]

It seems not surprising, then, that the Walt Disney Company, the purveyors of fantasy theme parks, entered the private residential development business in the 1990s. Its first complete city south of Orlando, called Celebration, is founded on postmodern simulation and a deep nostalgia for the past. "Celebration's planners envisioned a community reminiscent of the quaint villages that dot New England's landscape," said one journalist. "They wanted sidewalks and picket fences, a town not unrelated to Disney World's Main Street, USA, just a mile or so away. They wanted to bring back a way of life lost when suburbs appeared." "It's like an old time kind of place," says one resident. Ironically, clean, safe streets away from ethnically diverse urban centers were precisely the promise of the suburbs and gated, privatized, insular, and highly controlled, planned communities such as this may come close to delivering on the fantasy. As one resident puts it, "when I drive through those white picket fences I say whew and think I'm home and I don't have to go back out."[97]

While our dwellings may bristle with security devices and gated communities attempt to keep out the less desirable, some of the scrutinizing that goes on in some U.S. homes is directed more at family members and others on the inside rather than at strangers lurking about outside. With "babysitters-from-hell" in the movies; deranged, drug-using criminal teens on TV; and cheating celebrity spouses on the front page of the gossip rags, paranoia runs deep in the middle-class household. No matter the suspect, BrickHouse Security ("When You Need to Know") is one of many vendors that will sell you the technology to ease your fears and make everyone in your life "safe." For example, their sales pitch for "nanny cams" is quite compelling:

> Nanny cameras are critical tools for every parent or caregiver who needs to know their family is *safe*. Usually placed in the home, nanny cams provide *protection against the unknown. We've all heard the stories* of children suffering abuse at the hands of their babysitter. Setting up a nanny camera will *put your mind at ease*. You'll know for sure what's happening when you can't be there. Check out BrickHouse's extensive selection of affordable hidden cameras and nanny cams today. Because nothing is more important than your family's *safety*.
> If you suspect abuse, there is no better way to gather the evidence you need to bring a nanny or caregiver to justice than a hidden camera. These covert, easy-to-use devices will record your nanny's every move without them knowing.

Of course, the same technology can be used to keep an eye on your partner or spouse. BrickHouse can help there, as well:

> Catch cheaters with hidden spy cameras from BrickHouse Security. Covert cameras, including alarm clocks with night vision, are ideal bedroom spy cameras. For cheating spouse surveillance, a hidden camera can be housed in smoke detectors or standard AC outlets, giving you the vital footage you need to know for sure if your significant other has been faithful. Covert camera systems can even be hidden outside your home, to catch a spouse coming or going. Spy gear and other hidden cameras for sale through BrickHouse Security can give you the answers you need to know for sure if your suspicions are valid.[98]

Children and adolescents are particularly vulnerable to all kinds of surveillance ceremonies and techniques. It would seem that we are either frightened
of other people's "dangerous" teenagers or scared of what might become of
our own. For some parents, technology provides peace of mind and, once
again, the purveyors of "safety" and "protection" such as BrickHouse Security are there to comfort a worried parent:

> Tracking teen text messages and computer usage can keep your family mem-
> bers under 18 out of *a world of danger*. BrickHouse Security's teen computer
> security software and phone surveillance tools give you the ability to read chat
> logs, text messages, and more, ensuring that minors are not talking to anyone
> *looking to take advantage of them*. Our iPhone Spy Stick and Android Spy
> Stick can recover a variety of information from the newest smartphones. *Pro-
> tect* your kids against online predators with our sophisticated computer and
> cell phone monitoring devices and digital surveillance tools.[99]

Driving is a particular concern for the parents of teens. DriveCam Video
Systems sells camera technology "designed to make drivers more careful by
letting them know that someone is watching." The system is set up so that it
is only activated when "severe vehicle forces" such as hard breaking, corner-
ing, "aggressive," or "inattentive" driving is detected. At that point, the
"event recorder" captures and uploads video and data before and after the
action both inside and out of the vehicle. "Set the expectation for your teen to
NOT trigger the camera. They'll quickly learn to 'keep it green' by not
speeding, paying attention and scanning for hazards." The technology then
offers the driver "real-time feedback" and "self-correcting" opportunities
once they have internalized the boundaries of the gaze; kind of like an electronic dog fence. Reports generated are the basis for "driver analytics," a
process whereby a company "risk analyst" reviews the data and provides a
"report card" that not only rates the incidents—as those meeting, say, a
threshold of "concern," but "excellent" performance is noted as well—but
also "compares your teen's driving with the average from their peer group—
the most effective coaching and mentoring environment for novice drivers
ever created."

   The text from the company's website provides an extraordinary description of how this technology facilitates the exercise of disciplinary power:
micro-level movements of the body are examined in detail; surveillance is
continuous, automatic, and "anonymous" in that "feedback" is from an unknown third party; detailed, scientific-based knowledge is gathered and deployed as "corrective" and agents make "normalizing judgments" that provide the basis of penalties or rewards or privileges to accomplish the goal of
modifying behavior. All of it works efficiently, effectively, and productively:

DriveCam makes parenting easier by providing objective, third party feedback that teens listen to and video that enables fact-based discussions instead of emotion-based arguments. DriveCam makes it less expensive by reducing the chance of insurance premium increases from claims, unreimbursed repair costs, traffic fines and costly medical bills. DriveCam gives you peace of mind and a stronger relationship with your teen by giving you visibility into what's happening—and not happening—when your teen drives alone.

Using this program is an act of love and protection, like using a car seat . . . Parents who review videos with their teen, share the coaching tips from Drive-Cam and reinforce expectations find that the program requires very little effort, yet yields tremendous results. Teens are soon coaching and correcting themselves.

Have you noticed that most teens appear to listen to others more than their parents? DriveCam's objective, third-party feedback makes it simpler to be a parent by providing a fact-based comparison of your teen's driving risk to what it could be, along with suggestions on how to drive more safely. With DriveCam, you can be less of a judge that's "ruining their life" and more of the coach that's saving their life.[100]

Interestingly, the DriveCam website offers a number of video clips from their system catching kids getting into real accidents—I guess the system hadn't helped them yet—that offer frightening evidence of what can happen if you don't buy their product. How much does DriveCam cost? The camera is $495, installation is $50, and the monthly service fee is $30. "The cost is comparable to a cell phone or a sports club team fee, but can potentially save you thousands of dollars and heartache by preventing an expensive crash."[101]

For parents on a budget, they can pick up "The Car Chip Pro" from AlltrackUSA, the "hi-tech and yet economical way to monitor your teenager's driving. And in a compact package that's easy to install to boot!" Much like the Progressive Insurance "Snapshot," this device, which costs $79, plugs into your vehicle's onboard diagnostics connector and records "vehicle speeds driven, hard accelerations, hard decelerations/braking, time and date for each trip, distance traveled and more. It can even optionally beep at the driver if he/she surpasses speed, acceleration and braking levels that YOU define. Wow!" The same company sells "real-time" GPS tracking systems that will provide a fixed location of the vehicle and automatically e-mail or call the parent any time the teen drives too fast or goes somewhere they are not supposed to be, that is, outside a virtual fence drawn by the parent on a map. According to Mark Allbaugh from Alltrack, "It gives them [parents] control. I mean it's a way to help keep your kids in line, I think."[102] Yet Jim Katz, director of Rutgers University Center for Mobile Communications Studies, states that "I think over time parents will feel that if they don't have this they're not being good parents." Katz also thinks that the technology may give parents a false sense of security. "We can't just assume that if the software reports that our kid stayed in school, they ate properly, and that they passed the test, that everything is okay with that kid." And child psychiatrist Dr. Steve Scholzman argues that, "When kids feel crowded, they tend to do things that they actually might otherwise not do. You know, they'll take even greater risks, because they have a desire to sort of prove their independence and their individuality." Scholzman says tracking kids also undermines the trust that's critical to a teen's development and that they need enough freedom to make good choices on their own, "not just because they know mom and dad are watching." [103]

When teenagers try to step outside the trusting confines of home, they are likely to encounter other forms of social control. More than 150 U.S. cities now have curfews in place to restrict the movement of teenagers at night. Typically, they ban anyone under seventeen from being on the streets between the hours of 11 p.m. or midnight and 6 a.m. While instituting a curfew in Washington, D.C., a law enforcement official stated: "Our interest is not to go out, pick up and harass children. What we want to do is take these children out of harm's way." But curfew violators are subjected to an "automatic disciplinary process in which a violator is taken to a juvenile curfew center, where a parent or guardian is notified and the teenager is counseled." One fourteen-year-old youth complained, "They should catch the real criminals instead of trying to keep us in the house. I don't think it's fair." [104]

If these techniques can't keep kids under control or "out of harm's way," there is always the option of locking them up. For most poor children and children of color, this means a trip to the local juvenile detention center. I attended the opening-day ceremony of a multimillion-dollar regional facility of this kind in my hometown. Here, the emphasis seemed to be on impressing visitors that taxpayers had gotten their money's worth. We were treated to a tour that focused on security gadgets like the automatic door-locking system, surveillance cameras, and the listening devices installed in the inmates' rooms. Little attention was paid to kids or their problems. A representative of the Chamber of Commerce, which hosted the event, praised local politicians for bringing much-needed dollars and jobs to the city. Indeed, I could have been attending the ribbon cutting ceremony of a new frozen yogurt store.

If you are a white, middle-class teenager, you may find yourself shipped off to a psychiatric hospital or chemical dependency unit. During the last hundred years or so, behaviors which were once seen as instances of immorality or evil—such as drunkenness, drug use, sexual promiscuity, delinquency, and the like—have come to be reinterpreted as symptoms of sickness or disease. [105] Furthermore, increasing numbers and types of deviant behaviors are being treated in those institutions designed for the ill—hospitals and clinics—and with the sorts of psychological therapies deemed suitable to those who are seen as in trouble, rather than as causing trouble. Running away, incorrigibility, minor theft, and other forms of teenage "acting out" have been reclassified into psychiatric diagnoses such as "personality disorders" and "adjustment reaction to adolescence." As I like to say, I don't know anyone who didn't have an adjustment reaction to adolescence! In some of my previous research, I found that there was a dramatic increase in the 1980s in the use of private psychiatric facilities to control misbehaving youth.[106] Most of us have seen the commercials for these hospitals on TV. In most cases, they are likely profit-making operations owned by a large medical corporation and provide care and control of misbehaving or disturbed adolescents (and sometimes children) in return for third-party insurance money. Typically, kids are committed to these facilities as "voluntary" patients—after being checked in by their parents—and have no legal rights whatsoever. And, equally common, they are declared "cured" and released as soon as their parents' insurance coverage runs out.

SCHOOL DAYS, SCHOOL GAZE

If kids can't be trusted to act responsibly at home, they get even less benefit of the doubt at school. In urban and rural schools alike, the country's educational institutions have become security fortresses where increasing numbers of young people are subjected to daily surveillance ceremonies, mostly in the name of their own "safety." This trend has only accelerated in the wake of the awful school shootings in Kentucky, Oregon, Colorado, and the latest, in Newtown, Connecticut. In 1993, the federal government passed the Safe Schools Act: "A bill to help local school systems achieve Goal Six of the National Education Goals, which provides that by the year 2000, every school in America will be free of drugs and violence and will offer a disciplined environment conducive to learning, by ensuring that all schools are safe and free of violence."[107] Among other things, the bill allocated $175 million for metal detectors, security guards, and violence prevention programs. At the local level, some changes were striking. For instance, after an incident with a gun at a rural West Virginia high school that left one student wounded, outraged parents demanded the resignation of the principal and forced the school to institute new security measures. Within weeks, video cameras were installed to watch kids on their buses, follow them through the hallways, and monitor their classroom behavior. They are shuttled through metal detectors and X-ray scanners operated by security guards while drug-sniffing dogs searched their lockers and cars. As one journalist observed the scene, "At a guard shack outside Mount View High School, three teenagers who had been unruly on a school bus stopped for inspection recently. The guard wrote down their names and ran a hand-held metal detector over each. The youths turned on command and raised their hands over their heads." One young girl at the school, a fifteen-year-old, stated, "It feels like a prison in here. The older kids don't care because they've gotten used to it. But the younger ones like me are coming from schools where you're still playing with blocks."[108]

Echoing my theme of the blurring distinctions between the institutions and practices of the criminal justice system and those, as Foucault put it, out in the "free" state, Annette Fuentes argues in her book *Lockdown High: When the Schoolhouse Becomes a Jailhouse* that "When prisons are built faster than new schools as a solution to social and economic problems, a penal approach to school violence of any magnitude appears to be the logical fix even if there is little evidence that it works to make schools and students safer. . . . Every choice to adopt another punitive measure . . . has turned students into suspects, and moved the school house further down the slippery slope to the jailhouse."[109] Like me, Fuentes observes the penetration of prison culture into our institutions and daily lives.[110] The result: today, about 6 percent of public schools deploy metal detector checks on students. Security cameras are in 36 percent of all schools; nearly 64 percent of high schools, 42 percent of middle schools, and 29 percent of elementary schools.[111] In addition, drug testing (see chapter 4), lock-down procedures, zero-tolerance policies, mandatory suspensions, expulsions, and arrests have become commonplace. According to data collected from public school principals by the U.S. Department of Education from 2003 to 2006, 85 percent of principals reported locking or monitoring doors to the school building during the day, and 48 percent required identification cards or badges for faculty. Forty-five percent of the principals surveyed employed school security officers, including those employed by private security companies as well as local law enforcement officers. Fourteen percent of principals reported conducting random sweeps for contraband such as weapons and drugs, and 6 percent used random metal detector searches.[112]

And more is coming. In Phoenix, Arizona, the Royal Palm Middle School has installed biometric face scanners ostensibly to recognize registered sex offenders and missing children. The scanners are tied to local and national databases of sex offenders, missing children, and alleged abductors. "If it works one time, locates one missing child or saves a child from a sexual attack, I feel it's worth it," said Joe Arpaio, the infamous county sheriff who also put prisoners on chain gangs and issued them pink underwear.[113] Justice of the Peace Tommy Munoz of Bryan, Texas, orders truants to carry a hand-held GPS tracking unit with them at all times. The Attendance Improvement Management (AIM) program has been used in a number of locales across the United States. The student is required to key in a numeric code five times a day, such as when they leave home, when they get to school, after lunch, when they leave school, and when they make it home before curfew; for fifteen-year-olds or younger, the curfew is 8 p.m. while for sixteen or older, it's 9 p.m. And three to five times a week, truants carrying the device will receive a phone call from a counselor who will discuss how their day progressed and set goals for improvement.[114] In San Antonio, Texas, a school district is using RFID chips embedded in student badges to track their movements and whereabouts. The program, called the "Student Locator Project," is aimed at increasing student attendance rates, something that generates revenue for the school district. About 4,200 students at Jay High School and Jones Middle School are being required to wear "SmartID" card badges embedded with an RFID tracking chip which will make it possible for school officials to track students' whereabouts on campus at all times. One sophomore, fifteen-year-old Andrea Hernandez, who was suspended for refusing to wear the tracking device when she declared that the badge is a "mark of the beast" that goes against her religion, took the matter to court. Hernandez later lost her case when a judge ruled in favor of the school district claiming they have the right to expel the student for failing to abide by a school requirement.[115]

We can see how these kinds of practices are introduced, refined, and gain acceptance over time. A few years back, my then nine-year-old son came home from school one day to tell me that they had issued all the kids ID cards with barcodes on them. These relatively "dumb" barcode cards were used in the cafeteria to tally up their biweekly bill and in the library to keep track of books and materials a child had checked out. I dropped by my son's school one day only to find him and his classmates in a silent, orderly line waiting to eat lunch, their barcode "badges" dangling from their shirt pockets. It gave me a shudder. At the end of the cafeteria line, personnel stood with a laptop scanning the cards and the lunch items that the children had selected. When I went over and asked about the cards, one staff member excitedly described the wonderful advantages of the system: "This way we know, and can tell you exactly what items your child had for lunch, at exactly what time, on exactly what day!" "Gee," I said. "I guess my son will think twice about trying to sneak chocolate milk past me again." Seeing this scene nearly two decades ago, I anticipated then that some enterprising school administrator would get the idea to use this kind of technology to take attendance and monitor the children's whereabouts. I guess I was right.

In another example of the evolution of enhanced capabilities, while schools across the country were installing mostly analog video cameras in hallways, libraries, and cafeterias, administrators in Casino-rich Biloxi, Mississippi, took the next step, hanging expensive digital cameras in common areas but also in all of its five hundred classrooms. This installation makes nearly anything that takes place in any of the district's eleven public schools subject to oversight and instant replay. "Our whole purpose was to make our schools safer," the superintendent of schools declared in an interview. However, a while after the cameras were installed, principals in the district reported that they strictly used such replays to "confront only humdrum problems like clarifying the disappearance of a child's ice cream money or ensuring that students do not sleep in class." Like Bentham's overseer in the "inspector's lodge," one principal, Dr. Laurie A. Pitre, of North Bay Elementary, told a reporter that she frequently uses the computer in her office to look in on the school's classrooms. She stated that the cameras function "like truth serum." "When we have a he-said, she-said situation," Pitre reported, "9 times out of 10 all we have to do is ask children if they want us to go back and look at the camera, and they fess up." A fifth grader at the school said that she pretty much had adjusted to the presence of the cameras in the classroom except that one of her substitute teachers was fond of pointing to them and telling the pupils, "Be good or Dr. Pitre will see you."[116]

"Seeing you" is what administrators in Livingston, Tennessee, did when they recorded ten- to fourteen-year-old boys and girls undressing in changing areas in preparation for basketball. The images ended up being stored on a computer that was accessible through the Internet. The parents of the kids filed a federal lawsuit. The Director of Schools claimed that the cameras had been installed in a utility room that was later converted to a locker area. The plaintiffs, however, accused school officials of "callous indifference" to their children's privacy.[117] In another case in Penn Valley, Pennsylvania, parents sued their son's school accusing officials of watching him through his school-issued laptop's webcam, enabled through theft-tracking software while he was at home and did not know the camera was on. The suit claimed that an assistant principal informed the student "that the school district was of the belief that a minor plaintiff was engaged in improper behavior in his home, and cited as evidence a photograph from the webcam embedded in minor plaintiff's personal laptop issued by the school district." The laptop had not been reported lost so there would have been no need to engage the theft-tracking software; it was never revealed what the boy was supposedly doing in his room when the webcam was activated.[118]

While there appears to be a lot of observing of student bodies going on, other techniques are attempting to gaze into their minds. Again, applying a criminal justice and security mentality to our schools, post-Columbine public officials have been working with a variety of government agencies and security companies engaged in "threat assessment." In 2002, in coordination with the Department of Education, the National Threat Assessment Center of the U.S. Secret Service agency engaged in the Safe School Initiative with a focus on "targeted" school violence and the adaptation of earlier Secret Service research on assassination for its examination of incidents of school-based attacks.[119] The Secret Service outlines a step-by-step procedure for carrying out the threat assessment process "and set out 11 key questions that may provide members of the threat assessment team guidance in making judgments about whether a student of concern poses a threat." In a similar model, a private security company has been marketing the Mosaic computer program for more than ten years to help school authorities identify potentially violent students. The company has been creating "risk-assessment" programs for special law enforcement situations such as threats of domestic violence, and the safety of the Supreme Court and the governors of eleven states. The Mosaic program is based on a series of questions about a child's behavior developed from case histories of people who have turned violent:

> A development team of experts in psychology, law enforcement, victims' advocacy, prosecution, mental health, and threat assessment determines what areas of inquiry will produce the highest quality assessments. MOSAIC poses those questions to users, accompanied by a range of possible answers. MOSA-IC calculates the value of the answers selected by the assessor, and expresses the results on a scale of 1 to 10. MOSAIC automatically produces a full written report, describing the factors that were considered. [120]

Since administrators and teachers will be answering the questions with the students in absentia, one wonders how accurate the data for the forty questions asked can be. Would school personnel know, for example, if a student has experienced victimization by peers in the last eighteen months? It is not likely that even the most insightful school principal or staff member on campuses with hundreds of kids is going to know who is or is not being teased and tormented. Will certain young people who are simply "different" be singled out as being "dangerous"? The Mosaic software has all the makings of Foucault's examination, the ritualized knowledge-gathering activities in which case files are built out of the mundane details of people's lives. It contains normalizing judgments created by experts that attempt to assess an individual's behavior against some standard and judge them—with small, graduated distinctions—along a continuum; in this case, between docile and dangerous.

In the end, we have to ask ourselves, is all this "security" and surveillance of our children really called for? Does it make schools truly "safer?" If one reads the headlines, watches the television news, or listens to some politicians, one could conclude that our schools are decidedly dangerous places to be. Yet, despite the horrific instances of "targeted" school violence—tragedies that indeed call for investigations and prudent preventative actions—and other crimes and victimizations associated with schools, it's clear that children are in greater danger *off* school grounds than they are on them. [121] There are approximately 122,656 K–12 schools in the United States with more than fifty-five million students and the percentage of youth homicides occurring at school remains as it has for a number of years at less than 2 percent of the total number of youth homicides. In 2009, approximately 4 percent of students ages twelve to eighteen reported being victimized at school during the previous six months, 3 percent of those were reported thefts. In 2010, students experienced four serious violent victimizations per one thousand students at school and five serious violent victimizations per one thousand students away from school. At the same time, in total, 5,740 children and teens in the United States died from gunfire in 2009; the equivalent of a Columbine tragedy every day.[122]

Was there evidence that the Royal Palm Middle School in Phoenix had a problem with sex offenders entering the school when it installed facial recognition readers? Had the Northside Independent School District in San Antonio trouble finding students on its campus when it initiated the RFID-based "Student Locator Project?" Was the North Bay Elementary School in Biloxi, Mississippi, overrun with student misconduct before it mounted digital cameras in all of its classrooms? It's not likely that any of these cases warranted these kinds of responses. No, it seems that these tactics are the product of media-heightened fears and insecurities, our belief in technological solutions, "get-tough" approaches, counterproductive school funding policies, and our willingness to accept the claims of corporations and other private entities that have a vested interest in selling us "security." As Aaron Kupchik states in his book *Homeroom Security: School Discipline in an Age of Fear*, "Part of the problem is that Americans are so wedded to a particular solution to the problem of school crime despite a lack of evidence that the solution works. Strategies such as police in schools, security cameras, and zero-tolerance measures resonate with widely shared ideas about crime prevention: that more police and punishments will keep us (and our children) safe."[123]

NO. 2 PENCILS

Beyond the meticulous rituals children are subjected to as they move in and about school, we can't forget the classroom itself. For Foucault, the modern school represented a system of uninterrupted examination; tests and otherwise. Although the stated purpose of the institution is to disseminate knowledge *to* the students, it has long been involved in ritualized knowledge-gathering *about* them. Case files are built out of a series of hierarchical observations and normalizing judgments. With increased measuring and testing, we make finer and finer gradients that distinguish one student from another. In spite of the testers' claim that they are simply better able to measure a child's innate abilities, one can argue—from a social constructionist rather than positivist perspective—that the tests themselves "create" the very thing they purport to measure. For example, before there were IQ tests, one wonders whether there was anything like what we consider today to be "intelligence." Before the tests, we looked at two people and said that both seemed "kinda smart" or maybe that one was "not so bright." Once they take an IQ test, however, we can claim that one is nine, twelve, or twenty-five points "more intelligent" than the other.[124]

From the earliest grades, the process of sorting kids into categories begins, and their educational "careers" and identities begin to take hold. The smallest details of their performance, from penmanship to their ability to sit still, are measured and evaluated. After a battery of standardized tests, little Brandon or Brittany becomes the "slow learner," or it is decided that he has a "learning disability" or that she is "gifted" or maybe "just average." In one account by a family friend, this single mother was told that her daughter was "having problems" in the second grade. This prompted a meeting with the school's "intervention team"—a group of well-trained and well-intentioned professionals including the child's teacher, the principal, the school counselor, the district psychologist, a learning disabilities teacher, and a teacher of gifted children. The bad news was that the child's tests indicated that she had a "learning disability." The good news, however, was that she was also "gifted" (something that they would not have "discovered" if she had not been tested). This meant that the child was assigned an individual education plan (IEP), which is an even more detailed set of criteria and goals to be monitored and measured throughout the year. The IEP would follow throughout the child's educational career.

An amazing example of this mentality and the whole system of the examination with its case files, hierarchical observation, and normalizing judgments—uses barcode scanning to "revolutionize tracking a student's progress." The system, called *Learner Profile*, is used to build a database about an individual's academic and behavioral performance. Each category, from the smallest detail such as capitalization skills or listening skills, can be assigned barcodes with a scale of performance for each classification (e.g., "no understanding," "basic knowledge," or "mastery"). "Following the capitalization example," a journalist covering a story on the system writes, "a teacher reads a student paper, scans the student's bar code, . . . Beep! the category, capitalization . . . Beep! . . . and says the student shows a basic understanding . . . Beep!" And, of course, "if students are interacting while she is grading, she can pause in the middle and scan in a behavior field." The teacher thinks that the information collected will be more "comprehensive" than a standard grade card that "tells us so little." She would also like to see "self-motivated students use the system, setting goals and tracking their own progress." Here, once more, those under surveillance are encouraged to use the system to monitor themselves. Asked about the distracting nature of the incessant beeping noise—but perhaps more telling about this new meticulous ritual itself—the teacher said, "I've found that they get used to it pretty quickly."[125]

Another software system goes even a step further, putting everyone in the classroom under the gaze. Designed by researchers at my own university, the system is intended to place a child's classroom behavior in context and "help explain why children act the way they do." The software, run on a laptop, is used by an "outside observer" such as a school psychologist to systematize or "impose a discipline" on observations of the classroom environment. The software "helps the psychologist silently tabulate, every fifteen seconds, the teacher's behavior, the activity of the moment, the teaching materials at hand, and the configuration of the class—students working alone, one on one, in small groups." Despite the fact that one of the developers claims that, potentially, "everything can go wrong" (such that "people can take this, and in the worst case, use it to evaluate teachers under review"), a number of school districts in the United States and foreign countries have adopted the system. [126]

HARASSAMATICS AND THE DIGITAL SLAVES

Have you ever wondered why United Parcel Service (UPS) drivers are always in a hurry? A number I know and have spoken with—mostly in our building's elevator when they had no choice but to stand still—appear nearly frantic at times. I would guess most of us simply assume that employees with this company known for on-time deliveries have developed a culture of *esprit de corps* among its dedicated workers. Yet, there is much more going on behind the brown uniforms and consumer goodies that get dropped on our doorsteps. UPS describes their fleet of 100,000+ distinctive trucks as "Rolling Laboratories":

> We have created a proprietary system of telematics that combines a wealth of information about the behavioral and mechanical variables. . . . This enables us to use our delivery vehicles as "rolling laboratories" in which we collect data, test ideas, and hone our performance. . . . These delivery vehicles are equipped with sensors to provide information on how the vehicle performs mechanically and to report on: Speed, Direction, Braking, Performance of specific parts and components of the engine and drive train. . . . *In addition, information is gathered to optimize efficiency of delivery routes and driver behavior such as monitoring seat belt use. Drivers also receive detailed reports enabling them to compare their performance with benchmarks. . . .*
> To maximize the benefit of telematics, we bring our drivers into the process. *We give them and their managers' detailed reports on how their behaviors stack up against the results we strive for, such as accelerating and braking smoothly to conserve fuel. Having concrete data empowers them to optimize their behavior behind the wheel and make their "rolling laboratory" even more efficient.* [127]

According to a press release from UPS, truck-embedded "telematics"—the integrated use of telecommunications, informatics, and GPS technology— can help supervisors construct a detailed picture of the journey undertaken by a particular driver and vehicle fitted with sensors that generate more than two hundred vehicle-related variables from speed, RPMs, seatbelt use, the number of times the truck is placed in reverse, and the amount of time spent idling. At the end of each day, these data are automatically uploaded to UPS's enormous data center in Mahwah, New Jersey, to be analyzed and evaluated. And the latest generation of handheld devices the drivers carry let UPS load all the daily route information, track their whereabouts with GPS, and calculate their delivery times. "You can re-create the driver's day," Nigel Watson, a vice president in UPS's transportation technology group, proudly declares. [128]

But some employees writing on an independent blog for UPS drivers, had a different version of what telematics was all about:

[Entry #1]
Ever wonder why you never seem to be able to fall into a day to day, hum drum life, as a driver? It seems like you are always under pressure from so many angles when trying to do the job. You think you are getting it done to the boss's satisfaction, then you get hit from some other angle. Not enough lead cards. To many tracers. Production is off by 5 minutes. Driving the vehicle to hard. Not wearing the seatbelt. Not closing the bulkhead door. You've certainly heard all of these and many more. . . . The company knows that keeping you on edge and stressed makes you run harder. . . . You are obligated to give a fair days work, for a fair days pay. That fair day does not mean you have to sell your soul to the devil. Telematics is designed to steal more of that soul. The whole purpose of the system is to give them something to harass you about, even though you are doing the job. The system allows them to pick any point, and use it against you. The system should be known as Harassamatics. They tell you it's about safety, and seat belts, and backing. That's a bunch of crap. It's all about stealing your break time for their profit, and harassing you into a heightened state of frenzy about your job.
[Entry #7]
Telematics is all about assumption. Managers have always assumed that the drivers are sandbagging them. They assume that every driver is cheating and stealing from the company, they just haven't caught them yet. Telematics brings a whole new perspective to this world of assumption. . . . Every time Telematics has been thrown in my face, it has been presented to me that I was "taking extra break without recording it." In fact, I was dealing with irate, or disgruntled customers to the companies benefit. Of course the assumption was that I was stealing from the company. I was also being chastised for taking care of bodily functions. My comment to the manager is, "now you are the potty monitor." How many times did you go? How long did it take you to wipe? How far did you have to travel to go? Can't you consolidate your bathroom stops?
[Entry #9]
Telematics is being used by management as a harassment tool. They will soft speak you during implementation, telling you it's being put in for safety, not to be used for production, or harassment. The fact is its only purpose is to eliminate management, and make the surviving sups. more powerful amongst the

drivers. Sups. can sit at a desk and monitor 30 or more drivers at a time. They can pick the fly-sh-t out of the pepper of every minute of every day. They will do all of that.

Yet another driver wrote about telematics on a different section of the blog summing it up this way: "It's simple; you are being watched every second of every day."[129]

Surveillance and control have been central features of the world of work ever since people were hired to labor for someone else. As Karl Marx pointed out, nineteenth-century capitalism gave birth to the central problem of modern management: how to get workers to convert their potential labor power to labor done. A few centuries later, we have seen countless "solutions" to this dilemma come and go; from starvation and outright coercion, to company unions and Ford's 1920s high-paying incentive of "five dollars a day," to work teams and the latest prescription from this week's best-selling management guru.

Machines and technology have, in the last hundred years or so, played an important role in keeping industrial workers "on task," controlled, and docile, thus optimizing "efficiencies." This strategy was epitomized in the late nineteenth century by the emergence of the assembly line, which brought both the production process and the workers together in a centralized system. The "regime of production"—centered on mass production, high volume, standardized products using special purpose machinery—has been referred to as "Fordism." But "deindustrialization," globalization, the rise of the service industry, and the move toward more "flexible" use of labor—a new regime of production usually referred to as "Post-Fordist"—have generated a new class of white-collar and service workers that present a fresh challenge for management.[130] Today, corporate jargon is filled with terms such as gathering "intelligence," "the analytics of big data," "drilling down to the granular level," and "optimizing visibility and measurability." The result has been dramatic changes in the quality and quantity of watching and monitoring in the workplace itself and of those workers not tied to offices and desks. Workers who are increasingly deploying information and communication technologies (ICTs) in their work—computers and telecommunications equipment to store, retrieve, transmit, and manipulate data—find that these devices become the very tools that management uses to monitor and control their movements, behavior (what they can say, write, and do in the workplace), and productivity.

Surely, in a capitalist enterprise, an employer has a legitimate interest in checking in on an employee's activities at work to ensure that they are performing at acceptable levels, to protect business assets, be aware of security concerns, and address issues such as sexual harassment. However, in the United States at least, there appears to be little constraint, legal or otherwise, on management's ability and willingness to surveil employees at work. Moreover, such strategies may have the countereffects of creating a culture of suspicion, dampening employee morale, increasing their stress, and undermining creativity and productivity. While one could argue that employees using company equipment and resources during the workday have no "reasonable expectation of privacy," as Alan Westin argued years ago, an alternative viewpoint might suggest that the issue is not about privacy *per se*, but about the human dignity of employees and about personal integrity and autonomy. [131]

At first, the "personal" computer offered us an advanced, individualized tool for doing creative work. It spawned a whole generation of "hackers" and others that celebrated such machines and their liberating potential. But corporate America was, ultimately, not interested in workers' autonomy and liberation. It wanted the productivity gains the machines offered over a typewriter, calculator, or big mainframe computer, but it also wanted to eliminate the need for constant personalized supervision. In today's workplace, the friendly sounding "personal computer" has long since disappeared; it has been transformed into the more productive sounding "workstation" that is connected to a network. Those spending their days at one of these machines—as demanded by an extraordinary number of jobs and occupations—are vulnerable to managers who can use specialized software to scan all their e-mail and instant messages, review every keystroke and document created, accessed, changed, or edited, and produce video playback and screenshots of any activity on the computer.

With a few well-publicized harassment lawsuits against companies based on computer e-mail, many are arming themselves with sophisticated surveillance tools and monitoring employee e-mail, raising questions about the proper balance between employee autonomy and an employer's need to know. While some believe that employers have a right, if not an obligation, to investigate specific complaints, say, of computer-borne harassment, others think that firms are overreacting. According to the 2007 Electronic Monitoring and Surveillance Survey from American Management Association (AMA) and the ePolicy Institute, 43 percent of companies monitor e-mail, 73 percent of which use technology tools to automatically review e-mail, and 40 percent of which assign an individual to read and evaluate them. Of the 66 percent of all employers monitoring Internet connections, nearly all use software to block connections to what have been determined to be "inappropriate" websites—that figure represents a 27 percent increase since the 2001 AMA survey. Additional computer monitoring includes 45 percent of employers tracking content, keystrokes, and time spent at the keyboard while another 43 percent store and review computer files. In addition, 12 percent monitor the blogosphere to see what is being written about the company, and another 10 percent monitor social networking sites. Out of those firms surveyed, 28 percent who have fired workers for e-mail misuse did so for the stated reasons: violation of any company policy (64 percent); inappropriate or offensive language (62 percent); excessive personal use (26 percent); breach of confidentiality rules (22 percent); other (12 percent).[132]

In a press release announcing the results of their survey, Nancy Flynn, executive director of the ePolicy Institute and author of several books related to workplace computer use, states that, "Concern over litigation and the role electronic evidence plays in lawsuits and regulatory investigations has spurred more employers to monitor online activity. Data security and employee productivity concerns also motivate employers to monitor Web and e-mail use and content." She added, "Workers' e-mail and other electronically stored information create written business records that are the electronic equivalent of DNA evidence," noting that 24 percent of employers have had e-mail subpoenaed by courts and regulators and another 15 percent have battled workplace lawsuits triggered by employee e-mail, according to 2006 AMA/ePolicy research.[133]

To date, the U.S. Supreme Court has yet to hear an e-mail "privacy" case, although lower courts have generally upheld the rights of employers to use surveillance. Federal law, primarily the dated Electronic Communications Privacy Act of 1986 (ECPA), restricts the intentional interception of any wire, oral, or electronic communication, or the unauthorized access of stored communications, but exceptions contained in the law generally allow employers to monitor business-related phone calls, monitor communications, and to retrieve and access stored e-mail messages.[134] With billions of electronic mail messages flying about every day, few people, it seems, give much thought to how public they really are. This kind of correspondence is openly available to network administrators and others along the line, while "deleted" mail is often stored on system backups for quite some time. Defying hierarchy, even those from the upper echelons can have their correspondence scrutinized. In a stunning irony, it was, after all, the e-mail of Microsoft chairman Bill Gates that flatly contradicted his sworn testimony with regard to the federal government's 1994 antitrust suit against Microsoft. Like Nixon being thwarted by his own tapes, e-mail can function as a "machine in which everyone [is] caught," as Foucault writes, "those who exercise power, just as much as those over whom it is exercised."[135] The Microsoft case sent shivers down the spine of corporate America as e-mail came to be treated by government investigators and juries as the "real truth" of the hearts and minds of executives and CEOs alike.

Not long after the Gates episode, Amazon.com issued a directive instructing employees to purge e-mail messages that were no longer required for business or not subject to legal records requirements. This Amazon "document retention" policy was referred to as "Sweep and Keep." "In the past, message-retention policies have been primarily designed for disk space management," says Jim Browning, a senior research analyst at the Gartner Group, a consulting firm. "The new question is how quickly should e-mail be deleted to prevent it from becoming a danger to the organization?" The consulting firm suggests policies that help employees understand what is "appropriate business language." For example, in the new electronic workplace: "You talk about 'fair competition'; you don't talk about 'slaughtering' them. No warfare language. That way you have fewer messages you have to worry about in the files." Unlike policies prohibiting abusive or harassing electronic messages, the new rules attempt to suppress common forms of expression. As one observer states, "And when such exchanges must take place in writing, the prevailing philosophy would have them expunged as quickly and ruthlessly as possible."[136]

For years, so-called futurists have been predicting that the "information age" and its associated technologies would free us from the drudgery of long commutes and the confines of the office. "Telecommuting" was heralded as the means whereby we will find a new generation of happy, productive workers, who labor when and where they want. Indeed, the benefits of telecommuting for companies, individuals, and communities could be considerable. One study suggests that as many as fifty million workers—about 40 percent of the workforce, could work at least part of the time from home. Yet today, estimates are that only 2.5 million employees, excluding those who are "self-employed," consider their home their "primary place of business."[137] Why has telecommuting failed to catch on? It seems that organizational hierarchies and the dysfunctional social relation of work at most U.S. companies would suggest that employees are simply not trusted to work that independently.[138] As one sociologist states, "Managers are tempted to use 'face time' in the office as the *de facto* measurement of commitment and productivity. They are often suspicious about employees who work out of sight, believing they will shirk or drift if not under constant supervision."[139]

Even when employees are permitted to work remotely, technology provides management tools to facilitate their "supervision" and make sure workers are "on task." Some monitor computer use, assess progress on projects, and schedule meetings on shared calendars, while others require "virtual face time" via teleconferencing, e-mail, instant messaging, or phone calls. Take the case of Amy Johnson. Johnson works—interestingly, given the topic of this book (see chapter 4)—as a fingerprint technician for a company called Accurate Biometrics in Chicago. She telecommutes from her home in Dixon, Illinois, but as one journalist writes, "she might as well be sitting at a desk next to her boss in Chicago." Timothy Daniels, vice president of operations for Accurate Biometrics, uses a "security" program called InterGuard by Awareness Technologies to track Johnson's productivity and, for example, to check which websites she has visited. And like Bentham's "inspector," who can efficiently view many cells at once, Daniels can check up on all his employees, including sixteen who work in the office and twenty-four at home, to see if they are using their time on the computer effectively. Daniels says, "It enables us to keep a watchful eye without being over-invasive." Johnson and the other employees know that their computers are monitored, but she says, "It doesn't bother me. I'm not doing anything I shouldn't be doing." [140]

Corporate "downsizing" and decentralization, emerging global markets that demand instant availability, and a drive to boost productivity have created demand for the more flexible use of labor. The results are that people have an anxious preoccupation with work, that they are working more hours, and that the lines between work and personal time and life are blurring as corporations use the emerging technologies to harness workers' productivity. Although the "virtual office" may not have walls—much like the "virtual prison" of house arrest has no bars—for many of the thirty million traveling businesspeople—the so-called road warriors—new telecommunications devices have become "electronic leashes" that keep them "wired in" and monitored. For example, one company with another great name, Cbeyond, offers their "Mobile Workforce Manager," which they claim can help organize and reduce the cost of field-based operations by tracking and recording the locations, hours worked, and jobs performed by mobile employees. Bryan Melton, product manager for Cbeyond's Mobile Workforce, claims that,

> Many of our small business customers have trouble locating their mobile workers, and there were cases of "fudged" timesheets. Our Workforce Manager is great at tracking mobile employees through our web-based portal. It allows mapping—essentially, the business owner can sit at his desk and see "dots on a map" in real time. We also provide geo-fencing, limiting employees to a specific geographic location by tracking their whereabouts. Mobile workers can also now clock-in and out via their mobile devices, essentially making them electronic timesheets. Owners can also provide job scheduling/dispatching to their mobile workforce, so they're saving on fuel costs and mileage by dispatching jobs to the nearest worker, such as sending the nearest plumber to an emergency call. With our application you can be as efficient as possible with your mobile resources. It also generates detailed reports, and can do "bread crumb trails" which is a history of your mobile workforce—where they've been and what they've been doing all day. [141]

Similar capabilities for offices and other workplaces are enabled by Ekahau, Inc. ("Business Intelligence Through Location"), a "spin-off" company from Helsinki University in Finland that sells products worldwide. "Our mission is to provide the easiest, most cost effective and accurate positioning solutions for locating people, assets, inventory and other objects using wireless enterprise networks" (apparently "people" are considered just another "object").

Their "Badge and Pager provides accurate location for tracking people within your enterprise using your existing Wi-Fi network. These badges are the same size and shape of typical ID badges and fit easily on a lanyard with other credential cards or on a belt clip. . . . The Ekahau Real-time Location System provides an easy-to-use web-based user interface that displays the location of people on large campus floor plans [and] accurate real-time location provides a powerful way to remotely manage large areas and the workflow of large numbers of people."[142]

In another tactic reminiscent of the famous Hawthorne Works experiments of the 1920s, some companies are using sophisticated tracking devices to gather real-time information on how employees work and interact with each other. Sensors may be worn on lanyards or placed on office furniture to record how often staffers get up from their desks, consult other teams, and hold meetings. For instance, Bank of America wanted to find out if "face time" among call center teams matters to their productivity. It got ninety workers to wear badges with tiny sensors to record their movements and even the tone of their conversations. The data showed that the most productive workers belonged to close-knit teams with high-levels of interaction. Similarly, Cubist Pharmaceuticals did a sensor study of sales and marketing employees. For four weeks, company employees wore badges provided by Sociometric Solutions that collected data on their motions, whereabouts, voice levels, and conversational patterns. The information was merged with e-mail traffic data, along with the results of weekly surveys in which employees rated how energetic and productive they felt. Ben Waber, who runs Sociometric Solutions, says that a handful of managers have wanted to see the data on an individual employee, but his clients must sign contracts and consent forms prohibiting them from doing so. Yet, Waber claims that the individual level data can indicate from a worker's patterns of movement whether that employee is likely to leave the company or be a candidate for promotion. Kimberly-Clark deployed "space-usage" sensors beneath chairs and in conference rooms to examine where and when workers gather for formal and informal meetings. One journalist summed up these strategies this way: "Putting badges on workers is just the beginning of a broader trend, researchers say. As companies rethink their offices, many are looking into 'smart buildings,' wired with technologies that show workers' location in real time and suggest meetings with colleagues nearby."[143]

Meanwhile, recording workers' conversations is increasingly a part of the daily life of telephone operators, the "customer assistant" representatives of financial organizations, and the "sales associates" of catalog merchandisers. Many such organizations have decided that their employees—despite their "team spirit" and job titles that proclaim "we're a big happy family"—cannot be trusted to conduct business properly and need to have their calls monitored. "This call may be monitored," announces the recording, "for your protection and for training purposes." Since both sides of the conversation are recorded, it would seem that these businesses don't have confidence in their customers' integrity, either. With recordings, if a "dispute" or a complaint arises—from a customer or an employee—managers have the "truth" in hand.

The legions of customer service representatives and call center agents throughout the country (those that have not already been outsourced overseas) face the kind of grueling surveilled and rationalized workplaces once reserved for life on factory assembly lines. This type of workplace is facilitated by companies like NICE Systems ("Intent. Insight. Impact."), the self-proclaimed "worldwide leader of intent-based solutions that capture and analyze interactions and transactions, realize intent, and extract and leverage insights to deliver impact in real time." They deliver "real-time speech analytics technology," which

> analyzes spoken interactions as they occur, powering real-time agent guidance to help agents take the next-best-action and quickly address the customer issues. NICE Handle Time Optimization analyzes customer calls and categorizes them into call topics. It then breaks down agent handle time by topic. . . . The NICE solution identifies the discrete parts of calls and calculates average handle time for each. Call-part analysis can reveal agent knowledge gaps related to standard parts of customer calls such as up-selling. Here, too, real-time next-best-action recommendations and targeted training can help. [And] Drawing on NICE's Desktop Analytics, NICE Handle Time Optimization enables contact center managers to analyze agent desktop application usage during customer interactions and offline wrap-up time. The solution calculates handle time for agent applications such as CRM, billing and knowledge bases, and reports time spent on specific screens within these applications. With this information, managers can automate and simplify complex processes that slow average handle time. [144]

What does all this business-speak translate into for workers? A former employee of a call center in Kentucky run by Sitel, one of the firm's twenty-nine call centers in North America, was doing customer service representative work for Best Buy. He described his workplace this way:

> We made $8.00 per hour while in training and $8.25 per hour once we completed the training and took our seats on the floor. . . . You are watched by CC cameras and the phone lines are monitored (a common practice and one that is known to the agent). You log into a phone when you sit down to work, and you log on and off the phone for your time clock. You are given 30 seconds in-between calls to document the call you have just handled. If you go over the 30 secs., a supervisor will either come over to see what you are doing, or, as the lazy ones do, they will yell at you from across the room. . . . We were told that if we had to use the restroom that we had to go into our "break time" on the phone system (it clocks you in and out of everything) so that when your break

came around to get something to eat or drink, you had to take out your rest-room time. It was like being watched with a digital clock which tracked you down to the 1/10th of a second! In other words, it was like being a Digital Slave.[145]

It's not just office workers who are vulnerable to such monitoring. ICTs are transforming jobs throughout the entire occupational structure. Just look around. Restaurant workers wear vibrating beepers that literally prod them through their shift. Bookstore clerks don wireless headsets so they can stock shelves and answer phones and queries at the same time. Delivery people, auto-rental check-in clerks, parking and utility meter readers, and a host of others are carrying digital devices that keep tabs on their movements and keep track of their productivity. For instance, the transnational grocery giant TESCO has strapped electronic armbands on warehouse workers to monitor their work performance and break times. "The devices give a set amount of time for a task," said one employee, "such as 20 minutes to load packets of soft drinks. If they did it in 20 minutes, they would get 100 percent, but would get 200 percent if they were twice as fast." A Tesco spokesman referred to the bands as "Arm-mounted terminals."[146]

Bartenders may find themselves working under the watchful eye of the *BarMaxx RFID Solution*. Each liquor bottle is "chipped" when it arrives and is placed on an electronic scale fitted with BarMaxx's proprietary readers. The ID number and the bottle's weight—calculated to 4/1,000th of an ounce—is stored in the BarMaxx software. Every time a bottle is poured, the weight is reduced, and the software can then calculate the exact amount of that pour, based on the reduced weight. If a pour is too heavy or light or a bottle ends up missing, the systems sends an alert along with video footage to management. At the greenhouses of Eurofresh Farms, workers carry hand-held personally identified RFID readers. A description of each task to be completed is mounted on a wall along with an RFID tag beneath each de-scription. The employee selects the task about to be undertaken such as pruning or harvesting, and uses the handheld to read the tag associated with that task. If pruning, the worker simply proceeds to the appropriate row. At the front of each row, another RFID tag is mounted, with a unique ID number that identifies that particular row, along with all plants within it. The worker taps the row tag with their handheld, and a timestamp and row number are then stored on the reader. After moving on to another row, they tap the tag for that row, and so forth. Once finished, the staff proceeds to an upload terminal where the collected data are transferred to a central server. In this way, the company can track not only workers' productivity (how many rows each employee tended during a given shift, as well as how long that person spent in each row), but also how long it took the staff, in general, to care for plants in specific rows, based on their location or variety.

A restaurant chain in Utah deploys the RFID-enabled Table Tracker to identify where its customers have seated themselves and to measure how long it takes for an order to be served. [147] Hotel housekeeping staffs may have their performance measured by software fed through guest room phones. They must press, say, #1 from the phone when they enter the room and this records their "start clean time" in their digital file. When they are finished, they press #2 to mark the room as "ready for inspection." The system reports the actual clean time per room, the "forecasted time," and the difference to track housekeeper performance. [148] I saw a similar system at work recently at a large U.S. airport when a service worker came into the men's room and swept an RFID card over a reader on the wall. I asked him what that was about and he told me, "I have to do that in all the restrooms I service." Realizing what this likely meant, I probed, "Does it mean that your boss knows where you are?" He looked dejected and speaking quietly, looking from side-to-side, he said. "They know where I am all the time and how long it takes me to clean each restroom."

TESTING YOUR INTEGRITY

While all this monitoring and assessment is taking place in the workplace, it is likely that your employer began building a "case file" on you before you were even offered the job. As Foucault argued, disciplinary power—in this case, as it manifests itself between employer and potential employee—is enhanced by "the examination"; the use of the ritualized knowledge-gathering of the details of people's lives and activities and "normalizing judgments" that entail the assessment of an individual's behavior set against some standard or ideal. In the face of what employers claim is a rising tide of lawsuits, stringent hiring and firing regulations, drug use and alleged criminal activity in the workplace, post–9/11 security issues, as well as immigration status, corporations have turned to extensive pre-employment background checks and a series of other examinations to screen applicants. Ironically, although the EEOC restricts a potential employer from asking you "personal" questions in an interview such as "Are you married?" "Do you have children?" "Do you have any disabilities?" and the like, once you give your consent, pre-employment investigations can "drill down" into your:

Driving records	Neighbor interviews
Vehicle registration	Medical records
Credit records	Property ownership
Criminal records	Incarceration records
Social Security Number	Military records

Education records	State licensing records
Court records	Drug test records
Workers' compensation	Past employers
Bankruptcy	Personal references
Character references	Sex offender lists[149]

Larger firms often contract with background screening companies to conduct investigations, while others can simply go online and access sites like EmployersChoiceOnline.com that, given the name of an applicant, will access a variety of databases and online sources to unearth the "truth" about who they are. In hyperbolic justification of its services, this company claims, "In many ways, corporate America is at war. Companies are constantly under attack, often from within. Employee dishonesty, the proliferation of white-collar crime, and a myriad of internal threats such as lawsuits involving wage and hour disputes, sexual harassment claims and workers' compensation claims threaten to bring many employers down from the inside." But Tena Friery, research director at the Privacy Rights Clearinghouse, claims that, "There are a lot of things that potential employers can find out about you [and] this goes far beyond credit information and can include information about your personal characteristics and mode of living. One of the privacy concerns related to this is that there is no standard of relevance. The information that is gathered and disseminated doesn't have to apply to the specific job."[150]

Assuming you survive this kind of scrutiny, you may find yourself confronted with a pre employment "integrity test" (a favorite substitute for the lie detector, which was outlawed for most pre-employment situations back in 1988; I discuss the lie detector and the drug test in chapter 4, which focuses on surveillance and the body). Written integrity tests are used, supposedly, to measure a person's level of "honesty or dishonesty." Typically, testers will pose a set of questions that may come right out and ask whether you have committed various offenses (Have you ever stolen products from your place of employment?), or see what you would do under certain circumstances (If you saw a coworker taking money from the cash register would you report it to your supervisor?), or more subtly assess a person's values and attitudes (Do you agree with the idea of once a thief always a thief?). Despite the fact that the American Psychological Association has found that more than half of integrity-test publishers do not require any training or other qualifications of the people who administer their tests, and the U.S. Office of Technology Assessment found that over 95 percent of people who fail integrity tests are incorrectly classified as "dishonest," these tests are administered by an estimated six thousand organizations in the United States and taken by as many as five million people each year.[151]

Finally, an estimated 30 percent of all U.S. employers, from small businesses to Wal-Mart and General Motors, require applicants to take written "personality tests" that probe into aspects of their lives such as hygiene habits, sexuality, and family relationships (topics having little to do with on-the-job capabilities or performance). The 1990 Americans with Disabilities Act put some limits on the use of tests designed to reveal a physical or mental impairment. Like the integrity tests, psychologists question the validity of personality tests, yet one professional claims that it is their very limitations that make them so popular. "First of all," says organizational psychologist Dr. Ben Dattner, "they present a simplified view of human nature, and it can be reassuring to some people to be able to fit themselves and their colleagues into neat, predictable, pre-determined boxes. . . . Secondly, many of the most popular tests are non-evaluative, and convey an 'I'm OK, you're OK, we're just different' philosophy. . . . Finally, these assessments help people avoid unpleasant realities about real, underlying workplace conflict. For example, instead of needing to confront the real causes of conflict between two members of a team, such as real or perceived betrayals or destructive competition for limited resources, taking personality tests creates a reassuring, albeit false and oversimplified explanation for the conflict—one person is introverted and the other person is extroverted!"[152]

OK, now let's assume that you clear the background check, pass the integrity and psychological tests, the drug test (see chapter 4), and the physical exam and are offered a position. Once you are on the job, your supervisor is likely to add to your file through an ongoing monitoring and evaluation process made infinitely more systematic and thorough with a variety of inexpensive computer software programs. For example, Insperity's *Performance Now* package has "Built-in intelligence and support in a simple employee performance evaluation tool." The company goes on: "The most effective employee performance management programs are ongoing, not just an annual 'check-in.' *Performance Now* helps you track and measure goals throughout the year to ensure your employees are focused and more productive." Much like the barcode system being used to keep track of the smallest details about students' behavior, the "Employee Log" function "provides the mechanism to record specific examples of employee performance throughout the review period," this tool can thus be used to generate minute measurements of performance; evidence can be documented and tabulated, and penalties can be meted out when necessary. And like the teacher who would like to see the "self-motivated students use the system, setting goals and tracking their own progress," the makers of these kinds of products believe that the feedback provided to workers will give them the knowledge and self-awareness to increase their "productivity" and make themselves into "better" workers.

And with this tool, managers are relieved of the tasks of writing actual personal assessments of their employees. "*Performance Now* makes it easy to write complete, concise employee reviews that provide the type of feed-back to help your employees succeed. Simply choose from a list of elements, rate the employee's performance on a high-to-low scale, and watch *Performance Now*'s technology compose clear, concise, supporting text that translates your observations into meaningful words." In this way, the program generates a kind of "simulated" evaluation; only the appearance of a "real," "meaningful" appraisal is needed to create the necessary knowledge base of employee behavior. Just plug in the numbers and the program produces the sterile, legally safe text necessary to maintain the illusion of rigor. [153]

CONSUMING SURVEILLANCE

The relationship between consumerism and surveillance at this stage of late capitalism cannot be overstated. In fact, these two dimensions of postmodern life have become so intertwined that each presupposes the other; one cannot practically engage in consumption without being surveilled and many surveillance mechanisms are both dependent on and facilitated by consumption. Put another way, we now live in a "surveillance economy." [154] Each phase of the consumption cycle is replete with meticulous rituals of power: we are first targeted by sellers and advertisers based on their "intelligence" of our buying habits, "lifestyle" choices, and financial stature; when we do shop, our movements and activities are watched and observed (in stores and on-line); when we make a purchase, our identities and credit worthiness are confirmed and a record of our activities is stored; and finally additional gazes are secured through many of the very products and services that we are seduced into consuming. Each phase of consumption only serves to reinforce the next, creating an ever more sophisticated nexus and "granular" level analysis of the population.

All this came together and was illustrated nicely in a television commercial that appeared a few years ago called "Stinky Cheese" under the tag line of, "Know more, Sell more: IBM Business Intelligence." On the television screen we see a view of a food store through the somewhat distorted fish-eye effect of a panning video surveillance camera, as if we are looking through the camera. Two clerks appear on the screen in front of a display case:

Clerk 1: "Smell this stuff."

Clerk 2: "Ewwwwe."

Clerk 1: "It's green, it stinks, and it's . . . eight bucks!"

Clerk 1: "Marty" (both clerks waving their arms toward the video camera lens; the camera continues to pan slowly back and forth). "Marty. Hey Marty. . . . Who buys this stuff? It stinks."

Marty: "Well, Fletcher, the people who buy that stinky cheese also buy (keyboard typing) 92 percent of the miniature vegetables we sell" (more typing).

Marty: "Wow, look at the margins [profits] on miniature vegetables."

Clerk 1: "How can he know that?"

Clerk 2: "He's making it up."

Marty: "No, I'm not."

The closing caption reads: "Solutions for a Small Planet."

Some scholars go so far as to suggest that our participation in mass consumer culture has become a primary means of social integration and, in the broadest sense, social control in postmodern society. Like the shift from the brutal treatment of the offender in the classical age to the "gentle way" to punish in the modern era, social control, the argument goes, subtlety moves from the older, coercive forms of repression to the quiet seduction of the consumer market. Here any political discontent or social malfeasance is quickly absorbed into the stupefying complacency of the dominant consumer culture. Zygmunt Bauman declares, for example, that consumer conduct is moving "into the position of, simultaneously, the cognitive and moral focus of life, the integrative bond of society, and the focus of systemic management." Echoing Bauman, David Lyon adds, "Consuming, not working, becomes the hub around which the life-world rotates. Pleasure, once seen as the enemy of capitalist industriousness, now performs an indispensable role." Those unable or unwilling to consume at certain levels are sorted out as system "waste" (see chapter 5), undeserving of the efforts of seduction and more likely, it seems, to be subjected to the social control and surveillance practices of the penal/health/welfare complex.[155]

Today, an extraordinary amount of ritualized surveillance and monitoring takes place in our most mundane consumer activities—from our preferences in breakfast cereal, to the type of pain relief we take, or the magazines we read. Amazing amounts of personal, comprehensive information are collected and stored in an array of mostly private-sector databanks, offering access to this wealth of knowledge. For example, Acxiom Corporation (see chapter 5) based in Conway, Arkansas, has constructed the world's largest consumer database containing information about five hundred million active consumers worldwide, with about fifteen hundred data points per person. This is all quite a switch from a few hundred years ago. Think about it. Before the rise of modern, bureaucratic organizations and their knowledge-gathering activities, the people most "known" in society were elites—heroes, villains, royalty, heads of state, and religious leaders. Everyday folks were basically ignored—in their day and later by historians—in part, because there were few sources of information about them and, without a mass market for goods, there was no rationale for collecting any. But now it seems just the opposite. Today, those who have social power and wealth may use these resources to insulate and shield themselves from scrutiny as best they can while the rest of us are simply issued yet another account number.

In a marketplace overflowing with goods and services, the most effective and efficient way for sellers to bring order to this chaos—to increase their "targetability," as it is called—is by gathering up all the bits and pieces of our lives and reassembling them into highly individualized consumer profiles and portfolios. Indeed, the use of basic "demographic" data for mass marketing has given way to a finer mesh of personality profiling and market segmentation known by those in the trade as "psychographics" (examining attributes related to how a person thinks, feels, and behaves). As one marketing executive pitches it, "From a marketing perspective, demographics define what buyers commonly *need* whereas psychographics define what buyers *want*. Psychographics identifies aspirational behaviors that are much more powerful drivers than physical demographics."[156] For instance, a chain of child care centers wants to market itself to potential customers. Rather than wasting advertising and marketing dollars on broad swaths of the population, say, "Mothers, age twenty-five to thirty-four, household income more than $70,000," the goal would be "Women, first child between five and nine months, spends $1,500 a month online, lives more than 1,000 miles from parents and in-laws, lives within three miles of existing facility." In this case, "Social profile data, behavioral data and customer lifecycle data can now finally be leveraged to contact people who are ready to buy."[157]

This schema, like a number of other constellations of power/knowledge, has its roots in the rise of the human sciences and as such is designed to treat human beings as "objects" to be broken down, analyzed, and acted upon. Psychological studies are used to assess a wide range of behaviors, tastes, and preferences, while other social science techniques and methods, such as surveys, interviews, and focus groups, help to understand the potential customer. For example, much of psychographics marketing schemes are based on the "Values, Attitudes and Lifestyles" survey developed by social scientist Arnold Mitchell and his colleagues at the Stanford Research International group and draws on the work of Harvard sociologist David Riesman and psychologist Abraham Maslow. Surveys asking a series of questions based on "psychological traits and key demographics that drive consumer behavior" end up dividing U.S. adults into eight distinct types or "mindsets" that range from the "top" category called *"Innovator"* or "consumers [who] are on the leading edge of change, have the highest incomes, and such high self-esteem and abundant resources that they can indulge in any or all self-orientations" through categories of *"Thinkers"* "who are motivated by ideals," and are "mature, responsible, well-educated professionals." Next are *"Believers,"* a "low-resource group of those who are motivated by ideals. They are conservative and predictable consumers who favor American products and established brands" and there are *"Achievers," "Strivers," "Experiencers," "Makers,"* and finally the lowly group of just *"Survivors,"* who have the lowest incomes and "too few resources to be included in any consumer self-orientation. . . . They are the oldest of all the segments, with a median age of 61. Within their limited means, they tend to be brand-loyal consumers."[158]

Yet, it seems that even psychographics falls short. Like a number of social science research agendas these days, some marketing people want to "drill down" even further; to your brain. Citing the limitations of demographic and behavioral-based psychographics, neurology, it is claimed, offers hope that marketing strategists can determine how the human brain responds to pitches for different products. A recent (self-published) book and website by Brian Fabiano of Fabcom Marketing and Advertising Agency summarizes the movement:

> The idea behind neuromarketology is that our core brain responds to specific marketing messages, timing, and imagery. If we are able to understand what specific stimuli a person's core brain responds to, we can personalize marketing campaigns to the level of the individual. In order to do this, we must segment our target audience into subgroups that share similar values, characteristics, or beliefs. This will help us to identify their specific needs and expectations, which allows us to provide an individualized marketing campaign. [159]

In another everyday application of technology generally associated with law enforcement, some marketing strategies are using facial recognition systems to identify customers by age and gender (not actual individuals—for now). For example, Adidas has teamed up with Intel to install in stores digital walls with facial recognition built in. "If a woman in her 50s walks by and stops, 60 percent of the shoes displayed will be for females in her age bracket, while the other 40 percent will be a random sprinkling of other goods." Chris Aubrey, vice president of global retail marketing for Adidas, says, "If a retailer can offer the right products quickly, people are more likely to buy something," while the director of Intel's embedded and communications group says, "You can put this technology into kiosks, vending machines, digital signs. It's going to become a much more common thing in the next few years." An even more mundane use of this powerful technology is being touted by bar owners in Chicago. Set up in conjunction with video cameras, facial recognition scans the bars for the male to female ratio and age mixes of their crowds. A mobile app offers potential customers a real-time check of what the crowd looks like. "This helps people avoid those hit-or-miss nights," said Cole Harper, twenty-seven, co-founder of SceneTap, the company that makes the app. Sami Ari, twenty-seven, a social media marketer, is one of about eight thousand people who have downloaded the app. Aware that the system used facial recognition, the young man told a reporter, "I use it at least once a week to find a cool place for me and my friends to hang out." He added, "It's not that scary. I always get upset at new Facebook privacy settings, and then I get over it."[160]

OK, so let's say a product out there piques your interest—or the particular color, labeling, or generated association tickles that precise location of your brain—and you decide to buy. More than likely, you will do so with a credit or debit card. Currently, purchases with "plastic" are about 66 percent of all in-person sales; 31 percent are made with debit cards.[161] A credit card is a certificate of financial worth and an increasingly necessary key as well as a leash—to a vast electronic financial network. You can't rent a car without one, airlines will not accept cash for in-flight services, and even some stores and restaurants, like Standard Market in Chicago, are "plastic only." I notice that young people nearly always pay with credit or debit and I see there is a case for the iPhone that has a slot for a credit card on the back; that's all you need to carry. Even better, Google Wallet uses wireless technology called "near-field communications" to let you pay for stuff by tapping your phone on a merchant's Near Field Communication (NFC)-enabled terminal.

Why is all this happening? In the first place, cash and checks are cumbersome and expensive for stores and banks to deal with. Second, while credit card companies tempt us with the fast and "convenient" service, frequent flyer miles, "cash back" and other reward schemes, they take a "swipe fee" from the merchant whenever a customer uses a card; the more "swipes" the more revenue for them. And of course the banks that back the cards make their profits off the cards by charging exorbitant interest rates, annual fees, late fees, and the like. Third, merchants are willing to pay these fees, in part, because they know that behavioral economics tell us that people who use credit cards are willing to spend more than those who pay with cash; this is known as the "credit card premium." Finally, and most relevant for our discussion here, is the idea that a "cashless" society is a surveilled society. Every electronic purchase or transaction—with credit or debit cards and especially when used in combination with "loyalty" discount cards—provides a clearly readable "digital footprint" of our activities that can be used to build a profile of our purchases, habits, tastes, and even our movements and patterns of behavior. Using these cards at, say, a grocery store, instantly connects you to the computerized inventory of the store, which, of course, reflects the transactions of the barcode scanner at the checkout counter. These data can then be used by the store or sold to marketing firms to build a detailed portrait of your buying habits. Marketing firms are then able to sort you according to your perceived value in the marketplace and can ensure precise target marketing, making you susceptible to particular campaigns.

For example, an investigation into retail chain Target revealed how an in-house statistician figured out how to use point-of-purchase sales data to predict when customers might be expecting a baby. It begins when Target assigns every customer a "Guest ID" number that is the key to your individual electronic file. In it is not only your name, credit cards, address, and e-mail address but "your age, whether you are married and have kids, which part of town you live in, how long it takes you to drive to the store, your estimated salary, whether you've moved recently, what credit cards you carry in your wallet and what Web sites you visit. Target can buy data about your ethnicity, job history, the magazines you read, if you've ever declared bankruptcy or got divorced, the year you bought (or lost) your house, where you went to college, what kinds of topics you talk about online, whether you prefer certain brands of coffee, paper towels, cereal or applesauce, your political leanings, reading habits, charitable giving and the number of cars you own."[162]

Looking at the purchase data for all females who had signed up for Target baby registries in the past, the Guest Marketing Analytics Department found that women on the registry were buying larger quantities of unscented lotion around the beginning of their second trimester; sometime in the first twenty weeks, pregnant women bought mineral supplements; and later, when the women bought lots of cotton balls, scent-free soap, hand sanitizers, and washcloths, it signaled that they were close to their delivery date. Crunching these data, they identified some twenty-five products that, when scrutinized together, allowed them to assign each shopper a "pregnancy-prediction" score. And, by being able to estimate due dates to within a couple of weeks or so, the store is able to send coupons for these items timed to the stages of the customer's pregnancy.

A year or so after Target got the "pregnancy-prediction" model up and running, a man walked into a Target near Minneapolis and wanted to see the manager. "My daughter got this in the mail!" he said. "She's still in high school, and you're sending her coupons for baby clothes and cribs? Are you trying to encourage her to get pregnant?" The manager verified that the coupons had been addressed to the daughter, but having no idea about the marketing scheme, could not offer an explanation. The manager apologized and then called a few days later to again express his regrets for the incident. On the phone, however, the father had to confess. "I had a talk with my daughter," he said. "It turns out there's been some activities in my house I haven't been completely aware of. She's due in August. I owe you an apology."[163]

In this chapter, I began by describing a number of postmodern surveillance practices and meticulous rituals of power associated with the penal/health/welfare complex. Here we see how technologies such as electronically monitored house arrest, GPS, digital court dossiers, the RFID chipping of prisoners, as well as a variety of intrusive community corrections and welfare programs are supporting "hard" end-of-the spectrum accountability regimes being imposed on troublesome populations. We also see how highly advanced "crime-fighting" tools—most of them designed for the military and post–9/11 "security" challenges—are being deployed by ordinary police forces and emergency management agencies. It strikes me that these uses, often garnering prime media attention, demonstrate to the public the "high art of transparency," leaving many dazzled and awestruck. Moreover, the saturation of video throughout the society has firmly anchored the gaze as a dominant feature of our "looking culture;" a postmodern culture where even "big brother" has been rehabilitated into an "entertaining and benevolent pop-culture icon."

Media-generated fears, real tragedies like mass shootings, a pronounced emphasis on "safety" and "risk management," available Homeland Security funding, as well as the profit interests of those selling surveillance and security devices, has meant that public spaces, schools, homes, and other community settings are increasingly under the scrutiny of surveillance practices and those occupying those spaces subjected to meticulous rituals of power. Many of the technologies and strategies that have appeared in these places are the same as those deployed in the criminal justice system and serve, as they do in that system, to help maintain unbalanced and unequal authority relationships. Video cameras watch us on the street, our children at home, and at school; GPS tracks our teenager's whereabouts; and, like prisoners, high schoolers and the elderly are RFID "chipped" to follow their movements. Workplaces have become intensively surveilled spaces where microtechniques of monitoring and control are enhanced by the use of new ICTs. Employees are often treated with the mistrust of convicted felons where managers are able to monitor their every activity and movement with technologies like Mobile Workforce Manager that mimic the control and restrictions imposed on those doing time under "house arrest." Various ICTs, needed by workers to do their jobs, have the built-in capabilities of counting their keystrokes, recording their phone calls, and calculating their performance at meticulous levels. Digital case files are built from the time one applies for a job and are filed with deep background checks, personality tests, drug tests (see chapter 4), and an ongoing monitoring and evaluation process, all of which exceed by far the scrutiny contained in any probation or parole file.

Finally, with the help of universities and corporate research labs, "consumers" have become the *subject* of scientific inquiry as well as the *object* of its knowledge. Under the modern regime, it was the criminal and the deviant who were to be the targets of such scientific scrutiny and analysis. Today, while psychologists and criminologists have been turning to neurology and "behavioral genetics" (see chapter 5) to try to understand the conduct of the delinquents, the same science (and likely more resources) is being directed at understanding the behavior and mind of the consumer. In a "surveillance economy," where billions and billions are at stake, the key demographic and psychological traits, and even the brain of the consumer deserve such attention.

Chapter Four

Bodily Intrusions

I'm out on patrol with a community corrections surveillance officer. At 10:45 p.m. we pull into the driveway of a modest suburban house. "Pete" walks up, rings the doorbell, and, a minute or so later, a sleepy twenty-eight-year-old male answers in his nightclothes. Pete slips an alcohol scanner pipette to his face, the client breathes into the tube, and Pete takes his reading, says "good night," and walks back to the car to record his findings.—Staples, field notes

The iCup® drug testing kits are the most popular urine instant drug test kits that we sell! The drug test kits are easily administered at your workplace, clinic, home or other location.—Q Test, Inc., Linden, NJ

Tests of eyesight, skill and intelligence hardly prepare [a citizen] for Government demands to submit to the extraction of blood, to excrete under supervision, or to have these bodily fluids tested for the physiological and psychological secrets they may contain.—Supreme Court justices Marshall and Blackmun on drug testing and individual Fourth Amendment rights

In *Discipline and Punish*, Foucault begins his history of Western social control by recounting, in gruesome detail, the torture and execution of Damiens the regicide in Paris in 1757. Accused of trying to assassinate the king, Damiens was sentenced to make *amende honorable* on the scaffold before a large crowd in front of the Church of Paris. Foucault argues that this "carnival of atrocity," this public theater, was a political ritual, a symbol of the excessive power of the sovereign that could be invoked against anyone who challenged his authority. As the prisoner was tortured, he was forced to publicly confess and thereby set the seal of "truth" of the already-decided, secret proceedings of the magistrates. The confession was an act of the criminal playing the role of responsible, speaking subject. The disciplinary technique of public torture, then, was an elaborate display of power and knowledge inscribed on the body of the condemned.

But as Foucault demonstrates, in a relatively short time, torture as a public spectacle disappeared. Coinciding with the rise of the modern nation-state, a new form of political power took hold, entailing a new relationship between power, knowledge, and the body. With Enlightenment zeal, late eighteenth-century and early nineteenth-century philosophers, jurists, reformers, and state authorities asserted a new discourse on crime and punishment that placed themselves as "experts" at the center of justice practice. The body of the condemned man was now the property of society rather than that of the king. Here we see the gradual disappearance of public torture and the rise of rationally organized reformatory institutions. Within this new political regime, punishment was no longer aimed at torturing and destroying the body, but rather was intended to discipline it, to rehabilitate it, through meticulous rituals of power. As I have shown, this disciplinary power is advanced through the use of procedures such as the gaze, the examination, hierarchical observation, and normalizing judgments. With this modernist agenda of "rehabilitation," criminals would be understood and known in their individuality—through biography, observation, and behavioral analysis—with the ultimate aim being the transformation of their "soul." Punishment would no longer breed terror and exact a public confession; it would produce deterrence and private penance.

Now, while the king could reduce an offender's body to dust or the modern asylum could watch and attempt to train it, I want to argue that, today, we see a proliferation of postmodern surveillance and disciplinary technologies that are founded on deriving knowledge and evidence *from* the body. Why this shift? I want to argue that the modern regime of rehabilitation was premised, at least in part, on the appeal to the criminal's conscience, to what may "enlighten him from within," so that one might adhere to the social contract. Yet clearly, any behavior modification on the criminal's part was at the mercy of what we might call that individual's "privileged access" to one's inner self. In other words, criminals had to accept their own "rehabilitation"—their newly reformed and improved identities if you will—and change their ways accordingly. Rehabilitation, then, was premised on authorities trusting that the offender was, in fact, "a new man," and not simply on his "best behavior" while in custody.

But today, it is no longer considered effective or efficient to simply gaze *at* the body—incarcerate it or to train it in hopes of rendering it docile—rather, better that we surveil its inner evidences and secrets. How has this change come about? The legacy of the Enlightenment continues to foster our almost obsessive use of the physical, human, and clinical sciences to treat human beings as "objects" to be broken down, analyzed, and determined. Every day we are told that researchers at universities, foundations, and corporations have "unlocked the door" to something new about our bodies, minds, and behaviors. Yet such studies and discoveries—while carried out presumably for the "good" of humanity—are, nonetheless, indirectly and sometime very purposively, contributing to the creation of new tools for observing, assessing, classifying, and potentially controlling our bodies. (Think here of, say, the mapping of the human genome which *may* help us find a cure for cancer but *could* as well contribute to the creation of an entire class of people who are supposedly "predisposed" to "antisocial behavior" and need to be assessed and treated differently than others.) This also means that the ability of organizations—not just those involved in the justice system—to monitor, judge, or regulate our actions and behaviors *through* our bodies is being significantly enhanced.

Once put in place, these new techniques reduce the need to trust offenders to "mend their ways" or for suspects to "speak the truth," as in being at the scene of a crime, confessing to abusing prescription pain killers, driving after drinking alcohol, or even making "poor lifestyle choices" in what they eat. Rather, it is the individual's objectified body that will tell us what "we need to know" and "who they *really* are," as in the "known drug user," "sexual predator," the "undocumented alien," or someone "predisposed" to having an "obsessive personality disorder." I call this apparent revealing a "pornography of the self"; it is an obscene gaze that attempts to lay bare an individual's "true" identity and discover uncluttered by their family history, experience, or circumstances of events—the "truth" of their actions and behaviors. The resulting "information asymmetry," of course, helps authorities exercise disciplinary power and sustain their upper hand in confronting the suspected drug user, the diseased homosexual, deadbeat parent, or lying illegal immigrant. This is one of the "holy grails" of contemporary surveillance and social control: to circumvent the speaking subject by creating easily accessible and scientifically reliable ways to search for and reveal evidence of malfeasance or, ideally, to even predict deviance before it occurs.

We see some of this fantasy played out dramatically—if preposterously—in the seemingly endless forensics-themed television series, such as the *CSI* franchise, *Cold Case*, *Bones*, and *NCIS*, that portray young, attractive scientist-types wielding high-technology and solving case after case by challenging the veracity of each suspect's story through the collection of supposedly irrefutable evidence.[1] The reality, of course, is far less glamorous but still stumbling toward these goals. The security and justice system—with its ancillary organizations in the penal/ health/welfare complex—is today deploying a raft of techniques and devices intended to derive knowledge, or impose a form of accountability on individuals, through their bodies. However, this deployment certainly does not stop at the borders of the formal justice system. In this chapter, I explore a number of these domains of knowledge and power and show, once again, how they have leached out from the world of criminal justice into the everyday settings of the home, school, and work-place.

THE POLITICS OF "SUBSTANCE ABUSE"

This changing relationship between power, knowledge, and the body that I am describing is pointedly displayed in the practice of drug testing. Meshing well with the rhetoric of the 1980s "war on drugs" that blamed the defective character of the abuser for the country's drug and related problems, testing quickly became the weapon of choice in confronting the suspected drug user. Today, drug testing has become a ubiquitous part of the justice system and the everyday lives of millions of people.

Drug testing involves a two-part analysis of a bodily fluid (typically urine) to determine whether traces of drugs are present. The first part, a screening test, involves a relatively simple and inexpensive analysis using thin-layer chromatography. If the sample tests positive for drugs, a more sophisticated confirmation test employing GC/MS (gas chromatography/ mass spectrometry) may be performed. As the accuracy of inexpensive kits has improved, however, and depending on the context of the test (e.g., routine screening or exceptional, say, in the case of an accident) there is often little need for this next step. In addition to urine analysis, saliva can be tested and the use of hair samples has expanded rapidly. Both have important advantages over urine analysis. One distributor of saliva kits claims that, "The iScreen™ OFD—oral fluid drug testing kit—is a new integrated on-site, instant saliva drug test kit that makes corporate drug testing simple and easy with results provided in minutes" and with this test kit, there is, "No urine handling required," it "Eliminates 'shy bladder' or donor stating 'I can't go right now,'" and that the process is, "More dignified: donor feels less invasive."[2] Alternatively, hair testing is more comprehensive. According to one article on the technique, "Testing of urine specimens can detect a single instance of drug use in the prior one to three days, while hair testing can detect a pattern of repetitive use over a period of up to 90 days." When someone ingests a drug, the substance is circulated in the bloodstream and traces of it remain in hair follicles. Since hair grows at a rate of about one and a half inches a month, this method provides the ninety-day profile.[3]

The simplicity, efficiency, low cost of drug screening technology makes its use as a surveillance tool quite compelling in the worlds of prisons, community corrections, and substance abuse programs. The latest generation of urine analysis (UA) screening devices requires minimal steps on the part of the tester. As one distributor of kits declares,

> The iCup® drug test kit is the simplest-to-use, instant urine drug screening kit that provides quick results in seconds. Once the specimen is collected in the

all-inclusive drug testing kit, the lid is secured so there is zero exposure to the collector! The drug test kits start working immediately and results are revealed by simply peeling back the result label. A negative result is shown with two lines and a positive is shown with one line in the urine drug test panel. The iCup® drug testing kit can detect between three to 10 drugs instantly depending on your drug testing needs. [4]

I see drug testing, much like the electronic monitoring devices of house arrest, as an extraordinary example of a postmodern meticulous ritual of power. The practice is local and capillary as the collection of bodily fluids can be taken anywhere; an offender need not be institutionalized to be watched and monitored. It provides instant knowledge of an individual's behavior and codes a complex set of activities and behaviors into simple "yes" and "no" categories. The devices are lightweight and efficient; there is little need to collect heavy dossiers or engage in long interrogations in search of evidence or a confession. Random screening has the effect of making this form of surveillance operate "panoptically," since individuals never know when they might be tested.

The drug test constitutes what Steven Nock calls an "ordeal" or a form of surveillance intended to divulge the "truth" and thereby establish or maintain a reputation. [5] But it is also a ceremony of bodily objectification, an examination, in Foucault's terms, and a disciplinary drill. Nock describes the ideal conditions under which the ritual of the classic UA should be performed. It is worth quoting at length, since it offers us a glimpse of the ceremonial quality of the test:

> The actual administration of the drug test is done in a controlled situation where the applicant or employee can be watched or listened to while urinating. A photo identification must be presented to verify that the individual taking the test is who she or he claims to be. To guard against possible adulteration of the urine (many methods exist to confound urine tests), they must be conducted in such a way to eliminate the possibility of adding something to the sample, substituting another person's urine, or substituting a sample obtained during a drug-free period. Elaborate preparations and precautions are required. To prevent the applicant from concealing test-confounding substances under the fingernails, for example, the administrator of the test must witness the applicant thoroughly wash the hands. "Unnecessary" garments that might conceal things must be removed. A number of forms must be filled out to verify the chain of custody of the urine sample as it finds its way through the testing process. Both the subject of the test and the person monitoring it must fill out forms indicating that the test was, in fact, done at that time and place. The urine sample, itself, must be measured for temperature at the time of collection (to prevent the substitution of another person's urine). The sample is inspected also for color (to prevent the use of water). The urine must be kept in sight of both individuals throughout the entire process of preparing it for transmittal to the lab. [6]

During this meticulous ritual, the person being tested is forced to consent to the petty humiliation of the procedure and to the voyeuristic gaze of the tester, who must literally watch the person urinate. So while the person's "self" is embarrassed and ashamed, even, as Erving Goffman called it, "mortified," the body and its fluids, as the preceding description shows, are treated with extraordinary care because it is the body that holds "truth," not the self. The examination is pass/fail, employing the normalizing judgment, in local terms, of being "clean" or "dirty." Moreover, the technique evokes the legitimacy of science and technical objectivity as it disassociates the client's surveillance from any particular individual. That is, it seems as if you are not really being tested by "the boss," supervisor, or your probation officer, but rather by the test kit and the laboratory. Power is, therefore, seemingly exercised independently of the person who administers the procedure. As the maker of the testing kit described earlier put it, the procedure is "useful in case-management because both you and your client can watch as results develop." Here again, those watched become "partners" in constituting the gaze upon themselves.

Finally, the screening ceremony, performed enough times, becomes a disciplinary "drill." Like other surveillance ceremonies, we are at first apprehensive, unsure, and uncomfortable. But, much like the way we march through metal detectors at the airport, the test becomes routine and repetitive. Drug screening, then, acclimates clients to accept their own subjugation and encourages their general docility. They may even find themselves wanting to take the test as a way of trying to govern their own behavior and prove they are indeed "clean." As one house arrest client I interviewed told me, "I feel like, it's something to keep me honest. I've been clean for about six months right now and feel a whole lot better."[7]

Alternatively, of course, one can try to beat the test. Ken Tunnell documents the emergence of a vast counter-testing movement, what he calls the "detox industry" that sells products designed to produce a "false negative," or the nondetection of drugs despite their presence in the tests.[8] Tunnell recounts some of the farcical claims by manufacturers in this unregulated industry and their products such as herbal teas, pills, and liquids that can detox in a matter of hours, daily cleansing capsules for continual detoxing, and even shampoos that remove evidence from hair within ten minutes. Others sell "body flushers" and "clean" urine for purposes of substitution. Acting on a variety of "urban legends," F. Allan Hanson reports that people have attempted to alter their samples with salt, detergent, and other substances, while others have tried drinking large quantities of water or taking diuretics or, in one reported case, consuming the urine of pregnant women.[9]

According to the U.S. Department of Justice (DOJ), drug testing may take place at all stages of the criminal justice system: arrest, in the pretrial phase, during incarceration, probation, and parole. It serves several purposes according to DOJ: "1) *Inform judges for bail-setting and sentencing.* For example, a positive drug test at the time of arrest may result in a pretrial release condition that incorporates periodic drug testing. A subsequent failed drug test could result in revocation of bail or other more stringent release conditions. 2) *Indicate whether specified rules or conditions are being complied with.* If a defendant is being monitored while on pretrial release, probation, parole, work release, or furlough, a drug test can help ensure that he or she is remaining drug free. The results may be used in revocation hearings. Drug tests in prisons can also assist in monitoring drug use in correctional facilities and by inmates during temporary absences from the institution. 3) *Identify persons in need of treatment.* Drug tests can identify drug users who can be placed in treatment. Drug testing is also used to monitor persons undergoing drug treatment."[10]

In the house arrest and community corrections programs I have observed, drug testing was done routinely in the office and in the field. As a condition of their house arrest contract, clients were randomly tested at any time and a "hot" UA could get you an extended sentence or jail time. They even had to pay for their tests: $17 each time. In the other community corrections program, a screening might be conducted in the home, on a surveillance tour, when it was requested by an individual's probation officer, or when Pete the surveillance officer decided to, as he recounts, "pop them any time things don't look right." This was frequently the case with "John," a seventeen-year-old described as a "heavy marijuana" user who Pete told me had been caught "peeing dirty" on a number of occasions. "We can't seem to get it through his head to stay clean while he's on the program," the officer told me.

But does it take being arrested or committing a crime to find yourself urinating in a cup? Hardly. Three decades into the "war on drugs," testing has become an everyday surveillance ceremony for millions of our fellow citizens who have never used drugs or committed a crime. Current estimates put the number of Americans tested each year to be between twenty and twenty-five million, up from around seven million in 1996. One industry report asserts that the drug testing industry had $1.9 billion in sales in 2007.[11] The most common location for testing appears to be the workplace, where the vast majority of the tests are used in pre-employment screening rather than on current employees. Quest Diagnostics ("Employer Solutions: The Science of Employee Screening"), the world's leading provider of workplace diagnostic testing, processed more than 8.5 million drug tests in 2010. However, in certain occupational categories, drug and alcohol tests can take place under conditions of "reasonable cause" (or suspicion), after an accident, before treatment, and randomly, as during pre-employment. Much of this testing was spurred on by President Ronald Reagan's 1986 Executive Order 12564 stating that all federal employees may be tested for drugs; subsequent testing was mandated for specific occupations by the Department of Transportation and the Department of Defense. Today, it seems that the most common response to news reports of a plane crash, train derailment, or construction accident is: Were the individuals involved tested for drugs before or after the accident?

As pointed out earlier, hair sample analysis has expanded considerably, touted by companies like Psychemedics Corporation. Established in 1987, the firm claims that their testing

> offers significant advantages over urinalysis and creates a powerful deterrent for drug users. The primary difference is the wider window of detection with Psychemedics hair testing. . . . Additional advantages include: 1) Non-intrusive collection procedures; 2) Virtual elimination of test evasion through substitution or adulteration; and 3) Greater accuracy through test repetition capability. The combination of an increased window of detection and resistance to evasion makes hair testing far more effective than urinalysis in correctly identifying drug users. [12]

The company asserts that, "Our clients range in size from Fortune 500 companies to regional employers. Psychemedics' patented technology is utilized by over 10 percent of the Fortune 500 companies, major police forces, Federal Reserve Banks, schools and a variety of government and medical research programs" and "Over 200 schools in the United States and other countries use Psychemedics hair analysis as part of their drug-free school program. International schools include China, Indonesia, Japan, Malaysia, Philippines, Singapore, Thailand, Taiwan, and Venezuela." [13]

Indeed, if workplaces are the most common site for drug-testing adults, schools have become the primary location for surveilling kids for drug use. Following the U.S. Supreme Court decision that upheld the monitoring of student athletes (*Vernonia School District v. Wayne Acton*, 515 U.S. 646, 1995) and later, any student participating in extracurricular activities (*Board of Education of Independent School District No. 92 of Pottawatomie County v. Earls* 536 U.S., 2002) schools across the country began instituting drug-screening programs. The U.S. Department of Education does not keep figures on the number of school drug-testing programs, but according to one estimate done in 2008, 16.5 percent of U.S. public school districts have student random drug-testing programs with at least 1 percent of districts adding programs every year. [14]

One of those schools, Delaware Valley High School in Pennsylvania, made national headlines when it began testing every student who wants to join activities—from yearbook and chess club to sports and drama. "To test everybody just because they volunteer for something shows a basic lack of trust in students and families," said Sarah Casey, a seventeen-year-old senior who passed a drug test to participate in the environment club and the National Honor Society. "It's an invasion of privacy," said seventeen-year-old Jen Stangl, a senior who took the test to get a parking permit. "It was disgusting. I felt violated. They just presumed everyone was guilty."[15] Taking this one step further, however, Miami-Dade Public Schools launched a "voluntary" drug-testing program for all high school students, requiring consent from both parents and students. In 2011, with only a handful of local citizens present, the Belvidere Board of Education in Belvidere, New Jersey, approved a plan to let parents voluntarily have their middle school children— twelve-year-old sixth graders—subject to random drug and alcohol testing.[16]

Many, including some U.S. Supreme Court justices, believe that school-based drug testing programs are an effective deterrent to drug use. "We find that testing students," the justices declared, "is a reasonably effective means of addressing the School District's legitimate concerns in preventing, deterring, and detecting drug use." Yet, according to the available social science evidence, this does not seem to be the case. The authors of one major study, which spanned five years and included nearly 100,000 eighth graders and high school sophomores and seniors from 894 schools, drew a stark conclusion: "There are . . . no significant differences in marijuana use or the use of other illicit drugs as a function of whether or not the school has (a) drug testing of any kind, (b) drug testing of students based on cause or suspicion, or (c) drug testing of athletes. Nor is there evidence that the heavy drug-using segment of the student population, specifically, is deterred from using marijuana or other illicit drugs by random or for-cause testing."[17]

But with all this testing and about one-third of teens self-reporting drug use, there must be thousands of kids "peeing dirty," right? This doesn't seem to be the case. In the first two years of widespread drug testing at the San Bernardino, California, school district—one of the largest in the nation— only two students tested positive. In Cumberland County, Arkansas, which includes the city of Fayetteville, 15,087 students were enrolled in a random drug-testing program for athletes and students who participate in extracurricular activities. Over four years, 6,525 kids had undergone testing for drugs and alcohol and another 616 for steroids. The final results were sixty-nine positive tests for marijuana, three for alcohol, and one for amphetamine-methamphetamine.[18] Even in the arguments before the Supreme Court in the case of *Vernonia School District v. Wayne Acton* which helped spawn much of the school-based drug testing in the country, it was reported to the Court that the program in the Oregon high school found "two or three" positive drug tests in the five years it was in place. Justice Scalia asserted that this was evidence of the program's deterrent effect, while Justice Ginsburg claimed that one could just as easily read this as evidence that drugs were really not a problem in the first place. One certainly has to wonder that if the goal is to get kids to stop using drugs, then the millions of dollars spent on drug testing might be better utilized on drug education, counseling, and treatment programs.

But the drug testing of young adults does not stop at their workplace or school. Families are increasingly encouraged to use drug tests to check up on their kid's activities. The Food and Drug Administration (FDA) approved the first drug-testing kit for home use without a prescription in 1997. Just one year later, more than two hundred products were approved for such use. Today, parents can pick up testing kits at Target or Walgreens or "for privacy," simply order them over the Internet. According to a review of Internet-based home drug-testing products for parents published in the journal *Pediatrics*, makers and distributors encourage parents to "institute a 'home drug policy' that includes home testing as a means of preventing drug and alcohol use. These companies include testimonials from parents and teens to support their claims."[19] One, First Check Diagnostics provides assurance to parents that they offer, "accurate answers you are looking for to those difficult questions in the privacy of your own home. It is First Check's goal to give you the information you need, when you need it."[20] Another company claimed that testing is intended to enhance the love and care in the home: "It's about breaking down barriers of denial between parent and child."[21] But according to the authors of the *Pediatrics* article, "Drug testing could be associated with unanticipated consequences such as a decrease in honest communication between parents and teens," or a possible "delay in the diagnosis of a serious substance disorder," and that, in some cases, routine testing may encourage teens to become deceitful in an attempt to "beat the test."[22] In this way, we can see how the home can come to mimic more formal organizations such as workplaces, schools, and even "community corrections" programs where teens sign "contracts" with parents and where the household has a stated "drug policy" and deploys the latest technologies to enforce it.

Drug testing has generated a considerable amount of litigation over the issue of privacy, but many rulings seem to follow the now-established "greater good" argument. This reasoning holds that there is a "greater good" for society established at the cost of minimal individual invasion of privacy. For example, in a case in the late 1980s the California Court of Appeals held that drug and alcohol testing of job applicants did not violate the right of privacy set forth in the California Constitution. Interestingly, the court stated:

> Common experience with the ever-increasing use of computers in contemporary society confirms that the amendment was needed and intended to safeguard individual privacy from intrusion by both private and governmental action. If the right of privacy is to exist as more than a memory or dream, the power of both public and private institutions to collect and preserve data about individual citizens must be subject to constitutional control.[23]

But while the court concluded that collecting and testing of urine samples in this case intruded on the applicant's reasonable expectations of privacy, it decided, despite its spirited defense of personal privacy, that the "intrusiveness" of the drug screening was minimal. In most cases, the court claimed, applicants were required to take a pre-employment physical exam anyway, and in this case they were informed ahead of time that any job offer would be conditioned on consent to drug testing. Moreover, it was the court's opinion that the collection procedures were designed to minimize the intrusion into individual privacy (although this is generally not the opinion of people I have talked with over the years who have been tested). The court concluded that the applicants have a simple choice—either "consent to the limited invasion of their privacy resulting from the testing" or decline the test and the job.[24] Given that, in 2011, about 10 percent of Americans are unemployed, 1 in 382 homes are in foreclosure, and bankruptcies are at record levels, it hardly seems like a "choice" to either submit to a drug test or walk away from a job. To date, few states have enacted protective legislation against random testing, leaving private employers, in the vast majority of jurisdictions, to test anyone for any reason, or for no reason at all.

Much of the credit for a reported decline in drug use seems to go to the testing programs themselves. "Corporate programs make drug use more of a hassle and make it seem less socially acceptable" according to one drug program director. "There's no question they have driven down drug use."[25] The evidence offered for this turnaround is that the tests themselves are uncovering decreased drug use. For example, Quest Diagnostics claims a 13.8 percent positivity rate for urine drug tests for the U.S. workforce in 1988, a rate that it reports has dropped every year since to 3.6 percent in 2010. But, in fact, we do not know if such testing programs have much to do with whether or not people choose to use drugs. The lower rate may reflect normative changes in the culture, the impact of laws and incarceration rates, unemployment rates, the types of individuals applying for certain jobs, and the like.

CLEAN AND SOBER

As I pointed out in chapter 3, our society has taken to "medicalizing" behaviors that were once seen as immoral or evil. It would seem that in our contemporary culture—where the medical model dominates, and the "sick" and "survivor" roles have become a national obsession—it is far more agreeable to be the "victim" of a disease than it is to be considered personally weak or sinful. At one time, for example, excessive drinkers were simply "drunks" who did not have the moral backbone to resist temptation. Today, these individuals are said to suffer from alcoholism, a purported medical "disease" or addiction that, according to some, can curiously be "diagnosed" by just about anyone—family members, friends, counselors, and judges in courts of law. Part of this transformation has been the result of medical research that suggests various underlying biological explanations for the phenomenon.

But whatever physical "predisposition" there may be to abusing alcohol, drinking is primarily a behavioral activity that can be socially defined and constructed in many different ways. If we look cross-culturally and historically, we can see that what is defined as "problem" or "excessive" drinking varies widely from one setting to the next. Therefore, I would suggest that much of the contemporary definition of the situation comes both from today's "victim culture" and from the people who have an interest in framing alcohol (ab)use as a problem that only they themselves as "experts" can treat. Importantly, in this context, the expert response to and the control and treatment of alcoholics have been increasingly centered on the body and on a variety of therapeutic approaches. So, while "excessive" drinking has been medicalized, it has also been criminalized. The tolerance levels for blood alcohol—the legal definition of being "under the influence"—have been lowered, while penalties for drinking and driving, for underage consumption, and for public drunkenness have increased. Over the last couple of decades, state legislatures have passed hundreds of laws regulating drinking and driving. Each time the "tolerance" levels are lowered, lo and behold, more "drunk drivers" are arrested and these statistics are used to justify the continued definition of drinking and driving as a social problem. The result has been the emergence of new devices designed to assess the body for evidence of alcohol use and an explosion of public and private agencies geared to controlling and treating the alcohol user.

Mimicking many of the meticulous rituals and disciplinary drills present in drug testing, the use of alcohol is often tested by such means as the readily available Alcoscan Saliva Test, the Final Call Breath Tester, and others. Like drug-testing kits, these are quite simple portable devices that take little or no training to use. These devices are carried by law enforcement officials as they enable "field sobriety" checks on drivers, underage partygoers, and anyone else acting suspiciously. At my local Salvation Army shelter, all those looking for a bed at night are tested with a "breathalyzer." Anyone with a blood-alcohol content of more than 0.08 percent is turned away. Another popular device is a breathalyzer that is installed in a convicted drunk driver's vehicle. "Ignition interlock devices" analyze a driver's breath and disable the ignition if the driver has been drinking. Here the machine must be breathed into each time the person attempts to start the car. If alcohol is detected, the device will render the starter inoperable. The interlock will even start beeping periodically after the car is in motion, demanding another breath test to prevent the driver from drinking after the initial test (given all we now know about the performance of "distracted drivers," this seems questionable to me). More than half the states in the United States now require DUI ("driving under the influence") offenders to install the devices on their cars in order to drive to work while they have a suspended license or require the installation of the interlock for a period before relicensing. According to the Insurance Institute for Highway Safety, "In 15 states and 4 California counties, such a restriction is applied to all offenders, including first-time offenders. An additional 15 states apply the restriction to offenders with high BACs [blood alcohol content] (usually 0.15 percent or higher) and to repeat offenders, and 7 states apply the restriction only to repeat offenders."[26] Of course, the computerized interlock unit records the results of each test, which are routinely passed on to probation officers and judges to assess whether the client is "backsliding" into alcohol use.

Another type of drinking monitor was in place in the house arrest program where I interviewed clients. The Mitsubishi Electronic Monitoring System device that was installed in the offenders' homes, verified compliance with their house arrest contract by recording the offender's voice, taking their picture, and collecting breath samples for analysis. The results of the alcohol breath test are recorded in the computer and displayed on screen with the photo of the offender, which includes name, date, and time. In the other community corrections program I observed, alcohol testing was used during all surveillance tours. You would hardly notice as Pete slipped the tester up to the offenders' mouths as he approached them, and they seemed quite ready for the tester to appear. Most of the clients I saw were "clean," but occasionally one would "slip up," like seventeen-year-old "Eric," who registered a 0.064 blood-alcohol level. We drove by his house, and, although Pete said he was not supposed to be home from work until 9:00 p.m., his car was in the driveway, so Pete said we would "go ahead and catch 'em anyway." "Liar, liar, pants on fire," Pete says, getting back into the car. "Claims he is taking *Nyquil*. Yeah, right. . . . Anyway, we tell them not to take such medication when they are on the program."

Of course, all this running around the county that Pete had to do to test people for substance use is terribly inefficient and costly. Just a few years after I went along on these surveillance tours, the county began deploying "SCRAMx® which merges 'continuous alcohol monitoring' with house arrest anklet devices." Developed by Alcohol Monitoring Systems, the company offers these claims regarding its technology:

Raising the Accountability Bar
Greater accountability was one of the driving forces behind . . . SCRAMx®—which combines continuous alcohol monitoring (CAM) with house arrest technology in one device.

SCRAMx tests transdermally ("through the skin") for alcohol every half hour around the clock—and also monitors continuously for presence in the home during court-mandated hours. By delivering a facts-based, comprehensive profile of an offender's drinking patterns and schedule compliance to supervising authorities, the result is a more effective alternative to random testing or incarceration.

Flexible Monitoring Options

With SCRAMx, CAM can be used by itself or combined with house arrest as needed—depending on the offense, situation, or behavior while in the program. This gives you tremendous flexibility in how you manage your offenders, and enhances their compliance to the judge's orders. SCRAMx's dual functionality also lets you tailor sanctions for your higher-risk offenders and better protect community safety.

Leadership Advantage

SCRAMx is the industry leader in CAM and house arrest because it:

• Uses scientifically proven transdermal technology to monitor over 150,000 offenders in 40+ states.

Continuous Alcohol Monitoring + House Arrest [among the features]

• Automatically collects, stores, and downloads alcohol data to the SCRAMx base station.
• Date- and time-stamps readings for easy reporting and analysis.
• Downloads alcohol reporting schedules from SCRAMNET. . . [the] Central, secure repository where offender data is stored, analyzed, reported, and maintained [and] can be accessed 24/7 from any location using a standard and secure web browser. [27]

My local community corrections program had purchased twenty of the $2,000 bracelets that cost about $5 per day to operate but probationers are charged $10 per day in a program so the devices eventually pay for themselves, declared the county's chief executive probation officer. Another employee, a "risk reduction initiative" officer told the local paper how a SCRAM bracelet helped one of his probationers quit drinking after thirty-five years of alcohol abuse. "Their mindset has changed so much," he declared. Both gentlemen took pains to point out that the intent of the bracelets isn't necessarily to punish an offender caught drinking, but rather as a way to assess whether alcohol treatment needs to be stepped up for a particular offender. "We want the community to know this is designed to help," one said. [28]

The enforcement of "no alcohol" under many community corrections "contracts" underscores both the medicalizing and the criminalizing impact on what is, in fact, a legal substance (at least for the adults in the program). For some, it may be that program officials have decided that they have a drinking "problem," while for others, restricting alcohol is simply part of the overall project of transforming them into "productive members of society" (i.e., clean and sober people who go to work and pay taxes). For those not in a community corrections program, the "road to recovery" may begin at a detoxification hospital, a rehabilitation or treatment center, a private counselor, or at the ever-present Alcoholics Anonymous (AA) meeting. While it's clear that many people have sought relief from these agencies and organizations on their own, increasingly, others may find that they have been ordered to participate in such programs under the threat of the criminal justice system. Here we see a blurring of the distinction between legal/justice and medical/therapeutic practices and discourses.

For example, a first conviction of DUI in my home state of Kansas is a class B misdemeanor, the law calls for forty-eight hours of mandatory imprisonment, one hundred hours of public service, fines of at least $500, mandatory completion of an alcohol education program, plus court costs and evaluation fees, and suspension of driving privileges for thirty days and restricted privileges for another 330 days. One community-based, for-profit treatment center is "certified by the City and District Court to provide court ordered evaluation for DUI. . . . Following evaluation, we are certified to provide the court-required ADSAP—Alcohol and Drug Safety Action Education Treatment Program." This "evaluation" involves personal interviews with a counselor and a series of written tests designed to assess how much treatment someone requires. So it would seem that the same agency that is charged with evaluating an individual's status as a potential "problem drinker" is also in a position to benefit from the services that person is required, by law, to participate in—and the services that the agency just so happens to provide for a fee.

Another interesting example is the case of courts ordering violators to attend AA meetings. Here we see the assumed highly effective nature of the twelve-step model as well as how a primarily therapeutic program that has existed outside the law gets colonized and linked to the system, thereby enhancing disciplinary power. As most of us are aware, the AA "twelve-step" program has been widely emulated. It has been adapted by the spouses and children of alcoholics—the so-called codependents and enablers—as well as the overeaters, the oversexed, and other assorted "excessive" personalities. But despite its popularity and anecdotal evidence of success, only a couple of systematic evaluations have been conducted and the results have been equivocal.[29] Protective of the anonymity of participants, AA prohibits researchers from conducting any evaluative or clinical studies of its members. Not only are courts ordering people to participate in something they cannot say is effective, but, at a minimum, the fact that it is mandatory brings into question the idea that this is anything like "self-help." In this context, the twelve-step program becomes a disciplinary technique that provides a monitoring, surveillance, and social control function for the state.

THE "TRUTH" MACHINE

The availability and proliferation of drug and alcohol testing relieves work-place supervisors, athletic-team coaches, justice officials, and others of the tedious task of interrogating suspects while ritualized, random testing offers (they believe) a significant deterrent. But what if we think someone has stolen money from the cash register, sold industrial secrets, or just simply isn't telling us what we believe to be true? Deciding whether someone is lying has been the responsibility of another technology of bodily "truth," the polygraph. The idea behind this device dates back to Italian criminologist Cesare Lombroso (1836–1909) (who, incidentally, asserted that criminals are born with certain recognizable hereditary physical traits such as skull size). During the mid-nineteenth century, Lombroso began taking measurements of the blood pressure and pulse of suspects under interrogation. The technique was later "refined" in the United States; the first portable polygraph machine was developed in the 1920s and was used extensively in criminal investigation.[30]

Like the drug test, the polygraph evokes an extraordinary ceremonial procedure. Most of us have watched the scene on the TV or in the cinema at one time or another: A blood-pressure cuff, attached to a sphygmomanometer, is first wrapped around the person's upper arm. Then two tubes are wrapped around the person's upper and lower chest to measure any changes in respiration. Finally, two electrodes are placed on the index and second finger of one hand; these will assess any changes in the person's perspiration level. Data from these sensors are displayed to the examiner on a rotating paper chart, showing changes as spikes, peaks, and valleys, much like an earthquake monitor. The theory behind this is that, when a suspect is questioned about his or her activities, a "lie" will be detected by increases in blood pressure, respiration rate, and perspiration rate. The polygraph, like the drug test, is a portable machine that can be set up anywhere. And here, once more, the remarkable power of science and objectivity is conjured up to authenticate the "true self." As Hanson claims, "Some polygraph examiners, in an effort to heighten subjects' perception of the test as a professional procedure, go so far as to wear a white coat, stethoscope dangling from the neck, and to spray the air of the examining room with ethyl alcohol."[31]

Today there are, according to the American Polygraph Association, an estimated three thousand to four thousand polygraph examiners working in the United States. I wrote them but they told me that they don't keep data on the number of tests given, but it's in the hundreds of thousands across the world, claims Dan Sosnowski, board chairman and past president.[32] Polygraph testing is used by most major law enforcement agencies in the United States. Prosecutors use polygraph testing to assess a case before filing and to verify the truthfulness of witnesses. Defense attorneys use testing to determine defense strategy, courts and probation/parole officers are making regular polygraph testing a condition of probation/parole, and convicted sex offenders are being tested to ensure they are complying with the conditions of release. And lie-detector results may, under certain circumstances, be introduced as evidence in courts in about half of the states in the United States.[33] Congress, however, banned compulsory use of the polygraph in the private sector in 1988 when it passed the Employee Polygraph Protection Act. (The statute defines lie-detector tests broadly to include polygraphs, deceptographs, voice stress analyzers, psychological stress evaluators, and similar devices.) Yet the law exempted applicants and employees with jobs in numerous federal, state, and local law enforcement organizations including the national intelligence agencies, all the branches of the military, the Department of Energy as well as fire departments and in some industries such as armored car companies and drug manufacturers and distributors. Despite both federal and state regulations, it is still perfectly legal for employers who suspect losses or sabotage to hire private security firms to test suspected workers and dismiss those who fail.

In a culture laced with fear, mistrust, and uncertainly, the "polly" has ended up in some odd places as well. For example, Tonya Harp, thirty-one, took a polygraph test to reassure her boyfriend that a trip she took with a male friend was not a romantic tryst. A news article on the episode declared, "she had nothing but her word to back her up" and that she was "surprised when her boyfriend asked her to take the test." "I was, like, who takes lie-detector tests?" Harp said. "That's for criminals. I felt really stupid." But Harp said she felt better after passing the test. "It really saved our relationship," she said. The $400 test was conducted by Virginia Beach polygraph examiner David Goldberg, who says that he has tested about one hundred couples in the last year. "They come from all walks of life and across the age spectrum. Usually they seek to resolve issues about financial responsibility, addiction and other relationship issues—namely fidelity."[34]

In postmodern spectacular, numerous television shows have featured the polygraph as a central player, purportedly sorting truth from the lies of game show contestants, "celebrities," and assorted media characters. For example, on *The Moment of Truth* game show, contestants submit to a lie-detector test while answering personal questions to win cash prizes. On one show, polygamist Melanie Williams won $500,000 when she answered that she believed her father had sexual relations with a minor and the lie detector determined her truthful for the grand prize. *Lie Detector* claims to "[examine] the truth behind real-life stories ripped from the headlines" and its first episode featured a polygraph examination of Paula Jones, a woman who had accused Bill Clinton of sexual harassment. Jones answered "yes" when asked if Clinton had exposed himself to her in a hotel room, and the polygraph operator determined she was telling the truth. *Lie Detector* offered to test Clinton, but he did not respond to the request. One of the most popular television shows in Spain in the late 1990s was called *The Truth Machine*. This successful ninety-minute drama subjected politicians, businesspeople, and celebrities who had been accused of assorted infractions to the test so they could attempt to prove their innocence in the public's eye.

Yet, for all its alleged talent and apparent wizardry, the lie detector is a charlatan's tool. Its use has never been shown to accurately discern truth telling from deception. One conclusion of the most comprehensive study to date conducted by the National Academy of Sciences in 2002, was that: "There is essentially no evidence on the incremental validity of polygraph testing, that is, its ability to add predictive value to that which can be achieved by other methods." In other words, there is no indication that use of a polygraph is better at getting at the truth than a standard interview or interrogation. As David Lykken put it in his comprehensive study of the history and practice of lie detection, "we have no definitive scientific evidence on which to base precise estimates of the lie detector's validity. But we have enough evidence to say that an innocent person has nearly a 50/50 chance of failing a lie detector test, much worse than in Russian Roulette."[35] It seems that ex-CIA agent Aldrich Ames was willing to take those odds when he played his own game of Russian roulette. Ames was the former counterintelligence officer and analyst who, in 1994, was convicted of spying for the Soviet Union and Russia and compromised more CIA assets than had any Soviet mole in American history. When asked about how he managed to pass several agency lie-detector tests during his years in service he famously replied, "Well, they don't work."[36]

This begs the question: If the polygraph, despite its "scientific" underpinnings, is so seriously flawed, why is it used at all? The lie detector functions quite nicely in most situations as a way of coercing confessions and as a general form of surveillance. It does so by creating the illusion that the truth can, in fact, be had. Yet the "truth machine" is all smoke and mirrors; it generates knowledge through the simulation of the objective power of science. Since most people are not aware of its flaws and do not know how to "trick" the machine, they are likely to be very intimidated by the process. Like the black spot of the inspector's lodge of the panopticon, the lie detector leaves people uncertain about what it is capable of knowing. As Steven Nock states:

> If a subject believes that the ordeal works . . . there is strong incentive for the guilty to confess. The ritual aspect of the polygraph ordeal (the pretest interview, the connections of electrodes and straps to the body, the careful repetition of questions over and over) . . . sensitizes subjects—it frightens them. It helps convince them that there is no hope in fooling the ordeal. It makes lying seem senseless.[37]

It is said that it is often the case that individuals subjected to this ceremony are so terrified by its purported ability to reveal their inner secrets that they confess to activities having nothing to do with the present questioning or, incredibly, to crimes they are, in fact, innocent of committing. The disciplinary ritual is, therefore, capable of "creating" the very phenomena it seeks to uncover. Used judiciously, lie detectors may encourage self-surveillance and function as a deterrent to acting or behaving "inappropriately." In a culture where "everyone is so paranoid," disciplinary ceremonies like the polygraph remain popular devices despite the laws that prohibit their use. For example, following on the heels of the infamous case of Susan Smith—the South Carolina woman who rolled her car into a lake drowning her two children strapped into their car seats—the Justice Department issued a 220-page guide for law enforcement officials investigating cases of missing children. The report, written by the National Center for Missing and Exploited Children, claims that the police should assume that any child missing is in immediate danger and that they should search the home, even if the child has been reported missing from somewhere else, and they should quickly give the parents a polygraph test.

DEVICES AND DESIRES

The "pornography of the self" is taken to a different level of circumventing the speaking subject when even our most intimate, private thoughts are believed to be available for inspection. Dr. Kurt Freund, a Czech-Canadian physician and sexologist is credited for developing phallometry, or the "objective" measurement of sexual arousal in males in the 1950s. Based on some of the same principles as the polygraph, that is, the measurement of the flow of blood to a limb, the penile plethysmograph, PPG or "p-graph," is a narrow metal or rubber band that is placed around the penis of a male subject. The individual is then forced to watch visual displays of naked adults and children or, sometimes, to listen to audiotapes. The band, of course, measures variation in the circumference of the penis. (The female equivalent to penile plethysmography is vaginal photoplethysmography which optically measures blood flow in the vagina.) The accompanying computer software enables the examiner to know which stimulant produced an arousal and the relative degree of the erection.

According to one account, early in his career Freund was commissioned by the Czechoslovakian military to use penile plethysmography to detect recruits attempting to evade military service by falsely claiming to be homosexual. He was also involved in early attempts at "conversion therapy," a process designed to change the sexual orientation of homosexuals to heterosexuality through the use of behavioral aversive therapy (his research actual-

ly ended up demonstrating that conversion therapy was futile as he concluded that homosexual men simply lacked erotic interest in females). Later,
Freund's work focused on detection and diagnosis of sex offenders, particularly preference pedophiles, with a view to more appropriate treatment guide-
lines.[38]

Building on this work, the p-graph is presently being used, as one report
describes it, in "assessing deviant sexual arousal patterns in males who sexually offend" in over four hundred sex-offender treatment centers in forty
states in the United States, and in several countries around the world.[39]
Behavioral Technology, Inc. (BTI), a medical device manufacturer head-
quartered in Salt Lake City, claims that their MONARCH 21™ penile plethysmograph (PPG) was created "'by clinicians for clinicians' backed by
more than 40 years of clinical research" and that the "PPG is now recognized
as the only medical device that can accurately predict recidivism."[40] And
courts frequently mandate plethysmography as a term of supervised release
for sex offenders. Moreover, penile plethysmography and vaginal photoplethysmography have been deployed by sexologists at numerous universities
and research centers.[41]

Yet the technology is, according to one article, "emerging from behind
the locked doors of adult treatment centers and into the broader legal arena"
and is turning up in sentencing and parole decisions, custody fights, and the
like. For example, fathers have been subjected to p-graphs in child custody
disputes as lawyers seek to prove that they are—or are not—likely to abuse
their children. In a case in New York, a psychologist used the p-graph on a
father whose parental rights the county was trying to terminate. He concluded from the test that the father "did not become sexually aroused by
either male or female children." At a hospital in Phoenix in the early 1990s,
boys as young as ten who were accused of abusing other children were tested
with the p-graph. And, in an extraordinary case in Maine a few years back, a
police officer whose name was simply raised in a local sex-abuse case was
told he had to submit to a p-graph as a condition of keeping his job. In a
bizarre string of accusations, Officer Harrington was one of 170 other people,
including a U.S. Senator, who were accused of sexual impropriety by four
siblings. While no legal evidence was ever brought against him and he was
never formally charged, the district attorney said he had "doubts about the
man's character" and wanted "to be sure that the officer didn't have deviant
thoughts that might lead to dangerous behavior." Harrington was ordered to
see a sex therapist who requested that he take a sex-offender profile test as
well as the p-graph. The written exam determined that Harrington's "personality profile" was supposedly similar to that of about 6 percent of sex offenders. He later refused to take the p-graph. Some in the town suggested that this
was a sign of guilt, but some two thousand others began a petition drive to
support him. Three years after he was accused, Officer Harrington still had

has been long prison sentences for convictions and, for many finally released, they may be required to register as sex offenders. Some examples include:

- A man with HIV in Texas is serving thirty-five years for spitting at a police officer.
- A man with HIV in Iowa, who had an undetectable viral load, received a twenty-five year sentence after a one-time sexual encounter during which he used a condom; his sentence was suspended, but he had to register as a sex offender and is not allowed unsupervised contact with his nieces, nephews, and other young children.
- A woman with HIV in Georgia received an eight-year sentence for failing to disclose her HIV status, despite the trial testimony of two witnesses that her sexual partner was aware of her HIV-positive status.
- A man with HIV in Michigan was charged under the state's antiterrorism statute with possession of a "biological weapon" after he allegedly bit his neighbor.[54]

A disease like AIDS demonstrates how the body is becoming a contested terrain in the battle over questions of individual privacy and personal control of our bodies versus organizational demands, be they schools, hospitals, workplaces, or public health departments. The social control implications of the battle are clear, however. As Dorothy Nelkin and Laurence Tancredi state in their book *Dangerous Diagnostics*.

> Institutions must operate efficiently, controlling their workers, students, or patients in order to maintain economic viability. In some cases social controls are explicit, exercised through force; but more often institutions seek to control their constituents less by force than by symbolic manipulation. Sanctioned by scientific authority and implemented by medical professionals, biological tests are an effective means of such manipulation, for they imply that institutional decisions are implemented for the good of the individual. They are therefore a powerful tool in defining and shaping individual choices in ways that conform to institutional values.[55]

DIGITAL IDENTIFICATION

The demands of the criminal justice system for body-based evidentiary and archival knowledge are being met by hundreds of corporate "vendors" and grant-funded universities that are developing new technologies at the intersection of forensic, medical, and computer sciences. And, here again, we see where practices established first in the justice system proliferate outside its borders, where bigger markets for the technologies are cultivated and exploited, and their use becomes normalized in everyday life. Fingerprints, for example, have been used as evidence of personal identification in criminal

not gotten his job back and he filed a federal lawsuit against the town for violation of his civil rights. He was ultimately awarded a nearly $1 million judgment.[42]

Despite the fact that phallometry has been around for more than fifty years, the law seems ill-equipped to deal with questions of privacy and personal rights since there are no regulations regarding the use of these devices at this time. One therapist acknowledges that "a majority of people who undergo the assessment would prefer not to go through it. It's measuring the one thing left that is supposed to be private."[43] But more than the question of privacy is the issue of validity: is phallometry actually measuring the subject's inner, private self? Is the notion of a fixed sexual "identity" accurate? Is sexual arousal a sufficient predictor of future behavior? Can a "subject," much like the case of those who have been able to pass lie-detector tests, fake or suppress arousal? Or is this technology about making the body a domain of power and knowledge? Is it an attempt to draw lines—culturally and historically specific ones—between the "normal" and "deviant," and impose yet another form of accountability and control? As Foucault states, and as illustrated with the case of Officer Harrington cited earlier, when one wishes to create a "case" out of the "healthy, normal and law-abiding adult, it is always by asking him how much of the child he has in him, what secret madness lies within him, what fundamental crime he has dreamt of committing."[44]

REGULATING SEX AND TESTING FOR AIDS

"Dangerous" sexual behavior may also be a factor when authorities confront a disease such as acquired immune deficiency syndrome, or AIDS. According to the Centers for Disease Control and Prevention (CDC), in 2009, an estimated 1,178,350 persons aged thirteen and older were living with HIV, the virus that causes AIDS, and nearly eighteen thousand died of AIDS-related illnesses. Currently, thirty-five thousand to forty thousand new infections occur in the country every year and AIDS is one of the top three causes of death among African American men aged twenty-five to fifty-four and for African American women aged thirty-five to forty-four.[45] Since AIDS first appeared in the male homosexual community in the United States (as opposed to the sexually active heterosexual population in Africa), public health officials and politicians have had to involve themselves in what the *New York Times* once called "The Indelicate Art of Telling Adults How to Have Sex."[46]

What concerns health officials the most are public meeting places such as bars, bathhouses, and swingers clubs, where people go to have sex. Such places often operate legally and most fall under the jurisdiction of and are regulated by health departments. In most states, health codes prohibit a list of sexual acts from taking place in commercial facilities. Yet, medical experts argue that the crucial factor in AIDS transmission is not a matter of what kind of sex you have, but whether or not participants use a condom. The question of just how much "regulation" is to take place pits public health protection against civil liberties and personal freedom. Advocates of protecting the public contend that "reasonable intervention" involves education and inspection of businesses to see whether violations are occurring. Civil libertarians, on the other hand, argue that the government, besides making information available, has no business telling adults how they should have sex. [47]

But officials worry that the sex clubs—that have both homosexual and heterosexual patrons—are a particular danger because their customers tend to be young adults, men who have sex with men but who do not identify themselves as gay, and visitors from out of town who may not be aware of prevention practices. Moreover, these young men have come of age in a time when AIDS is considered a survivable disease and this has increased their willingness to engage in unprotected sex. In most cities, club owners have the responsibility of making sure that "high-risk" sex does not occur in their clubs; some hire "monitors" who patrol the premises, while others require patrons to sign a written pledge to use condoms. In New York, to make sure the clubs are in compliance, a dozen health inspectors are trained to do "spot checks." They are assigned to look for monitors and to see that the business itself is watching customers. "Closed rooms and poor lighting would raise a red flag," according to one journalist. [48]

The AIDS epidemic has also brought about a number of related problems having to do with testing for the disease, the privacy of test results, stigmatization, and the criminalization of HIV. The issues have arisen in a variety of settings. In the workplace, owners and managers fear the spread of diseases in their organizations and the potential for lawsuits against them. On the other side, workers, particularly those in "high-risk" occupations, fear contamination by the public they serve; while others, who may be contaminated themselves, worry about possible discrimination or losing their jobs or insurance if test results are made available. Olympic diver Greg Louganis spurred calls for mandatory testing of athletes when he announced in 1996 that he had AIDS and that he had tested positive for HIV before the 1988 Olympic Games. Louganis bled after cutting his head on a springboard during competition in the 1988 games. Three years after those games, National Basketball Association star Earvin "Magic" Johnson announced that he was HIV-positive, followed shortly after by boxer Tommy Morrison's public acknowledgment that he was also HIV-positive. Despite the fact that virologists have determined that the likelihood of HIV transmission in any sport is so infinitesimally small that it cannot even be quantified, calls for the mandatory

testing of athletes, in a variety of sports, from professionals to amateurs to high schoolers, have been proposed and required in some instances. [49]

At present, HIV testing is mandatory in the United States in certain cases including blood and organ donors, military applicants and active duty personnel, under certain circumstances federal and state prison inmates, and newborns in some states. As of January 2010, HIV testing is no longer mandatory for those wishing to immigrate to the United States or for refugees. [50] In an effort to stop the spread of HIV/AIDS, public health officials at the CDC recommend HIV testing for all pregnant women. HIV testing is provided to these women in two ways: "opt-in" or "opt-out." In certain states and locales, women may be offered HIV testing and may choose to "opt-in" and offer their consent to testing. In situations where there is "opt-out" testing, the HIV test is automatically included as part of routine prenatal care and thus a woman must specifically ask not to be tested and sign a form refusing HIV testing. In 2006, the CDC recommended that opt-out testing be the norm for all pregnant women and today more than forty-six states follow that recommendation. Yet HIV/AIDS advocacy groups contend that the "expanded focus on testing without counseling and written, informed consent will put people at risk for testing without their prior knowledge or approval—a clear violation of medical ethics and human rights." While acknowledging the need for more HIV testing, especially in the communities hit hardest by HIV/AIDS, these groups criticized the CDC for "delinking" HIV testing from HIV education, counseling, and prevention and focusing on written consent as the main barrier to testing. Many advocates contend that there is evidence of the effectiveness of voluntary HIV counseling and testing approaches, the importance of voluntariness and autonomy in healthcare decision making to marginalized populations, and the role of HIV testing as a gateway to comprehensive HIV health care and support services. [51]

The HIV/AIDS epidemic has generated widespread fear that has resulted in the stigmatization, mistreatment, and legal and illegal discrimination of people diagnosed with HIV. According to the Center for HIV Law and Policy, a national legal and policy resource and strategy center for people with HIV, thirty-six states and two U.S. territories now criminalize HIV exposure through sex, shared needles, and, in some through "bodily fluids," including saliva. [52] In all these cases, authorities are not required to provide proof of the intent to transmit HIV nor do they have to document the actual transmission of the infection from the defendant to the victim. The sentences handed to someone convicted of HIV exposure are often the most severe available and, according to the Center for HIV Law and Policy, "disproportionate to the actual or potential harm presented in the facts of the case, perpetuating the stigma that HIV-positive people are toxic and dangerous" and that "Studies show that these HIV-specific statutes and prosecutions have absolutely no effect on behavior, and in fact undermine public health goals." [53] The result

investigations and courtrooms in the United States for more than one hundred years. The DOJ publication, *The Fingerprint Sourcebook*, tells us that:

> On the palm side of each person's hands and on the soles of each person's feet are prominent skin features that single him or her out from everyone else in the world. These features are present in friction ridge skin which leaves behind impressions of its shapes when it comes into contact with an object. The impressions from the last finger joints are known as fingerprints. Using fingerprints to identify individuals has become commonplace, and that identification role is an invaluable tool worldwide. [56]

In the 1980s, the FBI began converting some forty million fingerprint cards and crime-history records into digitized files. That database has now morphed into the Integrated Automated Fingerprint Identification System (IAFIS), "the largest biometric database in the world" containing fingerprints and criminal histories (mug shots, scar and tattoo photos, physical characteristics like height, weight, hair, and eye color, as well as aliases) for more than seventy million "subjects" as well as more than thirty-one million "civil prints" of those who have served or are serving in the U.S. military or have been or are employed by the federal government. The IAFIS machine is fed by all but three U.S. states and territories. The FBI claims that the average response time in the IAFIS for an electronic "Tenprint Rapsheet Request" (TPRS) is three minutes and eleven seconds and 91.92 percent completed within fifteen seconds. IAFIS processed more than sixty-one million tenprint submissions in 2010. [57]

Echoing the principle of "smaller, lighter, faster, cheaper," the DOJ's *Fingerprint Sourcebook* states that, "Increasingly inexpensive computing power, less expensive fingerprint sensors, and the demand for security, efficiency, and convenience have led to the viability of automatic fingerprint algorithms for everyday use in a large number of applications." [58] Indeed. Beginning in 2012, the FBI will no longer accept prints produced by the manual rolling process using ink and what was the standard 8" x 8" fingerprint card. This messy, time consuming, and location-bound "old school" method has been replaced with "Live Scan" technology developed and deployed by companies like Cross Match Technologies. Live Scan enables quick uploading of the fingerprint image, in combination with personal descriptor information, to the FBI database. And in cities like Los Angeles and New York, portable fingerprint scanners are being deployed by police in the field. The NYPD has about twenty MorphoTrak® readers, sold to NYPD by MorphoTrust USA ("the leading U.S. provider of identity solutions designed to simplify, protect, and secure the lives of the American people"). [59] LAPD acquired five hundred mobile fingerprint scanners in 2005 and today most law enforcement agencies working in Los Angeles County are using mobile fingerprinting devices. [60]

Extolling the benefit of IAFIS, the FBI website offers "Latent Hit of the Year Award" videos (a latent or "partial" print is one that is made more readable through electronic, chemical, and physical processing techniques). The award is presented to a latent examiner or officer who worked a case where a latent print from a "cold case" is restored and submitted to IAFIS resulting in a "hit" of someone in the database and an arrest for a previous unsolved crime. The videos include a deep-voiced narrator, stagy music, and the dramatization of scenes from the cases that evoke more 1960s *Dragnet* than the latest episode of high-tech-filled *Cold Case*. In one, the investigating officer recounts the day when he got news of the "hit": "When I received the call that day, I was like a child on Christmas morning and opening the best present that you could ever receive." He goes on to say, "When I first saw Michael Moon sitting in court, it was a wonderful feeling to know that the person who had committed this murder thirty years ago would now face justice." The award winning latent examiner concludes, "Justice was served. We got the bad guys off the street." "Tap into the power of IAFIS," the narrator intones, "To learn more about using IAFIS latent services, go to fbi.gov."

It seems that the IAFIS system is certainly a powerful law enforcement tool and the results of its use are impressive: The FBI reports that in 2011 "Unsolved Latent Match" search "hits" through IAFIS were 10,015 and that year 211,737 fugitives were identified by the system.[61] Yet, while fingerprint analysis is firmly ensconced in the justice system and it appears, in the minds of jurors and the public as an infallible technique of personal identification, its limitations or associated problems are rarely acknowledged. So while the "science" of fingerprint identification, known as "dactyloscopy," has certain "objective" qualities, how that science is put into practice—the collection, storage, and examination of fingerprints—is embedded in a social context and is rife with "subjective" and interpretive processes.

This quality is revealed in the work of Simon Cole, in what he calls "fraud, fabrication and false positives" with the use of this technique.[62] For example, the police charged with collecting fingerprints can do a poor job or manipulate the evidence; the task of matching the "points" of similarity between two prints remains more art than science (especially with regard to "latent" print analysis) where there is a serious lack of standards to determine what is and what is not a match; and those who serve as expert witnesses in courtrooms have been able to testify with impunity and little oversight.

Some rather infamous cases reveal these problems:

Brandon Mayfield: Mayfield is an Oregon lawyer who was identified as a participant in the 2004 Madrid train bombings based on a fingerprint match by the FBI. The latent Print Unit processed a fingerprint collected in Madrid through IAFIS and among twenty possible hits identified Mayfield's as an "absolutely incontrovertible match." A short time later, however, the Spanish National Police claimed that the print did not match Mayfield and identified another man to whom they claimed the fingerprint did belong.

René Ramón Sánchez: Sánchez, a legal immigrant to the United States from the Dominican Republic, was arrested for drunk driving on July 15, 1995. During his booking, his fingerprints were placed on a card containing the name, Social Security number, and other identification for Leo Rosario, who was being booked at the same time. Leo Rosario had been arrested for selling cocaine to an undercover police officer. Five years later, while entering the United States at Kennedy International Airport, officials mistakenly identified Sánchez as Rosario and he was arrested. Despite not matching Rosario's physical description, authorities were willing to rely solely on the mislabeled fingerprint data.

Stephan Cowans: In 1997 in Roxbury, Massachusetts, Cowans was convicted of attempted murder after he was accused of shooting a police officer while fleeing a robbery. Two witnesses, including the victim, identified him as the perpetrator and an expert testified that a fingerprint lifted from a glass at the crime scene belonged to Cowans. Found guilty, Cowans was sentenced to thirty-five years in prison. After serving six years of his term, a comparison of Cowans's DNA and material recovered near the crime scene was tested at the urging of the New England Innocence Project, and it was not his. After reexamining the fingerprint found at the scene, the police acknowledged that it had been misidentified. The wrongful conviction led to the temporary closure of the police department's fingerprint unit and changes in how evidence is gathered and analyzed.

Craig D. Harvey: In 1993, Harvey, a New York State Police Trooper, was charged with and later admitted to fabricating fingerprint evidence in order to build cases against people who had already been identified as suspects. Harvey admitted he and another officer lifted fingerprints from items that a suspect had touched during booking. He attached the fingerprints to evidence cards and later claimed that he had lifted the fingerprints from the scene of the murder. The forged evidence was presented at trial and the defendant was sentenced to fifty years to life in prison. An investigation revealed that Harvey's behavior was not an isolated incident and that multiple troopers were involved in the nearly routine fabrication of evidence in criminal cases.[63]

Are these instances just a handful of anomalies or are they the tip of an iceberg of possibly thousands of wrongful convictions? A fingerprint match (or even the claim of a match) is a powerful and rarely questioned bit of information that can provide the police a certain degree of "leverage" in justifying the issuing of search warrants, making arrests, provoking suspects into confessions to crimes—possibly not committed—and swaying the decisions and actions of district attorneys, judges, and juries. Indeed, the possible prejudicial effect of a fingerprint examiner's court testimony came into stark relief in 2002 when Philadelphia federal judge Louis H. Pollak ruled that fingerprint evidence does not meet the standards of scientific testimony set by the Supreme Court almost a decade earlier. The judge ruled that an expert witness cannot testify that a suspect's prints "definitely match" those found at a crime scene. Rather, Pollak asserted that fingerprint experts could only point out the similarities between prints from a crime scene and those of a defendant, but he wrote, "what such expert witnesses will not be permitted to do is to present 'evaluation' testimony as to their 'opinion' that a particular latent print is in fact the print of a particular person."[64]

Another concern, rarely acknowledged but pointed out by Simon Cole, is that with "quality of life" policing in effect in major cities, "petty" offenders (e.g., turnstile jumpers, public drinkers, unlicensed street sellers) are now more likely to be arrested rather than warned or cited. This has a "net widening" effect, creating "criminals with a record" and "repeat offenders" out of those involved in minor crimes. Since "quality of life" offenders are more likely to be marginalized people, such as racial minorities, the poor, and immigrants, then they are more likely to be "in the system," that is, in the IAFIS database. This tends to create a "closed system": if those marginal folks are more likely to be arrested and more likely to be in the system, they are more likely to be identified in latent print "cold" searches and be the possible victims of "fraud, fabrication and false positives." As Cole adds, the IAFIS system can function to institutionalize racist and classist arrest patterns, thereby reinforcing and justifying various forms of typing and profiling. "As technology enables criminal identification networks to become increasingly comprehensive and omniscient, the threat to liberty may lie less in the state's ability to see everything and everybody than it is in the ability to pick and choose whom and what it sees."[65]

It appears that fingerprint technology is far too compelling and obliging to be confined to just criminal identification. Like Bentham, who argued that the panopticon could be adapted to fit a variety of institutional settings, today's manufactures see wide-ranging uses and markets for their products. East Shore Technologies, for example, states that their fingerprint scanning systems are suitable for a wide variety of settings including "supporting criminal justice, national identity cards, social welfare, driver licenses, voter registration, passports, immigration, and pension benefits."[66]

Seemingly one notch above on the social hierarchy from the criminal, the frequently mistrusted and often vilified welfare recipient became the target of a campaign of fingerprinting surveillance in the 1990s.[67] Based primarily on a few egregious cases of people collecting checks for multiple children not in their custody, politicians, technocrats, and corporate marketers declared that fraud and abuse was endemic and that fingerprinting technology would solve the problem and save taxpayers millions. In one news story in late 1994, then *NBC News* anchor Tom Brokaw was blunt about the perceived seriousness of the issue, leading off with, "To California tonight, where Los Angeles is trying to deal with *one of the country's major problems*—cheating on welfare."[68] Following an early demonstration project in San Diego set up "free" by the Unisys Corporation, Los Angeles County was the first to begin taking fingerprint images of all welfare recipients. The county's slogan for this program was, "Fingerprints for better service," and it projected to save $18 million by preventing fraudulent claims over five years (minus the $10.8 million needed for staff and equipment). By 2000, biometric identifiers were being used in welfare programs in more than twelve states.[69]

Yet just a few years after implementation, evidence of rampant multiple-case fraud and the supposed cost savings from stopping this practice never materialized. A study conducted by the Office of the Inspector General of the United States concluded that, "LA County identified 25 instances of suspected multiple-case fraud through recording and matching the fingerprints of over 280,000 AFDC recipients. However, 11 of the 25 matches were the result of processing errors" and that if the program is "principally a tool to prevent, detect and deter multiple-case fraud, available data did not clearly demonstrate the cost effectiveness specifically for this type of fraud." After the first couple of months in place, New York City's plan found few cases of duplicate claims. Among the 148,502 "Home Relief" recipients checked, the fingerprint screening system found just forty-three cases of "double dipping."[70]

Some "cost savings" were however produced by forcing the poor to have their prints scanned: many people simply stopped applying for assistance. As the OIG report on the LA county program stated, "significant savings occurred which related to the discontinuance of AFDC and food stamp assistance to a large number of cases in Los Angeles County." A similar thing happened in New York City where then mayor Rudolf Giuliani declared confidently that the fingerprinting had "scared off" the welfare cheats. Advocates for the poor, however, claimed that many people refused to submit to what they saw as a stigmatizing practice that criminalized them for being poor while one service provider to the poor in the Bronx in those early years stated, "we know that recent immigrants, Holocaust survivors, older people, political asylum seekers, psychiatric patients and those frequently most in need of government assistance are frightened by fingerprinting—frightened enough to forgo needed medical, food and housing assistance if fingerprinting is required."[71] Nearly twenty years after the movement to fingerprint welfare recipients started, the "early adopters" abandoned the practice; in 2007, then governor of New York Elliot Spitzer ended the provision and in 2011, California governor Jerry Brown signed a bill that terminated the requirement that food stamp recipients in the state be fingerprinted. [72]

Like criminals and the supposed welfare cheats, immigrants have been targeted for increased surveillance and scrutiny and biometric collection. Post–9/11, the United States Visitor and Immigrant Status Indicator Technology (US-VISIT) program has had U.S. Department of State consular officers and U.S. Customs and Border Protection officers collecting digital fingerprints and a photograph from all non-U.S. citizens between the ages of fourteen and seventy-nine when they apply for visas or arrive at major U.S. ports of entry. [73] Prints and photos are checked against a "look out" database which includes individuals that the U.S. government has judged to be terrorists, criminals, or illegal immigrants. This database contains records on over one hundred million people. Once in the country, immigrants—undocumented as well as documented—are more likely than others to encounter police engaging in "stop and frisk" style checks and, in major cities, "stop and scan" ceremonies facilitated by the portable technologies mentioned earlier. The Fourth Amendment of the U.S. Constitution is supposed to protect us from "unreasonable searches and seizures" regardless of citizenship or immigration status. In practice, "broad exceptions" seem to limit the need for the police to have probable cause and secure warrants, especially when dealing with immigrant groups who are already skittish about dealing with the police, less likely to know their rights, and more likely to voluntarily comply in an effort to avoid making trouble. For example, in Los Angeles, day laborers who congregate on certain street corners waiting to be picked up by contractors and homeowners alike, have been lined up by police to have their fingerprints scanned by handheld "MORIS" (Mobile Offender Recognition and Information System) devices and not only run through IAFIS, but the scans and other information about them are retained in the system. [74] As one legal analyst for the group Electronic Frontier Foundation summarized the situation:

> Undocumented people living within the United States . . . are uniquely affected by the expansion of biometrics collection programs. Under DHS's [Department of Homeland Security] Secure Communities program, states are required to share their fingerprint data—via the FBI—with DHS, thus subjecting undocumented and even documented immigrants in the United States to heightened fears of deportation should they have any interaction with law enforcement. Further, under data-sharing agreements between the United States and other nations, refugees' biometric data may end up in the hands of the same repressive government they fled. Should they ever be deported or repatriated, they could face heightened risks from discrimination or even ethnic cleansing within their former home countries. [75]

But like our "mug shot" ending up on our driver's licenses (my first license in New York State *did not* have a picture on it) and other ID cards, our association between fingerprinting and the criminal justice system seems to slowly fade with the mundane encroachment of these kinds of techniques into everyday life. For instance, when I returned to my campus fitness center after being away with an injury, I found, not unusually, a number of students, staff, and faculty were lined up at the entrance turnstile. Yet rather than handing over their ID cards with the embedded magnetic strip to be scanned by a student worker, each was placing their index finger on a small, square plastic box hooked up to a computer sitting on the desk. "Is that what I think it is?" I said to myself. Sure enough, I heard a low but audible "beep" as each person is cleared through the system while the staff member smiled and chirped, "Enjoy your workout!" When it was my turn, I handed over my beat-up ID card that had long since stopped scanning correctly and said, "Sorry, it needs to be entered manually." Befuddled, the student stumbled with the keyboard while the guy waiting behind me sighed out loud. The card was handed back to me and I was chastised with, "You really should get your fingerprint entered." Clearly I needed to "get with the program" and stop gumming-up the works with such "old school" technology.

More examples include:

- At Walt Disney World in Lake Buena Vista, Florida, a biometric measurement is taken from the finger of "guests" to make sure that a ticket is used by the same person from day-to-day. Disney claims they are not "fingerprints" *per se* and that the scans are deleted every thirty days.
- Many childcare centers are turning to biometric technology to ensure that only parents or authorized caregivers can enter and leave with a child.
- At most banks in the country, if you try to cash a check where you do not have an account, you will need to offer your thumbprint to a scanner and place another copy of it on the check.
- The California Department of Motor Vehicles has been collecting drivers' digitized fingerprints since 1990 for consolidated data storage and to help track identity theft.
- Avid Biometrics sells numerous products that deploy fingerprint control including door locks, flash and hard drives, valuables and gun safes, workplace attendance time clocks, and the like.
- Most computer manufacturers offer laptops with a fingerprint security feature and if a computer does not already come equipped with a fingerprint scanner, you can purchase a peripheral scanner that attaches to any computer via USB port for less than $40.

BEYOND THE FINGERPRINT

Of course, at this juncture, biometrics has gone well beyond fingerprinting. We now have a plethora of systems either in use or in advanced development that attempt to identify and isolate unique human characteristics or traits for purposes of identification, security, access control, and the like. Such traits include facial, iris, and ear shape recognition, handprints and "hand geometry" based on measurements of the hand—size of the palm, length and width of the fingers, distance between the knuckles—voice and signature verification, even vein recognition which uses the vascular patterns of an individual's palm, finger, and back of the hand as personal identification data. There are "keystroke dynamics," too, that track the patterns of rhythm and timing created when a person types. Gait recognition has also been developed and now features shoes outfitted with "Bio Soles" that use an algorithm that combines the measurements of a foot's shape and person's gait to create an anonymous ID that is stored on a tiny chip in the insole. This ID could be used to unlock a secure door or log into a computer system when an authorized person is within a certain range. "There is nothing to remember, nothing to swipe, nothing to touch, no backend system to incorporate the authenticity of the biometric," says Todd Gray, president of Autonomous ID, who stated that he started working on the idea in 2007 when Iraqi insurgents dressed in U.S. uniforms walked onto a base and abducted U.S. soldiers. Autonomous ID partnered with Carnegie Mellon University's Pedo-Biometrics Research and Identity Automation Lab to develop the technology. [76]

Deploying a system that combines multiple biometric technologies, U.S. Customs and Border Protection is testing a new system at border crossings in Arizona called the Automated Virtual Agent for Truth Assessments in Real-Time (AVATAR) to "detect liars." Itinerants stand before a kiosk and are asked a series of questions by the machine while "microphones monitor vocal pitch frequency and quality, an infrared camera monitors eye movement and pupil dilation, and a high definition camera monitors facial expression." Doug Derrick, a member of the University of Arizona team developing the AVATAR, thinks the kiosk will be a success. "What we're looking for is changes in human physiology," Derrick told CNN. "We've had great success in reliably detecting these anomalies—things that people can't really detect." [77] Will we see such a system appear at your local police station in the near future? How about at the mall or on street corners?

According to one industry report, the future of biometrics seems limitless:

> One of the world's fastest growing technologies, biometric has revolutionized the business security landscape at offices. Government organizations as well as financial and educational institutions, across the globe, are also enjoying the

advantages of its applications. . . . The corporate security and identity theft are also fueling growth in the global biometric market, which is expected to expand at a CAGR [Compound Annual Growth Rate] of around 21% during 2012–2014, as per the estimation carried out in our latest research. . . . [B]iometric technologies are being widely accepted and adopted in various civil and commercial applications, including Point of Sale, ATMs, [and] . . . e-commerce, financial services, and retail are set to emerge as the significant segments for biometrics vendors.[78]

IT'S IN THE GENES

More than fifteen years ago, I was reading the print edition of the *New York Times* and turned to a completely white and blank page except for two sentences written across the center: "Thank you for turning this page. We now have a sample of your DNA." This was a clever advertisement for the "science fiction" film called *Gattaca*. The 1997 movie offered a version of a future society driven by "liberal eugenics" where potential children are selected through a form of genetic diagnosis to ensure they possess the best hereditary traits of their parents. A genetic registry database uses biometrics to instantly identify and classify those so created as "valids" while those conceived by traditional means are derisively known as "in-valids."[79]

In reality, a decade before the film appeared, the FBI initiated the Combined DNA Index System, or CODIS, DNA identification system. This system has since been augmented by the authorization of the DNA Identification Act of 1994 with the establishment of the National DNA Index System, or NDIS, which contains DNA profiles contributed by federal, state, and local participating forensic laboratories. All fifty states, the District of Columbia, the federal government, the U.S. Army Criminal Investigation Laboratory, and Puerto Rico participate in NDIS. Currently, there are more than ten million profiles in the system from convicted offenders, arrestees from states that collect samples, detainees, forensic evidence from crime scenes, unidentified human remains, and missing persons.[80]

CODIS works much like the IAFIS database. While 99.9 percent of the human genome is identical across all individuals, there are variations in protein codes, and those distinctions, called a short tandem repeat (STR), are easily accessible and can be measured. The FBI examines thirteen core STRs to identify a particular individual. Deploying a matching algorithm, CODIS searches and compares the forensic sample against those stored in the index. A "forensic to forensic" match offers possible leads, connecting two or more previously unlinked cases whereas a "forensic to offender" match may offer a suspect in an otherwise unsolved case. A CODIS investigation, however, only produces a list of candidates; a "match" must be confirmed or disproved by a trained DNA analyst.

In my home state of Kansas, anyone arrested for or simply charged with a felony has their cheek swabbed and the sample is sent to the Kansas Bureau of Investigation (KBI) for profiling and submission to CODIS. Rachel Harmon, a forensic scientist with the KBI, calls the offender profiling process a "DNA factory," and the KBI can test eight hundred of the police-submitted samples per month. "CODIS never forgets," Harmon told a local newspaper reporter. "When we get a match, it's tremendous." In Kansas, more than eighty thousand DNA profiles have been entered in CODIS, and the system has aided in more than fifteen hundred Kansas criminal investigations, according to the FBI. "It only gets bigger and better," Harmon said. In 2011, the KBI had 284 "cold hit" matches using CODIS, including suspects in thirteen homicides and fifty-four rapes.[81]

But much like fingerprint matching, the determination of a DNA "match" relies on a certain degree of interpretation and judgment and the quality of evidence (it's much easier to exclude a suspect than it is determine a match). As one scholar writes, "In truth . . . teasing out a DNA fingerprint and determining the likelihood of a match between a suspect and a crime scene is a complicated process that relies upon probability to a greater extent than most people realize." She went on, "Sometimes, the DNA from crime scene evidence is in a very small quantity, poorly preserved, or highly degraded, so only a partial DNA profile can be obtained. When fewer than 13 STR loci are examined, the overall genotype frequency is higher, therefore making the probability of a random match higher as well."[82] Of course, DNA obtained from a crime scene can also be a match with someone who had a valid reason for being at the scene.

Despite these limitations, it seems police are now routinely collecting DNA evidence from crime scenes, from saliva on beer cans left behind by a burglar, from sweat on a baseball bat used in a beating, from blood on a bullet that passed through a suspect. Several years ago, a prosecutor in Wisconsin filed rape and kidnapping charges against a defendant who has no name. "John Doe" was known only by his DNA code, extracted from semen samples from three rapes, samples that have been tested after six years of storage in a police property room. "We know that one person raped these three women," said the prosecutor, Norman Gahn, assistant district attorney for Milwaukee County. "We just don't know who that person is. We will catch him." A warrant must identify the person to be arrested, and this one names "John Doe, unknown male with matching deoxyribonucleic acid profile."[83] Following Gahn, other prosecutors issued "John Doe" DNA warrants and legislatures responded by extending the statute of limitations in sexual assault cases. "That has been happening throughout the country," Gahn said in an interview years later, "all driven by DNA technology, and there's now a widespread belief that we don't need the statute of limitations anymore for those cases where you have a DNA profile. . . . And, of course, there are more DNA post-conviction motion statutes, which allow access to evidence for DNA testing for those convicted individuals who believe that such testing would exonerate them. Many changes have been made to the law—all driven by this great gift of forensic DNA testing." Gahn's original "John Doe" has never been apprehended. [84]

Another surveillance practice brought about by the "gift" of genetic evidence has been the appearance of police "DNA dragnets." The practice of sampling the DNA of people who are not actually suspects but merely live or work near a crime scene emerged in Britain in 1987. In that case, the police took swabs of four thousand men in Leicestershire before the rapist and killer of two girls was caught but only after he got another man to take the DNA test for him. In the United States in 1995, the Miami police took more than two thousand DNA samples in search of a killer of six prostitutes. The data ended up ruling out three suspects and the actual killer was caught only after neighbors found a prostitute tied up in his apartment. Detectives in Los Angeles in 1999 reopened the case of a 1985 killing of a sheriff's deputy and set about sampling 165 suspects. They had finished only the first twelve when a former colleague of the sheriff refused to comply. The police went to court to force him to submit to the test and matched his DNA. He killed himself before he could be arrested. [85]

Advocates of genetic forensics have called for a national databank of DNA, taken from every person at birth, for purposes of criminal identifications. This is a tempting position to take. As of July 2012, CODIS-NDIS has produced over 185,000 "hits" assisting in more than 177,500 investigations. [86] (How many have resulted in convictions is unknown.) In addition, it appears that our justice system is so deeply flawed—by eyewitness misidentification, improper forensics, false and coerced confessions, government misconduct, informants and snitches, bad lawyering, as well as racism and classism—that DNA evidence has helped right many judicial wrongs. According to the Innocence Project, a nonprofit legal clinic dedicated to exonerating wrongfully convicted people through DNA testing, there have been 297 postconviction DNA exonerations in the United States; 186 African Americans, 84 European Americans, 21 Latinos, 2 Asian Americans, and 4 whose race is unknown. Seventeen of the 297 people exonerated through DNA served time on death row while the average length of time served by exonerees is thirteen years. The total number of years served is approximately 3,944. Furthermore, the true suspects or perpetrators have been identified in 146 of the DNA exoneration cases, and since 1989, there have been tens of thousands of cases where prime suspects were identified and pursued—until DNA testing (prior to conviction) proved that they were wrongly accused.

Regardless of these apparent advantages, the idea of a national DNA bank raises a host of practical, legal, and ethical questions that have no easy answers. A recent attempt by Iceland to develop a population-based DNA collection project called deCODE reveals some of them. In 1998, the Icelandic Legislature awarded deCODE Genetics, Inc., a $200 million contract to generate a computerized database collecting medical records and DNA samples from the entire population of the island nation. From the start, opponents argued that the country was handing over a scientific monopoly on genetic research to a private company and that the issues of control over one's DNA, informed consent, and genetic privacy had not been adequately addressed. Many Icelanders refused to participate and suits were filed. Ultimately, a legal judgment from the Icelandic Supreme Court in 2003, based on these very concerns, effectively ended the program.[87]

Meanwhile, at the same time that we started collecting lots of DNA from criminals, some researchers have been exploring the possibility of a link between the two. With its roots dating to Darwin's biological evolution, Francis Galton (1822–1911) believed the principles of natural selection applied to behavior characteristics. "Behavioral genetics" is the study of the genetic underpinnings of behavioral "phenotypes" such as substance abuse, social attitudes, violence and criminality, mental abilities, nurturing, and homosexuality. In this research, actual DNA is not examined but rather inferred by the observed individual differences, called phenotypic variance, in a given trait through the examination of patterns of resemblance among individuals who are related genetically, environmentally, or in both ways. For instance, some humans in a population are taller than others; heritability attempts to identify how much genetics is playing a role in part of the population being extra tall. In one review article titled "Behavioral Genetics: The Science of Antisocial Behavior," the authors declare confidently that there has been a "paradigm shift" in the last decades in criminology "away from a culturally centered, social learning model towards a more balanced perspective in which both genetic and environmental factors are understood to explain the wide variations observed in human behavior."[88]

A number of sophisticated research programs have centered on the relationship between genes, environmental factors, and "antisocial behavior" and other terms like "aggression" and even "disruptive behavior," the majority it seems focus on child and adolescent behavior. Research designs have included studies of twins and adoptees in order to attempt to sort out biological from environmental influences. And summarizing the results of these studies, the authors of these quotes assert assuredly that, "Genetic influences are clearly important in antisocial behavior, including criminality. Numerous classical twin and adoption studies, as well as more recent studies of specific genes, support this conclusion. Heritability estimates suggest as much as one-half of the variation in propensity toward antisocial behavior can be explained by genetic differences among individuals."[89]

Yet these same researchers acknowledge that the definitions of "antisocial" behavior have varied widely across studies; from as broad as "violations of rules and social norms" to "specific forms of aggression, including self-defense or other reactive forms and proactive behaviors such as bullying." How have these behaviors been measured? "Some studies are based on official records such as police arrests, court convictions, or school records, while others rely on behavioral ratings provided by parents or teachers or on self-reporting." So, for all its scientism, "behavioral genetics" is ultimately rooted in such conceptually slippery and broad terms that, on any given day, many of us and our behaviors might be labeled as "antisocial." Moreover, years of research on the criminal justice system, the production of school "records," and teacher evaluations of student behavior have uncovered profound racial, class, and gender biases rendering any "objective" use of these data as highly questionable. And finally, while most researchers would contend that there is no "crime gene," the "holy grail" of this field seems to be finding inherited traits that are linked to aggression and, ultimately, to violent crime. But as one journalist notes, "Don't expect anyone to discover how someone's DNA might identify the next Bernard L. Madoff." Troy Duster, professor of sociology and bioethics at New York University, notes that this is precisely the problem. Duster argues that studies examine "not the remorseless and rapacious behavior of the rich and powerful, but the behavior of disadvantaged minorities. . . . Every era believes that the technology and the methodology have improved," Duster went on, "but the science itself is problematic."[90]

Much like drug-testing technology, genetic assessment has become "lighter" and "cheaper" and has therefore worked its way into everyday life in the arenas of medical testing, in civil and tort law, in paternity determinations, and even family genealogy. More than a decade ago, Myriad Genetics, Inc., announced a patented technology for "cheaper, more efficient, less resource-intensive DNA diagnostic tests" using DNA on silicon wafers, or biochips. The company has gone on to develop and market a variety of tests, including "the cornerstone technologies of biomarker discovery, high-throughput deoxyribo nucleuc acid (DNA) sequencing [as well as] new molecular diagnostic tests that are designed to assess an individual's risk for developing disease later in life (predictive medicine), identify a patient's likelihood of responding to drug therapy and guide a patient's dosing to ensure optimal treatment (personalized medicine), or assess a patient's risk of disease progression and disease recurrence (prognostic medicine)."[91]

In 2012, the cost of genetic testing can range from as little as $300 up to about $3,000 depending on the extent of the analysis. The Proton Semiconductor Sequencer from Ion Torrent Systems, Inc., can sequence *the entire human genome* in about eight hours for $1,000. "I think it's going to be just kind of crazy not to have your genetics known," Brian Naughton of 23andMe, another genetic testing company, told one reporter. "It would be kind of like not knowing if you are allergic to a drug or not knowing your family history of a disease."[92] According to the publicly funded website GeneTests, more than 2,500 diseases can now be identified through gene testing, compared with fewer than eight hundred in 2000.[93] And while DNA screening and testing offer real possibilities, as one journalist put it, "to transform medicine by predicting the risk of cancer or other severe diseases years in advance . . . the very nature of the tests creates the potential for catastrophic error because they're often used to make irreversible decisions, such as terminating a pregnancy or undergoing surgery to prevent cancer."[94] James Evans of the University of North Carolina, Chapel Hill, and the American College of Medical Genetics points out, "We don't just get MRIs on everybody who comes to the doctor's office. Not only would that be ridiculously expensive and uninformative," says Evans, "it could also lead to all kinds of false positives that would be highly problematic for those people."[95]

Privacy concerns, especially with direct-to-consumer testing kits, are another possible worry. "Your DNA might be sold, shared or used without your consent for testing and research," says Lori B. Andrews, a professor at the Chicago-Kent College of Law. "Some companies are just a front end for biotech companies that use it for research," she says.[96] In the legal arena, one study covering the period from January 1, 1995, to December 31, 2005, revealed 258 tort court cases where genetic tests or conditions were involved. Of those cases, over half appeared to involve the use of genetic information or genetic tests as a basis for determining liability or damages in the context of medical malpractice, child lead poisoning, negligence, domestic relations, and product liability/tobacco suits.[97] DNA evidence has also appeared in "toxic-tort cases" as proof of exposure, as proof of injury or increased risk of future injury or, conversely, to establish that exposure to a harmful substance or product was not the cause of the plaintiff's injuries. In some cases, claimants have introduced a negative test result to refute the defendant's claim.[98]

With the promise of determining the "truth" about who is and who is not the father of a child, DNA testing has also been introduced into the complex arena of sexual relations and family life. "Did you know that 1 out of 5 people have questioned paternity or know someone that has?" states the *Identigene* DNA Paternity Test Kit website. Sorenson Genomics of Salt Lake City sells the home test kit at Walgreens for about $28.00; the lab fees at another $129.[99] The test involves inside the cheek swabs from the child and the alleged father, although collection of the mother's cells is recommended as well to better certify results. No information about possible genetic disorders or other illnesses are revealed. *Identigene* and other websites pose a variety of predicaments people may find themselves in: "You are a mother and a little voice is asking, 'What if Eric is not the dad and it's really Michael?'" "What if I'm allowing my child to bond with a man who isn't really his father?" "What if you are NOT the father? It happens. A man can be unaware that a wife or girlfriend has been with someone else. And sometimes a woman manipulates the story or omits key information that would provide hints to the truth about paternity." "Your friends tell you rumors about your girlfriend's infidelity or you remember being broken up around the time the baby was conceived."[100]

A new blood test is now available that can determine paternity as early as the eighth or ninth week of pregnancy, without an invasive procedure that could cause a miscarriage. Ravgen, a small company in Columbia, Maryland, has been offering its test on a limited basis and another version of the test has been developed by a company in Silicon Valley called Natera, and is marketed by DNA Diagnostics Center, a leading provider of conventional paternity tests. Knowing who the father is before a child is born would permit a women to make a variety of decisions based on information not available before. For example, a woman might terminate a pregnancy if the preferred man is not the father or go to full term if he is. The test could influence a woman who learned that she was pregnant after a rape to give birth if she learned that the rapist was not the father. And a man who knows early on that he is indeed the future parent may be more willing to support the woman financially and emotionally during the pregnancy.[101]

Given the powerful implications of genetic knowledge, some suggest that, within a short time, most of us will have our DNA profile on record somewhere. In response, a number of states have passed laws protecting citizens against genetic discrimination in health insurance and employment situations, but the content of the laws has varied considerably. In an attempt to strengthen safeguards and create more uniformity, federal legislation in the form of the Genetic Information Nondiscrimination Act (GINA) was passed in 2008 (the National Association of Manufacturers, the National Retail Federation, the Society for Human Resource Management, and the United States Chamber of Commerce lobbied against it). The act forbids health plans and health insurers from denying coverage to a healthy individual or charging that person higher premiums based solely on a genetic predisposition to developing a disease sometime in the future. The legislation also bars employers from using individuals' genetic information when making hiring, firing, job placement, or promotion decisions. While GINA has been applauded as a step in the right direction, the Department of Health and Human Services (DHHS) acknowledges that GINA provides only a "baseline level of protection against genetic discrimination for all Americans." DHHS goes on to describe "What won't GINA do?"

- GINA's health coverage nondiscrimination protections do not extend to life insurance, disability insurance and long-term care insurance.
- GINA does not mandate coverage for any particular test or treatment.
- GINA's employment provisions generally do not apply to employers with fewer than fifteen employees.

- For health coverage provided by a health insurer to individuals, GINA does not prohibit the health insurer from determining eligibility or premium rates for an individual based on the manifestation of a disease or disorder in that individual. For employment-based coverage provided by group health plans, GINA permits the overall premium rate for an employer to be increased because of the manifestation of a disease or disorder of an individual enrolled in the plan, but the manifested disease or disorder of one individual cannot be used as genetic information about other group members to further increase the premium.
- GINA does not prohibit health insurers or health plan administrators from obtaining and using genetic test results in making health insurance payment determinations. [102]

With these fairly weak safeguards in place, genetic material will become increasingly important, perhaps a determining factor, in assessing an individual's predisposition to diseases and certain personality traits and their assumed links to behavioral patterns. Organizations such as workplaces, schools, hospitals, insurance companies, health and welfare agencies, courts, and those involved in law enforcement have incentives to store and use this kind of information. As with many medical discoveries, knowledge, and tests, we still seem ill-prepared as a society to deal with the social, legal, and ethical implications of DNA evidence. As the authors of the book *Dangerous Diagnostics* put it:

> The social meaning of this information . . . must be reconsidered in the context of an increasing sense of crisis—over criminal violence, the cost of health care services, the quality of education and the general state of the economy. . . . These economic and social imperatives are enhancing the social value of predictive testing and reinforcing the power of biological information well beyond the clinical context. [103]

HOW ARE WE FEELING TODAY?

The cost of health care and "economic imperatives" come into play in the context of employer-based healthcare plans. Despite the fact that a diminishing percentage of workers in the United States get health insurance through their jobs—down from 60.4 percent in December 2007 to 55.8 percent in April 2011—employment-based health insurance is still our most common form of coverage for the nonpoor and nonelderly, and the cost of providing that insurance is rising. In 2012, employers spent on average 8.5 percent of total compensation on health insurance costs, up from 5.5 percent in 2000, according to the Bureau of Labor Statistics. [104] These escalating expenditures reveal at least one fundamental contradiction of a healthcare system based primarily on employer-sponsored health insurance: employers have an economic incentive to control costs and, by extension, the health and personal behavior of their workers. Strategies for monitoring the bodies of employees have varied from compelling medical tests, to penalizing them for engaging in health harmful behaviors, to "incentivizing" them to offer up their health information and participate in various "wellness" programs. And all of these tactics contain various dimensions of the Foucaultdian "gaze," the examination, hierarchical observation, and normalizing judgments.

According to the Americans with Disabilities Act of 1990 an employer may not ask a job applicant to answer medical questions or take a medical exam before making a job offer. However, once a person has been hired, an employer can demand a "fitness for duty" examination or request a medical certification from an employee requesting leave under the Family and Medical Leave Act (FMLA). In either case, the employer is entitled only to information about the specific circumstances and not to a full health screening or medical history, and data gathered in medical examinations must be kept in a separate personnel file available only to those with a demonstrable need to know. All these sound like judicious protections of worker privacy and will prevent an employer from discriminating against an employee based on health reasons.

Yet, companies—especially larger corporations and other large employers like universities, have themselves been collecting vast amounts of detailed medical data on their employees through various "wellness" plans and programs. Most of the plans have been "soft," voluntary programs where employees who sign up receive discounts on healthcare premiums, free weight-loss and smoking-cessation programs, gym memberships, as well as counseling for emotional problems. But, in exchange for such discounts, employees must submit to a variety of tests and provide biometric data such as blood pressure, heart rate, cholesterol levels, and the like. As healthcare costs continue to rise and the country faces epidemic levels of obesity and diabetes and high rates of smoking and associated ills, companies seem to be moving toward making wellness programs a requirement of employment and using the data collected in them to confront the employees about their "unhealthy lifestyle choices" and challenging their claims for benefits resulting from workplace injuries or stress. One company leading the way in this tactic is the $2.7 billion lawn-care company, Scotts Miracle-Gro.

According to one case study of the company, Scotts employees undergo extensive health-risk assessments and those who refuse to pay $40 a month more in premiums. Deploying data-mining software, employees of Scotts onsite primary care and fitness center contractor, Whole Health Management, pour over the physical, mental, and family health histories of nearly every employee and match this information with insurance claims data. A health assessment questionnaire posed the following: "Do you smoke?

Drink? What did your parents die of? Do you feel down, sad, hopeless? Burned out? How is your relationship with your spouse? Your kids? Are you pregnant, diabetic, suffering from high cholesterol?" All tobacco use on the premises is banned. Employees identified as having "moderate to high risk" are assigned a "health coach" who designs an "action plan" and monitors their progress. Workers who don't submit to the plan pay an additional $67 a month for a total of $107 monthly penalty. "We tried carrots," says Benefits chief Pam Kuryla. "Carrots didn't work." One employee, Joe Pellegrini, a forty-eight-year-old executive, reports getting "another nagging phone call" at home from his coach: "Have you been to your doctor yet?" The woman inquires, "When are you going?" And then being told, "You need to lose weight and you really, really need to lower your cholesterol."[105]

The case of another employee, Scott Rodrigues, highlights the intrusiveness of the program as described by *Business Week* reporter Michelle Conlin in her article, "Get Healthy—Or Else":

> Rodrigues says he had been working at the company for about two weeks. He recalls a supervisor approaching him in the parking lot at the company's Cape Cod (Mass.) facility and urging him to get rid of the pack of Marlboro reds poking out of the dashboard of his decrepit Civic.
> Rodrigues knew Scotts was going tobacco-free on Oct. 1 as part of its effort to improve employee health and cut medical costs. He recalls the company's interviewer saying that once Rodrigues passed the 60-day probation, Scotts would help him quit his 15-year habit—paying for counseling, Nicorette, prescription drugs, hypnosis. Whatever it took.
> But on Sept. 1—which happened to be his 30th birthday—Rodrigues was fired. "Why?" he asked. "You failed your drug test," the boss replied. Rodrigues insisted it had to be a mistake. He didn't even keep beer in the fridge. Then his boss told him the drug was nicotine. "Five years ago, if you had told me, 'Hey, you better quit smoking or you might not get a job,' I would have laughed. Here I am five years later, and I can't get a job."[106]

BODY POLITIC(S)

While new surveillance and knowledge-gathering tactics can aim to uncover the body's inner evidences, some strategies may ensure docility by taking control of the body. In other words, if the surveillance, evidence, or threat of knowledge is not enough to render people controlled, we can always convince, cajole, or force their bodies into submission with various "treatments." Increasingly, these measures appear in the form of pharmacological interventions—some eschewing previous incarnations that were more physically invasive—and are offered to or forced on people in the name of social order, prudent public policy, or "for their own good." Interestingly, while we engage in a determined and quite costly effort to stop the use of illegal "drugs," we see fit to permit, even enforce by law, the use of legal "medication" regimes to control those bodies deemed out of control: in these cases, the old line of "Just say 'no'" becomes "Must say 'yes.'" Again, I see these examples reinforcing my idea that the body is the central target of many postmodern surveillance and social control practices.

In recent years, we have seen a number of these bodily based strategies deployed on a variety of people in different areas of social life. So, for example, back in 1993 in Arizona, a "welfare mother" had, under court order, the contraceptive Norplant surgically implanted in her arm to prevent her from having more children. About that same time, a California judge required a woman convicted of child abuse to use Norplant as a condition of her parole. These cases brought a call from various conservative politicians that, as a matter of public policy, welfare eligibility should be linked directly to long-term birth control. [107] In fact, twenty such measures were introduced in thirteen states during the 1990s. While none of these policies ultimately passed, the idea of mandatory contraception for welfare recipients has continued to circulate in various corners of the political discourse. Of course, as I have pointed out earlier, there have been many instances throughout U.S. history when we attempted to control the procreation of what were once quite openly called the "defective classes." What is so important now is that we need not go about rounding these people up in poorhouses and "reformatories" trying to watch and control their behavior as we did in the nineteenth and early twentieth centuries. The available pharmacological technology has the potential to make the whole business quite simple and more palatable, breaking down resistance and medicalizing and normalizing social control.

Yet another attempt to control women's reproduction is a program called Project Prevention (formally called CRACK, the acronym for Children Requiring a Caring Kommunity). For about twenty years now, the privately financed group has paid drug addicts and alcohol abusers in fifty states and the District of Columbia up to $300 to go on long-term birth control or, alternatively, to be permanently sterilized. The group's stated goals are, "to reduce the burden of this social problem on taxpayers, trim down social worker caseloads, and alleviate from our clients the burden of having children that will potentially be taken away." Project Prevention advertises its offer on its website, in public service announcements, in a collection of YouTube videos, on billboards in low-income neighborhoods, and through ads in clinics and homeless shelters with some declaring, "Don't let a pregnancy ruin your drug habit," and "She has her daddy's eyes . . . and her mommy's heroin addiction." "Project Prevention believes every baby deserves a sober start! GET BIRTH CONTROL GET $300 CASH. MAKE THE CALL TODAY: 888-30-CRACK." [108]

Project Prevention claims that by January 2012, "4,000 women severely addicted to drugs and/or alcohol, took part in our unique program paying them cash for long term or permanent birth control." Yet many see the program as a violation of informed consent, exploitive, coercive, and a form of eugenic population control.[109] The controversial founder of Project Prevention, Barbara Harris, once characterized drug-addicted women as having "litters" of babies and compared her program to the neutering and spaying of animals. "There is a much more constructive way of doing this," stated Dr. Hytham Imseis, an obstetrician at Presbyterian Hospital in North Carolina. Imseis says that research now suggests that a mother's drug addiction is not as dangerous for a child as once thought and that many of the adverse effects of that life are brought on by poverty and not drugs. "We need to focus on treatment," says Dr. Imseis, "rather than on this sort of strategy of sterilization of an entire population." He calls the cash incentive bribery and adds, "It's not about empowerment. It's about control, and when you try to control any particular group and as a society try to prevent them from reproducing, I think you've crossed a line."[110]

This tactic has been augmented with movements by state governments to exert some form of social control on women whose behavior is seen as dangerous to unborn children, a strategy the *New York Times* dubbed, "The Criminalization of Bad Mothers."[111] A number of "fetal rights" cases have appeared in recent years that attempted to hold women responsible for their conduct during pregnancy, especially their use of drugs or alcohol. In one early case, Jennifer Johnson of Seminole County, Florida, was convicted under a drug trafficking law. She was charged with using cocaine during her pregnancy and that by doing so she had delivered a controlled substance to a minor via her umbilical cord. She was sentenced to one year in a drug treatment program, fourteen years probation, and two hundred hours of community service. Johnson appealed her sentence and the Supreme Court of Florida overturned her conviction. In a more recent case, Amanda Kimbrough, a thirty-two-year-old Alabamian, delivered her third child, born premature at twenty-five weeks weighing just two pounds, one ounce, and lived only nineteen minutes. Kimbrough tested positive for methamphetamine. Six months later, the district attorney in Colbert County charged Kimbrough because her child died with "chemical endangerment of a child," a Class A felony that carries a mandatory sentence of ten years to life. At her trial, the state rested its case in just two days, and on the advice of her attorney, Kimbrough pleaded guilty and received the minimum sentence of ten years.

Men have also been the target of bodily social control in an attempt to suppress their sexual "urges." Surgical castration has been around for centuries but in the late 1800s, Indiana physician Dr. Harry Sharp surgically castrated nearly two hundred male prisoners to reduce their sex drive. His pioneering work prompted the state of Indiana to deploy physical castration in an attempt to reduce the recidivism of some prisoners and became the first state to legalize the sterilization of "mental defectives."[112] Today, as with control of women's reproduction, hormonotherapy permits highly effective and less permanent strategies for lowering a man's testosterone levels and these pharmacological interventions have been dubbed "chemical castration." The drug most commonly deployed is Medroxyprogesterone acetate or MPA, the ingredient used in Depo Provera which, despite its long history and established use, has never received approval from the FDA for use as a treatment for sexual offenders. In their law review article regarding the use of male castration for sex offenders in the United States, Drs. Charles L. Scott and Trent Holmberg point out that in 1996 California became the first state to authorize the use of either chemical or "voluntary" physical castration for certain sex offenders who were being released from prison. While considered extremely controversial at the time, the California law was followed by eight additional states that provide some form of castration for individuals who have been convicted of a sex offense and are being considered for parole or probation. Of the nine states, four permit the use of chemical castration only (Georgia, Montana, Oregon, and Wisconsin), four allow either chemical castration or voluntary surgical castration (California, Florida, Iowa, and Louisiana), and one (Texas) provides voluntary surgical castration as the only treatment option. [113]

The "Just say 'no'" becomes "Must say 'yes'" phenomena has been played out as well in the history of psychotropic "wonder drugs" for those mentally ill among us. These antipsychotic medications were first deployed in large state mental hospitals in the 1950s and replaced earlier physical treatments such as shackles, ice baths, lobotomies, and various "shock therapies." The drugs were so effective at "calming" out-of-control patients they were heralded as less permanent "pharmacological lobotomies" despite their debilitating physical side effects such as the "Thorazine shuffle" and Parkinson's like neurological problems. The psychotropic drugs were credited with helping us empty those same state mental hospitals during the "deinstitutionalization" period of the 1960s. Under the control of the drugs and the supposed care of new community mental health clinics, previously institutionalized individuals were released so that they could somehow go on to lead "full and productive lives in the community." [114]

Today, all but four states allow for psychiatric "involuntary treatment" that is administered despite an individual's objections, while forty-two states permit court-ordered "assisted outpatient treatment" or the forced medication of individuals who have a history of medication noncompliance as a condition of their release from a mental hospital. While the U.S. Supreme Court put limits on the forced medication of psychotic defendants in its 2006 ruling on *Sell v. United States*, we have seen a number of dramatic cases of this tactic in recent years. In 2003, a federal appeals court ruled that Arkansas officials could force convicted multiple-murderer Charles Laverne Singleton to take antipsychotic medication to make him sane enough to execute. Without the drugs, Singleton could not be put to death due to a U.S. Supreme Court decision, *Ford v. Wainwright*, that ruled an insane inmate cannot be executed. A justice writing for the majority in the Singleton decision wrote, astonishingly, that "Eligibility for execution is the only unwanted consequence of the medication."[115]

In 2011, Jared L. Loughner, who attempted to assassinate then congresswoman Gabrielle Giffords and killed six people, was forcibly medicated with antipsychotic drugs to make him fit to stand trial. Soon after, a federal appeals panel ruled that Loughner could refuse antipsychotic medication, since he "has not been convicted of a crime, is presumptively innocent and is therefore entitled to greater constitutional protections than a convicted inmate." However, the ruling stated that it "does not preclude prison authorities from taking other measures to maintain the safety of prison personnel, other inmates and Loughner himself, including forced administration of tranquilizers." Afterward, prison authorities resumed forcible treatment of Loughner, stating that the purpose of treatment was to stop the danger Loughner posed to himself. Further appeals to stop the involuntary treatment failed. On Tuesday, August 7, 2012, a judge found Loughner competent to stand trial and he pleaded guilty to the shootings.[116]

Concerning behavior far less threatening than murder, we see the confluence of psychiatric assessment and the dispensing of medications designed to control the mind and body played out in thousands of classrooms every day. Author Bronwen Hruska recalls her first experience with what she called, "Raising the Ritalin Generation":

> I remember the moment my son's teacher told us, "Just a little medication could really turn things around for Will." We stared at her as if she were speaking Greek. "Are you talking about Ritalin?" my husband asked. Will was in third grade, and his school wanted him to settle down in order to focus on math worksheets and geography lessons and social studies. The children were expected to line up quietly and "transition" between classes without goofing around. This posed a challenge—hence the medication. "We've seen it work wonders," his teacher said. "Will's teachers are reprimanding him. If his behavior improves, his teachers will start to praise him. He'll feel better about himself and about school as a whole."
> Will did not bounce off walls. He wasn't particularly antsy. He didn't exhibit any behaviors I'd associated with attention deficit or hyperactivity. He was an 8-year-old boy with normal 8-year-old boy energy—at least that's what I'd deduced from scrutinizing his friends. "He doesn't have attention deficit," I said. "We're not going to medicate him." The teacher looked horrified. "We would never suggest you do that," she said, despite doing just that in her previous breath. "We aren't even allowed by law to suggest that. Just get him evaluated." And so it began.[117]

According to the National Institute of Mental Health, attention deficit hyperactivity disorder (ADHD) is one of the most common childhood disorders. Surveys of parents tell researchers that about 9.5 percent or 5.4 million children four to seventeen years of age have been diagnosed with ADHD and parent-reported ADHD diagnoses increased 22 percent between 2003 and 2007. Approximately 75 percent of the kids diagnosed with ADHD are boys. And the prevalence of parent-reported ADHD diagnosis varies substantially by state, from a low of 5.6 percent in Nevada to a high of 15.6 percent in North Carolina. The recommended treatment for the condition is "a combination of medication and behavioral treatment" but "psychostimulants" such as Ritalin and Adderall are the mainstays.[118]

Initially a controversial diagnosis, ADHD has become a routinely accepted condition that is embedded in the organizational rituals of schools and in the everyday lives of millions of families. Psychiatrists, and increasingly neuroscientists, assert that there is overwhelming scientific evidence that proves the disorder really exists and it seems that the staggering number of children being labeled and treated as such has reinforced their "expert claims" and normalized its existence. Yet others inside and outside the psycho-medical establishment continue to raise questions about the legitimacy of the disorder and the use of drugs to treat it. Blame has been cast on a growing intolerance of normal childhood behaviors, especially in boys; doctors, teachers, and parents who are looking for a "quick fix" to deal with their own burdens and deficiencies, pharmaceutical companies cultivating new markets and their influence on doctors' decision making and appealing to parents through direct advertisements; and, as well, what some see as the intense pressure on kids to perform well and succeed in school.

On this last issue, it seems that school performance and grades have taken on heightened importance and that any behavior preventing a child from "settling down" is behavior that is taken far more seriously than in the past. The reality is that in a globalized, sink-or-swim, "knowledge-based" economy, a child's life chances may more than ever depend on their educational success and attainment. Parents know this and their anxiety about school performance is not only conveyed to children, but it makes them far more willing to turn to medications to control their kids' behavior once they are told that they are not performing at levels that teachers expect of them. In educational systems attempting to set high standards and "measurable goals" that are wrought with standardized testing and comparative national assessments, teachers and school administrators, whose jobs may be threatened, now have an added incentive to make sure that every child is capable of "making the grade."

In one study, children from 151 families from both the United States and Great Britain were interviewed about their experience being diagnosed with ADHD and being medicated with stimulants.[119] The authors tell us that the kids they spoke with living with ADHD tended to feel they benefit from being on these medications and do not think that it turns them into "robots." Reading the report, I was struck with the extent that the children—ages nine to fourteen years old—had a preoccupation with and had internalized the norms of "doing well" in school and behaviorally "being good." Listen to Camilla, from the United States, age ten:

> [With medication] I like, I finish my homework earlier and I don't get in trouble a lot anymore. I pay attention a lot more. . . . It feels great. . . . The medication, it like, changes, like, what you're doing and, like what you're thinking. Like all of a sudden, like, you know that you're not doing what the teacher told you to do, so then it just changes what, so then, so then, you can do the right thing what the teacher told you, so you can pay attention more better. [120]

According to the authors of the study, "Children invest in these values in part because it is an obligation they feel to their families . . . [and they] frequently noted that good grades in school made their parents happy." When an interviewer asked nine-year-old Miles from the United States, "What do you think makes a person a good person?" the boy responded, "When they don't do bad and when they get good grades." [121] A number of these issues came to the fore recently when a physician from Georgia revealed that while he routinely diagnoses children with ADHD, he calls the disorder "made up" and says that it simply provides justification to prescribe stimulants to treat what he considers "the children's true ill—poor academic performance in inadequate schools." [122] "I don't have a whole lot of choice," said Dr. Michael Anderson, a pediatrician for mostly poor and working class families outside Atlanta, told one journalist. "We've decided as a society that it's too expensive to modify the kid's environment. So we have to modify the kid." Jacqueline Williams, one of Anderson's clients, had all three of her kids diagnosed with ADHD. "My kids don't want to take it, but I told them, 'These are your grades when you're taking it, this is when you don't,' and they understood." Another family has a large basket of medications prescribed by Dr. Anderson on their kitchen shelf: "Adderall for Alexis, 12, and Ethan, 9; Risperdal (an antipsychotic for mood stabilization) for Quintn and Perry, both 11; and Clonidine (a sleep aid to counteract the other medications) for all four, taken nightly." In researching this article, the journalist spoke with a superintendent of a large California school district, who did not want to reveal his or her name, who suggested a connection between the rise in diagnosis rates of ADHD and the decline in school funding. "It's scary to think that this is what we've come to; how not funding public education to meet the needs of all kids has led to this," said the superintendent, referring to the use of stimulants in children without classic ADHD. "I don't know, but it could be happening right here. Maybe not as knowingly, but it could be a consequence of a doctor who sees a kid failing in overcrowded classes with 42 other kids and the frustrated parents asking what they can do. The doctor says, 'Maybe it's ADHD, let's give this a try.'"[123]

This chapter explores the proliferation of postmodern surveillance and disciplinary technologies that are founded on deriving knowledge and evidence from the body. I call this illumination a "pornography of the self" and it is the foundation of one of the key goals of contemporary surveillance and social control: to circumvent the speaking subject by creating easily accessible and scientifically reliable ways to search for and reveal evidence of deviance and malfeasance. Here I weave back and forth between the techniques and devices being deployed in the penal/health/welfare complex intended to derive knowledge and impose accountability on individuals through their bodies and the appearance of these or similar meticulous rituals of power have appeared in the everyday community settings of the home, school, and workplace. And again, in all these instances we see how advancing surveillance and accountability tactics help maintain unbalanced and unequal authority relationships.

How do we experience a situation where our bodies are becoming central targets of surveillance, knowledge gathering, and social control? It is said that the postmodern self personifies the multiple contradictions of the postmodern condition and may result in "intense emotional experiences shaped by anxiety, alienation, resentment, and detachment from others." [124] It seems to me that technologies or practices that permit our bodies to speak the truth, whether we want that voice to be heard or not, or alternatively, that control and restrict our bodies from being what they are, generate these very emotional states as they detach us from ourselves. Like the person whose capable mind is trapped in a degenerative frame, we are betrayed and abandoned by the physical expression of who we are. Hanson poetically describes this apparent double-cross in the case of the lie detector:

> The two machines commune together as the polygraph reaches out to embrace the subject's body with bands, tubes, and clips. The body responds lover-like to the touch, whispering secrets to the polygraph in tiny squeezes, twinges, thrills, and nudges. Both the machines are treacherous. The body, seduced by the polygraph's embrace, thoughtlessly prattles the confidences it shares with the subject's mind. The polygraph, a false and uncaring confidant, publishes the secrets it has learned on a chart to read. The subject as mind, powerless to chaperone the affair, watches helplessly as the carnal entwine of the machines produces its undoing. [125]

What are our options to resist this courtship? One is, of course, to behave, to stay clean, to "just say 'no '" The other strategy is to try to trick our bodies into not giving us away—a tactic that is sure to reinforce the personal troubles of the postmodern self and, if successful, to send the technicians scurrying to perfect a more reliable instrument.

Chapter Five

Wired.I.Am: The Digital Life 2.0

Ready or not, computers are coming to the people. That's good news, maybe better than psychedelics.—Stewart Brand, *Rolling Stone*, 1972

You have zero privacy anyway. Get over it.—Scott McNealy, CEO of Sun Microsystems, 1999

See absolutely everything visitors do on your webpage. Watch recordings of your visitors' full browsing sessions to discover exactly how they use your site. It's as if you're looking over their shoulder!—ClickTale, an industry leader in Customer Experience Analytics, 2012

Cell phones are tracking devices that make phone calls.—Jacob Appelbaum, security researcher, hacker, and privacy advocate, 2012

The history of the Internet—short for the more technical "internetwork" and once dubbed the "Information Superhighway"—mimics the creation of the Interstate Highway System; both were Cold War responses to the perceived post-Sputnik technological and nuclear threat of the former Soviet Union. In the late 1960s, with funding from the Pentagon's Advanced Research Projects Agency, researchers managed to get several computers talking to each other. A few years later, the National Science Foundation (NSF) created its own network, NSFNET, to provide scientists and researchers at universities greater access to its newly established supercomputer centers around the country. By 1993, there were two million computers attached to NSFNET and private companies took note of its success and began building their own. NSF outlined plans and funded a new "Internet" architecture, turning much of its development over to the private sector. [1]

The origins of the World Wide Web (Web)—the Internet's multimedia component combining text, sound, graphics, and video—came about in March 1989 when a British scientist working at a Swiss physics laboratory envisioned a system of networked "hypertext" documents: a form of nonsequential writing where the text can branch in different directions allowing the reader to choose a path. A couple of years later, the first piece of Web software was developed with the ability to view, edit, and send hypertext documents via the Internet. By the mid-1990s, researchers at the University of Illinois, supported by the NSF, released a graphical Web "browser" called Mosaic, a version of which later evolved into the software Netscape Navigator.[2]

Today, the Internet is at the center of our digitized communication and media storage and retrieval juggernaut. The number of Internet users worldwide is nearly 2.5 billion, or about 35 percent of the global population; that's an increase of 565 percent since the turn of the century. In 2012, 85 percent of American adults used the Internet and nearly 90 percent of U.S. households that had a computer at home subscribed to a broadband Internet service; five years before that number was just 65 percent of households. Cisco Systems, the maker of most networking hardware, estimates that by 2016, global Internet traffic will reach 1.3 zettabytes annually; growing fourfold from 2011 to 2016 (1 zettabyte is equal to about 250 billion DVDs or, put another way, the amount of visual information conveyed from the eyes to the brain of the entire human race in a single year). Yes, the Internet is that big.[3]

In the last few years, Internet connectivity has changed dramatically, drawing a staggering number of people more deeply into digital life. Cisco Systems claims that by 2016, there will be nearly 19 billion global network connections (fixed and mobile); the equivalent of two-and-a-half connections for every person on earth.[4] And thanks mostly to global manufacturing supply chains and low-cost labor in China (a country which, in 2012, accounted for one-fifth of the world's manufacturing output) the cost of computer hardware and other "digital devices" has plummeted. For example, even relatively expensive Apple computers have fallen precipitously. Adjusting for inflation, the 1984 Macintosh ($5,186) would cost almost $12,000 today; the current Apple iMac is just $1,299. Desktop and laptop PCs can be purchased for a few hundred dollars. And as of 2012, 85 percent of adults in the United States have a cell phone, 45 percent of them Internet capable "smartphones," 58 percent have a desktop computer, 61 percent have a laptop, and 18 percent have a tablet computer.[5] The result is that many middle-class American homes—wired up with broadband, internal networks, and wireless routers—are awash in computers, tablets, smartphones, and other wireless devices.

What are people in the United States doing when they are online? Survey data from the Pew Research Center tell us that among the top ten activities, using a search engine to find information and sending e-mail are tied at 91 percent followed by perusing hobby or interest (84 percent), accessing a map or driving directions (84 percent), checking the weather (81 percent), accessing health/medical information (80 percent), consumer research (78 percent), getting news (76 percent), going online just for fun or to pass the time (74 percent), and buying a product (71 percent). Social networking sites, once dominated by young adults, are now visited by 65 percent of Internet users—the majority of the total adult population.[6]

Pew has an online survey called "What Kind of User Am I?" that allows you to place yourself in one of several categories in their Pew "Typology of Information and Communication Technology Users." "Is Facebook your window to your social world?" the survey begins, "Is your mobile device the last thing you put aside before shutting the light out at night? Or does the deluge of digital information leave you flat and the ring of your cell phone leave you cranky?" The resulting categories range from the "Technologically Indifferent," one who makes little use of technology and finds it difficult to deal with to the most engaged "Digital Collaborator," who uses "information technology to work with and share your creations with others. You are enthusiastic about how ICTs [Information and Communications Technologies] help you connect with others and confident in your ability to manage digital devices and information. For you, the digital commons can be a camp, a lab, or a theater group—places to gather with others to develop something new."[7]

When I answered the survey questions for myself, I was somewhat chagrined to find out that, despite my actual ambivalence about pervasive ICTs, I fell into the "Digital Collaborator" group. As a graduate student in the social sciences in the early 1980s, I was drawn into using a personal computer as a practical writing and analytical tool. I owned the first model IBM PC, had a copy of the Mosaic web browser, and sent my first e-mail more than thirty years ago. Today, I struggle to regulate my level of "connectedness"; I have to make an effort not to take my smartphone when I go for a walk, decide if I can go on a totally "unplugged" vacation, or to not check e-mail when I am trying to write or just think without the distractions. These days, much of our daily lives and routines are saturated with Internet-related and dependent activities, be that at home, work, or school. I spend hours of my time planning and booking a vacation from my home computer (a job travel agents used to do); I watch as four young women sit adjacent to me in a restaurant nearly ignoring each other while each is texting and, somewhat ironically, posting pictures of their gathering on Facebook with their smartphones; my university, like many others, has directed faculty to offer "online" versions of their classes; and when the power has gone out in my office building, faculty and staff simply go home since they cannot do their jobs without computers and Internet connections. Conversations are peppered with, "Did you see that YouTube video of . . . ?" "Download our application online!" and so on. My plumber has a website. Every day I listen as my local

National Public Radio station personnel stumble through their readings of awkward dot-domain names. There is little doubt that the Internet, for better or worse, ranks as one of the most important social, cultural, and economic developments of our time. In 2006, "You" were chosen as *Time* magazine's "Person of the Year," recognizing the millions of people who anonymously contributed user-generated content to "wikis" (including Wikipedia), You-Tube, MySpace, Facebook, and the scores of other websites built around user-generated content.

In this chapter, I begin considering the postmodern qualities of the Web and I examine a number of surveillance and social control practices that have been developed for and facilitated by the Internet. Among these are strategies deployed in the criminal justice system, such as web-based "offender registries" but also the technologically driven tactics of surveillance and monitoring that have appeared in schools, workplaces, and homes. I also examine the "dataveillance" capabilities of the networks that facilitate the collection and exchange of information about individuals and that monitor the activities and locations of users on the network. Finally, I argue that the Web has enabled the "eroticization" of surveillance, thus contributing to a culture where watching and being watched is normalized in everyday life and serves to contribute to the postmodern blurring of the lines between the private and the public.

THE "ECSTASY OF COMMUNICATION"

Like the video camera, the Internet is a quintessentially postmodern technology, reflecting and reproducing many of the dominant themes of postmodern culture. "Surfing" the Web is a fluid and anchorless experience as we flow in and out of the endless mediascapes that form a pastiche of texts, images, and sounds. With instant access to a seemingly inexhaustible supply of information, we are equally enlightened, easily distracted, and sometimes overwhelmed by the magnitude of it all. The Internet compresses time as well as social and geographical space, undermining the experience of distance and exacerbating a sense of "placelessness." It is a life-world where formerly unique objects, located in a particular space, lose their singularity, their "aura," as Walter Benjamin called it, as they become accessible to anyone from anywhere.[8] Indeed, the entire Internet is a virtual simulation—the epitome of Jean Baudrillard's "ecstasy of communication"—where distinctions between "real" objects and their representations dissolve and our grip on the tangible fades.[9] The Web does not simply present an image to us, but rather it fundamentally alters the way we think about the world, determining what we see, and how we make sense out of it.[10] And like television and other forms of mediated life before it, questions of authenticity of experience and the truthfulness and reliability of information abound.

Kevin Kelly, one of the early enthusiastic cheerleaders of the new "wired" culture, captured much of postmodern life on and off "the Net" when he claimed that

> a person on the Internet . . . views the world decidedly decentralized, every far flung member a producer as well as a consumer, all parts of it equidistant from all others . . . and every participant responsible for manufacturing truth out of the noisy cacophony of ideas, opinions, and facts. There is no central meaning, no official canon, no manufactured consent. . . . Instead every idea has a backer, and every backer has an idea, while contradiction, paradox, irony, and multifaceted truth rise up in a flood. . . . People in a highly connected yet deeply fragmented society can no longer rely on a central canon for guidance. They are forced into a [post?] modern existential blackness of creating their own cultures, beliefs, markets, identities from a sticky mess of interdependent pieces. The industrial icon of a grand central or a hidden "I am" becomes hollow. Distributed, headless, emergent wholeness becomes the social ideal. [11]

Early promoters like Kelly, Stewart Brand, and John Perry Barlow brought a kind of communitarian perspective to the Web that merged with the "hacktivist," antisystem libertarian impulse of others. As Evgeny Morozov puts it, "These men emphasized the importance of community and shared experiences; they viewed humans as essentially good, influenced by rational deliberation, and tending towards co-operation. Anti-Hobbesian at heart, they viewed the state and its institutions as an obstacle to be overcome—and what better way to transcend them than via cyberspace?"[12] In this utopian view, the Internet would undermine political, economic, and social hierarchies, short-circuit institutional inequalities, and provide for more democratic participation. Through this technology, we would advance Marshall McLuhan's now classic idea of the "global village" with the Internet and new media offering us powerful new tools for fostering and sustaining social relations in new "cybernetic communities." Life on the Net, it was said, would be a place, much like the rest of social life, where people could work, shop, fall in love, read the news, debate politics, and join in associations with others who share common interests. On the Web, users could "pull" content from the medium, rather than have it "pushed" at them by traditional media. This "pulling" supposedly would empower consumers since they would have more choice to create their own reference points through a variety of "personalizing" features.

With no central authority, clearinghouse, or censoring mechanism, the Net, many argued, would democratize the technology of publication so that anyone could have a voice, publish their own website or blog, start a discussion group, and so on. The Web would offer a place where alternative forms of social, cultural, and political expression could flourish. For example, some have heralded the role that the Internet and social media played in political movements such as the "Arab Spring," the civil uprising that forced a number of rulers from power in places like Tunisia, Egypt, Libya, and Yemen, calling them "Twitter Revolutions." One Egyptian activist echoed this view when she tweeted that, "We use Facebook to schedule the protests, Twitter to coordinate, and YouTube to tell the world."[13]

There is little doubt that the Internet, digitization, and global communications technologies are truly amazing developments that have fundamentally altered our lives in countless ways. Yet, like most utopian visions, expectation and reality are often distant cousins. Twenty years down the road, many Internet "communities" look and function more like the physical "gated communities" I describe in chapter 3, where you must be registered to participate and where "moderators" or "admins" and others who have control can erase messages of those they disagree with or simply lock them out. Rather than the early idea of "open platforms" that offer users unrestricted access to applications and content, the Web is now dominated by "walled gardens" built by various service providers to give them control over the applications, content, and media offered and restrict access to others.[14] So, much like how news and entertainment in the United States is dominated by just a few companies—Time Warner, Disney, Viacom, News Corp., CBS, and NBC Universal—the control of the infrastructure, applications, software, and content is now dominated by just a handful of powerful corporate players. Comcast, ATT, and Time Warner Cable dominate the service provider markets and Google, Oracle, Apple, Microsoft, Yahoo, Amazon, Facebook, and eBay dominate the Web.[15] Increasingly, it is difficult to "pull" much of anything off the Web without being hit with a barrage of banners, flags, junk e-mail, or other forms of pushing from advertisers and promoters. Political debates and culture wars about pornography and sexual activity, hate speech, and other issues such as viruses, "spam" (fully 85 percent of all e-mail traffic in the world is spam), and hackers have brought about calls for regulatory legislation and censorship, euphemistically referred to as "content filtering." Today we are seeing the end of the "borderless" Internet, as nation-states assert their sovereignty and attempt to "territorialize" the network and bring it under their control. "The result is an Internet that differs among nations and regions that are increasingly separated by walls of bandwidth, language, and filters."[16]

And finally, we have seen a host of unpleasant consequences of the wired life not anticipated by its cheerleaders. Encouraged by the relatively inexpensive hardware and the proliferation of portable wireless devices such as laptops, smartphones, and tablets, Americans are staring at one kind of a screen or another for close to eight hours a day, more time than most sleep. The average teen grinds through an astounding 3,700 texts a month, a disturbing number of them while driving a car. "Internet addiction" has now been recognized as a disorder by the American Psychiatric Association while others are treated for compulsively gambling and watching pornography online. Neuroscientist Peter Whybrow claims that "the computer is like electronic cocaine," cycling us through manic and depressive episodes.[17] After surveying the growing body of scientific evidence on Internet use, Nicholas Carr, author of *The Shallows: What the Internet Is Doing to Our Brains*, says that the constant distractions and interruptions present in working on the Web are turning us into scattered and superficial thinkers.[18] Carr argues that, "People who read text studded with links, the studies show, comprehend less than those who read words printed on pages. People who watch busy multimedia presentations remember less than those who take in information in a more sedate and focused manner. People who are continually distracted by emails, updates and other messages understand less than those who are able to concentrate. And people who juggle many tasks are often less creative and less productive than those who do one thing at a time."[19] And since much of our time using the Internet at work involves sitting at desks and using repetitive motions deploying a keyboard and a mouse, deleterious physical consequences proliferate. One journalist posed the question, "Is Sitting a Lethal Activity?" while millions suffer from carpel tunnel syndrome, tendonitis, and back and shoulder injuries.[20]

If the Web was to become "much like the rest of social life," then we should have anticipated what it would look like today. Utopian visions aside, "cyberspace," the term coined by *dys*topic science fiction writer William Gibson, looks pretty much like the rest of our postmodern social space; both are deeply mired in consumer culture, corporate control, the fragmentation of information, hypersexuality, voyeurism, and surveillance.[21] As I have outlined, postmodern surveillance practices tend to have four main characteristics: they are technology-based, applied automatically and anonymously, and generate knowledge and evidence; they target the body as an object that can be watched and assessed; they are local and dispersed, operating in everyday life; and they manage to bring wide-ranging populations, not just the official "deviant," under scrutiny.

In what follows, I argue that the Internet and Web are consistent with this descriptive type. My point is not that the Web was designed specifically as a surveillance tactic but rather that, like any other tool, it can be adapted to and used for multiple purposes. So, clearly, the Internet is technologically driven and, as I will show, capable of collecting and storing massive amounts of information "quietly" and anonymously. With its visual capabilities, the Internet can be used to watch, monitor, and display our bodies to millions of people, with or without the permission of the person being watched. And much like Michel Foucault characterized the capillary nature of disciplinary power, as a network, the Internet extends out to the remotest corners of society, circulating throughout social life. It is, for now at least, like Kevin Kelly says: "distributed" and "headless." It is not operated from the "top down," but functions "bi-directionally" (e.g., a company can monitor their employees' work habits on the network while "hackers" can use the same system to infiltrate that corporation's files. At the same time, others are willingly making the details of their own lives available on the Web for others to see), appearing nearly everywhere, dispersed, and fragmented. And, again, while not specifically designed as a surveillance tool, I will show how the Internet and its assorted components and practices are indeed being used for this purpose.

A WEB OF SECURITY

In the realm of criminal justice, the Internet's capillary nature has brought an empowered gaze onto those no longer serving time behind bars and now needing to be watched over. In addition to "electronically monitored house arrest" and GPS tracking systems—both of which are run with the help of the Internet—web-based "offender registries" identify and provide the public information on the residential location of convicted reprobates. Like a digital "neighborhood watch" program, web-based registries increase the "pool of watchers" and enable each citizen to participate "in the labor of their own defense" and to perform their "mediated civic duty."[22] Following a number of high profile sex crimes or sexualized murder cases, President George W. Bush signed into law the Adam Walsh Child Protection and Safety Act of 2006 (the Adam Walsh Act). The act was intended "to protect the public from sex offenders and offenders against children . . . [and] establish a comprehensive national system for the registration of those offenders" in order to make sex offenders' information "accessible to anyone with the click of a button." Sex offender registration, then, is designed to maintain law enforcement and citizen surveillance over convicted offenders and aid in the investigation of new sex crimes.[23] In addition to the National Sex Offender website operated by the FBI, every state now has a Sex Offender Registry online and available for public use. In all fifty states, sex offenders who meet the registration criteria are required to register upon release, parole, supervised release, or probation. Intended to geographically identify convicted sex offenders, registries are typically searchable by zip code and geographic zone. The length of registration varies from state to state, depending on the offense and type of offender and ranging from ten years to life.

Picking up on the popularity of registries and rooted mostly in the perceived "safety" they bring as well as the punitive and stigmatizing nature of the tactic, legislatures and justice officials have broadened the offender field. Tennessee, Montana, Illinois, Minnesota, and a number of other states have created registries for those convicted of the sale, manufacture, or possession of methamphetamine. According to the 2005 bill in Tennessee, the purpose of online registry, which allows users to search for offenders by name or county of conviction, is, according to one report, "to empower communities." "It functions just like any other registry," said Tommy Farmer, director of the Tennessee Meth Task Force. "Not that their offenses are at all the same, but it's a very similar application to sex offender registries." The registry shows the name, offense, date of birth, date of conviction, and county of conviction of the offender; it does not, however show photographs of the offenders and they do not register annually. [24]

In my home state of Kansas, rather than build a separate database just for methamphetamine offenses, officials folded meth and all other drug offenders into an existing registry of violent and sex offenders. First-time offenders stay on the registry for ten years while repeat offenders are on it for life. The penalties for failing to keep the registry up-to-date are the same for all regardless of the offense. "It's a person-level crime (a violent felony) not to register, or failing to follow one of the rules of the registry," said Jennifer Roth, the legislative chair of the Kansas Association of Criminal Defense Lawyers to a reporter. "It's the same for everyone, regardless of whether your underlying offense was a violent crime or not." This could mean that a felony charge received for not maintaining your registry records could be more severe than that of your original offense. [25]

The online version of my hometown newspaper has the offender registry portal prominently displayed on the front page. In a box on the right-hand column between ads for a local pizzeria and the sports headlines—there is a color image of the back of a young man in a t-shirt and jeans with his hands in cuffs overlaying a map with colored pins on it. Below it reads: "We've mapped out all the registered sex, violent and drug offenders in Douglas County. Every week, we'll be updating the map to reflect any offenders who have moved in or out of the area. Check your neighborhood here." Selecting the link reveals a page with the following text:

> **Douglas County Registered Offender Map** The map below indicates all registered offenders in Douglas County. Red dots indicate sex offender, blue dots indicate violent offenders, green dots indicate drug offenders, and yellow dots indicate offenders with more than one offender designation. Offenders who have recently moved have a black dot inside their marker. **What is the Kansas Offender Registry?** The registry is an online service compiled by the Kansas Bureau of Investigation and lists the names, offenses, and addresses of Kansans convicted of certain sexual, violent, and drug crimes. **What type of information is available from the registry?** The registry includes home, work, and school addresses, as well as vehicle information and offenses committed for registered offenders, along with an updated picture. Citizens can sign up for alerts from the KBI, which will send out notifications when some-

one in a designated location changes an address. The registry also lists whether
or not an offender is compliant; that is, whether they verified their address with
law enforcement every several months as required by law.

Once you open the map and click on a pin, you have access to the person's
name, address—including a Google Street view of their residence—their
offense and year, age as well as a link to a photo, and any news article that
the paper did covering that individual's case.[26]
    Scholars argue that the appearance of sex offender registries are part-and-
parcel of the broader "get tough on crime" trend and follow a consistent
pattern of such laws being created following an isolated tragic incident often
involving a child, intense national media coverage, and ensuing "moral panic." While the dissemination of photos and addresses of known sex offenders
may serve to alert the public to possible "stranger danger," they unfortunately reinforce the idea that outsiders pose the greatest risk to children, when in
fact they are far more likely to be victimized by family members and ac-
quaintances.[27]
    Another postconviction, Internet surveillance, and monitoring tool is on-
line criminal record checks. Many states have made it easier for the public to
access the criminal histories of individuals, typically conducted for purposes
of employment screening, occupational licensing, and certifications. A
search engine request for "criminal background checks" reveals hundreds of
Web pages of private companies with names like "Criminal WatchDog,"
"BeenVerified," and "Intellius" who, for a fee, will conduct searches of
publicly available sources aggregated into proprietary databases. "Official"
repositories include "PACER" for federal criminal records and nearly every
state offers online criminal records searches (also for a fee).[28]
    According to one scholarly investigation, changes in access laws have
"combined with a greater ease of access afforded by technological developments, have fed a growing reluctance by employers to hire ex-offenders."[29]
Indeed, "blanket" ads for jobs stating, "Do Not Apply with Any Misdemean-
ors or Felonies" have meant that sixty-five million Americans—about one in
four adults with criminal convictions—are essentially locked-out of the job
market.[30] This situation has existed despite the fact that there is no evidence
that a previous conviction predicts the likelihood of any particular individual
creating a safety or security threat at work. Moreover, "A record may include
a wide swath of misleading information; not only is a criminal record difficult to interpret, it may include arrests that were dropped because of factual
innocence." Even worse, both commercially and even FBI background
checks have been found to have high levels of inaccuracy. "The bottom line,"
one advocacy group claims, "is that a criminal record can be a blunt, misleading tool to determine whether a worker poses a risk on the job."[31]

And finally, another example of how the Internet is facilitating surveillance and monitoring in the world of crime, justice, and security comes from the borderlands between Texas and Mexico. Here, the state-funded pilot program called the Texas Virtual BorderWatch was set up, which consists of a network of web-based cameras, online 24/7, and equipped with night-vision technology that can be viewed through a dedicated portal. The program allows anyone with an Internet connection to view the border as part of a "virtual posse" to watch for smuggling and illegal immigration.[32] In true neoliberal fashion, the program has morphed into a privately funded entity called, oddly, "BlueServo." Here is how they describe themselves:

> BlueServo[SM] deployed the Virtual Community Watch, an innovative real-time surveillance program designed to empower the public to proactively participate in fighting border crime.
> The BlueServo[SM] Virtual Community Watch[SM] is a FREE service consisting of a network of cameras and sensors along the Texas-Mexico border. . . . Users will log in to the BlueServo[SM] website and directly monitor suspicious criminal activity along the border via this virtual fence.
> Citizens can sign up as Virtual Texas Deputies[SM] to participate in border surveillance through this social network. Virtual Texas Deputies[SM] from around the country will monitor the streaming video from these cameras 24/7 and report any suspicious activities directly to the Border Sheriffs via email. All emails regarding suspicious activity will be submitted anonymously.
> This service will provide millions of dollars in benefits to local border Sheriffs, with the public acting as additional pairs of eyes for Deputies on the ground. This extra surveillance will allow the public to directly participate in reducing crime and improving their communities. It is a well-established fact that citizen involvement in community watch programs such as this one reduces crime.[33]

Exploiting the idea of "crowdsourcing"—that is, soliciting contributions from a large group of people rather than from, say, employees, and in this case online, as well as through social networking—the Texas Virtual BorderWatch helps increase the "pool of watchers" and transforms the citizenry into what Mark Andrejevic calls "interactive citizen-soldiers." As indicated, when the "Virtual Texas Deputies" spot something on one of the cameras, they report it via e-mail or on the group's Facebook page where users leave comments such as "on camera 4 . . . four to five people ran from left to right" or "swimmers on cam 13 now" to alert the sheriffs to border crossers. If a number of them report the same movement in the same area, border patrol agents move in.[34]

In postmodern fashion, "Virtual Texas Deputies" are just that: simulated law enforcement agents who can voyeuristically join in on a mediated surveillance experience justified for its altruistic intent. Robert Fahrenkamp, a truck driver in South Texas, claims that when he logs into blueservo.net, it "gives me a little edge feeling, like I'm doing something for law enforcement as well as for our own country."[35] Moreover, by linking itself to the Web, the system compresses social and geographical space, inviting anyone, anywhere to participate. Donald Reay, executive director of the Texas Border Sheriff's Coalition, says that "virtual deputies" have come from as far away as Australia. "They said in good Australian fashion, 'Hey, mate, we've been watching your border for you from the pub in Australia,'" Reay told a reporter.[36] Finally, comments by BlueServo user Rob Abernethy, a forty-two-year-old factory worker from Lincolnton, North Carolina, seem to reflect the mesmerized and bored postmodern subject when he told a reporter for CNN that watching BlueServo is "no worse than any other form of quick entertainment," adding that, "It's no different than watching *Everybody Loves Raymond* reruns. . . . It's just something to do."[37]

Sex offender registries, state-run online criminal background checks, and the Texas Virtual BorderWatch are criminal justice and "security" projects situated on the "hard" end of my spectrum of social control and reflect a number of postmodern surveillance themes. Each strategy exploits advanced information and communications technologies; digital repositories centralize information, some knitted together from multiple sources, and the Internet facilitates access and distribution of that information while surveillance cameras serve to generate new knowledge and evidence. All three strategies target the body as an object that can be watched directly or its description and prior behaviors packaged into digital case files. Much like disciplinary power itself, these tactics are capillary in nature, each circulating detailed information about individual lives—their geographic and social locations, and, in one case, even "real-time" views of potential threats—into the mundane, everyday settings of home offices, business cubicles, and, with mobile devices, even coffee shops and the like. And although all three strategies were initiated "from the top," that is, by the state, they operate bi-directionally, empowering the gaze of ordinary citizens—neighbors, business owners, and factory workers—creating what has been called a "synopicon"; a mechanism that makes possible the surveillance of the few by the many.[38]

"NOW EVERYTHING IS TRANSPARENT"

Of course, the Web appears now in innumerable areas of social life, working its way, like the roots of a rhizome, into the everyday settings of a wide range of institutions and organizations.[39] It does so by demonstrating extraordinary productivities and efficiencies and, in many cases, intentionally or not, advancing surveillance and accountability tactics that help maintain unbalanced and unequal authority relationships. For example, augmenting the surveillance practices already in place in schools across the country, many districts now produce and share detailed student performance measures with parents via the Web. PowerSchool (another interesting choice for a name) is, according to its owner Pearson, the giant international media and education company, "the fastest-growing, most widely used web-based student information system, supporting 10 million students in all 50 states and over 65 countries. *PowerSchool* enables today's educators to make timely decisions that impact student performance while creating a collaborative environment for parents, teachers and students to work together in preparing 21st century learners for the future."[40]

PowerSchool delivers amazing capabilities. Here is how Pearson Education describes some of its features:

> **Student and Parent Access** As a *PowerSchool* parent, you can check to see whether or not your child is in class right now, find out what tonight's homework is, confirm that last night's homework was handed in, and view your child's final grades as they exist in the teacher's grade book at this very moment. You can also track the formative progress of your child's performance on state standards, register to receive alert notifications, review the daily comments from teachers, and much more.
>
> **PowerTeacher** All classes, rosters, student demographic information, grading periods, standards, rubrics and grades scales are automatically loaded. As teachers use *PowerTeacher*, all data flows back to your central database in real time, providing all stake-holders, including parents and students with instant visibility to assignments, scores, grades, comments and progress toward each standard.
>
> *PowerTeacher Mobile* for the iPad untethers teachers from their desktop or laptop and allows them to record scores and make observations while roaming the classroom, gymnasium, blacktop, science lab or even on a field trip. [41]

There are about a dozen additional components to the system including tracking data on Immunization Screenings, Health Screenings, Family Management ("you can be sure that all of your families are correctly linked together and displaying accurate demographic data"), Address Management and Boundary Validation ("leverages Google mapping technology to validate student addresses, including the ability to visually determine whether an address is within district and school boundaries"), as well as Class Scheduling, Prerequisite Checking and Teacher Recommendations, Multiple Language Options, and more than two hundred built-in reports that examine minute student-based details. Reports run the gamut from "Discipline Log-A list of student discipline incidents by date . . . gender, ethnicity" to "Lunch Transactions—Report listing all lunch transactions for the student along with the current lunch balance." By weaving in health and immunization records as well as "Family Management" and residential mapping, the system becomes a "dense," information-rich corpus of each student's life.

Speaking about one of the main functions of PowerSchool, the real-time reporting of individual student progress, guidance counselor Karolyn Misa from Bogota, New Jersey, was quoted in a news article saying, "It really cut down on the lapse between when the student misses something and when we know it." Misa adds, "It gives me more leverage in terms of working with a student and staying on top of them." In the same article, the vice principal of the school, Damian Kennedy, said, "We always felt that it was important to have more communication with the parents and guardians of the kids [and now] they can actually view a real live teacher grade book of their students, with past and upcoming assignments. If a parent says, 'Hey, do you have any homework?' they can go online and see what's due on Monday," he said. Kennedy characterized life with the system this way: "Now everything is transparent." He went on, "We're very confident that it's going to be something that will help our students and our families open up communications with the school and help the students do better and improve their academics."[42]

As I suggested in chapter 3, from the viewpoint of disciplinary theory, the modern school is brimming with incessant examinations, assessments, and ritualized knowledge gathering. Seen from this perspective, PowerSchool intensifies and multiplies these effects by further routinizing and systematizing meticulous rituals of power and normalizing judgments about a student's performance and behaviors. For example, a "disciplinary incident" taking place on the playground or in the hallway, once handled informally or even forgotten before the teacher or vice principal returns to their office, is now easily noted on an iPad and becomes part of the "Disciplinary Log." In addition, with enhanced "transparency," the system attempts to invest, colonize, and link together the institutions of school and family—a relationship previously based more on informal, personal arrangements—as partners in the new surveillance network. As Pearson Education puts it, "online access to schedules, grades, homework, and attendance information makes it easy for parents and teachers to stay in close contact with student progress. In turn, this holds students more accountable for their own academic performance."

This linking, then, obviously creates a finer mesh of social control, permitting administrators and parents to vigilantly, remotely, and instantly monitor the behavior, whereabouts, and performance of students (a dream come true for the "helicopter parent"). But more, much like the Web that it operates on, PowerSchool empowers the gaze in a variety of directions, connecting all of the parties—administrators, teachers, parents, and students—in a hierarchical arrangement where individuals carry out the act of watching others while they themselves are being watched. In this way, they are all enmeshed in the disciplinary workings of the project.

For instance, not long after the system's adoption, teachers and administrators are likely to begin making normalizing judgments about a parent's "involvement" in their child's education as indicated by their level of engagement with PowerSchool. Indeed, one built-in report is called "Parent/ Student Net Access Log," which lists each time a parent accesses the parent portal, reporting the date, time, access type (phone or Internet), and the duration of the access. "But we reported on PowerSchool that Brittany was missing several homework assignments," parents will hear. "Didn't you check it?" Likewise, although the system has been supposedly "designed by teachers, for teachers" for the stated purpose of the "management" and assessment of their students, administrators can use the system to monitor teachers' activities on and through PowerSchool, the use of which has now become part of their job and performance criteria. A vigilant principal can tell which teachers are logged in and using the system, which ones have and have not taken attendance, entered their grades, and the like, as well as read their comments to parents. In 2013, the Clarksville-Montgomery County School district fired a twenty-seven-year veteran high school science teacher for being "negligent in her duties and insubordination." During an appeal hearing, the attorney representing the school system told the school board that the teacher "failed to update students' grades on the school system's online PowerSchool site and would not respond to parents' emails."[43] And even administrators are not immune; PowerSchool-generated "metrics" form the basis of cross-school and even cross-district comparisons, putting individual principals under scrutiny of the superintendent who, in turn, is under the watch of the school board.

Finally, students are encouraged to internalize the gaze on themselves through self-monitoring and self-discipline. "Students now have portable access to PowerSchool right from their iPhone®, iPod touch® or iPad®!" (There's even "an app for that!"). "PowerSchool for Students provides real-time access to: Attendance, School Announcements, Assignments, Assignment Scores, Teacher Comments . . . *PowerSchool for Students* is now available in the App Store!" To add to kids' relentless texting, PowerSchool offers the grade-obsessed, college-bound high school student up-to-the-minute feedback on their progress. "With the end of the school year looming ominously in the future," one news story goes, "seniors at Bismarck High School [ND] are feeling the pressure to prepare for the coming year in college. Several seniors started preparing months ago for important scholarships or the chance to earn spots in the program of their choice." Senior Michael Long told the reporter, "Homework has always come first, and I check *PowerSchool* every day and applied for every scholarship possible."[44]

It does not take much imagination to see the Web integrating and delivering images from the school's video camera system, data from RFID ID scans, and drug-testing results to an administrator or parent's screen. The fear and mistrust generated in a post-Columbine/Red Lake/Virginia Tech/New-town world are real, and these security "solutions" present themselves as attractive options.

"TOTAL BEHAVIORAL VISIBILITY"

The Web and "performance monitoring" come into play with a different twist in the workplace, revealing a certain paradox. On the one hand, we have thousands of companies trying to get us online, visiting their Web pages, buying their products, reading their news or sports coverage, and trading their stocks. On the other hand, the very technology that permits us to do this is installed in our workplaces where managers insist that computers and other company recourses be reserved only for appropriately "productive" uses. Firms are concerned about hostile work environments created by employees accessing adult-oriented websites, engaging in illegal activity, or leaking trade secrets, for example. The Web, then, is seen as both a source of and a threat to workplace productivity and security. The latest 2007 survey by the American Management Association and the ePolicy Institute found that 66 percent of companies surveyed monitor websites visited by employees. Typically, firms call on outside vendors who sell "Internet access management systems" for help. One dealer, Awareness Technologies, sells a bundle of products under the name InterGuard: "InterGuard defends your business from all insider threats . . . Webfiltering, Employee Monitoring and Laptop Recovery." They describe their webfiltering product this way:

> Blocking inappropriate web surfing is critical not only to ensuring the security of your organization, but also to ensuring that your employees are productive, but web surfing is only a part of how employees spend their time. InterGuard Webfiltering is designed to *extend your visibility* beyond a simple list of URLs and give you a true understanding of whether or not your employees are acting in a safe and productive manner.
> While other webfiltering applications are simply designed to enforce acceptable use policies, InterGuard Webfiltering helps define the policies that it enforces by giving you *total transparency* into how your employees spend their time. *With InterGuard, you'll see everything from everywhere.* No exceptions.[45]

With this system, a company can block specific websites or whole categories such as shopping, gambling, or job hunting websites. "Alert key words" generate actual screenshots of any activity carried out on computers producing video-like playback that "captures incontrovertible evidence." Journalist James Vlahos described how he saw firsthand the capabilities of another such system:

There's a man in Salt Lake City who knows what I did last summer. Specifically, he knows what I did on Aug. 24, 2007. He knows that I checked my EarthLink e-mail at 1:25 p.m., and then blew a half an hour on ESPN's Web site. He also knows that my wife, Anne, wanted new shoes, from Hush Puppies or DSW, and that she synced her electronic planner—"she has quite a busy schedule," the man noted—and downloaded some podcasts. We both printed out passes for free weeklong trials at 24 Hour Fitness, but instead of working out, apparently spent the evening watching a pay-per-view movie. It was *Bridge to Terabithia* or *Zodiac*, he thinks.[46]

The "man" was Joe Wilkinson, who works for Raytheon Oakley Systems, another company specializing in "insider risk management." Wilkinson had agreed to demonstrate the system after he used the Web to install an "agent" from the company's software SureView on Vlahos's home computer that reported back to Wilkerson all the activity that took place there. "Total Behavioral Visibility" is Raytheon Oakley's motto, and here we are, back again to the panoptic model, where a few can watch the many.[47]

Shifting to another setting, the same principles and procedures of "insider risk management" are now being applied by parents to their kids' wired lives. Seeing a new market opportunity, security companies like Symantec, Trend Micro, and Infoglide, as well as new start-ups, are cashing in on the insecurities and anxieties of the worried parents of the digital age. Symantec alone claims it added a million new subscribers to its Norton Online Family service in 2012. While not exactly as "military grade" capable as Raytheon's Sure-View, some companies sell products for the home that mimic the kind of "granular" level analysis, offer comparable features, and use similar terminology as those offered by sophisticated corporate Internet monitoring programs. For instance, for $9.95 per month, web-based uKnowKids.com, which dubs itself "The Best Parenting Tools in the World," offers the "world's first Parental Intelligence System that leverage[s] the team's tremendous knowledge of Internet security and risk management to help parents keep their social and mobile kids safe. . . . Our technology helps protect kids from predators, bullies and sexting. Unlike parental control software, uKnowKids enables parents to 'have their child's back' without constantly looking over his or her shoulder."[48] Here are some of the features:

> **Knowing your child is safe on Facebook, Twitter and Instagram.** uKnow-Kids automatically pulls all of your child's Facebook, Twitter and Instagram activities so that you can monitor what your child is doing online quickly and easily. Save time viewing all your child's social activities in one easy to understand dashboard.
> **Does your child have an Android or iPhone?** uKnowKids collects text messages, contacts, images, downloaded applications, check-ins and location history allowing you to understand what your child is doing with his or her smart phone in a matter of minutes . . . receive alerts for risky text messages, and

check to see if they have downloaded any apps you may not be comfortable
with.

And what exactly is "Parental Intelligence"?

> **Insight and Real-time Analytics** Our Parental Intelligence System adds a
> layer of insight and analytics to your uKnowKids Dashboard. Analyzing your
> child's numerous digital activities, our system crunches the data to find pat-
> terns and trends and translates it back to parents in a form that is easy to
> understand. [The webpage displays various pie-charts and graphs and looks
> like some kind of corporate report.]
> **Push Notifications for Risky Situations** As a parent, nothing is more impor-
> tant than protecting your child from dangerous situations and potential harm.
> Our Parental Intelligence System automatically flags keywords and phrases
> (relating to violence, sexual content, and more) and sends you a push notifica-
> tion via email or text.

And the product can translate cryptic teenage slang and texting shorthand
into words that even a "tool" of an adult can understand.

Computer security professional Dan Sherman of Jackson, New Jersey,
makes sure his two daughters' digital lives take place with his oversight. He
has loaded filters on home computers that block porn sites and track all
website activity, set parental controls, and limited access to all digital devices
owned by his family, and tracks his thirteen-year-old daughter's Facebook
account with MinorMonitor, which will alert him to the appearance of any
key words such as bullying or alcohol. When asked by a journalist if he
thought all this might make his daughters think he does not trust them,
Sherman replied, perceptively and realistically, that they should learn the
lesson that they will be monitored throughout their lives, "It's not any different from any employer." And internalizing the gaze of her parents, Sherman's thirteen-year-old recalled a recent episode when she stopped herself
from criticizing a classmate for spreading rumors about her on Facebook
because she knew her parents would not approve of her behavior: "Having
your parents monitor makes you think twice about what you put [online],"
she said.[49]

LOCATION, LOCATION, LOCATION

The old real estate adage about the importance of locality takes on new
meaning in a wired world. An extraordinary number of people now connect
to the Web via mobile devices and "location-based services" are made possible through the integration of the Internet, cellular networks, and GPS-
capable handheld devices. Location-based services enable you to do things
like navigate your way in a city, see your position or that of others on a map

in real time, help you find restaurants, stores, and other nearby points of interest or even track, analyze, and store data about your daily jog. In this section, I will introduce several examples of corporate-developed, location-based services that identify the whereabouts and enhance the visibility of individuals to others.

As I have already covered, electronic monitoring and GPS tracking in the criminal justice system has become commonplace, but so, too, has the remote monitoring of "mobile employees," their work vehicles, as well as cars driven by young adults. Now, the "real-time" tracking of cell phones with built-in GPS has been "normalized" since the introduction of AT&T's FamilyMap service, Verizon's Chaperone, and Sprint's Family Locator services. Adding these features is no different than upgrading your data plan—they cost $5 to $10 a month—and can show tracked phone locations on a web-based map. A more "robust" model comes from the vendor uKnowKids.com that I introduced previously. This company offers "Amazing Family Location Tools" as part of their "Premier Plan." Here is how they describe the service:

> **Find your child's location at any time, with any phone**
> uKnowKids family location tools include an unparalleled location-on-demand feature. You can locate your child . . . with the click of a button. No more wondering if your child is going where they said they were, no more worrying where they are if they are a few minutes past curfew. . . . Not knowing how to find out where your child is at any given time is an age old problem. . . . uKnowKids collects location coordinates from your child's social network checkins, geo-tagged posts and cell phone. His or her last known location will always appear on your Family Map for you to view at any time.
> **Location History, Geo-fences, and Scheduled Check ins**
> Three location monitoring tools no parent should be without. Every 30 minutes uKnowKids will capture your child's location so at the end of the day you can view where they have been. . . . In addition, uKnowKids offers you the unique ability to create "geo-fences" on our Family Map. A "geo-fence" is created by selecting a location and a perimeter around that location. . . . You will have the option to receive alerts when your child arrives and/or departs from your specified location. [50]

These extraordinary features suggest that the system is far more "advanced" than the ones we see operating in the criminal justice system. Is this kind of surveillance on the "soft" or "hard" end of the spectrum of social control? The bleary state of postmodern culture may mean that it is difficult to tell.

Of course, location-based services offer many other nifty capabilities. Early on, start-ups like "Foursquare" merged location and social networking to permit users to "check in" at different venues such as restaurants, stores, coffee shops, and so forth, using a mobile website, text messaging, or a device application. [51] By "checking in," you choose to broadcast your location to people you have identified as friends and they then know where you are. You also can earn points and "badges" for your check-ins and, if you "check in" enough times, you can even become the "mayor" of a location and earn special deals for doing so. The company tells us, "Foursquare is a free app that helps you and your friends make the most of where you are. When you're out and about, use Foursquare to share and save the places you visit." Youthful founder and CEO of Foursquare Dennis Crowley spoke in altruistic tones about the company's mission: "We can give all this data back to people to make their lives a little better."[52]

Cool, right? A "free," user-controlled way of linking up and socializing with your friends. The system even stores your past locations: "easily jump to all your past check-ins from any month or year, and even filter them by who you were with, what type of place you were at, or which neighborhood, city, or country you were in. We'll show you your check-in photos, comments, and friends who were there." And since Foursquare is integrated with Facebook and Twitter, your "check-in" can appear on those sites, as well. To date, the Foursquare "community" has over thirty million people worldwide with more than three billion check-ins daily.

But there is more. Foursquare goes on, "And, when you're looking for inspiration for what to do next, we'll give you personalized recommendations and deals based on where you, your friends, and people with your tastes have been." Hmm . . . For all of its attempts to make our lives "better," Foursquare had to have a business plan to make money and survive. In other words, it had to "monetize" location and the associated information it was collecting about its users.[53]

So, like so many other "free" web-based services, you pay not with your dollars but with your data. Foursquare is selling *you* and your location to businesses in the area that want your patronage and Foursquare becomes the delivery system that allows brands to pay for advertising messages to consumers who are in the vicinity of a restaurant, store, or other businesses. This is called "contextual advertising;" the more you use Foursquare, the more they learn about your "tastes," habits, and movements. Foursquare is very open about how important your data is: "Remember: each time you check in, you're teaching us about the restaurants, bars, and shops you like." Foursquare can break down the data they have collected about what types of customers visit what stores and other venues and sell it to them. In the near future, users of Foursquare might get alerts on their phones when they pass by a store that carries an item on their Amazon "wish list."

Responding to the question of privacy issues with the use of Foursquare, cofounder Naveen Selvadurai states that, "Users decide if they want to push to Twitter or Facebook, over what information they want to share and send" and that "There is a lot of misunderstanding about location based services. On Foursquare, if you don't want people to know you are on a date or with a friend at a certain place, then you don't have to let people know."[54] In spite of the technical ability to "opt out," the work of behavioral economist Alessandro Acquisti suggests that, while we profess to value our privacy, many of us are hurried and distracted, don't monitor our activities that closely, and can be easily enticed to turn over our data in exchange for a "deal" or other reward. [55]

This is the genius of Foursquare; it takes advantage of these qualities and, by using the appeal of social networking, the provision of "recommendations," and competitive games, it keeps people contributing to the exchange and "nudges" them to patronize one business over another. In this way, while a "soft" form of social control, Foursquare and others like it are attempting to use rewards or privileges to accomplish their goal of modifying behavior; to transform the fickle consumer into the tractable participant. "Training" a person to "check in" wherever they go, then, is another variant of meticulous rituals of power; this is a small, knowledge-gathering strategy, enhanced by new information and communications technologies, that is faithfully repeated without resistance—indeed with enthusiastic participation—as it produces accomplices in certain consumer conduct. When I think of this "training," I cannot help but envision rats in the operant conditioning chamber invented by radical behaviorist B. F. Skinner (1904–1990) that stumble upon the lever, which when pressed, produces a food pellet. Once rewarded, they press it over and over again.

One final point related to location-based services, Foursquare, and surveillance. Not long ago, a geolocation iPhone application called "Girls around Me" was created by Russian-based i-Free Innovations. The app used publicly available information from Foursquare to enable men (or anyone) to locate women in the vicinity on a map and even pull up information about them and their photos from their Facebook profiles. When you opened the app, the design consisted of James Bond–style silhouettes of naked women dancing and posing provocatively. On their website promoting the app, it stated, "In the mood for love, or just after a one-night stand? Girls around Me puts you in control! Reveal the hottest nightspots, who's in them, and how to reach them. . . . Browse photos of lovely local ladies and tap their thumbnail to find out more about them." They go on, "Girls around Me is the perfect complement to any pick-up strategy. And with millions of chicks checking in daily, there's never been a better time to be on the hunt." In a short time, the app was downloaded over seventy thousand times.

Word of the app eventually went viral and John Brownlee, a writer for the blog *The Cult of Mac*, wrote a piece calling the app "creepy" and a potential "tool for rapists and stalkers." [56] Criticism grew as others pointed out that, although the women brought under the gaze of Girls around Me had signed up for Facebook and did indeed "check in" with Foursquare, they had not "opted in" to the Girls around Me "service" nor were they aware that they were being surveilled in this way. Sensing a publicity nightmare, Foursquare pulled the plug on the application's access to its technology. In response, i-Free Innovations stated that they were simply exploiting the technology as others were doing. "Girls around Me app was designed to make geo-social exploration of popular venues easy and visual. We follow the geo-social trend for mobile devices that is supported by numerous location sharing services, networks and apps. Many other mobile apps provide the same or more extended functionality using location data provided by . . . [the] major social networks," and that "since the app's launch we've seen numerous positive comments from users who claimed that the app helped them to discover 'hot spots'—venues that are popular among girls or boys. . . . [W]e believe it is unethical to pick a scapegoat to talk about the privacy concerns."[57]

DATA MINING FOR E-GOLD

The business of buying and selling goods and services over the Internet, or "e-commerce," has in the last twenty years produced staggering entrepreneurial success stories and colossal failures. During the "innovation" stage of the late 1990s, Internet-related companies were all the rage and they helped to generate a historic speculative bubble as investors, ignoring basic business principles and economic logic, wanted "in" at all costs. Described prophetically by then Federal Reserve Board chairman Alan Greenspan as "irrational exuberance," the market for the "dot-com" stocks peaked to historic highs on March 10, 2000—and then the bottom fell out. Within months, the tech-laden Nasdaq Composite stock index lost 78 percent of its value and many companies simply evaporated. E-commerce then entered a "consolidation" phase as firms like Amazon weathered the downturn and came away bigger and more powerful while "brick-and-mortar" firms began to use the Web to enhance their existing businesses. By 2006, e-commerce is said to have entered its current "reinvention" stage, as social networking and Web 2.0 applications (e.g., social networking, blogs, wikis, video sharing sites, hosted services) have helped reinvigorate e-commerce and encourage new business models.[58]

A leading market research firm predicted that e-commerce and online retail sales in the United States in 2012 would reach $226 billion, an increase of 12 percent over 2011, with consumers' average yearly online spending increasing from $1,207 per person in 2011 to $1,738 per person by 2016. Online sales are expected to grow from 7 percent of overall retail sales to close to 9 percent by 2016. This analysis credits the growth to greater comfort level by consumers with purchasing various goods online, enhanced Web shopping capabilities with mobile and tablet devices, innovative shopping models that divert spending away from physical stores (e.g., flash sales, subscription models), online loyalty programs, and aggressive promotional offers from Web retailers. Many people shop online daily. In 2011,167 million consumers, or 53 percent of the U.S. population, purchased something online. That number is expected to grow to 192 million, or 56 percent of the population, by 2016.[59]

With so much at stake, the practitioners of e-commerce are willing to draw upon all the marketing schemes, "psychographics," and other "data mining" techniques I have already mentioned to identify, track, and collect copious amounts of information on potential customers. The goal of all this "dataveillance" energy is to target desirable "prospects" for highly individualized courting and, ultimately, to turn the capricious buyer into a responsive customer. As I pointed out in chapter 3, the extent of this monitoring suggests that we are now living in a "surveillance economy" where specialized companies collect, process, aggregate, deploy, or sell comprehensive and detailed information about us. To these companies, we are not consumers but rather commodities that are bundled and sold off to advertisers. For example, "data compilers" collect a wide variety of information from both public databases, like property ownership and the like, and third-party sources in order to assess a consumer's financial status, sex, race/ethnicity, buying habits, hobbies, health status, travel preferences, Internet providers, and social networks. One of the biggest compilers, Acxiom Corporation, based in Conway, Arkansas, has constructed the world's largest consumer database containing information about five hundred million active consumers worldwide, with about 1,500 data points per person.[60] The company manages customer databases for or works with forty-seven of the Fortune 100 companies and even provided the government with information about eleven of the nineteen hijackers following the 9/11 terrorist attacks. Acxiom uses their vast data warehouse to engage in "database marketing," a form of personalized direct marketing that statistically models customer behavior to select the best customers to pitch products and services to; the more data, the more accurate the targeting and personalization. Acxiom offers its work with Macy's department store as a retail case study:

> At Macy's, the customer is definitely "Queen," and every decision is made with her in mind. . . . When it comes to customer intelligence, Macy's sets a high threshold. "Knowing her" now means not only capturing her basic household and customer information such as primary addresses, email addresses, and phone numbers; but also having secondary addresses, purchase and promotional history, demographics, attitudinal data, survey responses, and online activity with Macy's. With Acxiom's InfoBase®, the nation's largest repository of customer intelligence, Macy's can ensure CIM [Customer Intelligence at Macy's] records reflect a multidimensional view of her. InfoBase enhances CIM customer records with details such as buying activity and preference outside of Macy's, behavioral data, as well as life stage events like births, marriages or home purchases. . . . It also allows the retailer to focus invest-

ments on reaching and engaging only those people who are Macy's target customers, while reducing investment in unproductive marketing activities. [61]

Yet another type of company, called an ad-trading platform, profiles Internet users and auctions off online access to them to marketers in a practice called "real-time bidding." A company called BlueKai, for example, enables its customers like Kayak and Expedia to target and track more than two hundred million of us based on what we browse and buy online. Here is how one journalist describes the process if, say, you were planning a vacation to Hawaii and visited a travel website like Expedia:

> With the travel site's cooperation, BlueKai puts a cookie on your computer that records the fact that you have looked up flights from San Francisco to Maui with a seven-day advance purchase. BlueKai's extensive partnership network enables it to follow more than 160 million people every month who are looking to buy things like cars, financial services, retail and consumer goods or travel accommodations. By sorting users into categories based on our interests and purchasing power—"midscale thrift spenders," for example, or "safety-net seniors"—BlueKai's software helps advertisers determine how much each of us is worth following, and at what price. Advertisers for Hawaiian hotels, restaurants, car-rental companies, souvenir shops and so on then place bids starting at one or two cents for each anonymous consumer. The winning bidder—the Maui Hyatt Regency, for instance—next goes to an advertising exchange, like Google's DoubleClick Ad Exchange, which conducts a separate auction to determine what the Hyatt has to pay to send you an ad whenever you show up on a Web page that has a relationship with Double-Click. The Hyatt bids against the entire pool of other would-be advertisers who may not know that you want to vacation in Hawaii and therefore bid less to send you an ad. The automated auction is conducted in real time, which means that as soon as the Maui Hyatt wins the auction, its ad shows up within milliseconds of your loading a given Web page. [62]

So, if you are interested in what Macy's has to offer or looking for a place to stay in Hawaii, doesn't all this make perfect sense? After all, who wants all that annoying "junk mail" for products and services we're not interested in? Setting aside for the moment concerns about vast, centralized databases of personal information that we have little control over, these companies are involved in a process of "social sorting" that ranks and classifies some people as high-value "target customers" while others are summarily dismissed as low-value and not worthy of attention; the latter folks are known in industry parlance as simply "waste." [63] One result of these strategies is "personalized pricing," a tactic used, for example, by the travel site Orbitz. After some data mining told the company that Mac users spend 30 percent more on hotel rooms than Windows users, the company began sending ads to Mac users for hotels that are 11 percent more expensive than the ones that other users were seeing.

Data about a person's race or ethnicity may also be used to target them for ads for "ethnic" foods or products. Joel R. Reidenberg, professor at the Fordham Law School says, "At the same time, this is ethnic profiling. The people on this list, they are being sold based on their ethnic stereotypes."[64] These forms of "web lining" and "digital discrimination" help to reinforce social and economic inequalities and may even affect a person's life chances. For example, traditional credit scores have been around for some time and many companies have ranked consumers by their socioeconomic status. Today, we have data brokers that produce "e-scores," an algorithmic-generated assessment of your likelihood of spending money on certain goods and services. The score is a product of your occupation, salary, home value, as well as your spending and shopping habits. A company called eBureau calculates the scores of about twenty million American adults each month, selling off their names to a variety of businesses looking to target certain customers. The CEO of eBureau, Gordy Meyer, claims that the scores help his clients answer questions any business has about possible customers. "Are they legitimate?" Meyer asks. "Are they worth pursuing? Are they worth spending money on?"[65]

But, since banks, insurance companies, and large employers may deploy these data, access to quality health services, getting a competitive mortgage rate, knowledge about educational opportunities, even getting a job may depend on the quality of your "digital DNA." And once tagged with a low e-score or pigeon-holed as "waste" or another low desirability category, it may become exceedingly difficult to shed that classification since the very opportunities not offered might be the ones that permit us to move out of these boxes. Although the scores may be helpful for companies, as one journalist put it, "they may send some consumers into a downward spiral, locking them into a world of digital disadvantage." Frank Pasquale, a professor at Seton Hall University School of Law, says, "I'm troubled by the idea that some people will essentially be seeing ads for subprime loans, vocational schools and payday loans while others might be seeing ads for regular banks and colleges, and not know why." The lack of awareness on the part of the consumer is a central issue. Ed Mierzwinski, consumer program director at the U.S. Public Interest Research Group in Washington, "There's a nontransparent, opaque scoring system that collects information about you to generate a score—and what your score is results in the offers you get on the Internet," he says. "In most cases, you don't know who is collecting the information, you don't know what predictions they have made about you, or the potential for being denied choice or paying too much."[66]

CU SEE ME

In retrospect, the marriage of inexpensive video technology and the Internet was inevitable. The original matrimony was made in a college computer lab at the University of Cambridge and predates the Web itself. The "coffee camera" began with an experiment in networking in 1991, when researchers from several parts of the building put the technology they were developing to work to ensure that they knew when a fresh pot of coffee had been brewed. Output from a video camera pointed at the coffee machine was posted on their computers into still pictures, updated every second or two. Today, there are millions of "webcams" worldwide—open access ones, closed-loop systems, and "pay-per-view" ones—"jacked" into the Web creating a vast conglomeration of human voyeurism, exhibitionism, and narcissism.[67] The cameras have become standard equipment on laptops, tablets, and televisions or can be purchased separately as an "add-on" feature to many devices. Webcams and their use, like other video technologies, reflect both our serious and playful fascination with the camera's gaze.

The array of topics, territories, and targets of webcams that can be accessed through the Web is simply astonishing. A leading portal, "Earth-Cam—Where the World Watches the World," claims to be "the premiere network of scenic webcams and offers a complete searchable database of interesting places and views from around the world . . . [and] is viewed by fans in 192 countries and ranks among the top 1% of all websites." The site includes everything from views of major monuments around the world, to a supposedly haunted house in Sweden, to a lava lamp in someone's home in Thailand. There are views of a chicken coop in Bradford, England; pandas in the Washington, D.C., zoo; a birdfeeder in Estes Park, Colorado; a casino in Las Vegas; and a pizza joint in Goiânia, Brazil. "EarthCam Mobile" permits people to access EarthCam's network of live webcams on mobile devices and the WebCamStore is EarthCam's full-service e-commerce site selling webcam technology.

In addition to all this "virtual tourism"—that from time to time happens to "capture" people's foibles that then go viral—and views of incredibly mundane settings, webcams have been put to more "productive" uses. The devices have been installed in various organizations for video conferencing, in schools for a host of learning applications, and of course as "Voiceover IP" video chat over the Internet with software such as Skype. In addition, a company called TrueLook sells systems for time-lapse video for construction sites "to more effectively control costs, manage subcontractors, reduce travel expense, handle scheduling conflicts, and create a visual audit trail . . . for remote construction management" as well as resort marketing webcams, and live-event webcams. The company claims that "Our cameras have delivered over 2.2 billion images from every continent on the globe."[68]

A popular service offered by daycare centers to parents is streaming video feeds of their child's room, playground, and other parts of the facility. (Of course this kind of system is only open to those with accounts and the like, but given the ability of hackers and others to infiltrate much more sophisticated schemes, one has to wonder how really secure they are.) One company, "WatchMeGrow . . . Anywhere," pitches their services to daycare operators asserting that, "Offering WatchMeGrow will give your school a marketing edge—families are increasingly including 'webcams' in their childcare center selection. . . . WatchMeGrow video helps you extend your 'open door' policy so your families can see all the great things going on at your childcare center." Indeed, posted "Parent Testimonials" tell us quite a lot about the anxieties of working parents, the potent fear in the culture, the meaning of surveillance for family members, as well as the acceptance, nay, *request* for this form of monitoring.

> I can watch my daughter during the day. I see what she is doing and what she is not doing. She ask [*sic*] me most days when I pick her [*sic*] "did you watch me on the camera today."—Georgia

> I think it's a great idea, gives you peace of mind . . . you can watch your baby grow in a safe environment with people that care and have nothing to hide.—Nevada

> I could see what he was doing which created the trust much more quickly. With all that's going on today, I honestly cannot understand why a daycare provider wouldn't provide this option.   New Hampshire

> It made going back to work easier after the birth of our second child. Now that my oldest has started kindegarted [*sic*], I am going through withdrawal. Why can't you be everywhere?—Texas

> We love knowing that we can check up on the kids at any time and see what's happening and see the teachers. Our five-year-old asks us daily if we watched him.—Florida

> I feel that if the childcare center can trust their employees with our kids, they can trust that we, as parents, we will see that our kids are in hands that really do care.—North Carolina

Like the PowerSchool system discussed earlier, WatchMeGrow engenders multidirectional gazes that reinforce the hierarchical structure of this setting. So while parents and family members are permitted to "check-up" on their kids, they are able to view the staff's behavior as they interact with the children as well as the status and condition of the facility, a reflection of the owner's performance. The owner/director, in turn, can systematically monitor the center's employees "24/7 from anywhere and always know that your employees are maintaining your high standards." And demonstrating the productive and "corrective" elements of this postmodern surveillance scheme, the vendors of WatchMeGrow submit that administrators can "Raise Accountability—Your staff will perform better when they know you may be observing" as well as provide "Enhanced Training—Seeing is believing—you can train your teachers more effectively by showing them video of their interactions." Finally, like the adaptive quality that Bentham saw in the design of his panopticon, where "Persons of any description are to be kept under inspection," this system of surveillance is marketed as a tool to be deployed not only on children, but also on a variety of other clientele including the elderly, pets at kennels, and office workers.

RESTLESS VOYEURS

Webcams, whether aimed at the Eiffel Tower or a chicken coop in England, contribute to postmodern "placelessness" and offer images that are cybernetic simulations and virtual representations of "real" places and experiences. This technology has spawned a variety of other gazes, as well. For instance, one segment of the hypersexualized Internet is "reality" pornography, which includes amateur porn and other erotic material produced to look like spontaneous, authentic, and "real" sexual escapades, as opposed to the theatrics and predictableness of "mainstream" commercial porn. Following the postmodern adage, "The illusion has become real and the more real it becomes, the more desperately they want it," the quest in this "pornscape" is, as Ruth Barcan argues, to capture authenticity, "brazenness" or "rawness."[69] For example, a search of webpages devoted to "voyeurism" reveals hundreds involved in the distribution, exchange, and sale of erotic pictures and video supposedly taken of people without their knowledge. (Whether any of these images are "real" voyeurism or simply staged is anyone's guess and, of course, this goes to my point.) One site, called Peepholecam.com, includes "hidden" Webcam footage from devices supposedly set up by landlords and others with "Over 1,000 movies and 900,000 Archived Pictures!" Other sites contain images from restrooms, hotels, clothing-store dressing rooms, tanning booths, and high school locker rooms as well as clips from "up skirts" (where cameras are positioned in such a way so as to look up women's clothing in public places). Enterprising "e-pornographers" have tried to convert the "bored" housewife, the college coed, "your best friend's mother," and other adolescent male fantasies into cash by setting up "real-life" voyeuristic scenarios. Although the bulk of these images involve "ordinary" people, celebrities are high-valued targets and, as I mentioned in chapter 3, when "caught on tape" paparazzi-style photos and video of them flood the Internet, their amateur-looking "private" sex tapes going viral.

While the availability and viewing of these and other kinds of erotic material is not, strictly speaking, a postmodern surveillance practice as I have specifically defined it—there is not a clear disciplining and social control intent in all this—I discuss them here because I argue that this "eroticization" of surveillance promotes a culture where watching and being watched is both fetishized and normalized in everyday life and in commonplace settings. Moreover, voyeuristic and other pornscapes, facilitated by webcams and the Internet, serve to reinforce the postmodern blurring of the lines between the private and the public. Here, we see the proliferation of webpages set up by people who install webcams in their homes and charge others a fee to watch them go about their daily lives. As Peter Weibel suggests, this phenomenon unites "the pleasure principle of the voyeur, to see everything, and the pleasure principle of the exhibitionist, to show all" and contributes to a shift "from private drives to public norms."[70]

One of the innovators in this practice was then college junior Jennifer Ringley, who, in 1996, thought it would be fun to hook up a digital camera to her computer and let it post a photo to the Web every two minutes. She later created JenniCAM, added more cameras and, to offset the cost, began to charge for access to the website. At its peak, her site received five hundred thousand visits in a day. The cameras in her apartment, one in the bedroom and one in the living room, were on twenty-four hours a day, seven days a week. How did this young woman feel about her public performance? On her then website, Ringley tried to explain her site and her motivations; I think her answers are very much a reflection of the attributes of the postmodern self and its contradictions:

Why are you giving up your privacy like this?
Because I don't feel I'm giving up my privacy. Just because people can see me doesn't mean it affects me—I'm still alone in my room, no matter what. And as long as what goes on inside my head is still private, I have all the space I need. On the other hand, if someone invented a TelepathyCam where you could hear everything I was thinking, I must admit I'd be a bit more squeamish. *wink*

You're naked sometimes, is this pornography?
Pornography is in the eye of the beholder. Myself, I do not think this constitutes pornography. Most often, pornography is defined as something explicit which is made with the clear intention of arousing the viewer. Yes, my site contains nudity from time to time. Real life contains nudity. Yes, it contains sexual material from time to time. Real life contains sexual material. However, this is not a site about nudity and sexual material. It is a site about real life.

Called the first "life caster," "Internet star," and even "conceptual artist," Ringley shut down her site on December 31, 2003, citing PayPal's antinudity policy. Out of the public gaze for a while, Ringley stated, "I really am enjoying my privacy now. I don't have a web page; I don't have a MySpace page. It's a completely different feeling, and I think I'm enjoying it."[71]

But Ringley had started something. Today, millions of people use social media, YouTube, and other new media formats to promote themselves and hope that their popularity measured by the number of "views" and "hits" they generate will turn them into "Must-Follow" personalities.[72] This activity, once again, reflects the video-centeredness of the contemporary period and how the Internet facilitates what Derber calls our "pursuit of attention" and "democratization of celebrity."[73] After all, this is a media where it seems anyone can become a "star"—a bored college student like Jennifer Ringley, a mediocre actor like Perez Hilton, or a former telemarketer like Matt Drudge.

Hollywood picked up on the theme of entertainment voyeurism with the film, *The Truman Show*. The movie's central character, Truman Burbank, has his entire life, from birth on, broadcast live to the world "without commercial break and without interruption." Five thousand cameras record Truman's life; yet in this case, he does not have a clue that his wife, boss, friends, and strangers are all actors. Speaking of the film at the time, yet possibly indicative of the postmodern JenniCAM phenomena, film critic Janet Maslin defined "Trumania" as an "obsessive national interest in the surreal ordinariness of Truman Burbank" that is manifested "by a willingness to find the most nondescript of Truman's experiences more poignant and meaningful than one's own."[74] Of course, following JenniCAM and Truman, "reality" television became all the rage where, as David Bell suggests, the "logics, aesthetics and cultural understandings of reality shows like *Big Brother* are intimately enmeshed in the culture of surveillance. For example, the omnipresence of the camera's gaze on set and the countless ways that contestants respond to being filmed, both consciously and unconsciously, make shows like *Big Brother* experiments in surveillance as much as they are supposed experiments in interpersonal relations. . . . It teaches us all about how to act in front of an ever-watchful camera, and about the power of images caught on camera."[75]

Ever since Jennifer Ringley became a "ewebrity," hundreds of "personal" websites have appeared touting "true" and "real" amateur exhibitionists. The range of these sites seems to run the gamut from noncommercial websites run by people who participate in subcultures of exhibitionism to high-trafficked, profit-making portals that bring together hundreds of wanna-be actors, strippers, and porn industry "stars" who will cavort, strip, and masturbate for the audience for payment. One portal I accessed, with only a few mouse clicks, had more than 1,300 virtual peepshows taking place in living rooms and bedrooms around the world where spectators and performers text back and forth, and where "private" chats and Skype sessions are optional. "Tips" are made with purchased tokens. Another variant of self-made exhibitionism is produced with cell phones. A "camera phone cutie" snaps a shot of oneself, and posts it to a website, and as Bell argues, "the intimacy of the camera user connection is further played on in images where the phone appears in shot, almost like a sex toy."[76]

In these and other cases, new technologies such as powerful smartphones and inexpensive, high quality webcams and other equipment have "democratized access to image-making technologies and to circuits of both amateur and commercial exchange of images"[77] and, as Bell points out, have created a "surveillance aesthetic—where the technologies and staging of pornographic images plays on ideas of surveillance, voyeurism, and exhibitionism and where the technologies of surveillance structure the narrative, the action and most importantly the 'look' of porn."[78]

Although the panopticon exemplified modern surveillance within the confines of the modern disciplinary institution, I would argue that the Internet is capable of facilitating and delivering prototypical *post*modern surveillance practices. The strategies I have introduced are technologically advanced, dispersed and locally situated, automated, knowledge-gathering procedures that watch or assess the body, and are aimed at surveilling and disciplining a variety of subjects—from "official" deviants to all potential ones. As Foucault prophetically notes, "[T]he massive, compact disciplines are broken down into flexible methods of control, which may be transferred and adapted."[79] Disciplinary power, in these cases, is exercised in a multidirectional, capillary network; it appears nearly everywhere, dispersed and fragmented. At the same time, it links individuals and organizations in a complex web of empowered gazes that reinforce and reproduce hierarchical relations. The Net, then, for all its hyperbolic promise of liberation and freedom, must also be understood as a potential tool for fostering and maintaining unbalanced and unequal authority relationships.

As I have shown here, the Internet facilitates meticulous rituals of power across my continuum of social control. On the "hard" side, it enables the state to increase the "pool of watchers" by eliciting the help of the citizenry to keep track of sex offenders, restrict the employment opportunities of convicted criminals, and engage in border surveillance in protection of the "homeland." These "synoptic" surveillance ceremonies make possible the watching of the few by the many. In the "middle ground" of my spectrum are tactics like PowerSchool, "insider risk management" schemes in the work places, and geotracking capabilities of uKnowKids. Finally, on the "softer" side, companies like Foursquare are using location-based social networking to learn about people's "tastes," habits, and movements and to poke and prod them to make certain choices. Other firms use the Internet in ritualized knowledge-gathering activities that build extensive case files out of the smallest, most mundane details of our lives, often without us even knowing. By increasing the amount of knowledge they have about us, private companies create "information asymmetry," and by decreasing the amount of control we have over that information, these firms shift the balance of power in their favor. We are thus vulnerable to being "targeted" for marketing campaigns that bring all the "intelligence" gathered about us together with the power of the human sciences in an attempt to shape and influence our choices, behaviors, and social and cultural activities. One outcome is the "social sorting" of the populace into "high-value" people who need to be courted and offered "the best" treatment and "low-value" ones who can summarily be dismissed as system "waste." The discriminatory practices of social sorting are likely to enhance the life-chances of some while diminishing those of others.

But more, webcams "jacked in" to the Net contribute to the "ecstasy of communication": a deluge of images—voyeuristic gazes and exhibitionist delights—cascading into our screens from anywhere at any time. To reiterate Denzin, "The postmodern person is a restless voyeur, a person who sits and gazes (often mesmerized and bored) at [a] screen. This is a looking culture, organized in terms of a variety of gazes."[80] The Internet promotes many of these contemporary gazes; gazes that not only reveal the private and make it public, but that obliterate the very distinction between the two. Webcams, once installed in "public" spaces, do not distinguish between those who choose to be on camera and those who do not, while video voyeurs can position their cameras in "private" spaces and sell their files to e-pornographers. At the same time, Web exhibitionists can transform their "private" spaces at home into "sets" to display their bodies—for fun or profit—to anyone willing to watch them eat breakfast, change their clothes, or have sex. "Obscenity begins when there is no more spectacle," Baudrillard reminds us, where there are "no more illusions, when everything becomes immediately transparent, visible, exposed in the raw and inexorable light of information and communication."[81]

Chapter Six

The Anatomy of Visibility

It had to be like a faceless gaze that transformed the whole social body into a field of perception: Thousands of eyes posited everywhere, mobile attentions ever at the alert, a long hierarchized network.—Michel Foucault[1]

What I apprehend immediately when I hear the branches cracking behind me is not that there is someone there; it is that I am vulnerable; that I have a body which can be hurt; that I occupy a place and I cannot in any case escape from this space in which I am without defense—in short, I am seen. Jean Paul Sartre[2]

In the future, everyone will be famous for fifteen minutes.—Andy Warhol

The purpose of this book has been to describe and examine some of the surveillance and disciplinary techniques that have become part of contemporary life. Guided by the ideas of Michel Foucault, I have centered my observations on the intersection of power, knowledge, and the body. Most generally, I have included microtechniques of discipline—often enhanced by the use of new information and visual, communication, and medical technologies—that target and treat the body as an object to be watched, assessed, and manipulated. This anatomy of visibility is built on local, meticulous rituals of power; knowledge-gathering activities that involve surveillance, information, and evidence collection and analysis that increasingly compose our daily lives as students, workers, consumers, and community members. I have argued that these new disciplinary techniques must be understood as a product both of important, long-term processes set in motion with the onset of modernity and of the cultural context of postmodernity.

I have drawn my examples from and moved back and forth between the official justice system and everyday life. Much like the reformers of the nineteenth century, contemporary advocates of "community-based" punishment and social control seek to make justice more effective and more efficient. Yet, as I have shown, as they have gone about decentralizing the justice system, we have seen how some the discourses, techniques, and procedures used in the justice system have been adapted for use in schools, workplaces, and other community institutions. One of my goals has been to show how we appear to be building a community *of* corrections, a tendency to normalize and accept the presence of formal social control in our daily lives. "But perhaps the most important effect of the carceral system and its extension well beyond legal imprisonment is," according to Foucault, "that it succeeds in making the power to punish natural and legitimate, in lowering at least the threshold of tolerance to penalty."[3]

But how did all this happen? "There was no revolution," one astute journalist declared, "no totalitarian takeover, no war bringing the collapse of world-wide democracy. But by an invention here and a new computer application there, American culture is nearing the point forwarded by those who feared technology could breed a new kind of oppression."[4] Yet, while many of us are subjected to this new despotism, few, it would seem, see or appreciate the implications of this "quiet" revolution. We seem to exhibit what Marshall McLuhan called "narcissus narcosis," a syndrome that is like self-hypnosis in which people appear oblivious to how new technologies are invading and changing every aspect of their daily lives.[5] One reason, as I have tried to show, is that these surveillance practices often work in the background; we may not even know they exist, and even if we do, they rarely, in and of themselves, give cause for serious concern. Take, for example, the near universal and long accepted practice of "tagging" of merchandise in stores to prevent shoplifting. If we were confronted as we left a business and were "patted down" physically, people would be outraged. Yet, since the technology permits us to be "electronically" frisked, we generally consent to this surveillance ceremony. Another potent reason for "narcissus narcosis" is that a case is often made how a new system or device will "solve" one problem or another, be more efficient, make our lives easier, or even be entertaining. Consider the location-based social networking service Foursquare. Here, more than thirty million people have been willing to broadcast their whereabouts in a way that permits the company to learn about their preferences, habits, and movements and to sell off their location to businesses in the area. Yet, participation is considered "cool" and you can win points and get great "deals." Even the more confrontive disciplinary rituals such as random drug screens are quickly routinized into common, everyday practices that soon lose their sense of transgression. "Who cares if my employer tracks my web usage?" someone will declare; "What difference does it make if some big company knows all about me?" another asks. "People should be tested for drugs," most seem to say; "They can test me, I have nothing to hide." Fragmented and piecemeal, quiet and habitual—and often convincingly productive—meticulous rituals elicit only minor resistance.

Yet these new habits, no matter how small or seemingly trivial, have their own significance, for they define a certain mode of political investment in "the soft machine," as William S. Burroughs called our bodies. That is, meticulous rituals of power are the concrete ways in which our bodily lives are shaped, manipulated, and controlled by public and private organizations and by the people who have authority over us. These are the politics of social control in the workplace, the school, the home, and the community. They are also the politics of our "virtual" database(d) identities, who controls them, and how the processes of "big data" analytics contribute to social sorting. But since these kinds of practices often appear as a "nudge" here and a "twist" there, and are often dispersed and decentered, designed into the flows of everyday existence, few of us experience them as anything like "oppression." Yet, taken together, these "small acts of cunning," a term Foucault coined, constitute the building blocks of what I would argue is a rapidly emerging postmodern disciplinary society; a society increasingly lacking in personal privacy, individual trust, or viable public life that supports and maintains democratic values and practices.

I do not claim that the surveillance techniques I have identified are put in place with impunity, that they are universally accepted, or even that they work in accordance with their proponents' claims. Development is uneven; implementation is problematic, and some resistance is always present. People do fake drug tests, employers make exceptions, and probation officers work with violators trying to avoid revocations. There is competition among providers of new technology, some of it designed to thwart the efforts of others. Like the invention of the penitentiary itself, the new techniques are said to embody all the ideal virtues of justice—preventing crime or deviance, protecting property, or insulating us from harm—while being more effective, less expensive, and more "civilized" than what came before. The prison, for example, was more "humane" than the scaffold; now that the reality of the penitentiary can no longer be concealed (or its cost tolerated), electronic monitoring is "kinder and gentler" and more practical than the institution. Or take drug testing. Urine analysis is relatively cumbersome and invasive; people resent it. Testing hair follicles is not only more effective, it is less intrusive. Each failure, it seems, only serves to justify and bring about a new generation of disciplinary devices.

BIG BROTHER IS US

When I speak about "everyday surveillance," someone invariably asks, "Who is doing all this? Who's behind it? Who is 'big brother'?" "There is no 'big brother,'" I tell them; "we are him." Rather than appear simply "from the top down" or originate from a small group of identifiable individuals or even a particular organization, the new surveillance and social control practices I have identified here are advanced, I argue, directly or indirectly, by all of us. They are not orchestrated by only a few or as part of some master plan that is simply imposed on us; rather, disciplinary power expands "bi-directionally," flowing from top to bottom and vice versa. So while President Ronald Reagan can issue an executive order that demands that all federal workers be tested for drugs, an ex-auto mechanic can start marketing and selling video cameras to school districts for their buses. While Congress can pass the sweeping "Patriot Act," just forty-five days after the 9/11 attacks, an employer in your hometown is likely to be conducting "integrity" testing of all job applicants. A government agency or giant corporation may set out to create a new surveillance gadget, but it seems just as likely that a university professor will develop one—or, more importantly, the basis for a potential one—for no other reason than "curiosity," or to get promoted. A young computer software designer may develop a new program because its capabilities are "cool," rather than seeing it as a possible employee-monitoring tool.

This is not to suggest that everyday surveillance emerges "by accident." Some people have a vested interest in creating and selling new surveillance technologies, while others may be in a position to exercise this kind of control and benefit from it. Yet even they are, ultimately, not exempt from the gaze of that "long hierarchized network" Foucault refers to. We are all involved and enmeshed within a grid of power relations that are highly intentional and purposeful, arrangements that can be more or less hierarchical and unequal but are never simply one-directional. So while a police officer can video record all interactions she has with the public, the department can use those same digital files to evaluate her behavior as well. Similarly, a teacher can deploy "Student Information System" to organize all the "normalizing judgments" made about students, only to find that school administrators can use the same program to assess the teacher's "performance" in the classroom.

Everyday surveillance, I would argue, is being built on a foundation of seduction, desire, fear, and salvation. We all advance disciplinary power when we go about naively—and with blind faith and sometimes arrogance—trying to "make things better" and always assuming that, in fact, we can. This applies to anyone, across the political spectrum. "The road to hell," the saying goes, "is paved with good intentions." While some of the effects I have described in this book may be the "unintended consequences" of such good intentions, they are consequences nonetheless, and, it seems, they are rarely considered in the public discourse. We extend the bounds of everyday surveillance when we turn our backs on the important relationship between knowledge and power, when we take science—physical, medical, and social—at its word or assume that all technological change is always "for the better" and represents "progress." There are often seemingly very compelling reasons why decisions are made to test people for drugs, to fingerprint welfare recipients, or to put surveillance cameras on school buses. After all, we need to "deal with the problem" (even if we have little idea of just what the problem actually is) or, better yet, because "something might happen." Why not take steps to prevent it? We are easily seduced by the image of a protected, peaceful order. We are a people who like things to "work," to be efficient, to be predictable, to "make sense." We are easily persuaded and charmed by politicians promising "security," school administrators ensuring well-behaved children, and developers offering us the "serene fortress" of the gated community. We desire to eliminate risk, but at what price? If we could choose, our ideal would, of course, be a "free" society that is also free of crime and deviance. Since this is not going to happen, is the alternative a highly controlled society that is crime free? Singapore ranks as one of the top countries in the world in "Order and Security" and "Effective Criminal Justice"; yet it scores as one of the lowest in "Freedom of Speech" and "Freedom of Assembly." Put another way, is it worth surviving the risks of life only to end up "living" in a surveillance society?

We support, actively or passively, the creation of disciplinary practices, irrationally believing that they will be deployed exclusively "on those other folks," only to find that we have become the next targets. We facilitate everyday surveillance as well when we consume products that either make us the potential targets of surveillance or, alternatively, give us the tools to watch others. Here, the daily act of consumption—so central to the organization of late capitalism—becomes directly tied to the distribution and spread of disciplinary technology. Seduced by the market's desires and our overwhelming dependence on it, we have become, to paraphrase Mark Poster, "individuals plugged into the circuits of our own panoptic control."[6] If the company hasn't already done so, we are quite willing to "wire" ourselves in as we rush to buy the latest products that offer us access to the "Net," the "Web," and "cell" phones (the irony of this new terminology should not be ignored). We post pictures of ourselves, families, and friends on the Web so anyone can see us. We also install the device to monitor our kids' texting, to keep an eye on their driving, or even to test them for drugs. We buy the videocams and use them to document our own movements, or we turn them on our friends, neighbors, or strangers and post them on YouTube for the world to see. In a media saturated life where seemingly anyone can be a "star," everybody gets their fifteen minutes of fame. News networks will pay handsomely for amateur tapes of "important" events that they can then broadcast over and over again. In a culture of voyeurs, there is always plenty of footage.

The imperative of more and more surveillance and social control is also a function of fear. Steven Nock claims that increased formal surveillance results from our need to establish "reputations" and trust because, in a society of strangers, "How can we trust the people we see but do not know; those who live near us, who work near us, who must sometimes be counted on to help us?"[7] Yet, I would argue that, in our contemporary culture, it would seem that the "stranger" is more than someone without a reputation; what we really fear is the stranger assumed to exist within us all. In our sometimes hysterical culture, everyone is a potential suspect; otherwise, why would people who have established, "good" reputations still be subjected to surveillance ceremonies? Nock cites the example of the "highly respected civic leader" who is trusted. "His word is believed; his promise accepted."[8] Yet, at the height of the war on drugs, a proposal was made in my hometown that five city commissioners present themselves for drug screening in order to make a public statement that the town was "drug-free." The commissioners voted against the proposal, three to two, and the editor of the local newspaper proceeded to question the motives of those who had voted against it. The message is clear: If you refuse to consent to surveillance rituals, you must have something to hide.

It seems that increasingly we trust no one. As I have argued, our primary sources of cultural knowledge, the popular media, have turned everyday life into a theatrical drama pumped into our homes and media devices twenty-four/seven where the most compelling stories are those that recount lives filled with uncertainty, unpredictability, and tragedy. "Watch out! You could be next!" the media seems to scream out. We therefore become convinced that our only recourse against the apparent tide of problems we face is to "keep an eye on" everyone and we are seduced into believing that even our own subjection is an unfortunate but necessary condition. Is fear an irrational response then? No. Not only are the media accounts powerfully convincing, but also our fears are grounded in a certain reality. The United States is a relatively dangerous place; again, I am *not* suggesting that crime, youth violence, drugs, and other social ills are not "real." What I am saying is that we need to be aware of the role played by the media in shaping the process of how we come to "know" and believe we understand the nature of those problems.

This cultural hysteria—generated by docudramas, prime-time sensational "journalism," made-for-TV movies "based on the true story," and panic-laden Internet blogs—creates a fertile market for those selling "science" and the technological "fixes" they claim will bring knowledge and certainty to ease our fears. Political problems become technical ones when we are gripped by fear and we long for the salvation of easy "solutions." But what have we bargained for when we surrender the fundamental problem of social control to predominately corporate science and technology? Ironically, while the videocam is used to "create" this hysteria through television and the other outlets, it is offered as our salvation as well. "Just put up a camera," they say, and the problems will go away. In the case of the school bus, for example, once the camera is in place, no one has to bother teaching children *why* they should behave. This begs the question, how will they act when they are not under the gaze of the camera? Of course, the logical outcome of this "solution" is to make sure that they are always under its watchful eye.

How do we maintain anything deserving to be called a democratic society in the face of all this? I am not referring simply to the act of voting (although that is an issue also) as much as I am to the notion of democracy as an ongoing, daily accomplishment that is practiced and maintained both in human relationships and by mediating institutions. Democracy in this sense means not only ensuring our constitutionally given rights but also fostering what we might call the characteristics of a "good society"; a society where citizens are able to maintain a degree of trust in the individuals and organizations that they encounter; a society that is "civil" in every sense of the word; a society that ensures human rights and respects individual privacy and dignity, while at the same time balancing a concern for the "common good."[9] For years, social and political scholars have asserted that a fundamental characteristic of such a society is a viable public life—one that includes both public space (e.g., streets, parks, community markets, meeting places, schools) and a civic discourse (such as "public opinion"). If Enlightenment reason and democratic ideals offer us any hope, it is in the notion that people can come together and rationally decide what is in their best interest and for the common good.

But in today's culture, how is this possible? As more and more of this "public" space is brought under the gaze of surveillance, and as meticulous rituals permeate our daily lives, "there is nowhere to hide," as Gary Marx puts it. "A citizen's ability to evade this surveillance is diminishing. To venture into a shopping mall, bank, subway, sometimes even a bathroom is to perform before an unknown audience."[10] Even if this kind of surveillance is relatively "seamless," as I have argued, it may function to undermine our willingness to participate in civic life and "to speak our minds as clearly, openly, and imaginatively as we can."[11] Like those subjected to the gaze of the panopticon, we are increasingly "awed to silence" as Bentham put it, systematically manipulated and progressively unable to question corporate influence, challenge public officials, or engage in political dissent. We become, in essence, a "docile" citizenry, disciplinary subjects rather than democratic ones.

Increasingly driven out of the public sphere, we retreat to the "private life" of home only to find that, increasingly, it is not private at all. Here, public opinion has been replaced by the mass-mediated "storytelling" of high-profile media stars who "inform" us about how to vote and what is and what is not a "social problem." Our homes are nodes on telecommunication networks that offer corporations unprecedented access to our habits, buying preferences, and financial status. Meanwhile, new technologies can be used to convert some people's homes into "virtual" prisons as they are remotely monitored under the watchful eye of the criminal justice system, or, in other instances, similar devices enable suspicious parents to monitor their teens whereabouts, video record the babysitter, or to rifle through each other's e-mail. With the contemporary blurring of boundaries between notions of "public" and "private," between "real" freedom and its simulation, it is easy to see how "democracy" could become little more than a media illusion on the postmodern landscape.

BACK FROM THE ABYSS

All this sounds pretty bleak, doesn't it? Now that we have arrived at the crumbling edge of the cliff, it's time to turn to me and say, "OK, now what? You brought us here; what do we do about it?" This is the point in which many "cultural critics" end their books by offering some vague and hopeful agenda for the future, evoking some ideal society that will somehow miraculously spring forth from the rubble. Well, I have no such plan to offer. For me to put forward prescriptions for what is to be done would not only be a stunning display of hubris, it would contradict much of what I have written here. As I see it, my role as a sociologist is not to tell people what to do but to ask questions about aspects of social life that most take for granted; to look for patterns where ones seemingly do not exist; and to use theories and ideas to try to make sense out what I see. I offer this book in that spirit. Some readers may respond to this by saying, "See, it's easy to be critical and much harder to come up with solutions." But I don't agree; *both* are extremely difficult. The first step, I would argue, is *understanding*; to learn that there is, indeed, a crumbling ledge out there to be cautious of; to see it through the haze of confusion, accepted wisdom, and just plain foolishness.

Since advocating leaping into the abyss would effectively end our discussion here, let's assume, rather, that we choose to confront the surveillance society, to challenge the inevitably of these developments, and to try to shake off our "narcissus narcosis." Let's further assume that, while possible, a radically different society is not likely to emerge anytime soon. After all, much of what we live with today is grounded in a legacy of Western thought and practice dating back several centuries and is firmly lodged in the basic day-to-day functioning of the society. Given these assumptions, what can we do as individuals to counter new surveillance and disciplinary practices or to at least temper their excesses? One strategy that we might adopt—a tactic animated by the analysis I have offered here—is to engage in modest forms of active resistance. If we accept the premise that meticulous rituals of power and surveillance take place in the form of "local" micropractices that are present in our everyday lives, then the sites of opposition are right before us. They are in our own homes, workplaces, schools, and communities.

While we can support large scale political movements to demand better privacy protections, restrain the authority of employers, and broadly support the value of human dignity over efficiency and imagined security, the saying, "Think Globally, Act Locally" seems fitting. While potent institutional forces conspire to drive us deeper into a culture of surveillance, we are in fact active agents in building the world we live in; nothing is inescapable. As Foucault put it, "Where there is power, there is resistance."[12] So, resist media hysteria and rather than buy a home drug test kit, build trust with your kids by talking openly and honestly with them about both the allure and the dangers of drug use. Debate your business partners when they claim that a new computer monitoring system will make your employees more productive by pointing out that such a system may also undermine their morale and commitment to your company. When a school board member in your community proposes that students wear RFID tags, demand a reasoned explanation and evidence why this tactic is really necessary. Next time you telephone a business and a recording tells you that your call is being monitored "for your protection," ask to speak to a supervisor, and tell that person that you disapprove of the practice. If your state legislature debates the merits of drug testing welfare recipients, call your representative's office and ask her or him to justify their support for it. As Foucault reminds us, "One of the tasks, one of the meanings of human existence—the source of human freedom—is never to accept anything as definitive, untouchable, obvious, or immobile. No aspect of reality should be allowed to become a definitive and inhuman law for us."[13]

Notes

1. EVERYDAY SURVEILLANCE

1. Since I began working in the area of surveillance about twenty years ago, there are now dozens of books, hundreds of articles, and even an academic journal devoted to the topic. Today, surveillance studies is a vital, interdisciplinary field, and I will cite work from this area throughout the book. For a comprehensive overview of the field, see Kirstie Ball, et al., *Routledge Handbook of Surveillance Studies* (New York: Routledge, 2012). Also John Gilliom and Torin Monahan, *SuperVision: An Introduction to the Surveillance Society* (Chicago: University of Chicago Press, 2013); David Lyon, *Surveillance Studies: An Overview* (Malden, MA: Polity, 2007); Sean Hier and Joshua Greenberg, eds., *The Surveillance Studies Reader* (Maidenhead, UK: Open University Press, 2007); and the online, open-access journal, *Surveillance and Society.*

2. The term social control has a long history in sociology. See E. A. Ross, *Social Control: A Survey of the Foundations of Order* (New Brunswick, NJ: Transaction Publishers, 2009 [1901]); Jack Gibbs, *Norms, Deviance, and Social Control: Conceptual Matters* (New York: Elsevier, 1981), Stanley Cohen, and Andrew Scull, *Social Control and the State* (New York: St. Martin's Press, 1983).

3. This kind of informal social control may still be operating in small, rural communities throughout the United States, although through the process of urban and suburbanization, the percentage of the total population living is such communities is relatively small. Moreover, the market penetration of corporate convenience stores, Wal-Mart, and others means that not only do we see fewer and fewer small shop owners but we see the importation of the kind of technological store surveillance regimes I am characterizing here.

4. In fact, our "virtual" doppelgängers may be "better" representations of our "real" selves. Can you remember all the videos you watched last year? Netflix, HuLu, or Amazon can tell you. Mark Poster, "Databases as Discourse; or, Electronic Interpellations," in *Computers, Surveillance, and Privacy*, eds. David Lyon and Elia Zureik (Minneapolis: University of Minnesota Press, 1996), 175–192.

5. Donald Lowe, *The Body in Late Capitalism USA* (Durham, NC: Duke University Press, 1995).

6. See Bruce Western, *Punishment and Inequality in America* (New York: Russell Sage, 2007), and Becky Pettit, *Invisible Men: Mass Incarceration and the Myth of Black Progress* (New York: Russell Sage, 2010).

7. This perspective is rooted in recent "neoliberal" models of managing the "risk society" where "risk" becomes the concept for the understanding of how dangers are both identified and

responded to technologically. See Ericson V. Richard, *Policing the Risk Society* (Toronto: University of Toronto Press, 1997). This phenomenon has been referred to as "actuarial justice" where the criminal justice system serves a kind of "waste management function." Malcolm Feeley and Jonathan Simon, "Actuarial Justice: The Emerging New Criminal Law," in *The Futures of Criminology*, ed. David Nelken (London: Sage, 1994), 173–201.

8. The idea of the "postmodern" has gone out of fashion in many academic circles. However, I find many of the ideas and concepts developed around this notion to still be highly relevant to understanding contemporary culture. This position is articulated well by Steven Best and Douglas Kellner in *The Postmodern Adventure: Science, Technology and Cultural Studies at the Third Millennium* (New York: Guilford Press, 2001).

9. In the field of crime and punishment studies, some, like myself, have argued that a new, postmodern penology has taken hold in contemporary justice practice (See Malcolm Feeley and Jonathan Simon, "The New Penology: Notes on the Emerging Strategy of Corrections and Its Implications," *Criminology* 30, no. 4 (1992): 449–474; Jonathan Simon, "From Confinement to Waste Management: The Post-Modernization of Social Control," *Focus on Legal Studies* 8, no. 2 (1993): 6–7, while others such as David Garland contend that no such transition has taken place and have defended the "persistence of penal modernism." David Garland, "Penal Modernism and Postmodernism," in *Punishment and Social Control*, eds. Thomas Blomberg and Stanley Cohen (New York: Aldine de Gruyter, 1995), 45–74. I contend, rather than representing a historical rupture, postmodern developments as I describe them here should be seen as extensions of disciplinary power that invest, colonize, and link up preexisting institutional forms.

10. Best and Kellner, *Postmodern Adventure*, 6.

11. Michel Foucault, *Discipline and Punish: The Birth of the Prison*, trans. A. M. Sheridan (New York: Pantheon, 1977). Foucault was one of the most influential thinkers of the late twentieth century and his ideas have appeared in the work of scholars across the social sciences, humanities, law, architecture, and medicine. Bibliographies of his writing, lectures, and interviews can be found on websites such as http://foucaultsociety.wordpress.com.

12. There is an enormous literature on the development and influence of technology on social life. For some recent titles see Wenda K. Bauchspies, Jennifer Croissant, and Sal Restivo, *Science, Technology, and Society: A Sociological Approach* (Malden, MA: Wiley-Blackwell, 2005); Wenceslao J. Gonzalez, *Science, Technology and Society: A Philosophical Perspective* (A Coruña, Spain Netbiblo, 2005); and Barry M. Dumas, *Diving into the Bitstream: Information Technology Meets Society in a Digital World* (New York: Routledge, 2012).

13. On these examples, see Rob Tillyer, Charles F. Klahm, and Robin S. Engel, "The Discretion to Search: A Multilevel Examination of Driver Demographics and Officer Characteristics," *Journal of Contemporary Criminal Justice* 28, no. 2 (2012): 184–205; Shaun L. Gabbidon, "Profiling by Store Clerks and Security Personnel in Retail Establishments. An Exploration of 'Shopping While Black,'" *Journal of Contemporary Criminal Justice* 19, no. 3 (2003): 345–364; Christine I. Williams, "Racism in Toyland," *Contexts* 4 (2005): 28–32; Torin Monahan, "Dreams of Control at a Distance: Gender, Surveillance, and Social Control," *Cultural Studies=Critical Methodologies* 9, no. 2 (2009): 286–305; Heather McLaughlin, Christopher Uggen, Amy Blackstone, "Sexual Harassment, Workplace Authority, and the Paradox of Power," *American Sociological Review* 77, no. 4 (2012): 625–647; Elisa Puvia and Jeroen Vaes, "Being a Body: Women's Appearance Related Self-Views and Their Dehumanization of Sexually Objectified Female Targets," *Sex Roles* 68, no. 7–8 (2013): 484–495.

14. As Haggerty and Ericson put it, "we are witnessing a rhizomatic leveling of the hierarchy of surveillance, such that groups which were previously exempt from routine surveillance are now increasingly being monitored." See Kevin D. Haggerty and Richard V. Ericson, "The Surveillant Assemblage," *British Journal of Sociology* 51, no. 4 (2000): 606.

15. David Lyon, ed., *Surveillance as Social Sorting: Privacy, Risk and Digital Discrimination* (New York: Routledge, 2003). See also Oscar Gandy Jr., *The Panoptic Sort: A Political Economy of Personal Information* (Boulder, CO: Westview, 1993).

16. Diana Crane, *The Sociology of Culture* (Cambridge: Blackwell, 1994). See also Clifford Geertz, *The Interpretations of Cultures* (New York: Basic, 1973).

17. In fact, I treat the content of a good number of news stories as my "data" and I often quote and paraphrase journalists and the people that they have interviewed in my text and cite the sources. While this quasi-content analysis of news sources has its obvious limitations, historians and cultural analysts have been using newspapers as legitimate sources for years. See Vernon Dibble, "Four Types of Inference from Documents to Events," *History and Theory* 3, no. 2 (1963): 203–221; Elizabeth Ann Danto, *Historical Research* (Oxford: Oxford University Press, 2008); Bridget Somekh and Cathy Lewin, *Theory and Methods in Social Research* (London: Sage, 2011).

2. THE SCAFFOLD, THE PENITENTIARY, AND BEYOND

1. Alice Morse Earle, *Curious Punishments of Bygone Days* (Rutland, VT: Charles E. Tenant, 1972), 144–145.

2. W. David Lewis, *From Newgate to Dannemora* (Ithaca, NY: Cornell University Press, 1975), 117–120.

3. Michel Foucault, *Discipline and Punish: The Birth of the Prison*, trans. A. M. Sheridan (New York: Pantheon, 1977). It should also be pointed out that the "birth of the prison" did not end physical punishment. Inmates at penitentiaries, mental asylums, and poorhouses as well as children in houses of refuge and reformatories were subjected to systematic corporal punishment and physical and mental abuse, to say nothing of various "treatments." See David J. Rothman, *The Discovery of the Asylum: Social Order and Disorder in the New Republic* (Boston: Little, Brown, 1971) and his *Conscience and Convenience: The Asylum and Its Alternatives in Progressive America* (Boston: Little, Brown, 1980).

4. "Applying the Death Penalty," *New York Times*, Letters to the Editor, Ernest van Den Haag, November 18, 1994, 34(A). See, for example, "Six Lashes in Singapore," *Newsweek*, March 14, 1994, 29.

5. Letter to H. Zangger (1917). Alan Lightman, *A Sense of the Mysterious: Science and the Human Spirit* (New York: Vintage, 2006), 110.

6. Steven Best, "Foucault, Postmodernism, and Social Theory," in *Postmodernism and Social Inquiry*, eds. David R. Dickens and Andrea Fontana (New York: Guilford Press, 1994), 28.

7. Foucault, *Discipline and Punish*.

8. As Steven Best points out, for Foucault, although all knowledge is connected to forms of power, not all knowledge systems reinforce systems of domination and can actually be used against them. "Foucault . . . did not ask social scientists to abandon 'truth and method,' rather he asked them only to acknowledge the political character of all their knowledge and to be sensitive to the ways in which knowledge and truth are intertwined with power." Best, "Foucault, Postmodernism, and Social Theory," 43.

9. Michel Foucault, "Afterword: The Subject of Power," in *Michel Foucault: Beyond Structuralism and Hermeneutics*, eds. Hubert L. Dreyfus and Paul Rabinow (Berkeley: University of California Press, 1983), 209.

10. I wrote about these developments in a previous book entitled, *Castles of Our Conscience: Social Control and the American State, 1800–1985* (New Brunswick, NJ: Rutgers University Press, 1991), 19–25. I reproduce some of this material here since I think understanding this history is crucial to making sense of our present-day situation.

11. Lawrence Friedman, *A History of American Law* (New York: Simon and Schuster, 1973), 250.

12. Orlando Lewis, *The Development of American Prisons and Prison Customs, 1776–1845* (1922; reprint, Albany: Prison Association of New York, 1967), 18; Staples, *Castles of Our Conscience*, 19–25.

13. Staples, *Castles of Our Conscience*, 69.

14. Thomas Dumm, *Democracy and Punishment: Disciplinary Origins of the United States* (Madison: University of Wisconsin Press, 1987), 120.

15. Margaret O. Kirk, "Firms Turn to Hair Drug Tests to Find Out Who Makes the Cut," *Sun Sentinel*, January 26, 1996, accessed April 23, 2013, http://articles.sun-sentinel.com/1996-01-26/business/9601250644_1_hair-analysis-hair-test-urine.

16. Foucault, *Discipline and Punish*, 143.

17. Robert M. Emerson and Sheldon M. Messinger, "The Micro-Politics of Trouble," *Social Problems* 25 (1977): 121–134.

18. Images of the panopticon design can be found on the Internet.

19. Jeremy Bentham, *The Panopticon Writings*, ed. Miran Bozovic (London: Verso, 1995), 34.

20. Jeremy Bentham, *The Works of Jeremy Bentham*, vol. 4, ed. Sir John Bowring (London: Tait, 1843), 79.

21. Foucault, *Discipline and Punish*, 201–202.

22. Jeremy Bentham, *The Panopticon Writings*, 95.

23. Foucault, *Discipline and Punish*, 205, 216, 206.

24. Foucault, Discipline and Punish, 205.

25. Kevin Haggerty calls on us to "Tear Down the Walls" of the panopticon because he argues that the idea has outlived its usefulness, has become a theoretical straightjacket, and is unable to capture the complexity of contemporary surveillance processes and practices. I feel this is the case especially when one considers the number of narrow readings of Foucault that focus exclusively on the panoptic mechanism and ignore the other dimensions of disciplinary power. However, I also agree with Zygmunt Bauman when he states, "As I see it, the panopticon is alive and well, armed in fact with muscles so mighty that Bentham or even Foucault could not or would not have imagined them." See Kevin Haggerty, "Tear Down the Walls: On Demolishing the Panopticon," in *Theorizing Surveillance: The Panopticon and Beyond*, ed. David Lyon (Cullompton: Willan, 2006), 23–45; and Zygmunt Bauman and David Lyon, *Liquid Surveillance: A Conversation* (Cambridge: Polity, 2013), 55.

26. Foucault, *Discipline and Punish*, 211.

27. Foucault, *Discipline and Punish*, 297.

28. Dreyfus and Rabinow, *Michel Foucault*, xxvi.

29. Foucault, *Discipline and Punish*, 209; emphasis added. For an interesting analysis, see Nicholas Gane, "The Governmentalities of Neoliberalism: Panopticism, Post-Panopticism and Beyond," *Sociological Review* 60 (2012): 611–634.

30. See Steven Best and Douglas Kellner, *The Postmodern Adventure: Science, Technology and Cultural Studies at the Third Millennium* (New York: Guilford Press, 2001) for an excellent statement of this position. Also Nicos P. Mouzelis, *Modern and Postmodern Social Theorizing: Bridging the Divide* (Cambridge, UK: Cambridge University Press, 2008), and Brendan Edgeworth, *Law, Modernity, Postmodernity: Legal Change in the Contracting State* (Aldershot, UK: Ashgate, 2003).

31. See Fredric Jameson, *Postmodernism, or, The Cultural Logic of Late Capitalism* (London: Verso, 1992), and Ernest Mandel, *Late Capitalism* (London: Verso, 1978). Some have called it "fast capitalism," referring to "the impact of information and communication technologies on self, society and culture in the 21st century." See the online journal, *Fast Capitalism*, www.fastcapitalism.com.

32. Donald Lowe, *The Body in Late Capitalism USA* (Durham, NC: Duke University Press, 1995), 20.

33. Vaclav Havel, "The New Measure of Man," *New York Times*, July 8, 1994, accessed April 25, 2013, www.nytimes.com/1994/07/08/opinion/the-new-measure-of-man.html.

34. In the world of art, architecture, and the cinema, "postmodern" generally refers to the mixing, blending, and bending of traditional styles and media, the creation of pastiche, "remixing" older songs in music, and the like.

35. Jean Baudrillard, *The Ecstasy of Communication*, New Edition, trans. Bernard Schütze and Caroline Schütze (Boston: Semiotext(e), 2012).

36. Sherry Turkle, *Life on the Screen: Identity in the Age of the Internet* (New York: Simon & Schuster, 1995), 235, and her *Alone Together: Why We Expect More from Technology and Less from Each Other* (New York: Basic, 2012).

37. Alec Charles and Gavin Stewart, eds., *The End of Journalism* (New York: Peter Lang, 2011); and Howard Tumber and Marina Prentoulis, *Journalism and the End of Objectivity* (London: Bloomsbury, 2012).

38. Joseph Turow, *Breaking Up America: Advertisers and the New Media World* (Chicago: University of Chicago Press, 1998).

39. Norman K. Denzin, *Images of Postmodern Society: Social Theory and Contemporary Cinema* (Newbury Park, CA: Sage, 1991), 9. For example, in 2013, political commentator Bill O'Reilly had *two* "history" books on the bestseller list.

40. Actual text from local TV news, Channel 9, Kansas City, 10 p.m., June 10, 1997. See Barry Glassner, *Culture of Fear: Why Americans Are Afraid of the Wrong Things* (New York: Basic, 1999); and Jeff Ferrell and Neil Websdale, *Making Trouble: Cultural Constructions of Crime, Deviance, and Control* (Hawthorne, NY: Aldine De Gruyter, 1999).

41. Lydia Saad, "Perceptions of Crime Problem Remain Curiously Negative: More See Crime Worsening Rather Than Improving," *Gallup*. Last updated October 22, 2007, www.gallup.com/poll/102262/perceptions-crime-problem-remain-curiously-negative.aspx.

42. See the General Social Survey, a personal interview survey of U.S. households conducted by the National Opinion Research Center, accessed October 5, 2010, www.icpsr.umich.edu.

43. "Heroin Ads Are Needle-Sharp," *Lawrence Journal-World*, June 18, 1996, 4(A).

44. See among others, Lara Abigail Bazelon, "Exploding the Superpredator Myth: Why Infancy Is the Preadolescent's Best Defense in Juvenile Court," *New York University Law Review* 75 (2000): 1 38.

45. David Harvey, *A Brief History of Neoliberalism* (New York: Oxford University Press, 2007); and Colin Crouch, *The Strange Non Death of Neo-liberalism* (Cambridge: Polity, 2011).

46. Loïc Wacquant characterizes these developments this way: "The soft touch of libertarian proclivities favoring the upper class gives way to the hard edge of authoritarian oversight, as it endeavors to direct, nay dictate, the behavior of the lower class. 'Small government' in the economic register thus begets 'big government' on the twofold front of workfare and criminal justice." Loïc Wacquant, "Crafting the Neoliberal State: Workfare, Prisonfare, and Social Insecurity," *Sociological Forum* 25 (2010): 214.

47. Wacquant, "Crafting the Neoliberal State," 205.

48. Keith Humphreys and Julian Rappaport, "From the Community Mental Health Movement to the War on Drugs: A Study in the Definitions of Social Problems," *American Psychologist* 48 (1993): 892–901.

49. According to Humphreys and Rappaport, "From the Community Mental Health Movement to the War on Drugs," 895, budget authority for federal spending on interdiction, law enforcement, treatment, and prevention of drug abuse rose 679 percent during the decade 1981–1991. In 1988, the majority of people arrested in America's twenty-two largest cities were classified as "cocaine users."

50. "Get tough" suddenly meant "Go broke!" according to Ronald Corbett and Gary T. Marx, "Critique: No Soul in the New Machine: Technofallacies in the Electronic Monitoring Movement," *Justice Quarterly* 8 (1991): 399 414. By 1987, thirty-seven states were under court-ordered mandate to end prison overcrowding, claims Joan Petersilia in *Expanding Options for Criminal Sentencing* (Santa Monica, CA: RAND, 1987).

51. David L. Altheide, "Gonzo Justice," *Symbolic Interaction* 15 (1993); and David L. Altheide and R. Sam Michalowski, "In the News: Fear a Discourse of Control." *Society* 40 (2010): 475–503.

52. Stanley Cohen anticipated some of these developments in his important work, *Visions of Social Control: Crime, Punishment and Classification* (Cambridge: Polity, 1985) and "The Punitive City: Notes on the Dispersal of Social Control," *Contemporary Crisis* 3 (1979): 339–363.

53. Mike Davis, *City of Quartz* (London: Verso, 1990), 257.

3. THE GAZE AND ITS COMPULSIONS

1. Jean Baudrillard, *Simulations* (New York: Semiotext(e), 1983), 25.

2. See my work on house arrest including William G. Staples and Stephanie Decker, "Between the 'Home' and 'Institutional' Worlds: Tensions and Contradictions in the Practice of House Arrest," *Critical Criminology* 18 (2010): 1–20; William G. Staples, "'Where Are You and What Are You Doing?' Familial 'Back Up Work' as a Collateral Consequence of House Arrest," in *Who's Watching: Daily Practices of Surveillance among Contemporary Families*, eds. Margaret Nelson and Anita Garey (Nashville, TN: Vanderbilt University Press, 2009), 33–53.

3. For more on "hyperreality" see Baudrillard, *Simulations*, 11. For research on the anxiety of house arrestees, see John Holman and James Quinn, "Dysphoria and Electronically Monitored Home Confinement," *Deviant Behavior* 13 (1992): 21–32; and Staples and Decker, "Between the 'Home' and 'Institutional' Worlds." Other work on the experience of house arrest includes Sylvia Ansay, "When Home Is a Prison Cell: The Social Construction of Compliance in House Arrest," unpublished doctoral dissertation. Gainesville: University of Florida (1999); Randy R. Gainey and Brian K. Payne, "Understanding the Experience of House Arrest with Electronic Monitoring: An Analysis of Quantitative and Qualitative Data," *International Journal of Offender Therapy and Comparative Criminology* 44 (2000): 84–96.

4. Josh Kurtz, "New Growth in a Captive Market," *New York Times*, December 31, 1989, 12(E); and *Arizona Republic*, May 13, 1992, 5(B).

5. Currently, house arrest programs tether nearly twelve thousand individuals to central monitoring systems in the United States. See Todd Minton, "Prison and Jail Inmates at Midyear 2011—Statistical Tables." Bureau of Justice Statistics, U.S. Department of Justice Office of Justice Programs, http://bjs.gov/content/pub/pdf/jim11st.pdf; and Doris Layton MacKenzie, *What Works in Corrections: Reducing the Criminal Activities of Offenders and Delinquents* (New York: Cambridge University Press, 2006).

6. Kutz, "New Growth in a Captive Market," 12(E).

7. The New Generation III Alcohol and Marijuana Sensing House Arrest Ankle Bracelet with Active GPS, accessed April 15, 2013, www.housearrestbracelet.com.

8. Shadowtrack: Nothing Tracks Like Shadowtrack, accessed April 15, 2013, http://shadowtrack.com.temp.guardedhost.com.

9. Ronald Corbett and Gary T. Marx, "Critique: No Soul in the New Machine: Technofallacies in the Electronic Monitoring Movement," *Justice Quarterly* 8 (1991): 399–414.

10. Michel Foucault, *Discipline and Punish: The Birth of the Prison*, trans. A. M. Sheridan (New York: Pantheon, 1977), 200.

11. Foucault, *Discipline and Punish*, 206.

12. Matt Mangino, "The Cautionary Instruction: Tracking Sex Offenders for Life," *Community Voices*, November 2, 2012, accessed November 15, 2012, http://communityvoices.sites.post-gazette.com/index.php/news/ipso-facto/34776-the-cautionary-instruction-tracking-sex-offenders-for-life; and Evan Halper, "Gov. Wants State to Track Gangs, *Los Angeles Times*, accessed April 15, 2013, http://americancityandcounty.com/issue20070101/governor-wants-state-track-gangs.

13. A former student of mine who was employed as an ISO officer supplied this information. I must ensure confidentiality of this individual and of the agency.

14. See note 13.

15. Vanessa G. Hodges and Betty Blythe, "Improving Service Delivery to High-Risk Families: Home-Based Practice," *Families in Society: Journal of Contemporary Human Services* 73 (1992): 259–265.

16. Leonard J. Woods, "Home-Based Family Therapy," *Social Work* 33 (1988): 211–214.

17. Foucault, *Discipline and Punish*, 211.

18. Shaun Assael, "Robocourt," *Wired*, March 1994, 106.

19. Assael, "Robocourt," 106.

20. Corbett and Marx, "Critique: No Soul in the New Machine," 400.

21. "Sheriff's Video Patrol Auditioning Begins," *Lawrence Journal-World*, March 6, 1994, 3(B).

22. "Sheriff's Video Patrol Auditioning Begins," 1(B); *Foucault, Discipline and Punish*, 177.

23. Randall Stross, "Wearing a Badge, and a Video Camera," *New York Times*, April 6, 2013, accessed April 15, 2013, www.nytimes.com/2013/04/07/business/wearable-video-cameras-for-police-officers.html?pagewanted=all.

24. Chris Woodyard, "Latest Tech Gear Turns Police into RoboCop," *USA TODAY*, October 15, 2012, accessed December 13, 2012, www.usatoday.com/story/money/cars/2012/10/15/robocop-raytheon-motorola-police/1629989/; and Carolyn Duffy Marsan, "How Wearable Cameras Aid Law Enforcement," *STATETECH*, July 17, 2012, accessed November 15, 2012, www.statetechmagazine.com/article/2012/07/how-wearable-cameras-aid-law-enforcement.

25. "Local Woman Creates TV Show to Track Down Deadbeat Parents," *Daily Review*, January 8, 2010, accessed July 11, 2012, http://thedailyreview.com/news/local-woman-creates-tv-show-to-track-down-deadbeat-parents-1.532192.

26. "'Life on the Beat' Bolsters Police Image," *Lawrence Journal-World*, May 29, 1998, 6(D).

27. David Firestone, "New Police Policy Opens Doors to TV," *New York Times*, July 16, 1994, accessed October 12, 2012, www.nytimes.com/1994/07/16/nyregion/new-police-policy-opens-doors-to-tv.html.

28. Roger Cohen, "In Sarajevo, Victims of a 'Postmodern' War," *New York Times*, May 21, 1995, accessed April 12, 2013, www.nytimes.com/1995/05/21/world/in-sarajevo-victims-of-a-postmodern-war.html.

29. "High-Tech Devices Utilized by U.S. Military in Bosnia," National Public Radio, *All Things Considered*, March 15, 1996.

30. "Law Enforcement Agencies Obtaining Record Amount of Surplus Military Equipment," *Public Intelligence*, August 29, 2012, accessed January 23, 2013, http://publicintelligence.net/leas-obtaining-military-equipment.

31. "Bayonets Given to Police Force," *Lawrence Journal-World*, November 2, 1997, 9(A).

32. Paul Roberts, "Boston's Logan Airport Uses Thermal Imaging to Boost Security," *CIO*, July 1, 2003, accessed September 2012, www.cio.com/article/31937/Boston_s_Logan_Airport_Uses_Thermal_Imaging_to_Boost_Security.

33. Spencer Ackerman, "Handheld Radar Senses Life behind the Wall," *Wired*, October 26, 2010, accessed July 23, 2012, www.wired.com/dangerroom/2010/10/handheld-radar-senses-life-behind-the-wall; "Solicitation: Sensors and Surveillance Technologies," U.S. Department of Justice, 2006, www.ncjrs.gov/pdffiles1/nij/sl000757.pdf.

34. Woodyard, "Latest Tech Gear Turns Police into RoboCop"; David Hayes, "'Pings' Assist in Missing-Persons Cases," *Kansas City Star*, June 7, 2007, accessed, August 23, 2012, www.kansascity.com/115/story/139639.html; Thomas J. Lueck, "From Database to Crime Scene: Network Is Potent Police Weapon," *New York Times*, June 6, 2007, accessed July 23, 2012, www.nytimes.com/2007/06/07/nyregion/07real.html; Alex Pearlman, "Domestic Police Forces, Universities Using Drones Despite Privacy Concerns," *Global Post*, September 26, 2012, accessed January 13, 2013, www.globalpost.com/dispatches/globalpost-blogs/rights/domestic-drones-UAVs-FAA-oversight; Tom Hays, "New York City Police Eye Trucks as Potential Vehicles for Terrorists," *Seattle Times*, June 12, 2007, accessed October 12, 2012, http://seattletimes.com/html/nationworld/2003744093_nytrucks12.html; Joseph Straw, "New Views on Airport Screening," *Security Management*, no date, accessed April 12, 2013, www.securitymanagement.com/article/new-views-airport-screening-004586?page=0%2C2; "District, Police Looking at Camera Technology" *YourHub.com*, May 23, 2007, accessed July 3, 2010, http://denver.yourhub.com/CastleRock/Stories/News/Law/Story~311308.asp; Carol Eisenberg, "Airport Protection System on the Way," *New York Newsday*, June 6, 2007, accessed April 16, 2013, www.newsday.com/news/airport-protection-system-on-the-way-1.653043; "Chicago Police Have New Toy," *Impact Lab*, June 1, 2007, accessed April 16, 2013, www.impactlab.net/2007/06/01/chicago-police-have-a-new-toy/; Milton J. Valencia, "Eyes Opened to Find the Missing," *Telegram and Gazette*, May 21, 2007, accessed April 16,

2013, www.telegram.com/apps/pbcs.dll/article?AID=/20070531/NEWS/705310733/1008/NEWS02.

35. Kim Zetter, "TSA Investigating 'Don't Touch My Junk' Passenger," *Wired*, November 16, 2010, accessed August 12, 2012, www.wired.com/threatlevel/2010/11/tsa-investigating-passenger. See also Mark B. Salter, ed., *Politics at the Airport* (Minneapolis: University of Minnesota Press, 2008); and Harvey Molotch, *Against Security: How We Go Wrong at Airports, Subways, and Other Sites of Ambiguous Danger* (Princeton, NJ: Princeton University Press, 2012).

36. Torin Monahan, "'War Rooms' of the Street: Surveillance Practices in Transportation Control Centers," *Communication Review* 10 (2007): 367–389.

37. Automated Traffic Surveillance and Control (ATSAC) System, accessed January 23, 2013, http://trafficinfo.lacity.org/html/atsac_1.html.

38. Torin Monahan, *Surveillance in the Time of Insecurity* (New Brunswick, NJ: Rutgers University Press, 2010), 99.

39. "Fact Sheet AQMD's High Emitter Repair or Scrap (HEROS) Program," August 2007, accessed September 23, 2012, www.aqmd.gov/news1/2007/remotesensingfactsheet.html.

40. "New Turnpike System Lets Drivers Glide Past Lines at Toll Booth," *Lawrence Journal-World*, October 7, 1995, 10(B).

41. Chris Newmarker, "E-ZPass Records Out Cheaters in Divorce Court," *NBCNews.com*, August 10, 2007, accessed November 11, 2012, www.nbcnews.com/id/20216302/econstruct%20her%20movements.

42. "Q&A: Red Light Cameras," *Insurance Institute for Highway Safety*, June 2012, accessed December 2, 2012, www.iihs.org/research/qanda/rlr.aspx.

43. Hunton and Williams, LLP, "OnStar Announces Reversal of Controversial Vehicle Data Collection Proposals," *Privacy and Security Information Law Blog*, September 30, 2011, accessed December 12, 2013, www.huntonprivacyblog.com/2011/09/articles/onstar-announces-reversal-of-controversial-vehicle-data-collection-proposals/.

44. Joan Lowy, "Car Black Boxes Raise Privacy Concerns," *Huffington Post*, December 7, 2012, accessed April 14, 2013, www.huffingtonpost.com/2012/12/07/car-black-box_n_2255110.html.

45. Progressive Insurance, accessed February 12, 2013, www.progressive.com/auto/snapshot-common-questions.aspx.

46. Teletrac Corporation, accessed January 21, 2013, www.teletrac.com.

47. Smart Card Alliance, accessed February 12, 2013, www.smartcardalliance.org/pages/alliance.

48. "Examples of RFID Use in Different Industries," *Knowledgeleader*, June 2006, accessed November 30, 2012, www.theiia.org/download.cfm?file=97597.

49. Katherine Albrecht and Liz McIntyre, *SPYCHIPS: How Major Corporations and Government Plan to Track Your Every Move with RFID* (Nashville, TN: Thomas Nelson, 2005), 3.

50. Examples in the next two paragraphs come from, "News," *RFID Journal*, accessed February 11, 2013, www.rfidjournal.com/article/archive/1/7.

51. See also *RFID: Applications, Security, and Privacy*, eds. Simson Garfinkel and Beth Rosenberg (New York: Addison-Wesley Professional, 2005); and Torin Monahan and Jill A. Fisher, "Implanting Inequality: Empirical Evidence of Social and Ethical Risks of Implantable Radio-Frequency Identification (RFID) Devices," *International Journal of Technology Assessment in Health Care* 26 (2010): 370–376; and Jill A. Fisher and Torin Monahan, "Tracking the Social Dimensions of RFID Systems in Hospitals," *International Journal of Medical Informatics* 77 (2008): 176–183.

52. Mark Andrejevic, "The Kinder, Gentler Gaze of Big Brother: Reality TV in the Era of Digital Capitalism," *New Media* 4 (2002), 252.

53. James Vlahos, "Surveillance Society: New High-Tech Cameras Are Watching You," *Popular Mechanics*, October 1, 2009, accessed March 12, 2013, www.popularmechanics.com/technology/military/4236865.

54. New York Civil Liberties Union, *Who's Watching?: Video Camera Surveillance in New York City and the Need for Public Oversight*, Fall 2006, accessed October 14, 2012, www.nyclu.org/files/publications/nyclu_pub_whos_watching.pdf.

55. Ben Palosaari, "Big Brother Has Arrived in Sugar Creek, and He Wants to Know If You're Speeding," *Pitch*, September 20, 2010, accessed September 22, 2012, http://blogs.pitch.com/plog/2010/09/big_brother_has_arrived_in_sugar_creek_and_he_wants_to_know_if_youre_speeding.php; Eric Roper, "Police Cameras Quietly Capture License Plates, Collect Data," *Star Tribune*, August 10, 2012, accessed November 12, 2012, www.startribune.com/local/minneapolis/165680946.html?refer=y; Karen Ann Cullotta, "Chicago Links Street Cameras to Its 911 Network," *New York Times*, February 21, 2009, accessed October 10, 2012, www.nytimes.com/2009/02/21/us/21cameras.html?emc=tnt&tntemail0=y; Kim Zetter, "$30,000 Will Buy Your Name on a Surveillance Camera," *Wired*, July 31, 2008, accessed January 12, 2012, www.wired.com/threatlevel/2008/07/30000-will-buy.

56. Despite the fact that 99 percent or more of the activity recorded is of law abiding behavior, the police and the public seems convinced that if one thief or assailant is caught because of video surveillance then it is well worth the expense, the intrusion into public space, and even possible abuses of the systems. In the Boston case, however, it was a private surveillance camera above the door of a restaurant that captured the images of the Tsarnaev brothers and just five days before the incident the FBI told Boston police that the finish line of the marathon was an "area of increased vulnerability" yet no additional measures were apparently taken. All this is somewhat ironic since the Boston police department has a history of using surveillance tactics to monitor the behavior of the city's citizenry. Boston police have been found to routinely spy on ordinary citizens engaged in peaceful, constitutionally protected activities and then created criminal "intelligence reports" on the lawful political activity of peace groups, local leaders, and professors.

57. Clive Norris and Gary Armstrong, *The Maximum Surveillance Society: The Rise of CCTV* (Oxford: Berg Publishers, 1999).

58. For recent research on the effectiveness of video surveillance, see Adam Schwartz, "Chicago's Video Surveillance Cameras: A Pervasive and Poorly Regulated Threat to Our Privacy," *Northwestern Journal of Technology and Intellectual Property* 4/ (2013): 47–60; Brandon C. Welsh and David P. Farrington, "Is CCTV Effective in Preventing Crime in Public Places?" in *Evidence-Based Policing*, ed. Eveline De Wree, et al., (Antwerp: Maklu-Publishers, 2010), 263–281; Brandon C. Welsh and David P. Farrington, "Surveillance for Crime Prevention in Public Space: Results and Policy Choices in Britain and America." *Criminology and Public Policy* 3 (2004): 497–525; Aaron Doyle, et al., *Eyes Everywhere in the Global Growth of Camera Surveillance* (London: Routledge, 2011).

59. "Big Brother Is Definitely Watching You: Shocking Study Reveals UK Has One CCTV for Every 32 People," *Daily Mail*, March 3, 2011, accessed January 12, 2013, www.dailymail.co.uk/news/article-1362493/One-CCTV-camera-32-people-Big-Brother-Britain.html.

60. Vlahos, "Surveillance Society."

61. Vlahos, "Surveillance Society."

62. Zachary H. Sacks, "More Employers Turning to Surveillance to Combat WC Fraud." *Workcompcentral*, November 5, 2012, accessed January 12, 2013, https://ww3.workcompcentral.com/columns/show/id/8049000efcdc4ef4a04578c3e416f61ej.

63. "Millwood and Hickory Trails Hospitals (IP Surveillance)," DLINK Corporation, no date, accessed March 11, 2013, www.dlink.com/us/en/resource-centre/case-studies/millwood-and-hickory-trails-hospitals.

64. Jonathan Turley, "Your Right to Record," *Los Angeles Times*, November 8, 2011, accessed February 22, 2013, http://articles.latimes.com/2011/nov/08/opinion/la-oe-turley-video-20111108.

65. Richard A. Oppel Jr., "Taping of Farm Cruelty Is Becoming the Crime." *New York Times*, April 6, 2013, accessed April 12, 2013, www.nytimes.com/2013/04/07/us/taping-of-farm-cruelty-is-becoming-the-crime.html?pagewanted=all.

66. Tami Abdollah and Amanda Covarrubias, "Extracurricular Videos Roil Campus," *Los Angeles Times*, February 8, 2007, accessed March 23, 2013, http://articles.latimes.com/2007/feb/08/local/me-classvideo8; and Katharine Q. Seelye, "Cameras, and Rules against Them, Stir

Passions in Delivery Rooms," *New York Times*, February 2, 2011, accessed August 27, 2012, www.nytimes.com/2011/02/03/us/03birth.html?pagewanted=all&_r=0].

67. "Britain's Raciest Surveillance Videos Stir Outrage," *Lawrence Journal-World*, March 18, 1996, 8(D).

68. Lili Berko, "Surveying the Surveilled: Video, Space, and Subjectivity," *Quarterly Review of Film and Video* 14 (1992): 61–91.

69. David Lyon, "The New Surveillance: Electronic Technologies and the Maximum Security Society," *Crime, Law and Social Change* 18 (1992): 159–175.

70. YouTube, "Frequently Asked Questions," accessed February 12, 2012, www.youtube.com/t/faq.

71. Catherine Holahan, "Google Is Watching You," *Business Week*, June 22, 2007, accessed November 25, 2012, www.businessweek.com/technology/content/jun2007/tc20070622_338015.htm.

72. Torin Monahan, "Dreams of Control at a Distance: Gender, Surveillance, and Social Control," *Cultural Studies-Critical Methodologies* 9 (2009): 286–305; Lorraine Bayard de Volo, "Service and Surveillance: Infrapolitics at Work among Casino Cocktail Waitresses," *Social Politics* 10 (2003): 347–376; Hille Koskela, "Video Surveillance, Gender, and the Safety of Public Urban Space: 'Peeping Tom' Goes High Tech?" *Urban Geography* 23 (2002): 257–278; Gary T. Marx, "Technology and Gender: Thomas I. Voire and the Case of the Peeping Tom," *The Sociological Quarterly* 43 (2002): 409–433; William G. Staples and Joane Nagel, "Gary's Gone . . .: Comment on The Case of the Pepping Tom: Technology and Gender by Gary T. Marx," *Sociological Quarterly* 43 (2002): 447–452.

73. Gilbert Cruz, "Trooper Controlled Camera on the Strip," *Tuscaloosanews.com*, September 16, 2003, accessed April 16, 2013, www.tuscaloosanews.com/article/20030916/NEWS/309160346.

74. John Stearns, "2 Fort McDowell Casino Officials Fired over Photos," *Arizona Republic*, June 5, 2004, accessed April 1, 2013, www.azcentral.com/arizonarepublic/local/articles/0605casinophotos05.html.

75. Time's Up: 2005-02-24 NYPD Cameras Invade - CBS TV2, accessed April 14, 2013, http://www.times-up.org/2005-interest/2005-02-24-nypd-cameras-invade-cbs-tv2 and Jim Dwyer, "Police Video Caught a Couple's Intimate Moment on a Manhattan Rooftop," *New York Times*, December 22, 2005, accessed April 14, 2013, www.nytimes.com/2005/12/22/nyregion/22rooftop.html?.

76. Vicki Smith, "2 FBI Workers Accused of Spying on Teenage Girls Trying on Prom Dresses at W.Va. Mall," *Star Tribune*, April 20, 2009, accessed February 12, 2013, www.startribune.com/sid=43310262.

77. Charles Derber, *The Pursuit of Attention: Power and Ego in Everyday Life* (New York: Oxford University Press, 2000), xi.

78. Matt Snyders, "One of the YouTube Assault Perps Already on Probation for Robbery," November 19, 2009, accessed January 12, 2013, http://blogs.citypages.com/blotter/2009/11/one_of_the_yout.php.

79. Andrew Greenstein, "Teens Videotape Themselves Trashing Stores," *WOKV*, December 20, 2011, accessed, January 12, 2013, www.wokv.com/news/news/local/teens-videotape-themselves-trashing-stores/nF6JB/.

80. Associated Press, "Video: Homeless Man Beaten in Wall by Two Laughing N.J. Youths," *NJ.com*, December 19, 2011, accessed January 12, 2013, www.nj.com/news/index.ssf/2011/12/video_homeless_man_beaten_in_w.html.

81. "Abu Ghraib," *New York Times*, accessed January 12, 2013, http://topics.nytimes.com/topics/news/international/countriesandterritories/iraq/abu_ghraib/index.html.

82. "Neighborhood Cameras on The Blink," *WSOC-TV*, Charlotte, NC, March 4, 2004, accessed March 12, 2013, www.wsoctv.com/news/news/neighborhood-cameras-on-the-blink/nG4sJ.

83. Will Reisman, "City's Crime Cameras Shortsighted," *San Francisco Examiner*, March 20, 2008, accessed March 12, 2013, www.sfexaminer.com/local/city-s-crime-cameras-shortsighted.

84. "Spy Cameras Fail to Focus on Street Crime," *Washington Times*, August 13, 2006, accessed March 12, 2013, www.washingtontimes.com/news/2006/aug/13/20060813-121827-2123r/.

85. "Camera Keeps Eye on Treasurer's Office," *Lawrence Journal-World*, December 17, 1997, 5(B).

86. Associated Press, "Dunkin' Donuts Facing Suit over Listening Devices," *Telegraph*, July 29, 1994, accessed February 23, 2013, www.news.google.com/newspapers?nid=2209&dat=19940729&id=foJKAAAAIBAJ&sjid=zpMMAAAAIBAJ&pg=2417,744483.

87. Associated Press, "Dunkin' Donuts Wants Surveillance Stopped," *Lakeland Ledger*, May 28, 1994, accessed February 23, 2013, http://news.google.com/newspapers?nid=1346&dat=19940528&id=xNwvAAAAIBAJ&sjid=cvwDAAAAIBAJ&pg=6812,4615337.

88. "Audio Surveillance Reduces Theft for Goodwill Industry Stores," Barix.com, accessed February 23, 2013, www.barix.com/real-stories/security/audio-surveillance-complements-video/.

89. Michael Kelley, "US Government Plans to Install Sophisticated Audio Surveillance on Public Buses." *Business Insider*, December 10, 2012, accessed February 23, 2013, www.businessinsider.com/us-plans-audio-surveillance-on-buses-2012-12.

90. Julie Banovic, "Intelligent Lights Make Up Wireless Network Used for Entertainment and Safety," *ABC Action News, WXYZ*, November 28, 2011, accessed February 23, 2013, www.wxyz.com/dpp/news/region/oakland_county/intelligent-lights-make-up-wireless-network-used-for-entertainment-and-safety.

91. Steven Greenhouse, "At the Bar: Secret Tape-Recording," *New York Times*, September 16, 1994, accessed February 23, 2013, www.nytimes.com/1994/09/16/us/bar-secret-tape-recording-debate-that-divides-old-line-ethicists-new-wave.html.

92. L. M. Sixel, "One-third of Workers with Beefs Tape Their Bosses," *Houston Chronicle*, February 3, 2011, accessed February 29, 2013, www.chron.com/business/sixel/article/One-third-of-workers-with-beefs-tape-their-bosses-1684505.php.

93. Juan Gonzalez, "Angry Employees at Central Park's Boathouse Restaurant Secretly Taping Their Bosses," *New York Daily News*, January 11, 2011, accessed February 29, 2013, www.nydailynews.com/new-york/angry-employees-central-park-boathouse-restaurant-secretly-taping-bosses-article-1.154359.

94. "Saints on Report: 1,000 Percent False," *Fox Sports*, April 4, 2012, accessed February 29, 2013, http://msn.foxsports.com/nfl/story/Mickey-Loomis-New-Orleans-Saints-deny-eavesdropping-042312.

95. Associated Press, "Angry Voice Mail from Baldwin Goes Public," *NBC News*, April 20, 2007, accessed February 29, 2013, www.nbcnews.com/id/18220258/site/todayshow/ns/today-entertainment/t/angry-voice-mail-baldwin-goes-public.

96. Timothy Egan, "Many Seek Security in Private Communities," *New York Times*, September 3, 1995, accessed February 29, 2013, www.nytimes.com/1995/09/03/us/the-serene-fortress-a-special-report-many-seek-security-in-private-communities.html?pagewanted=all&src=pm.

97. Yet one visitor commented: "Before I came here my sister told me it creeped her out, it was too perfect. It is kinda Stepford wife-like." Lyn Riddle, "At Celebration, Some Reasons to Celebrate," *New York Times*, March 7, 1999, accessed February 29, 2013, www.nytimes.com/1999/03/07/realestate/at-celebration-some-reasons-to-celebrate.html; see also, Jackie Craven, "Celebration, Florida," *About.com*, accessed February 29, 2013, http://architecture.about.com/od/plannedcities/ss/celebration.htm.

98. BrickHouse Security, accessed February 29, 2013, www.brickhousesecurity.com/. Emphasis added.

99. BrickHouse Security, accessed February 29, 2013, www.brickhousesecurity.com/.

100. DriveCam, accessed February 29, 2013, www.drivecam.com/our-markets/family.

101. DriveCam, accessed February 29, 2013, www.drivecam.com/our-markets/family.

102. All Track USA, accessed February 29, 2013, www.alltrackusa.com.

103. "Technology Lets Parents Track Kids' Every Move," *National Public Radio*, August 29, 2006, accessed February 29, 2013, http://m.npr.org/story/5725196.

104. Michael Janofsky, "Teen-Agers in Washington Face New Curfew," *New York Times*, July 7, 1995, accessed February 29, 2013, www.nytimes.com/1995/07/07/us/teen-agers-in-washington-face-new-curfew.html; National News Briefs, "Curfews in More Cities, Survey of Mayors Shows," *New York Times*, December 1, 1997, accessed February 29, 2013, www.nytimes.com/1997/12/01/us/national-news-briefs-curfews-in-more-cities-survey-of-mayors-shows.html; and Michael deCourcy Hinds, "Philadelphia Adopts Tough New Truant Policy, with Handcuffs, Too," *New York Times*, February 9, 1994, accessed February 29, 2013, www.nytimes.com/1994/02/09/us/philadelphia-adopts-tough-truant-policy-with-handcuffs-too. html.

105. Now classic statements on medicalization are, Peter Conrad and Joseph Schneider, *Deviance and Medicalization: From Badness to Sickness* (St. Louis, MO: Mosby, 1980); and Malcolm Spector, "Beyond Crime: Seven Methods to Control Troublesome Rascals," in *Law and Deviance*, ed. H. L. Ross (Beverly Hills, CA: Sage, 1981), 127–158.

106. William G. Staples, *Castles of Our Conscience: Social Control and the American State, 1800–1985* (New Brunswick, NJ: Rutgers University Press, 1991), 138–145; William G. Staples and Carol A. B. Warren, "Mental Health and Adolescent Social Control," in *Research in Law, Deviance and Social Control: A Research Annual*, eds. Steven Spitzer and Andrew Scull (Greenwich, CT: JAI Press, 1988), 113–126.

107. S. 1125 (103rd): Safe Schools Act of 1993, accessed March 5, 2013, www.govtrack.us/congress/bills/103/s1125.

108. "Even Small Schools Adding Security," *Lawrence Journal-World*, January 25, 1994, 8(B).

109. Annette Fuentes, *Lockdown High: When the Schoolhouse Becomes a Jailhouse* (New York: Verso, 2011), 26.

110. See also Michelle Brown, *The Culture of Punishment: Prison, Society, and Spectacle* (New York: New York University Press, 2009).

111. Annette Fuentes, *Lockdown High*, 89.

112. U.S. Department of Education, *Issue Brief: Public School Practices for Violence Prevention and Reduction: 2003–04* (Washington, DC: National Center for Education Statistics, 2007); and U.S. Department of Education, *School Crime and Safety, 2007* (Washington, DC: National Center for Education Statistics, 2007).

113. Michelle Rushlo, "Phoenix Installs Face Scanners in School," *Boston Globe*, December 15, 2003, accessed March 3, 2013, www.boston.com/news/nation/articles/2003/12/15/phoenix_installs_face_scanners_in_school/.

114. Shannon Dillon, "Judge Orders Truants to Carry GPS Tracking Device," *KBTX-TV Channel 3*, January 19, 2010, accessed March 3, 2013, www.kbtx.com/home/headlines/82119747.html.

115. "Texas School Tracking IDs Can Be Required of Students, Judge Rules," *Huffingtonpost.com*, January 8, 2013, accessed March 3, 2013, www.huffingtonpost.com/2013/01/09/texas-school-tracking-ids_n_2439465.html.

116. Sam Dillion, "Cameras Watching Students, Especially in Biloxi," *New York Times*, September 24, 2003, accessed March 3, 2013, www.nytimes.com/2003/09/24/nyregion/cameras-watching-students-especially-in-biloxi.html?pagewanted=all&src=pm.

117. Dillion, "Cameras Watching Students."

118. Nicole Bliman, "Student Says School Webcam Spied on Him at Home," *CNN.com*, February 19, 2010, accessed March 3, 2013, www.cnn.com/2010/CRIME/02/19/laptop.suit/index.html; and David Kravets, "School District Halts Webcam Surveillance," *Wired*, February 19, 2010, accessed March 3, 2013, www.wired.com/threatlevel/2010/02/school-district-halts-webcam-surveillance/.

119. *Threat Assessment in Schools: A Guide to Managing Threatening Situations and to Creating Safe School Climates* (Washington, DC: U.S. Secret Service and U.S. Department of Education, 2002), 143.

120. Mosaic Threat Assessments, LLC, accessed March 3, 2013, www.mosaicmethod.com/?page=what_is_mosaic.

121. *Indicators of School Crime and Safety: 2011* (Washington, DC: U.S. Department of Education and U.S. Department of Justice, 2012), accessed March 3, 2013, www.bjs.ojp.usdoj.gov/content/pub/pdf/iscs11.pdf.

122. Children's Defense Fund, "Protect Children, Not Guns," March 23, 2012, accessed March 3, 2013, www.childrensdefense.org/child-research-data-publications/data/protect-children-not-guns-2012.html.

123. Aaron Kupchik, *Homeroom Security: School Discipline in an Age of Fear* (New York: New York University Press, 2010), 4; and Torin Monahan and Rodolfo Torres, eds., *Schools under Surveillance: Cultures of Control in Public Education* (New Brunswick, NJ: Rutgers University Press, 2009).

124. See Carl Milofsky, *Testers and Testing: The Sociology of School Psychology* (New Brunswick, NJ: Rutgers University Press, 1989), and F. Allan Hanson, *Testing Testing: Social Consequences of the Examined Life* (Berkeley: University of California Press, 1993).

125. "Grades Go High-Tech in Cordley Class," *Lawrence Journal-World*, October 23, 1994, 1(B); and Houghton Mifflin, Learner Profile, accessed March 3, 2013, www.learnerprofile.com/index.cfm.

126. Of course, there never seems to be any question about such software being "progress." The headline reads, "KU-Developed Software Beneficial to Schools: Computer Helps in Classroom," *Lawrence Journal-World*, November 26, 1995, 8(B).

127. United Parcel Service, "Leadership Matters—Telematics," accessed March 21, 2013, www.ups.com/content/us/en/bussol/browse/leadership-telematics.html. Emphasis added.

128. Chris Murphy, "UPS: Positioned for the Long Haul," *Information Week*, January 17, 2009, accessed March 21, 2013, www.informationweek.com/ups-positioned-for-the-long-haul/212900815?itc=edit_in_body_cross.

129. "Denver Brown . . . A View from the Driver's Side," accessed March 21, 2013, www.denverbrown.com/TELEMATICS.html.

130. Brian Zirkle and William G. Staples, "Negotiating Workplace Surveillance," in *Electronic Monitoring in the Workplace: Controversies and Solutions*, ed. John Weckert (Hershey, PA: Idea Group, 2005), 79–100; Lucas D. Introna, "Opinion: Workplace Surveillance Is Unethical and Unfair," *Surveillance and Society* 1 (2003): 210–216.

131. Alan Westin, *Privacy and Freedom* (New York: Atheneum, 1967).

132. American Management Association and ePolicy Institute, "2007 Electronic Monitoring & Surveillance Survey," February 28, 2008, accessed March 21, 2013, http://press.amanet.org/press-releases/177/.

133. American Management Association, "2007 Electronic Monitoring and Surveillance Survey."

134. See relevant entries in my *Encyclopedia of Privacy*, Vols. 1 and 2 (Westport, CT: Greenwood Publishers, 2006).

135. Michel Foucault, *Power/Knowledge: Selected Interviews and Other Writings, 1972–1977*, ed. Colin Gordon (New York: Pantheon, 1980), 156.

136. Amy Harmon, "Corporate Delete Keys Busy as E-Mail Turns Up in Court," *New York Times*, November 11, 1998, accessed March 25, 2013, www.nytimes.com/1998/11/11/business/corporate-delete-keys-busy-as-e-mail-turns-up-in-court.html?pagewanted=all&src=pm; and see also Viktor Mayer-Schönberger, *Delete: The Virtue of Forgetting in the Digital Age* (Princeton, NJ: Princeton University Press, 2011).

137. Scott H. Matthews and Eric Williams, "Telework Adoption and Energy Use in Building and Transport Sectors in the United States and Japan," *Journal of Infrastructure Systems* 11(2005): 21–30; and Telework Research Network, "How Many People Telecommute?" *Telework Research Network*, accessed March 24, 2013, www.teleworkresearchnetwork.com/resources/people-telecommute.

138. Pam Kruger, "Survey: 1 In 3 Employees Are Stressed Out, Underpaid and Overworked," *Wall Street Journal*, March 3, 2013, accessed March 25, 2013, http://jobs.aol.com/articles/2013/03/06/americans-stressed-underpaid-overworked-survey/.

139. Jennifer Glass, "It's About Work, Not the Office," *New York Times*, March 7, 2013, accessed March 25, 2013, www.nytimes.com/2013/03/08/opinion/in-defense-of-telecommuting.html?pagewanted=all&_r=0.

140. Sue Shellenbarger, "'Working from Home' without Slacking Off," *Wall Street Journal*, July 11, 2012, accessed March 25, 2013, http://online.wsj.com/article/ SB10001424052702303684004577508953483021234.html.

141. Richard Grigonis, "Keeping Tabs on Road Warriors," *Technology Marketing Corporation*, May 2009, accessed March 25, 2013, www.tmcnet.com/voip/0509/location-based-services-here-there-and-everywhere.htm.

142. Ekahau Corporation, "Wi-Fi Pager and Badge Tag," accessed March 25, 2013, www.ekahau.com/images/stories/documents/datasheets/b4_datasheet_letter.pdf.

143. Rachel Emma Silverman, "Tracking Sensors Invade the Workplace," *Wall Street Journal*, March 7, 2013, accessed March 25, 2013, http://online.wsj.com/article/ SB10001424127887324034804578344303429080678.html#

144. NICE Systems, accessed March 25, 2013, www.nice.com.

145. Kim Bhasin, "Former Employee Says Working at an Outsourced Best Buy Call Center Is Like Being a 'Digital Slave,'" *Business Insider*, July 6, 2012, accessed March 25, 2013, www.businessinsider.com/former-employee-describes-conditions-at-outsourced-best-buy-call-center-2012-7.

146. Kevin Rawlinson, "TESCO Accused of Using Electronic Armbands to Monitor Its Staff," *Independent*, February 12, 2013, accessed March 25, 2013, www.independent. co.uk/news/business/news/tesco-accused-of-using-electronic-armbands-to-monitor-its-staff-8493952.html.

147. Examples from the two paragraphs come from, "News," *RFID Journal*, accessed March 25, 2013, www.rfidjournal.com/article/archive/1/7.

148. Resort Data Processing, Inc., "Housekeeping Management-Hotel Hospitality Software Solutions," accessed March 25, 2013, www.resortdata.com/rdpwin/newmodules/housekeepingscheduling/housekeepingoverview.htm.

149. Privacy Rights Clearinghouse, "Fact Sheet 16: Employment Background Checks: A Jobseeker's Guide," Revised February 2013, accessed March 25, 2013, www.privacyrights.org/ fs/fs16-bck.htm.

150. Amy B. Crane, "The ABCs of Pre-Employment Background Checks," *Bankrate.com*, February 16, 2005, accessed March 25, 2013, www.bankrate.com/brm/news/advice/ 20050216a1.asp.

151. Annie Murphy Paul, *The Cult of Personality Testing: How Personality Tests Are Leading Us to Miseducate Our Children, Mismanage Our Companies, and Misunderstand Ourselves* (New York: Simon and Schuster, 2010).

152. Ben Dattner, "The Use and Misuse of Personality Tests for Coaching and Development," *Psychology Today*, June 13, 2008, accessed March 25, 2013, psychologytoday.com/ blog/minds-work/200806/the-use-and-misuse-personality-tests-coaching-and-development.

153. Performance Now description, accessed March 25, 2013, www.pcrush.com/product/ Business-Management-Software/90043/Knowledge-Point-Performance-Now-v.4.0-Complete-Product].

154. Even the *Wall Street Journal* declares so. See the graphics on "The Surveillance Economy," accessed April 17, 2013, http://online.wsj.com/article/SB100008723 963904433896045780264739540943366.html.

155. Zygmunt Bauman, *Intimations of Postmodernity* (London: Routledge, 1992), 49; David Lyon, *Postmodernity* (Minneapolis: University of Minnesota Press, 1994), 66. See also Zygmunt Bauman and David Lyon, *Liquid Surveillance* (Cambridge, UK: Polity, 2012); and Pierre Bourdieu, *Distinction: A Social Critique of the Judgment of Taste* (London: Routledge, 1984).

156. Marketance. "How to Use Psychographics to Improve Demographic Market Segmentation," *Marketance.com*, accessed March 29, 2013, http://marketance.com/how-to-use-psychographics-to-improve-demographic-market-segmentation.

157. Jamie Beckland, "The End of Demographics: How Marketers Are Going Deeper with Personal Data," *Mashable*, June 30, 2011, accessed March 29, 2013, http://mashable.com/ 2011/06/30/psychographics-marketing.

158. Ensight Business Report No. 45, March 2011, www.ensight.ro/newsletter/no45/ art1_1_en.html.

159. Brian Fabiano, *Neuro Marketology: Harness Converging Technologies and Diverging Audiences to Create Dynamic One to One Marketing and Astonishing ROI* (Phoenix: FabCom Publishing, 2010) and www.neuromarketology.com.

160. Shan Li and David Sarno, "Facial Recognition Is Latest Marketing Tool," *Seattle Times*, August 28, 2011, accessed March 29, 2013, http://seattletimes.com/html/businesstechnology/2016036009_btadfacescans29.html.

161. Gregory Karp, "Cash vs. Credit Mindset," *Chicago Tribune*, December 15, 2011, accessed March 29, 2013, http://articles.chicagotribune.com/2011-12-15/news/sc-cons-1215-karpspend-20111210_1_credit-cards-card-balances-debit-cards.

162. Charles Duhigg, "How Companies Learn Your Secrets," *New York Times*, February 16, 2012, accessed March 31, 2013, www.nytimes.com/2012/02/19/magazine/shopping-habits.html?pagewanted=1&_r=2&hp.

163. Duhigg, "How Companies Learn Your Secrets."

4. BODILY INTRUSIONS

1. There is an emerging literature on the "CSI Effect." See for example, Tamara F. Lawson, "Before the Verdict and Beyond the Verdict: The CSI Infection within Modern Criminal Jury Trials," *Loyola University Chicago Law Journal* 41 (2009): 132–142.

2. Qtest, Inc., accessed October 12, 2012, www.qtestinc.com/index.html.

3. Phyllis Korkki, "The Count: Workers May Lie about Drug Use, but Hair Doesn't," *New York Times*, December 12, 2009, accessed October 12, 2012, www.nytimes.com/2009/12/13/business/13count.html.

4. Qtest, Inc., accessed October 12, 2012, www.qtestinc.com/index.html.

5. Steven L. Nock, *The Costs of Privacy: Surveillance and Reputation in America* (New York: De Gruyter, 1989).

6. Nock, *The Costs of Privacy*, 102.

7. William G. Staples and Stephanie K. Decker, "Technologies of the Body, Technologies of the Self: House Arrest as Neo-Liberal Governance," in *Surveillance and Governance: Crime Control Today*, ed. Mathew Deflem (Bingley, UK: Emerald/JAI Press, 2008), 131–149.

8. Ken D. Tunnell, *Pissing on Demand: Workplace Drug Testing and the Rise of the Detox Industry* (New York: New York University Press, 2004).

9. F. Allan Hanson, *Testing Testing: Social Consequences of the Examined Life* (Berkeley: University of California Press, 1993), 128.

10. U.S. Department of Justice, Office of Justice Programs, Bureau of Justice Statistics, *Fact Sheet: Drug Testing in the Criminal Justice System*, March 1992, accessed October 12, 2012, www.ncjrs.gov/pdffiles/dtest.pdf.

11. BCC Research and Market Forecasting, accessed October 12, 2012, www.bccresearch.com/report/drug-testing-technology-markets-phm013e.html.

12. Psychemedics Corporation, accessed October 12, 2012, www.psychemedics.com. See also their webpage, "School Drug Testing," accessed October 12, 2012, www.schooldrugtesting.com.

13. Psychemedics Corporation and "School Drug Testing." See also John Gilliom, *Surveillance, Privacy, and the Law: Employee Drug Testing and the Politics of Social Control* (Ann Arbor: University of Michigan Press, 1996).

14. Student Drug Testing Coalition, accessed October 12, 2012, www.studentdrugtesting.org.

15. "Drug-Test the Chess Club?" *USA Weekend*, November 20–22, 1998.

16. Dean Praetorius, "NJ School District Votes on Middle School Drug Tests," *Huffington Post*, May 25, 2011, accessed October 12, 2012, www.huffingtonpost.com/2011/01/12/middle-school-drug-tests_n_808268.html.

17. Ryoko Yamaguchi, Lloyd D. Johnston, and Patrick M. O'Malley, "Drug Testing in Schools: Policies, Practices, and Association with Student Drug Use," *Youth, Educ. and Society*

Occasional Papers 2 (2003), accessed October 14, 2012, www.yesresearch.org/publications/occpapers/YESOccPaper2.pdf.

18. Earl Vaughan, "Cumberland County Schools Ends Random Drug Testing Program for Athletes," FayOberserver.com, accessed October 14, 2012, http://fayobserver.com/articles/2011/07/14/1108339.

19. Sharon Levy, et al. "A Review of Internet-Based Home Drug-Testing Products for Parents," *Pediatrics* 113 (2004): 720–726.

20. First Check Diagnostics, Inc., accessed October 14, 2012, www.firstcheckfamily.com.

21. Cited in Hanson, *Testing Testing*, 128.

22. Levy, et al. "A Review of Internet-Based Home Drug-Testing Products for Parents," 725.

23. *Hill v. National Collegiate Athletic Assn.* 7 Cal.4th 1 (1994) Supreme Court of California, January 28, 1994, accessed October 14, 2012, www.leagle.com/xmlResult.aspx?page=9&xmldoc=199487Cal4th1_18.xml&docbase=CSLWAR2-1986-2006&SizeDisp=7.

24. Mark E. Brossman, "Workers Gain Privacy Rights by Legislation, Judicial Action," *National Law Journal*, April 9, 1990, 28.

25. Joseph B. Treaster, "Testing Workers for Drugs Reduces Company Problems," October 10, 1993, accessed October 14, 2012, www.nytimes.com/1993/10/10/nyregion/testing-workers-for-drugs-reduces-company-problems.html?pagewanted=all&src=pm.

26. Insurance Institute for Highway Safety, "DUI/DWI laws," April 2013, accessed April 18, 2013, www.iihs.org/laws/dui.aspx.

27. Alcohol Monitoring Systems, "The SCRAMx System," accessed August 14, 2011, www.alcoholmonitoring.com.

28. Shaun Hittle, "Leg Bracelets Succeed in Keeping Offenders from Alcohol, County Finds," *Lawrence Journal-World*, June 27, 2010, accessed 8/14/2011, www2.ljworld.com/news/2010/jun/27/leg-bracelets-succeed-keeping-offenders-alcohol-co.

29. See Diana C. Walsh, et al., "A Randomized Trial of Treatment Options for Alcohol-Abusing Workers," *New England Journal of Medicine* 325 (1991): 775–781; and Project MATCH Research Group, "Matching Alcoholism Treatments to Client Heterogeneity: Project MATCH Posttreatment Drinking Outcomes," *Journal of Studies on Alcohol* 58 (1997): 7–29.

30. David T. Lykken, *A Tremor in the Blood: Uses and Abuses of the Lie Detector* (New York: Plenum, 1998), xxi.

31. Hanson, *Testing Testing*, 68.

32. Cindy Clayton, "Va. Beach Polygraph Examiner Puts True Love to the Test," *Virginian-Pilot*, February 14, 2011, accessed August 14, 2011, www.hamptonroads.com/2011/02/va-beach-polygraph-examiner-puts-true-love-test.

33. Lykken, *A Tremor in the Blood*, xvi; U.S. Congress, Office of Technology Assessment, 1983, in Nock, *The Costs of Privacy*, 89–90.

34. Clayton, "Va. Beach Polygraph."

35. Lykken, *A Tremor in the Blood*, xvi; U.S. Congress, Office of Technology Assessment, 1983, in Nock, *The Costs of Privacy*, 89–90. See also National Research Council, *The Polygraph and Lie Detection* (Washington, DC: National Academies Press, 2003).

36. Stein, Jeff, "Lie Detectors Lie (Tell the C.I.A.)," *New Yrok Times*, February 19, 1995, accessed March 12, 2012, www.nytimes.com/1995/02/19/opinion/lie-detectors-lie-tell-the-cia.html.

37. Nock, *The Costs of Privacy*, 90–91.

38. Association for the Treatment of Sexual Abusers, "Remembering Kurt Freund 1914–1996," Vol. 18, no. 4 (Fall 2006), accessed April 17, 2013, http://newsmanager.commpartners.com/atsa/issues/2006-09-15/2.html.

39. Glen Kercber, "Use of the Penile Plethysmograph in the Assessment and Treatment of Sex Offenders," Report of the Interagency Council on Sex Offender Treatment to the Senate Interim Committee on Health and Human Services and the Senate Committee on Criminal Justice, January 1999, accessed March 11, 2012, www.dshs.state.tx.us/csot/csot_pleth.pdf; Alan Hyde, *Bodies of Law* (Princeton, NJ: Princeton University Press, 1997); Abby Goodnough and Monica Davey, "For Sex Offenders, a Dispute over Therapy's Benefits," *New York*

Times, March 6, 2007, accessed March 11, 2012, www.nytimes.com/2007/03/06/us/06civ-il.html?pagewanted=all.

40. Behavioral Technology, Inc., accessed March 11, 2012, www.btimonarch.com/page.php/monarch21PPG/Monarch-21-PPG.html.

41. Daniel Bergner, "What Do Women Want?" January 22, 2009, *New York Times*, accessed March 11, 2012, www.nytimes.com/2009/01/25/magazine/25desire-t.html.

42. "Debatable Device: Privacy, Technology Collide in a Dispute over Intimate Test," *Wall Street Journal*, February 3, 1993, 1.

43. "Debatable Device," 1.

44. Michel Foucault, *Discipline and Punish: The Birth of the Prison*, trans. A. M. Sheridan (New York: Pantheon, 1977), 193.

45. Centers for Disease Control and Prevention, "HIV/AIDS Statistics and Surveillance," accessed March 13, 2012, www.cdc.gov/hiv/topics/surveillance/basic.htm#dpdhi.

46. Mireya Navarro, "The Indelicate Art of Telling Adults How to Have Sex," *New York Times*, May 16, 1993, accessed March 13, 2012, http://select.nytimes.com/gst/abstract.html?res=F70617F9355E0C758DDDAC0894DB494D81.

47. David W. Webber, *AIDS and the Law* (New York: Aspen Publishers, 2007).

48. Navarro, "The Indelicate Art."

49. Casey Kovacic, "Out of Bounds: HIV and AIDS Discrimination in American Athletics," *Willamette Sports Law Journal* 1 (2008): 2–16; Karin Gopal Sankaran, et al., *HIV/Aids in Sport: Impact, Issues, and Challenges* (Champaign, IL: Human Kinetics, 1999).

50. Kaiser Family Foundation, "Updated Fact Sheet: HIV Testing in the United States," accessed July 6, 2012, www.kff.org/hivaids/upload/6094-12-2.pdf.

51. The Center for HIV Law and Policy, "Testing," accessed July 6, 2012, www.hivlawandpolicy.org.

52. The Center for HIV Law and Policy, "Testing," accessed July 6, 2012, www.hivlawandpolicy.org.

53. The Center for HIV Law and Policy, "Positive Justice Project: HIV Criminalization Fact Sheet," accessed July 6, 2012, www.hivlawandpolicy.org/resources/view/560.

54. The Center for HIV Law and Policy, "Ending and Defending against HIV Criminalization: State and Federal Laws and Prosecutions," Vol. 1, CHLP's Positive Justice Project, First Edition, Fall 2010 (Revised through 2012), accessed July 6, 2012, www.hivlawandpolicy.org/resources/view/564.

55. Dorothy Nelkin and Laurence Tancredi, *Dangerous Diagnostics: The Social Power of Biological Information* (1989; reprint, Chicago: University of Chicago Press, 1994), 160–161.

56. National Institute of Justice, Office of Justice Programs, *The Fingerprint Sourcebook* (Washington, DC, 2011), 7.

57. Federal Bureau of Investigation, "Integrated Automated Fingerprint Identification System-Fact Sheet," accessed July 12, 2012, www.fbi.gov/about-us/cjis/fingerprints_biometrics/iafis/iafis_facts.

58. *The Fingerprint Sourcebook*, 31.

59. Rocco Parascandola, "NYPD Gets High-Tech Upgrade with New Portable Fingerprint Scanner," accessed July 12, 2012, www.articles.nydailynews.com/2010-09-18/local/27075699_1_crime-victims-nypd-handheld-devices.

60. Leo M. Norton, "Who Goes There? Mobile Fingerprint Readers in Los Angeles County," *Police Chief* (June 2009), accessed July 12, 2012, www.policechiefmagazine.org/magazine/index.cfm?fuseaction=display_arch&article_id=1824&issue_id=62009.

61. Federal Bureau of Investigation, "Integrated Automated Fingerprint Identification System-Fact Sheet."

62. Simon A. Cole, *Suspect Identities: A History of Fingerprinting and Criminal Identification* (Cambridge, MA: Harvard University Press, 2002).

63. Eric Lichtbau, "U.S. Will Pay $2 Million to Lawyer Wrongly Jailed," *New York Times*, November 30, 2006, accessed July 16, 2011, www.nytimes.com/2006/11/30/us/30settle.html?_r=0; "Man wrongly convicted in Boston police shooting found dead," *Boston Globe*, accessed July 16, 2011, www.boston.com/news/globe/city_region/breaking_news/2007/10/man_wrongly_con.html; "An Officer's Guilt Casts Shadow on Trials," *New York Times*, March

4, 1993, accessed July 16, 2011, www.nytimes.com/1993/03/04/nyregion/an-officer-s-guilt-casts-shadow-on-trials.html; "Police Investigation Supervisor Admits Faking Fingerprints," *New York Times*, July 30, 1993, accessed July 16, 2011, www.nytimes.com/1993/07/30/nyregion/police-investigation-supervisor-admits-faking-fingerprints.html.

64. Andy Newman, "Judge Rules Fingerprints Cannot Be Called a Match," *New York Times*, January 11, 2002, accessed July 16, 2011, www.nytimes.com/2002/01/11/us/judge-rules-fingerprints-cannot-be-called-a-match.html?pagewanted=all&src=pm.

65. Cole, *Suspect Identities*, 258.

66. East Shore Technologies, Inc., accessed July 16, 2011, www.east-shore.com.

67. Shoshana Magnet, "Bio-Benefits: Technologies of Criminalization, Biometrics, and the Welfare System," in *Surveillance: Power, Problems, and Politics*, eds. Sean P. Hier and Joshua Greenberg (Vancouver: University of British Columbia Press, 2009), 169–183. See also John Gilliom, *Overseers of the Poor: Surveillance, Resistance, and the Limits of Privacy* (Chicago: University of Chicago Press, 2001).

68. "Fingerprinting Welfare Recipients to Stop Double-Dipping, Fraud," *NBC Nightly News*, November 1, 1994, accessed August 16, 2012, https://archives.nbclearn.com/portal/site/k-12/browse/?cuecard=5829. Emphasis added.

69. Department of Health and Human Services, Office of the Inspector General, "Review of the Ongoing Los Angeles County Fingerprinting Demonstration Project" (2003), accessed August 16, 2012, http://oig.hhs.gov/oas/reports/region9/99500054.pdf; Magnet, "Bio-Benefits."

70. Kimberly J. Mclarin, "Welfare Fingerprinting Finds Most People Are Telling Truth," *New York Times*, September 29, 1995, accessed July 16, 2011, www.nytimes.com/1995/09/29/nyregion/welfare-fingerprinting-finds-most-people-are-telling-truth.html.

71. Jeffrey Plaut, Coordinator, City-Wide Welfare Advocacy Network, Bronx, "When Welfare Tries Fingerprints," *New York Times*, April 23, 1992, accessed July 16, 2011, www.nytimes.com/1992/04/23/opinion/l-when-welfare-tries-fingerprints-256092.html. See also Harry Murray, "Deniable Degradation: The Finger-Imaging of Welfare Recipients," *Sociological Forum* 15 (2000): 39–63.

72. Kathleen Lucadamo, "Gov's Healthy Overhaul of Food Stamps: Spitzer to Nix Fingerprinting, 2G Max in Bank," *New York Daily News*, June 5, 2007, accessed July 16, 2011, www.nydailynews.com/news/gov-healthy-overhaul-food-stamps-article-1.221927; and Patrick McGreevy, "Gov. Jerry Brown Ends Fingerprinting for Food Stamp Recipients," October 6, 2011, accessed July 16, 2011, http://latimesblogs.latimes.com/california-politics/2011/10/gov-jerry-brown-ends-fingerprinting-for-food-stamp-recipients.html.

73. Department of Homeland Security, "Office of US-VISIT- Overview," accessed July 16, 2011, www.dhs.gov/us-visit-office.

74. Jennifer Lynch, "From Finger Prints to DNA: Biometric Data Collection in U.S. Immigrant Communities and Beyond," Electronic Frontier Foundation (2012), accessed July 16, 2011, www.policechiefmagazine.org/magazine/index.cfm?fuseaction=display_arch&article_id=1824&issue_id=62009.

75. Lynch, "From Finger Prints to DNA," 3.

76. John Roach, "Your Feet May Soon Be Your Password," *NBC News*, accessed July 18, 2011, www.nbcnews.com/technology/futureoftech/your-feet-may-soon-be-your-password-905968. On facial recognition, see Kelly Gates, *Our Biometric Future: Facial Recognition Technology and the Culture of Surveillance* (New York: New York University Press, 2011).

77. "Border Patrol Kiosk Detects Liars Trying to Enter U.S.," *Homeland Security News Wire*, August 21, 2012, accessed July 18, 2011, www.homelandsecuritynewswire.com/dr20120821-border-patrol-kiosk-detects-liars-trying-to-enter-u-s.

78. "Biometrics Market Set to Grow by 21 Percent CAGR from 2012 to 2014," *Homeland Security News Wire*, May 16, 2012, accessed July 24, 2012, www.homelandsecuritynewswire.com/dr20120516-biometrics-market-set-to-grow-by-21-percent-cagr-from-2012-to-2014.

79. IMDB, "Gatttica," accessed July 24, 2012, www.imdb.com/title/tt0119177/.

80. Federal Bureau of Investigation, "Biometric Analysis—CODIS—CODIS Brochure," accessed July 12, 2012, www.fbi.gov/about-us/lab/codis/codis_brochure.

81. Shaun Hittle, "DNA database helps provide missing links in unsolved cases," *Lawrence Journal-World*, February 13, 2012, accessed July 13, 2012, www2.ljworld.com/news/2012/feb/13/dna-database-helps-provide-missing-links-unsolved-/.

82. Karen Norrgard, "Forensics, DNA Fingerprinting, and CODIS," *Nature Education* 1 (2008), accessed July 13, 2012, www.nature.com/scitable/topicpage/forensics-dna-fingerprinting-and-codis-736.

83. Bill Dadman, "A Rape Defendant With No Identity, But a DNA Profile," *New York Times*, October 07, 1999, accessed July 13, 2012, www.nytimes.com/1999/10/07/us/a-rape-defendant-with-no-identity-but-a-dna profile.html.

84. National Center for Victims of Crime, "Profiles in DNA: An interview with Norman Gahn," accessed July 13, 2012, www.victimsofcrime.org/our-programs/dna-resource-center/profiles-in-dna/norman-gahn.

85. David M. Halbfinger, "Police Dragnets for DNA Tests Draw Criticism," *New York Times*, January 4, 2003, accessed July 16, 2011, www.nytimes.com/2003/01/04/us/police-dragnets-for-dna-tests-draw-criticism.html; and Rebecca Leung, "DNA Dragnet," *CBS NEWS-60 Minutes*, February 11, 2009, accessed July 16, 2011, www.cbsnews.com/2100-18560_162-642684.html.

86. Federal Bureau of Investigation, "Biometric Analysis—CODIS – Statistics," accessed July 12, 2012, www.fbi.gov/about-us/lab/codis/ndis-statistics.

87. Robin McKie, "Icelandic DNA Project Hit by Privacy Storm," *Observer*, May 16, 2004, accessed July 12, 2012, www.guardian.co.uk/science/2004/may/16/genetics.research.

88. Laura Baker, et al., "Behavioral Genetics: The Science of Antisocial Behavior," *Law and Contemporary Problems* 69 (2006), 7.

89. Baker, "Behavioral Genetics," 44.

90. Patricia Cohen, "Genetic Basis for Crime: A New Look," *New York Times*, June 19, 2011, accessed July 16, 2011, www.nytimes.com/2011/06/20/arts/genetics-and-crime-at-institute-of-justice-conference.html; and Daniel Goleman, "New Storm Brews on Whether Crime Has Roots in Genes," *New York Times*, September 15, 1992, accessed July 16, 2011, www.nytimes.com/1992/09/15/science/new-storm-brews-on-whether-crime-has-roots-in-genes.html.

91. Reuters Business Profile: Myriad Genetics Inc., accessed July 16, 2011, www.reuters.com/finance/stocks/companyProfile?symbol=MYGN.O.

92. Rob Stein, National Public Radio, "Will Low-Cost Genome Sequencing Open 'Pandora's Box'?" *NPR: Morning Edition*, October 2, 2012, accessed October 3, 2012, www.npr.org/blogs/health/2012/10/02/161110956/will-low-cost-genome-sequencing-open-pandoras-box.

93. GeneTests Medical Genetics Information Resource, University of Washington, Seattle, 1993–2012, accessed October 3, 2012, www.genetests.org.

94. Robert Langreth, "Fumbled DNA Tests Mean Peril for Breast-Cancer Patients, *Bloomberg*, September 9, 2012, accessed October 3, 2012, www.bloomberg.com/news/2012-09-10/fumbled-dna-tests-mean-peril-for-breast-cancer-patients.html.

95. Stein, "Will Low-Cost Genome Sequencing Open 'Pandora's Box'?"

96. Jane E. Brody, "Buyer Beware of Home DNA Test," *New York Times*, September 1, 2009, accessed October 3, 2012, www.nytimes.com/2009/09/01/health/01brod.html.

97. Diane E. Hoffmann and Karen H. Rothenberg, "Judging Genes: Implications of the Second Generation of Genetic Tests in the Courtroom" *Maryland Law Review* 66 (2007): 858–922.

98. Anthony G. Hopp, "DNA Evidence in Toxic-Tort Cases: Still We," *Andres Litigation Reporter*, accessed October 3, 2012, www.edwardswildman.com/files/Uploads/Documents/Hopp-DNAEvidence[1].pdf.

99. Identigene, LLC, "Identigene Helps Fatherhood Matters Inc. with I.AM.A.FATHER Campaign," accessed October 4, 2012, www.dnatesting.com/blog/dnatesting.

100. Identigene, LLC, "IDENTIGENE DNA Paternity Test—How It Works," accessed October 4, 2012, www.dnatesting.com/blog/dnatesting/tag/dna-sample-collection/.

101. Andrew Pollack, "Before Birth, Dad's ID," *New York Times*, June 19, 2012, accessed October 4, 2012, www.nytimes.com/2012/06/20/health/paternity-blood-tests-that-work-early-

in-a-pregnancy.html?pagewanted=all. See also Alain Pottage, "The Socio-legal Implications of the New Biotechnologies," *Annual Review of Law and Social Science*, (2007): 321–344.

102. Department of Health and Human Services, "'GINA'—The Genetic Information Non-discrimination Act of 2008," April 6, 2009, accessed October 6, 2012, www.genome.gov/Pages/PolicyEthics/GeneticDiscrimination/GINAInfoDoc.pdf.

103. Nelkin and Tancredi, *Dangerous Diagnostics*, ix–x.

104. Jonnelle Marte, "Get Paid to Stay Healthy," *Wall Street Journal*, October 5, 2012, accessed October 6, 2012, http://articles.marketwatch.com/2012-10-05/finance/34253423_1_health-savings-accounts-wellness-programs-health-costs; Diane Stafford, "Percentage of Health Coverage at Work Is Declining, Study Says," *Kansas City Star*, May 22, 2012, accessed October 6, 2012, www.kansascity.com/2012/05/22/3622489/percentage-of-workers-with-employer.html.

105. Michelle Conlin, "Get Healthy—Or Else: Inside One Company's All-Out Attack on Medical Costs," *Bloomberg Businessweek*, February 26, 2007, accessed October 6, 2012, www.businessweek.com/stories/2007-02-25/get-healthy-r-else.

106. Conlin, "Get Healthy—Or Else."

107. While many of these politicians want to *force* birth control on some, they want to *limit* access to birth control for other women.

108. Project Prevention, "Objectives," accessed October 6, 2012, www.projectprevention.org/objectives.

109. National Advocates for Pregnant Women, "C.R.A.C.K." accessed October 6, 2012, www.advocatesforpregnantwomen.org/issues/crack.

110. Beth Shayne, "Program Pays Drug Addicts $300 to Get Sterilized," *WCNC.com*, May 19, 2010, accessed October 6, 2012, www.wcnc.com/news/local/Drug-addicts-can-get-steril-ized-for-cash-94203844.html.

111. Ada Calhoun, "The Criminalization of Bad Mothers," *New York Times*, April 25, 2012, accessed October 4, 2012, www.nytimes.com/2012/04/29/magazine/the-criminalization-of-bad-mothers.html?pagewanted=all.

112. Charles L. Scott and Trent Holmberg, "Castration of Sex Offenders: Prisoners' Rights Versus Public Safety," *Journal of the American Academy of Psychiatry Law* 31 (2003): 502–509.

113. Scott and Holmberg, "Castration of Sex Offenders," 503.

114. William G. Staples, *Castles of Our Conscience: Social Control and the American State, 1800–1985* (New Brunswick, NJ: Rutgers University Press, 1991); Gerald N. Grob, *From Asylum to Community: Mental Health Policy in Modern America* (Princeton, NJ: Princeton University Press, 1991); Andrew Scull, *Decarceration: Community Treatment and the Deviant* (Englewood Cliffs: Prentice Hall, Inc., 1977).

115. Adam Liptak, "State Can Make Inmate Sane Enough to Execute," *New York Times*, February 11, 2003, accessed October 4, 2012, www.nytimes.com/2003/02/11/us/state-can-make-inmate-sane-enough-to-execute.html.

116. Adam Liptak, "State Can Make Inmate Sane Enough to Execute"; Jacques Billeaud, "Loughner Loses Appeal over Forced Medication," *Seattle Times*, March 5, 2012, accessed October 4, 2012, http://seattletimes.com/html/nationworld/2017670737_apuscongressmanshot-suspect.htm; Fernanda Santos, "Life Term for Gunman After Guilty Plea in Tucson Killings," *New York Times*, August 7, 2012, accessed October 4, 2012, www.nytimes.com/2012/08/08/us/loughner-pleads-guilty-in-2011-tucson-shootings.html.

117. Bronwen Hruska, "Raising the Ritalin Generation," *New York Times*, August 18, 2012, accessed August 19, 2012, www.nytimes.com/2012/08/19/opinion/sunday/raising-the-ritalin-generation.html?pagewanted=all.

118. Centers for Disease Control and Prevention, "Attention-Deficit/Hyperactivity Disorder (ADHD)," accessed October 11, 2012, www.cdc.gov/ncbddd/adhd/index.html; PubMed, "Attention deficit hyperactivity disorder, ADD; ADHD; Childhood hyperkinesis," March 25, 2012, accessed October 11, 2012, www.ncbi.nlm.nih.gov/pubmedhealth/PMH0002518/.

119. Ilina Singh, "Voices on Identity, Childhood, Ethics and Stimulants Children Join the Debate," *Voices.com*, accessed October 11, 2012, www.adhdvoices.com/documents/VoicesReport2012.pdf.

120. Singh, "Voices on Identity."

121. Singh, "Voices on Identity."

122. Alan Schwarz, "Attention Disorder or Not, Pills to Help in School," *New York Times*, October 9, 2012, accessed October 11, 2012, www.nytimes.com/2012/10/09/health/attention-disorder-or-not-children-prescribed-pills-to-help-in-school.html.

123. Schwarz, "Attention Disorder or Not." See also David Healy, *Pharmageddon* (Los Angeles: University of California Press, 2012), and Robert Whitaker, *Anatomy of an Epidemic: Magic Bullets, Psychiatric Drugs, and the Astonishing Rise of Mental Illness in America* (New York: Broadway, 2011).

124. Norman K. Denzin, *Images of Postmodern Society: Social Theory and Contemporary Cinema* (Newbury Park, CA: Sage, 1991), vii.

125. Hanson, *Testing Testing*, 93,

5. WIRED.I.AM: THE DIGITAL LIFE 2.0

1. National Science Foundation, "A Brief History of NSF and the Internet," August 13, 2003, accessed April 17, 2013, www.nsf.gov/news/news_summ.jsp?cntn_id=103050.

2. See Evgeny Morozov, "Two Decades of the Web: A Utopia No Longer," *Prospect*, June 22, 2011, accessed April 17, 2013, www.prospectmagazine.co.uk/magazine/morozov-web-no-utopia-twenty-years-short-history-internet; David J. Eck, *The Most Complex Machine: A Survey of Computers and Computing* (New York: A. K. Peters, 1995); Katie Hafner and Matthew Lyon, *Where Wizards Stay Up Late: The Origins of the Internet* (New York: Simon and Schuster, 1996).

3. "World Internet Users and Population Stats," accessed April 17, 2013, www.internetworldstats.com/stats2.htm; Leichtman Research Group, Inc., "Nearly 90% of Us Computer Households Subscribe to Broadband," accessed April 17, 2013, www.leichtmanresearch.com/press/090412release.html; Cisco Systems, Inc., "Visual Networking Index," accessed April 17, 2013, www.cisco.com/en/US/netsol/ns827/networking_solutions_sub_solution.html.

4. Cisco Systems, Inc., "Visual Networking Index."

5. Joanna Brenner, Pew Internet and American Life Project, "Mobile," January 31, 2013, accessed April 17, 2013, http://pewinternet.org/Commentary/2012/February/Pew-Internet-Mobile.aspx.

6. Pew Internet and American Life Project, "Trend Data (Adults)," accessed April 17, 2013, http://pewinternet.org/Trend-Data-(Adults)/Online-Activites-Total.aspx.

7. Pew Internet and American Life Project, What Kind of Tech User Are You?" accessed April 17, 2013, http://pewinternet.org/Static-Pages/Participate/What-Kind-of-Tech-User-Are-You.aspx.

8. Walter Benjamin's "The Work of Art in the Age of Mechanical Reproduction," in *Illuminations: Essays and Reflections*, eds. Walter Benjamin and Hannah Arendt (New York: Harcourt, 1968), 219–253. In the end, Benjamin asserts that the loss of authenticity may be advantageous because it democratizes and politicizes art. His Frankfurt School colleagues, however, were convinced that the capitalist culture industry would commodify and standardize art to its and society's detriment.

9. Jean Baudrillard, *The Ecstasy of Communication*, new ed., trans. Bernard Schütze and Caroline Schütze (Boston: Semiotext(e), 2012).

10. David Weinberger, *Everything Is Miscellaneous: The Power of the New Digital Disorder* (New York: Holt Paperbacks, 2008), and *Small Pieces Loosely Joined: A Unified Theory of The Web* (New York: Basic, 2003); F. Allan Hanson, *Technology and Cultural Tectonics: Shifting Values and Meanings* (New York: Palgrave, forthcoming).

11. Kevin Kelly, "The Electronic Hive: Embrace It," in *Computerization and Controversy: Value Conflicts and Social Choice*, 2nd ed., ed. Rob Kling (San Diego: Academic Press, 1996), 76–77.

12. See Evgeny Morozov, "Two Decades of the Web." and his *The Net Delusion: The Dark Side of Internet Freedom* (New York: Public Affairs, 2011).

13. Philip N. Howard, "The Arab Spring's Cascading Effects," *Pacific Standard*, accessed April 17, 2013, www.psmag.com/politics/the-cascading-effects-of-the-arab-spring-28575.

14. Dwayne Winseck, "Netscapes of Power: Convergence, Network Design, walled Gardens, and Other Strategies of Control in the Information Age," in *Surveillance as Social Sorting: Privacy, Risk and Digital Discrimination*, ed. David Lyon (New York: Routledge, 2003), 176–198.

15. Robert W. McChesney, *Digital Disconnect: How Capitalism Is Turning the Internet against Democracy* (New York: New Press, 2013); Jack Goldsmith and Tim Wu, *Who Controls the Internet?: Illusions of a Borderless World* (New York: Oxford University Press, 2008).

16. Goldsmith and Wu, *Who Controls the Internet?*, viii.

17. Tony Dokoupil, "Is the Web Driving Us Mad?" *Daily Beast*, July 9, 2012, accessed April 22, 2013, www.thedailybeast.com/newsweek/2012/07/08/is-the-internet-making-us-crazy-what-the-new-research-says.html.

18. Nicholas Carr, *The Shallows: What the Internet Is Doing to Our Brains* (New York: W. W. Norton, 2011). See also Sherry Turkle, *Alone Together: Why We Expect More from Technology and Less from Each Other* (New York: Basic, 2011); Mark Bauerlein, *The Digital Divide: Arguments for and Against Facebook, Google, Texting, and the Age of Social Networking* (New York: Tarcher, 2011).

19. Nicholas Carr, "How the Internet Is Making Us Stupid," *Telegraph*, August 27, 201, accessed April 17, 2013, www.telegraph.co.uk/technology/internet/7967894/How-the-Internet-is-making-us-stupid.html.

20. James Vlahos, "Is Sitting a Lethal Activity?" *New York Times*, April 14, 2011, accessed April 17, 2013, www.nytimes.com/2011/04/17/magazine/mag-17sitting-t.html?_r=0.

21. As the Web becomes "much like the rest of social life" it mimics what Kuntsler calls the "Sameness of the Suburban Landscape" where "we drive up and down the gruesome, tragic suburban boulevards of commerce, and we're overwhelmed at the fantastic, awesome, stupefying ugliness of absolutely everything in sight." In this case, we "surf" up and down a mediascape that looks increasingly like those suburban thoroughfares, plastered with the familiarity of franchised advertisements, company logos, and virtual "box stores" ready to sell or, popularly, auction, any conceivable commodity. And we see Disney and other media conglomerates teaming up with the likes of powerhouse Google, Microsoft and the like to saturate the Web with their cultural products, making it look like the all-too-familiar mainstream of Hollywood, cable and tabloid television, HBO, MTV, and the rest. See James Howard Kuntsler, *Home from Nowhere: Remaking Our Everyday World for the Twenty-first Century* (New York: Simon and Schuster, 1996).

22. Doug Tewksbury, "Crowdsourcing Homeland Security: The Texas Virtual Border-Watch and Participatory Citisenship," *Surveillance and Society* 10 (2009): 249–262, accessed April 18, 2013, www.surveillance-and-society.org.

23. Richard G. Wright, "Sex Offender Post-Incarceration Sanctions: Are There Any Limits?" *New England Journal of Criminal and Civil Confinement* 34 (2008): 17–50; H.R. 4472 (109th): Adam Walsh Child Protection and Safety Act of 2006, accessed April 17, 2013, www.govtrack.us/congress/bills/109/hr4472.

24. Jeff Lambert, "Tennessee's Meth Offender Registry Copied and Reviled," *TimesNet-News*, August 24, 2008, accessed April 18, 2013, www.timesnews.net/article.php?id=9007847.

25. Lambert, "Tennessee's Meth Offender Registry Copied and Reviled."

26. Douglas County Registered Offender Map, accessed April 18, 2013, www2.ljworld.com/registered-offenders.

27. Wright, "Sex Offender Post-Incarceration Sanctions"; Roxanne Lieb, Vernon Quinsey and Lucy Berliner, "Sexual Predators and Social Policy," *Crime and Justice* 23 (1998): 43–114.

28. Patricia M. Harris and Kimberly S. Keller, "Ex-Offenders Need Not Apply: The Criminal Background Check in Hiring Decisions," *Journal of Contemporary Criminal Justice* 21 (2005): 6–30.

29. Harris and Keller, "Ex-Offenders Need Not Apply," 6.

30. Michelle Natividad Rodriguez and Maurice Emsellem, "65 Million 'Need Not Apply': The Case for Reforming Criminal Background Checks for Employment," *National Employ-

ment Law Project (2011), accessed April 13, 2013, www.nelp.org/page/-/SCLP/2011/65_Million_Need_Not_Apply.pdf?nocdn=1.

31. Rodriguez and Emsellem, "65 Million 'Need Not Apply,'" 7. An interesting variant on the public records check are private databases set up to collect names of employees in the retail industry that have been accused of stealing. These extra-legal databases have thousands of subscribers from some of the biggest names in retail. Typically, the databases provide few details about the circumstances of the theft incidences and most cases do not even involve criminal charges. An investigation by two journalists into the databases suggests that many employees, interrogated by store security personnel, often feel coerced into confessing to having done something wrong. Without due process procedures and protections, they are not likely to understand that their statements are taken as admission of guilt. See Stephanie Clifford and Jessica Silver-Greenberg, "Retailers Track Employee Thefts in Vast Databases," *New York Times*, April 2, 2013, accessed April 23, 2013, www.nytimes.com/2013/04/03/business/retailers-use-databases-to-track-worker-thefts.html?hpw&_r=0.

32. Tewksbury, "Crowdsourcing Homeland Security."

33. BlueServo, "About BlueServo," accessed April 12, 2013, www.blueservo.net/about.php.

34. Tewksbury, "Crowdsourcing Homeland Security." Mark Andrejevic, "Interactive (In)Security," *Cultural Studies* 20 (2006): 441–458.

35. John Burnett, *All Things Considered*, "A New Way to Patrol the Texas Border: Virtually," *National Public Radio*, February 23, 2009, accessed April 3, 2013, www.npr.org/templates/story/story.php?storyId=101050132.

36. Burnett, "A New Way to Patrol the Texas Border."

37. "New Technologies Help Border Patrol and Border Crossers, Respectively," huffingtonpost.com, August, 8, 2011, accessed April 3, 2013, www.huffingtonpost.com/2011/08/22/technology-helps-border-c_n_931639.html.

38. Thomas Mathiesen, "The Viewer Society: Michel Foucault's 'Panopticon' Revisited," *Theoretical Criminology* 1 (1997): 215–234.

39. Kevin D. Haggerty and Richard V. Ericson, "The Surveillant Assemblage," *British Journal of Sociology* 51 (2000): 605–622.

40. Pearson School Systems, "PowerSchool," accessed April 13, 2013, www.pearsonschoolsystems.com/products/powerschool.

41. Pearson School Systems, "Products, PowerSchool," accessed April 13, 2013, www.pearsonschoolsystems.com/products/powerschool.

42. Devin Mcginley, "Bogota Parents Can Now Track Grades Online," Northjersey.com, March 15, 2013, accessed April 12, 2013, www.northjersey.com/news/198396531_Bogota_parents_can_now_track_grades_online.html?page=all.

43. Mark Hicks, "Clarksville-Montgomery County School Board Upholds Gray's Dismissal," *Leaf Chronicle*, March 12, 2013, accessed April 12, 2013, www.theleafchronicle.com/article/20130312/NEWS01/303120065/Clarksville-Montgomery-County-School-Board-upholds-Grays-dismissal.

44. Kaelee Heidt, "The Future Is Not Far for High School Seniors," *Bismarck Tribune*, March 4, 2013, accessed April 13, 2013, http://bismarcktribune.com/lifestyles/fashion-and-style/the-future-is-not-far-for-high-school-seniors/article_a7e403e8-7f8d-11e2-a72f-001a4bcf887a.html.

45. Awareness Technologies, Inc., accessed April 15, 2013, www.awarenesstechnologies.com. Emphasis added.

46. James Vlahos, "Surveillance Society: New High-Tech Cameras Are Watching You," *Popular Mechanics*, January 2008, accessed April 3, 2013, www.popularmechanics.com/technology/military/4236865.

47. Vlahos, "Surveillance Society," and Raytheon Company, "Insider Threat and Counterintelligence Solutions," accessed April 17, 2013, www.raytheon.com/capabilities/products/cybersecurity/insiderthreat/index.html.

48. uKnow.com, accessed April 17, 2013, www.uknowkids.com.

49. Somini Sengupta, "'Big Brother'? No, It's Parents," *New York Times*, June 5, 2012, accessed April 20, 2013, www.nytimes.com/2012/06/26/technology/software-helps-parents-monitor-their-children-online.html?pagewanted=all&_r=0.

50. uKnow.com.

51. Foursquare, "About Foursquare," accessed April 20, 2013, www.foursquare.com/about.

52. Kai Ryssdal, "'Checking in' with Foursquare CEO Dennis Crowley," *American Public Media: Market Place*, June 25, 2012, accessed April 20, 2013, www.marketplace.org/topics/business/corner-office/checking-foursquare-ceo-dennis-crowley.

53. Anne Marie Kelly, "Three Reasons Why Foursquare's New Advertising Model Might Work," *Forbes*, August 22, 2012, accessed April 20, 2013, www.forbes.com/sites/annemarie-kelly/2012/08/22/three-reasons-why-foursquares-new-advertising-model-might-work.

54. Cecilia Kang, "Foursquare Founder Selvadurai Talks about Privacy, Future," *Washington Post*, April 8, 2011, accessed April 20, 2013, www.washingtonpost.com/blogs/post-tech/post/foursquare-founder-selvadurai-talks-about-privacy-future/2011/04/08/AFGYa21C_blog.html.

55. Somini Sengupta, "Letting Down Our Guard with Web Privacy," *New York Times*, March 30, 2013, accessed April 20, 2013, www.nytimes.com/2013/03/31/technology/web-privacy-and-how-consumers-let-down-their-guard.html?hpw.

56. John Brownlee, "This Creepy App Isn't Just Stalking Women without Their Knowledge, It's a Wake-Up Call about Facebook Privacy," *Cult of Mac*, March 30, 2012, accessed April 10, 2013, www.cultofmac.com/157641/this-creepy-app-isnt-just-stalking-women-without-their-knowledge-its-a-wake-up-call-about-facebook-privacy; Irina Raicu, "Case Study on Online Privacy—'Girls around Me,'" Markkula Center for Applied Ethics, Santa Clara University, June 2012, accessed June 19, 2013, www.scu.edu/ethics/practicing/focusareas/technology/internet/privacy/girls-around.html.

57. Scott Austin and Andrew Dowell, "'Girls around Me' Developer Defends App after Foursquare Dismissal," *Wall Street Journal*, March 31, 2012, accessed June 19, 2013, http://blogs.wsj.com/digits/2012/03/31/girls-around-me-developer-defends-app-after-foursquare-dismissal/.

58. Kenneth Laudon and Carol Guercio Traver, *E-Commerce 2012*, 8th ed. (New York: Pearson Education, 2012).

59. Lauren Indvik, "U.S. Online Retail Sales to Reach $327 Billion by 2016," *Mashable*, February 27, 2012, accessed April 10, 2013, http://mashable.com/2012/02/27/ecommerce-327-billion-2016-study.

60. Acxiom Corporation, accessed April 20, 2013, www.acxiom.com; Natasha Singer, "Mapping, and Sharing, the Consumer Genome," *New York Times*, June 16, 2012, accessed April 20, 2013, www.nytimes.com/2012/06/17/technology/acxiom-the-quiet-giant-of-consumer-database-marketing.html?pagewanted=all.

61. Acxiom Corporation, "Retail Case Study," accessed April 20, 2013, www.acxiom.com/site-assets/case-study/case-macys-view-across-touchpoints.

62. Jeffery Rosen, "Who Do Online Advertisers Think You Are?" *New York Times*, November 30, 2012, accessed April 19, 2013, www.nytimes.com/2012/12/02/magazine/who-do-online-advertisers-think-you-are.html. See also, Natasha Singer, "Your Online Attention, Bought in an Instant," *New York Times*, November 17, 2012, www.nytimes.com/2012/11/18/technology/your-online-attention-bought-in-an-instant-by-advertisers.html.

63. See, for example, Bart W. Schermer, "The Limits of Privacy in Automated Profiling and Data Mining," *Computer Law and Security Review* 27 (2011), 45–52; Ethan Cohen-Cole, "Credit Card Redlining," *Federal Reserve Bank of Boston*, Quantitative Analysis Unit Working Paper No. QAU08-1, February 9, 2009, accessed April 23, 2013, http://ssrn.com/abstract=1098403; Michael Powell, "Bank Accused of Pushing Mortgage Deals on Blacks," *New York Times*, June 6, 2009, accessed April 23, 2013, www.nytimes.com/2009/06/07/us/07baltimore.html; Lori Andrews, "Facebook Is Using You," *New York Times*, February 4, 2012, accessed April 23, 2013, www.nytimes.com/2012/02/05/opinion/sunday/facebook-is-using-you.html; Marcia Stepanek, "Weblining Companies Are Using Your Personal Data to Limit Your Choices—and Force You to Pay More for Products," *Business Week*, accessed April 23, 2013, www.businessweek.com/2000/00_14/b3675027.htm.

64. Singer, "Mapping, and Sharing, the Consumer Genome."

65. Natasha Singer, "Secret E-Scores Chart Consumers' Buying Power," *New York Times*, August 18, 2012, accessed April 20, 2013, www.nytimes.com/2012/08/19/business/electronic-scores-rank-consumers-by-potential-value.html?pagewanted=all.

66. Singer, "Secret E-Scores."

67. Phillip Tabor, "I Am a Videocam." In *The Unkown City: Contesting Architecture and Social Space*, eds. Iain Borden, et al. (Cambridge, MA: MIT Press, 2002): 122–137.

68. TrueLook Professional Webcam Systems, Inc. "FAQ," accessed April 20, 2013, www.truelook.com/resources/faq.

69. From the film *Wall Street*, quoted in Norman K. Denzin, *Images of Postmodern Society* (Newbury Park, CA: Sage, 1991), 82. Ruth Barcan, "In the Raw: 'Home-Made' Porn and Reality Genres," *Journal of Mundane Behavior* 3 (2002): 87–108. See also Katrien Jacobs, *Netporn: DIY Web Culture and Sexual Politics* (Lanham, MD: Rowman & Littlefield, 2007).

70. Peter Weibel, "Pleasure and the Panoptic Principle," in *Rhetorics of Surveillance from Bentham to Big Brother*, eds. Thomas Y. Levin, Ursula Frohne, Peter Weibel (Cambridge, MA: MIT Press, 2002), 207–233.

71. "Behind the Scenes with Jennifer Ringley," segment of "Webjunk" on VH1, posted to IFILM on March 18, 2007, accessed April 18, 2013.

72. Daniel Trottier, *Social Media as Surveillance: Rethinking Visibility in a Converging World* (Burlington, VT: Ashgate, 2012); Jean Burgess and Joshua Green, *YouTube: Online Video and Participatory Culture* (Cambridge, UK: Polity, 2009).

73. Charles Derber, *The Pursuit of Attention: Power and Ego in Everyday Life* (New York: Oxford University Press, 2000), xi.

74. Janet Maslin, "So, What's Wrong with This Picture?" *New York Times*, June 5, 1998, accessed April 19, 2013, www.nytimes.com/1998/06/05/movies/film-review-so-what-s-wrong-with-this-picture.html. Maslin goes on to say, "What if our taste for trivia and voyeurism led to the purgatory of a whole life lived as show-biz illusion? What if that life became not only the ultimate paranoid fantasy but also achieved pulse-quickening heights of narcissism?"

75. David Bell, "Surveillance Is Sexy," *Surveillance and Society* 6 (2009), 209.

76. Bell, "Surveillance Is Sexy," 206.

77. Barcan, "In the Raw," 88.

78. Bell, "Surveillance Is Sexy," 204.

79. Michel Foucault, *Discipline and Punish: The Birth of the Prison*, trans. A. M. Sheridan (New York: Pantheon, 1977), 211.

80. Denzin, *Images of Postmodern Society*, 9.

81. Baudrillard, *The Ecstasy of Communication*, 26.

6. THE ANATOMY OF VISIBILITY

1. Michel Foucault, *Discipline and Punish: The Birth of the Prison*, trans. A. M. Sheridan (New York: Pantheon, 1977), 214.

2. Jean-Paul Sartre, "The Other and His Look," in *To Freedom Condemned*, ed. Justin Treller (New York: Philosophical Library, 1960), 37.

3. Foucault, *Discipline and Punish*, 301.

4. "Surveillance Extends Everywhere," *Lincoln Star*, May 19, 1994, 7.

5. Marshall McLuhan, *Understanding Media: The Extensions of Man* (New York: McGraw-Hill, 1964).

6. Mark Poster, "Databases as Discourse; or, Electronic Interpellations," in *Computers, Surveillance, and Privacy*, eds. David Lyon and Elia Zureik (Minneapolis: University of Minnesota Press, 1996), 184.

7. Steven L. Nock, *The Costs of Privacy: Surveillance and Reputation in America* (New York: Aldine de Gruyter, 1989), 3.

8. Nock, *The Costs of Privacy*, 2.

9. See Robert N. Bellah, Richard Madsen, William M. Sullivan, Ann Swindler, and Steven M. Tipton, *The Good Society* (New York: Knopf, 1991). The communitarian sociologist Amitai Etzioni argues that excessive protection of individual privacy, in certain situations, may threaten the common good. See Amitai Etzioni, *The Limits of Privacy* (New York: Basic, 1999). Deciding what is best for the "common good," however, is a political process.

10. Gary T. Marx, quoted in Lili Berko, "Surveying the Surveilled: Video, Space, and Subjectivity," *Quarterly Review of Film and Video* 14 (1992), 86.

11. Jeffrey C. Goldfarb, *The Cynical Society* (Chicago: University of Chicago Press, 1991), 182.

12. Michel Foucault, *The History of Sexuality: An Introduction* (New York: Vintage Books, 1990), 95.

13. Michel Foucault, "Power, Moral Values, and the Intellectual: An Interview with Michel Foucault by Michael Bess," *History of the Present* 4 (1988), 1.

Selected References

Agre, Philip, and Marc Rotenberg, eds. *Technology and Privacy: The New Landscape*. Boston: MIT Press, 1997.

Albrecht, Katherine, and Liz McIntyre. *SPYCHIPS: How Major Corporations and Government Plan to Track Your Every Move with RFID*. Nashville, TN: Thomas Nelson, 2005.

Altheide, David. "Electronic Media and State Control: The Case of Azscam." *Sociological Quarterly* 34, no. 1 (1993). 53–69.

———. "Gonzo Justice." *Symbolic Interaction* 15, no. 1 (1993): 69–86.

Altheide, David L., and R. Sam Michalowski. "In the News: Fear a Discourse of Control." *Society* 40, no. 3 (2010): 475–503.

American Management Association and the ePolicy Institute. "2007 Electronic Monitoring and Surveillance Survey." February 28, 2008. Accessed March 21, 2013.

Andrejevic, Mark. "The Kinder, Gentler Gaze of Big Brother: Reality TV in the Era of Digital Capitalism." *New Media and Society* 4, no. 2 (2002): 251 270.

———. "Surveillance in the Digital Enclosure." *Communication Review* 10, no. 4 (2007): 295–317.

Baker, Laura, et al. "Behavioral Genetics: The Science of Antisocial Behavior." *Law and Contemporary Problems* 69, 1 2 (2006): 7 46.

Ball, Kirstie. "Workplace Surveillance: An Overview." *Labor History* 51, no. 1 (2010): 87–106.

Ball, Kirstie, and Frank Webster, eds. *Intensification of Surveillance: Crime, Terrorism and Warfare in the Information Age*. London: Pluto Press, 2003.

Ball, Kirstie, Kevin Haggerty, and David Lyon, eds. *Routledge Handbook of Surveillance Studies*. London: Routledge, 2012.

Barcan, Ruth. "In the Raw: 'Home-made' Porn and Reality Genres." *Journal of Mundane Behavior* 3 (2002): 87–108.

Barnard-Wills, David. *Surveillance and Identity: Discourse, Subjectivity and the State*. Burlington, VT: Ashgate, 2012.

Bauchspies, Wenda K., Jennifer Croissant, and Sal Restivo. *Science, Technology, and Society: A Sociological Approach*. Malden, MA: Wiley-Blackwell, 2005.

Baudrillard, Jean. *The Ecstasy of Communication* (New Edition), trans. Bernard Schütze and Caroline Schütze. Boston: Semiotext(e), 2012.

———. *Simulations*. New York: Semiotext(e), 1983.

Bauerlein, Mark. *The Digital Divide: Arguments for and against Facebook, Google, Texting, and the Age of Social Networking*. New York: Tarcher, 2011.

Bauman, Zygmunt. *Intimations of Postmodernity*. London: Routledge, 1992.

Bauman, Zygmunt, and David Lyon. *Liquid Surveillance: A Conversation.* Cambridge: Polity, 2013.

Bayard de Volo, Lorraine. "Service and Surveillance: Infrapolitics at Work among Casino Cocktail Waitresses." *Social Politics* 10, no. 3 (2003): 347–376.

Beckett, Katherine, and Steve Herbert. *Banished: The New Social Control in Urban America.* New York: Oxford University Press, 2010.

Bell, David. "Surveillance Is Sexy." *Surveillance and Society* 6, no. 3 (2009): 203–212.

Bellah, Robert N., Richard Madsen, William M. Sullivan, Ann Swindler, and Steven M. Tipton. *The Good Society.* New York: Knopf, 1991.

Benjamin, Walter. "The Work of Art in the Age of Mechanical Reproduction." In *Illuminations: Essays and Reflections*, edited by Walter Benjamin and Hannah Arendt, 219–253. New York: Harcourt, 1968.

Bentham, Jeremy. *The Panopticon Writings.* Edited by Miran Bozovic. London: Verso, 1995.

———. *The Works of Jeremy Bentham*, Vol. 4, edited by Sir John Bowring (London: Tait, 1843).

Berko, Lili. "Surveying the Surveilled: Video, Space, and Subjectivity." *Quarterly Review of Film and Video* 14, no. 1–2 (1992): 61–91.

Best, Kirsty. "Living in the Control Society: Surveillance, Users and Digital Screen Technologies." *International Journal of Cultural Studies* 13, no. 1 (2010): 5–24.

Best, Steven. "Foucault, Postmodernism, and Social Theory." In *Postmodernism and Social Inquiry*, edited by David R. Dickens and Andrea Fontana, 25–52. New York: Guilford Press, 1994.

Best, Steven, and Douglas Kellner. *The Postmodern Adventure: Science, Technology and Cultural Studies at the Third Millennium.* New York: Guilford Press, 2001.

Blanchette, Jean-François, and Deborah G. Johnson. "Data Retention and the Panoptic Society: The Social Benefits of Forgetfulness." *Information Society* 18, no. 1 (2002): 33–45.

Bourdieu, Pierre. *Distinction: A Social Critique of the Judgement of Taste.* London: Routledge, 1984.

Brighenti, Andrea. "Visibility: A Category for the Social Sciences." *Current Sociology* 55, no. 3 (2007): 323–342.

Brossman, Mark E. "Workers Gain Privacy Rights by Legislation, Judicial Action." *National Law Journal*, April 9, 1990, 28.

Brown, Michelle. *The Culture of Punishment: Prison, Society, and Spectacle.* New York: New York University Press, 2009.

Browne, Simone. "Digital Epidermalization: Race, Identity and Biometrics." *Critical Sociology* 36, no. 1 (2010): 131–150.

Burgess, Jean, and Joshua Green. *YouTube: Online Video and Participatory Culture.* Cambridge, UK: Polity, 2009.

Campbell, Nancy D. "Suspect Technologies: Scrutinizing the Intersection of Science, Technology, and Policy." *Science, Technology, and Human Values* 30, no. 3 (2005): 374–402.

Carr, Nicholas. *The Shallows: What the Internet Is Doing to Our Brains.* New York: W. W. Norton, 2011.

Charles, Alec, and Gavin Stewart, eds. *The End of Journalism.* New York: Peter Lang, 2011.

Cohen, Stanley. "The Punitive City: Notes on the Dispersal of Social Control." *Contemporary Crisis* 3, no. 4 (1979): 339–363.

———. *Visions of Social Control: Crime, Punishment, and Classification.* Cambridge: Polity, 1985.

Cohen, Stanley, and Andrew Scull. *Social Control and the State.* New York: St. Martin's Press, 1983.

Cole, Simon A. *Suspect Identities: A History of Fingerprinting and Criminal Identification.* Cambridge, MA: Harvard University Press, 2002.

Conrad, Peter, and Joseph Schneider. *Deviance and Medicalization: From Badness to Sickness.* St. Louis: Mosby, 1980.

Corbett, Ronald, and Gary T. Marx. "Critique: No Soul in the New Machine: Technofallacies in the Electronic Monitoring Movement." *Justice Quarterly* 8, no. 3 (1991): 399–414.

Crane, Diana. *The Sociology of Culture.* Cambridge: Blackwell, 1994.

Crouch, Colin. *The Strange Non-death of Neo-liberalism*. Cambridge: Polity, 2011.

Dandeker, Christopher. *Surveillance, Power and Modernity: Bureaucracy and Discipline from 1700 to the Present*. Cambridge: Polity, 1990.

Danto, Elizabeth Ann. *Historical Research*. Oxford: Oxford University Press, 2008.

Davis, Mike. *City of Quartz: Excavating the Future in Los Angeles*. London: Verso, 1990.

Decew, Judith Wagner. *In Pursuit of Privacy: Law, Ethics and the Rise of Technology*. Ithaca, NY: Cornell University Press, 1997.

Denzin, Norman K. *Images of Postmodern Society: Social Theory and Contemporary Cinema*. Newbury Park, CA: Sage, 1991.

Derber, Charles. *The Pursuit of Attention: Power and Ego in Everyday Life*. New York: Oxford University Press, 2000.

Dibble, Vernon. "Four Types of Inference from Documents to Events." *History and Theory* 3, no. 2 (1963): 203–221.

Doyle, Aaron, Randy K. Lippert, and David Lyon, eds. *Eyes Everywhere: The Global Growth of Camera*. New York: Routledge, 2012.

Dreyfus, Hubert L., and Paul Rabinow, eds. *Michel Foucault: Beyond Structuralism and Hermeneutics*. Berkeley: University of California Press, 1983.

Dumas, Barry M. *Diving into the Bitstream: Information Technology Meets Society in a Digital World*. New York: Routledge, 2012.

Dumm, Thomas. *Democracy and Punishment: Disciplinary Origins of the United States*. Madison: University of Wisconsin Press, 1987.

Earle, Alice Morse. *Curious Punishments of Bygone Days*. Rutland,VT: Charles E. Tenant, 1972.

Eck, David J. *The Most Complex Machine: A Survey of Computers and Computing*. New York: A. K. Peters, 1995.

Edgeworth, Brendan. *Law, Modernity, Postmodernity: Legal Change in the Contracting State*. Aldershot, UK: Ashgate, 2003.

Emerson, Robert M., and Sheldon M. Messinger. "The Micro-Politics of Trouble." *Social Problems* 25, no. 2 (1977): 121–134.

Ericson, Richard V. *Policing the Risk Society*. Toronto: University of Toronto Press, 1997.

Ericson, Richard V., and Kevin D. Haggerty, eds. *The New Politics of Surveillance and Visibility*. Toronto: University of Toronto Press, 2006.

Etzioni, Amitai. *The Limits of Privacy*. New York: Basic, 1999.

Feeley, Malcolm, and Jonathan Simon. "Actuarial Justice: The Emerging New Criminal Law." In *The Futures of Criminology*, edited by David Nelken, 173–201. London: Sage, 1994.

———. "The New Penology: Notes on the Emerging Strategy of Corrections and Its Implications." *Criminology* 30, no. 4 (1992): 449–474.

Ferrell, Jeff, and Neil Websdale. *Making Trouble: Cultural Constructions of Crime, Deviance, and Control*. Hawthorne, NY: Aldine de Gruyter, 1999.

Fisher, Jill A., and Torin Monahan. "Tracking the Social Dimensions of RFID Systems in Hospitals." *International Journal of Medical Informatics* 77, no. 3 (2008): 176–183.

Fitzpatrick, Tony. "Critical Theory, Information Society and Surveillance Technologies." *Information, Communication and Society* 5, no. 3 (2002): 357–378.

Foucault, Michel. "Afterword: The Subject of Power." In *Michel Foucault: Beyond Structuralism and Hermeneutics*, edited by Hubert L. Dreyfus and Paul Rabinow, 208–226. Berkeley: University of California Press, 1983.

———. *Discipline and Punish: The Birth of the Prison*. Translated by A. M. Sheridan. New York: Pantheon, 1977.

———. *Power/Knowledge: Selected Interviews and Other Writings, 1972–1977*. Edited by Colin Gordon. New York: Pantheon, 1980.

Fraser, Nancy. *Unruly Practices: Power, Discourse, and Gender in Contemporary Social Theory*. Minneapolis: University of Minnesota Press, 1989.

Friedman, Lawrence. *A History of American Law*. New York: Simon and Schuster, 1973.

Fuentes, Annette. *Lockdown High: When the Schoolhouse Becomes a Jailhouse*. New York: Verso, 2011.

Gabbidon, Shaun L. "Profiling by Store Clerks and Security Personnel in Retail Establishments. An Exploration of 'Shopping While Black.'" *Journal of Contemporary Criminal Justice* 19, no. 3 (2003): 345–364.

Gainey, Randy R., and Brian K. Payne. "Understanding the Experience of House Arrest with Electronic Monitoring: An Analysis of Quantitative and Qualitative Data." *International Journal of Offender Therapy and Comparative Criminology* 44, no. 1 (2000): 84–96.

Gandy, Oscar, Jr. *The Panoptic Sort: A Political Economy of Personal Information*. Boulder, CO: Westview, 1993.

Gane, Nicholas. "The Governmentalities of Neoliberalism: Panopticism, Post-panopticism and Beyond." *Sociological Review* 60, no. 4 (2012): 611–634.

Garfinkel, Simson, and Beth Rosenberg, eds. *RFID: Applications, Security, and Privacy*. New York: Addison-Wesley Professional, 2005.

Garland, David. *The Culture of Control: Crime and Social Order in Contemporary Society*. Chicago: University of Chicago Press, 2001.

———. "Penal Modernism and Postmodernism." In *Punishment and Social Control*, edited by Thomas Blomberg and Stanley Cohen, 45–74. New York: Aldine de Gruyter, 1995.

Gates, Kelly. *Our Biometric Future: Facial Recognition Technology and the Culture of Surveillance*. New York: New York University Press, 2011.

Geertz, Clifford. *The Interpretations of Cultures*. New York: Basic, 1973.

Gibbs, Jack. *Norms, Deviance, and Social Control: Conceptual Matters*. New York: Elsevier, 1981.

Gilliom, John. *Overseers of the Poor: Surveillance, Resistance, and the Limits of Privacy*. Chicago: University of Chicago Press, 2001.

———. *Surveillance, Privacy, and the Law: Employee Drug Testing and the Politics of Social Control*. Ann Arbor: University of Michigan Press, 1996.

Gilliom, John, and Torin Monahan. *SuperVision: An Introduction to the Surveillance Society*. Chicago: University of Chicago Press, 2013.

Glasser, Dara J., Kenneth W Goodman, and Norman G Einspruch. "Chips, Tags and Scanners : Ethical Challenges for Radio Frequency Identification." *Knowledge Creation Diffusion Utilization* 9, no. 2 (2007): 101–109.

Glassner, Barry. *Culture of Fear: Why Americans Are Afraid of the Wrong Things*. New York: Basic, 1999.

Goldfarb, Jeffrey C. *The Cynical Society*. Chicago: University of Chicago Press, 1991.

Goldsmith, Jack, and Tim Wu. *Who Controls the Internet?: Illusions of a Borderless World*. New York: Oxford University Press, 2008.

Gonzalez, Wenceslao J. *Science, Technology and Society: A Philosophical Perspective*. A Coruña, Spain Netbiblo, 2005.

Grob, Gerald N. *From Asylum to Community: Mental Health Policy in Modern America*. Princeton, NJ: Princeton University Press, 1991.

Hafner, Katie, and Matthew Lyon. *Where Wizards Stay Up Late: The Origins of the Internet*. New York: Simon and Schuster, 1996.

Haggerty, Kevin. "Tear Down the Walls: On Demolishing the Panopticon." In *Theorizing Surveillance: The Panopticon and Beyond*, edited by David Lyon, 23–45. Cullompton: Willan, 2006.

Haggerty, Kevin D., and Richard V. Ericson. "The Surveillant Assemblage." *British Journal of Sociology* 51, no. 4 (2000): 605–622.

Haggerty, Kevin D., and Amber Gazso. "Seeing Beyond the Ruins: Surveillance as a Response to Terrorist Threats." *Canadian Journal of Sociology* 30, no. 2 (2010): 169–187.

Hanson, F. Allan. *Technology and Cultural Tectonics: Shifting Values and Meanings*. New York: Palgrave, forthcoming.

———. *Testing Testing: Social Consequences of the Examined Life*. Berkeley: University of California Press, 1993.

Harris, Patricia M., and Kimberly S. Keller. "Ex-Offenders Need Not Apply: The Criminal Background Check in Hiring Decisions." *Journal of Contemporary Criminal Justice* 21, no. 1 (2005): 6–30.

Harvey, David. *A Brief History of Neoliberalism*. New York: Oxford University Press, 2007.

Healy, David. *Pharmageddon*. Los Angeles: University of California Press, 2012.

Hier, Sean, and Joshua Greenberg, eds. *The Surveillance Studies Reader*. Maidenhead, UK: Open University Press, 2007.

Hodges, Vanessa G., and Betty Blythe. "Improving Service Delivery to High-Risk Families: Home-Based Practice." *Families in Society: Journal of Contemporary Human Services* 73, no. 5 (1992): 259–265.

Hoffmann, Diane E., and Karen H. Rothenberg. "Judging Genes: Implications of the Second Generation of Genetic Tests in the Courtroom." *Maryland Law Review* 66, no. 4 (2007): 858–922.

Holman, John E., and James F. Quinn. "Dysphoria and Electronically Monitored Home Confinement." *Deviant Behavior* 13, no. 1 (1992): 21–32.

Humphreys, Keith, and Julian Rappaport. "From the Community Mental Health Movement to the War on Drugs: A Study in the Definitions of Social Problems." *American Psychologist* 48, no. 8 (1993): 892–901.

Hyde, Alan. *Bodies of Law*. Princeton, NJ: Princeton University Press, 1997.

Jacobs, Katrien. *Netporn: DIY Web Culture and Sexual Politics*. Lantham, MD: Rowman and Littlefield, 2007.

Jameson, Fredric. *Postmodernism, or, The Cultural Logic of Late Capitalism*. London: Verso, 1992.

Kelly, Kevin. "The Electronic Hive: Embrace It." In *Computerization and Controversy: Value Conflicts and Social Choice*, 2nd ed., edited by Rob Kling, 76–77. San Diego: Academic Press, 1996.

Koskela, Hille. "Video Surveillance, Gender, and the Safety of Public Urban Space: 'Peeping Tom' Goes High Tech?" *Urban Geography* 23, no. 3 (2002): 257–278.

Kovacic, Casey. "Out of Bounds: HIV and AIDS Discrimination in American Athletics." *Willamette Sports Law Journal* 1 (2008): 2–16.

Krier, Dan, and William G. Staples. "Seen but Unseen: Part-time Faculty and Institutional Surveillance and Control." *American Sociologist* 24, no. 3–4 (1993): 119–134.

Kuntsler, James Howard. *Home from Nowhere: Remaking Our Everyday World for the Twenty-first Century*. New York: Simon and Schuster, 1996.

Kupchik, Aaron. *Homeroom Security: School Discipline in an Age of Fear*. New York: New York University Press, 2010.

Lemke, Thomas. "'The Birth of Bio-politics': Michel Foucault's Lecture at the Collège de France on Neo-liberal Governmentality." *Economy and Society* 30, no. 2 (2001): 190–207.

Levin, Thomas Y., Ursula Frohne, and Peter Weibel, eds. *Rhetorics of Surveillance from Bentham to Big Brother*. Cambridge, MA: MIT Press, 2002.

Levy, Sharon, et al. "A Review of Internet-Based Home Drug-Testing Products for Parents." *Pediatrics* 113, no. 4 (2004): 720–726.

Levy, Sharon, Shari Van Hook, and John Knight. "A Review of Internet-Based Home Drug-Testing Products for Parents." *Pediatrics* 113, no. 4 (2004): 720–726.

Lewis, Orlando. *The Development of American Prisons and Prison Customs, 1776–1845*. Albany: Prison Association of New York, 1967 (1922 Reprint).

Lewis, W. David. *From Newgate to Dannemora*. Ithaca, NY: Cornell University Press, 1975.

Lieb, Roxanne, Vernon Quinsey, and Lucy Berliner. "Sexual Predators and Social Policy." *Crime and Justice* 23 (1998): 43–114.

Lightman, Alan. *A Sense of the Mysterious: Science and the Human Spirit*. New York: Vintage, 2006.

Lorenz, Chris. "If You're So Smart, Why Are You Under Surveillance? Universities, Neoliberalism, and New Public Management." *Critical Inquiry* 38, no. 3 (2012): 599–629.

Lowe, Donald. *The Body in Late Capitalism USA*. Durham, NC: Duke University Press, 1995.

Lykken, David T. *A Tremor in the Blood: Uses and Abuses of the Lie Detector*. New York: Plenum, 1998.

Lyon, David. *The Electronic Eye: The Rise of Surveillance Society*. Minneapolis: University of Minnesota Press, 1996.

———. "The New Surveillance: Electronic Technologies and the Maximum Security Society." *Crime, Law, and Social Change* 18, no. 1–2 (1992): 159–175.

————. *Postmodernity*. Minneapolis: University of Minnesota Press, 1994.

————, ed. *Surveillance as Social Sorting: Privacy, Risk and Digital Discrimination*. New York: Routledge, 2003.

————. *Surveillance Studies: An Overview*. Malden, MA: Polity, 2007.

————, ed. *Theorizing Surveillance: The Panopticon and Beyond*. Abingdon, UK: Willan, 2006.

Lyon, David, and Elia Zureik, eds. *Computers, Surveillance, and Privacy*. Minneapolis: University of Minnesota Press, 1996.

MacKenzie, Doris Layton. *What Works in Corrections: Reducing the Criminal Activities of Offenders and Delinquents*. New York: Cambridge University Press, 2006.

Mattelart, Armand. *The Globalization of Surveillance*. Cambridge, UK: Polity, 2010.

Magnet, Shoshana. "Bio-Benefits: Technologies of Criminalization, Biometrics, and the Welfare System." In *Surveillance: Power, Problems, and Politics*, edited by Sean P. Hier and Joshua Greenberg, 169–183. Vancouver: University of British Columbia Press, 2009.

Mandel, Ernest. *Late Capitalism*. London: Verso, 1978.

Mark Andrejevic. *iSpy: Surveillance and Power in the Interactive Era*. Lawrence: University Press of Kansas, 2007.

Marx, Gary T. "Technology and Gender: Thomas I. Voire and the Case of the Peeping Tom." *Sociological Quarterly* 43, no. 3 (2002): 409–433.

Mathiesen, Thomas. "The Viewer Society: Michel Foucault's 'Panopticon' Revisited." *Theoretical Criminology* 1, no. 2 (1997): 215–234.

Mayer-Schönberger, Viktor. *Delete: The Virtue of Forgetting in the Digital Age*. Princeton, NJ: Princeton University Press, 2011.

McChesney, Robert W. *Digital Disconnect: How Capitalism Is Turning the Internet against Democracy*. New York: New Press, 2013.

McGrath, John E. *Loving Big Brother: Performance, Privacy and Surveillance Space*. New York: Routledge, 2004.

McLaughlin, Heather, Christopher Uggen, and Amy Blackstone. "Sexual Harassment, Workplace Authority, and the Paradox of Power." *American Sociological Review* 77, no. 4 (2012): 625–647.

McLuhan, Marshall. *Understanding Media: The Extensions of Man*. New York: McGraw-Hill, 1964.

Milofsky, Carl. *Testers and Testing: The Sociology of School Psychology*. New Brunswick, NJ: Rutgers University Press, 1989.

Molotch, Harvey. *Against Security: How We Go Wrong at Airports, Subways, and Other Sites of Ambiguous Danger*. Princeton, NJ: Princeton University Press, 2012.

Monahan, Torin. "Dreams of Control at a Distance: Gender, Surveillance, and Social Control." *Cultural Studies-Critical Methodologies* 9, no. 2 (2009): 286–305.

————, ed. *Surveillance and Security: Technological Politics and Power in Everyday Life*. New York: Routledge, 2006.

————. *Surveillance in the Time of Insecurity*. New Brunswick, NJ: Rutgers University Press, 2010.

————. "'War Rooms' of the Street: Surveillance Practices in Transportation Control Centers." *Communication Review* 10, no. 4 (2007): 367–389.

Monahan, Torin, and Jill A. Fisher. "Implanting Inequality: Empirical Evidence of Social and Ethical Risks of Implantable Radio-frequency Identification (RFID) Devices." *International Journal of Technology Assessment in Health Care* 26, no. 4 (2010): 370–376.

Monahan, Torin, and Rodolfo D. Torres, eds. *Schools under Surveillance: Cultures of Control in Public Education*. New Brunswick, NJ: Rutgers University Press, 2010.

Morozov, Evgeny. *The Net Delusion: The Dark Side of Internet Freedom*. New York: Public Affairs, 2011.

Mouzelis, Nicos P. *Modern and Postmodern Social Theorizing: Bridging the Divide*. Cambridge, UK: Cambridge University Press, 2008.

Murray, Harry. "Deniable Degradation: The Finger-Imaging of Welfare Recipients." *Sociological Forum* 15, no. 1 (2000): 39–63.

Nelkin, Dorothy, and Laurence Tancredi. *Dangerous Diagnostics: The Social Power of Biological Information*. 1989. Reprint, Chicago: University of Chicago Press, 1994.

Nock, Steven L. *The Costs of Privacy: Surveillance and Reputation in America*. New York: Aldine de Gruyter, 1989.

Norris, Clive, and Gary Armstrong. *The Maximum Surveillance Society: The Rise of CCTV*. Oxford: Berg Publishers, 1999.

Paul, Annie Murphy. *The Cult of Personality Testing: How Personality Tests Are Leading Us to Miseducate Our Children, Mismanage Our Companies, and Misunderstand Ourselves*. New York: Simon and Schuster, 2010.

Petersilia, Joan. *Expanding Options for Criminal Sentencing*. Santa Monica, CA: RAND, 1987.

Pettit, Becky. *Invisible Men: Mass Incarceration and the Myth of Black Progress*. New York: Russell Sage, 2010.

Poster, Mark. "Databases as Discourse; or, Electronic Interpellations." In *Computers, Surveillance, and Privacy*, edited by David Lyon and Elia Zureik, 175–192. Minneapolis: University of Minnesota Press, 1996.

Project MATCH Research Group. "Matching Alcoholism Treatments to Client Heterogeneity: Project MATCH Posttreatment Drinking Outcomes." *Journal of Studies on Alcohol* 58, no. 1 (1997): 7–29.

Puvia, Elisa, and Jeroen Vaes. "Being a Body: Women's Appearance Related Self-Views and Their Dehumanization of Sexually Objectified Female Targets." *Sex Roles* 68, no. 7–8 (2013): 484–495.

Raab, Charles, and David Mason. "Privacy, Surveillance, Trust and Regulation." *Information, Communication and Society* 7, no. 2 (2004): 249–251.

Ross, E. A. *Social Control: Control a Survey of the Foundations of Order*. New Bruswick, NJ: Transaction Publishers, 2009 (1901).

Rothman, David J. *Conscience and Convenience: The Asylum and Its Alternatives in Progressive America*. Boston: Little, Brown, 1980.

———. *The Discovery of the Asylum: Social Order and Disorder in the New Republic*. Boston: Little, Brown, 1971.

Salter, Mark B., ed. *Politics at the Airport*. Minneapolis: University of Minnesota Press, 2008.

Sankaran, Karin Gopal, et al. *HIV/Aids in Sport: Impact, Issues, and Challenges*. Champaign, IL: Human Kinetics, 1999.

Sartre, Jean-Paul. "The Other and His Look." In *To Freedom Condemned*, edited by Justin Treller, 37. New York: Philosophical Library, 1960.

Schermer, Bart W. "The Limits of Privacy in Automated Profiling and Data Mining." *Computer Law and Security Review* 27, no. 1 (2011): 45–52.

Schwartz, Adam. "Chicago's Video Surveillance Cameras: A Pervasive and Poorly Regulated Threat to Our Privacy." *Northwestern Journal of Technology and Intellectual Property* 11, no. 2 (2013): 47–60.

Scott, Charles L., and Trent Holmberg. "Castration of Sex Offenders: Prisoners' Rights versus Public Safety." *Journal of the American Academy of Psychiatry Law* 31, no. 4 (2003): 502–509.

Scull, Andrew. *Decarceration: Community Treatment and the Deviant*. Englewood Cliffs, NJ: Prentice Hall, 1977.

Sheller, Mimmi, and John Urry. *Mobile Technologies of the City*. London: Routledge, 2006.

Simon, Jonathan. "From Confinement to Waste Management: The Post-Modernization of Social Control." *Focus on Legal Studies* 8, no. 2 (1993): 6–7.

Solove, Daniel J. *The Digital Person: Technology And Privacy in The Information Age*. New York: New York University Press, 2006.

Somekh, Bridget, and Cathy Lewin. *Theory and Methods in Social Research*. London: Sage, 2011.

Spector, Malcom. "Beyond Crime: Seven Methods to Control Troublesome Rascals." In *Law and Deviance*, edited by H. L. Ross, 127–157. Beverly Hills, CA: Sage, 1981.

Staples, William G. *Castles of Our Conscience: Social Control and the American State, 1800–1985*. New Brunswick, NJ: Rutgers University Press, 1991.

———. *Encyclopedia of Privacy*. Vols. 1–2. Westport, CT: Greenwood, 2006.

————. "'Where Are You and What Are You Doing?' Familial 'Back Up Work' as a Collateral Consequence of House Arrest." In *Who's Watching: Daily Practices of Surveillance among Contemporary Families*, edited by Margaret Nelson and Anita Garey, 33–53. Nashville, TN: Vanderbilt University Press, 2009.

Staples, William G., and Stephanie Decker. "Between the 'Home' and 'Institutional' Worlds: Tensions and Contradictions in the Practice of House Arrest," *Critical Criminology* 18 (2010): 1–20.

————. "Technologies of the Body, Technologies of the Self: House Arrest as Neo-Liberal Governance." In *Surveillance and Governance: Crime Control Today*, edited by Mathew Deflem, 131–149. Bingley, UK: Emerald/JAI Press, 2008.

Staples, William G., and Joane Nagel. "'Gary's Gone . . .': Comment on the Case of the Pepping Tom: Technology and Gender by Gary T. Marx." *Sociological Quarterly* 43, no. 3 (2002): 447–452.

Staples, William G., and Carol A. B. Warren. "Mental Health and Adolescent Social Control," in *Research in Law, Deviance and Social Control: A Research Annual*, edited by Steven Spitzer and Andrew Scull, 113–126. Greenwich, CT: JAI Press, 1988.

Tabor, Phillip. "I Am a Videocam." In *The Unkown City: Contesting Architecture and Social Space*, edited by Iain Borden, et al., 122–137. Cambridge, MA: MIT Press, 2002.

Tewksbury, Doug. "Crowdsourcing Homeland Security: The Texas Virtual Border Watch and Participatory Citizenship." *Surveillance and Society* 10, no. 3/4 (2009): 249–262. Accessed April 18, 2013, http://www.surveillance-and-society.org.

Tillyer, Rob, Charales F. Klahm, and Robin S. Engel. "The Discretion to Search: A Multilevel Examination of Driver Demographics and Officer Characteristics." *Journal of Contemporary Criminal Justice* 28, no. 2 (2012): 184–205.

Trottier, Daniel. *Social Media as Surveillance: Rethinking Visibility in a Converging World*. Burlington, VT: Ashgate, 2012.

Tumber, Howard, and Marina Prentoulis. *Journalism and the End of Objectivity*. London: Bloomsbury, 2012.

Tunnell, Ken D. *Pissing on Demand: Workplace Drug Testing and the Rise of the Detox Industry*. New York: New York University Press, 2004.

Turkle, Sherry. *Alone Together: Why We Expect More from Technology and Less from Each Other*. New York: Basic, 2011.

————. *Life on the Screen: Identity in the Age of the Internet*. New York: Simon and Schuster, 1995.

Turow, Joseph. *Breaking up America: Advertisers and the New Media World*. Chicago: University of Chicago Press, 1998.

————. *The Daily You: How The New Advertising Industry Is Defining Your Identity and Your Worth*. New Haven, CT: Yale University Press, 2011.

————. *Niche Envy: Marketing Discrimination in the Digital Age*. Cambridge, MA: MIT Press, 2006.

Vaidhyanathan, Siva. *The Googlization of Everything: (And Why We Should Worry)*. Berkeley: University of California Press, 2011.

Wacquant, Loïc. "Crafting the Neoliberal State: Workfare, Prisonfare, and Social Insecurity." *Sociological Forum* 25, no. 2 (2010): 197–220.

Walsh, Diana C., et al. "A Randomized Trial of Treatment Options for Alcohol-Abusing Workers." *New England Journal of Medicine* 325, no. 11 (1991): 775–781.

Webber, David W. *AIDS and the Law*. New York: Aspen Publishers, 2007.

Weibel, Peter. "Pleasure and the Panoptic Principle." In *Rhetorics of Surveillance from Bentham to Big Brother*, edited by Thomas Y. Levin, Ursula Frohne, and Peter Weibel, 207–233. Cambridge: MIT Press, 2002.

Weinberger, David. *Everything Is Miscellaneous: The Power of the New Digital Disorder*. New York: Holt Paperbacks, 2008.

————. *Small Pieces Loosely Joined: A Unified Theory of The Web*. New York: Basic, 2003.

Welsh, Brandon C. "Surveillance for Crime Prevention in Public Space: Results and Policy Choices in Britain and America." *Criminology* 578, no. 252 (2004): 497–526.

Welsh, Brandon C., and David P. Farrington. "Is CCTV Effective in Preventing Crime in Public Places?" In *Evidence-based Policing*, edited by Eveline De Wree, et al., 263–282. Antwerp: Maklu-Publishers, 2010.

———. "Public Area CCTV and Crime Prevention: An Updated Systematic Review and Meta-Analysis." *Justice Quarterly* 26, no. 4 (2009): 716–745.

———. "Surveillance for Crime Prevention in Public Space: Results and Policy Choices in Britain and America." *Criminology and Public Policy* 3, no. 3 (2004): 497–525.

Western, Bruce, *Punishment and Inequality in America*. New York: Russell Sage, 2007.

Westin, Alan. *Privacy and Freedom*. New York: Athencum, 1967.

Whitaker, Robert. *Anatomy of an Epidemic: Magic Bullets, Psychiatric Drugs, and the Astonishing Rise of Mental Illness in America*. New York: Broadway, 2011.

Willcocks, Leslie P. "Michel Foucault in the Social Study of ICTs: Critique and Reappraisal." *Social Science Computer Review* 24, no. 3 (2006): 274–295.

Williams, Christine I. "Racism in Toyland." *Contexts* 4 (2005): 28–32.

Winseck, Dwayne. "Netscapes of Power: Convergence, Network Design, Walled Gardens, and Other Strategies of Control in the Information Age." In *Surveillance as Social Sorting: Privacy, Risk and Digital Discrimination*, edited by David Lyon, 176–198. New York: Routledge, 2003.

Wise, J. Macgregor. "An Immense and Unexpected Field of Action: Webcams, Surveillance and Everyday Life." *Cultural Studies* 18, no. 2–3 (2004): 424–442.

Wood, David Murakami. "The 'Surveillance Society': Questions of History, Place and Culture." *European Journal of Criminology* 6, no. 2 (2009): 179–194.

Woods, L. J. "Home-Based Family Therapy." *Social Work* 33, no. 3 (1988): 211–214.

Wright, Richard G. "Sex Offender Post-Incarceration Sanctions: Are There Any Limits?" *New England Journal of Criminal and Civil Confinement* 34, no. 1 (2008): 17–50.

Zirkle, Brian, and William G. Staples. "Negotiating Workplace Surveillance." In *Electronic Monitoring in the Workplace: Controversies and Solutions*, edited by John Weckert, 79–100. Hershey, PA: Idea Group, 2005.

Zurawski, Nils. "Video Surveillance and Everyday Life: Assessments of Closed-Circuit Television and the Cartography of Socio-Spatial Imaginations." *International Criminal Justice Review* 17, no. 4 (2007): 269–288.

Zwick, Detlev, and Janice Denegri Knott. "Manufacturing Customers: The Database as New Means of Production." *Journal of Consumer Culture* 9, no. 2 (2009): 221–247.

Index

About the Author

William G. Staples grew up on the south shore of Long Island, New York. He has been a commercial fisherman, taxicab driver, plumber's apprentice, and pizza chef. He studied sociology at the University of Oregon, the University of Southern California, and UCLA. Staples is currently professor of sociology and founding director of the Surveillance Studies Research Center at the University of Kansas. In addition to the first edition of *Everyday Surveillance*, his previous books include *Castles of Our Conscience: Social Control and the American State, 1800–1985* (1991), with his fellow sociologist brother, Clifford L. Staples, *Power, Profits, and Patriarchy: The Social Organization of Work at a British Metal Trades Firm, 1791–1922* (2001), and the two-volume reference work, *The Encyclopedia of Privacy* (2006). He lives in Lawrence, Kansas.